# LANGUAGE
# REVITALIZATION

# LANGUAGE REVITALIZATION

## Policy and Planning in Wales

*Edited by*

COLIN H. WILLIAMS

*Published on behalf of the
Board of Celtic Studies of the
University of Wales*

UNIVERSITY OF WALES PRESS
CARDIFF
2000

British Library Cataloguing-in-Publication Data.
A catalogue record for this book is available from the British Library.

ISBN 0–7083–1667–0

Typeset by Mark Heslington, Scarborough, North Yorkshire
Printed in Great Britain by Bookcraft, Midsomer Norton, Avon

*To the teaching staff of Ysgol Gyfun Rhydfelen (1962–9) for their
inspiration, professional dedication and sense of common humanity,
which made school life a daily joy.*

# Contents

# List of Figures

# List of Tables

# Preface and acknowledgements

I would first like to thank all the contributors for their original and insightful contributions as well as for their generous co-operation. Promoters of language revival activities are on trial, their interpretations, actions and policy recommendations deserve the closest scrutiny by academics and committed critics. But they also deserve encouragement, support and political leadership to see their efforts come to fruition. I believe that taken together the chapters in this volume represent a significant contribution to the current debate on the role of the Welsh language and of bilingualism in society. While broadly sympathetic to current attempts to promote the Welsh language several of the contributors offer trenchant criticisms of the failings of government efforts, the lack of adequate resources and the inability of many professional agencies to deliver a thorough, comprehensive bilingual service at the point of customer demand.

My special thanks go to my co-researchers at Cardiff University, Jeremy Evas and Maite Puigdevall i Serralvo for their informed discussions and professional assistance. The encouragement of Professor Glyn E. Jones, my former Head of Department, was especially significant, first in inviting me to work at Cardiff and subsequently in ensuring that language policy issues were given a prominent place within the Department of Welsh at Cardiff University. This commitment has been maintained by his successor Professor Sioned Davies, who, together with my colleague Dr E. Wyn James, has provided encouragement at every stage. I moved to Cardiff from Canada where I remain an Adjunct Professor at the Department of Geography, University of Western Ontario. I would like to thank Professor Roger King, Head of Department, Professor Mireya Folch-Serra and Professor Don Cartwright, together with Patricia Chalk of the Cartography Section, for their intellectual engagement and valued support.

This work has been supported by a number of agencies whose grants or invitations to participate in language-related focus groups have proved especially stimulating. Bwrdd yr Iaith Gymraeg have sponsored the research investigations of several of the contributors and co-organized a European Conference on Community Language Planning in 1998 which drew many of the contributors together. We have profited from the supportive environment created by its former chair, Lord Dafydd Elis Thomas, and its current chair, Rhodri Williams.

John Walter Jones, Gwyn Jones and Eifion Davies have been especially helpful in providing information and opportunities to meet to discuss language revitalization efforts. The several visits of Nick Gardner to Wales from the Basque Country to act as a special adviser to the Language Board enabled us to continue a long-standing friendship and led to the preparation of Chapter 11.

I would also like to thank the European Cultural Foundation and the European Parliament for their gracious invitation to join an expert standing panel occupied with the question 'Which Languages for Europe?' Our discussions in these meetings have been very influential in broadening out the conception of language revitalization. In similar vein I would like to thank Joe Shields of the Modern Language Section of the Council of Europe, Strasbourg, for involving me in their activities in several East European contexts concerned with issues of minority rights, bilingual education and group conflict.

A co-operative project 'On Small Nations in the New Europe', undertaken with Dr Milan Bufon, Department of Geography, Ljubljana University and supported by the Slovene Ministry of Science, the ZRS Koper Research Institute and the British Council, has also been immensely useful in articulating European trends on ethnic, political and language-related issues.

Several individuals and organizations have responded to our request for information and have shared their research findings with us. Many are acknowledged in the footnotes accompanying the chapters. Dr Stephen May, Department of Sociology, Bristol University, and Professor Guy Lachapelle, Vice-Rector, Concordia University, Montreal, kindly sent academic papers which were very useful for the educational and comparative analyses. For help on current Irish developments I would like to thank Nollaig Ó Gadhra, Helen Ó Murchu, Nora Welby, Glór na nGael and Peadar Ó Flatharta, Dublin.

Hywel Evans, Menter a Busnes and the Department of Linguistic Policy, Generalitat de Catalonia, have been very generous in sharing data, policy documents and in supporting several aspects of the collaborative work which Maite Puigdevall i Serralvo and I have undertaken in the use of lesser-used languages in small and medium-sized enterprises. A grant from the ESRC, No. R000 22 2936, to investigate the 'Bilingual Context, Policy and Practice of the National Assembly' has advanced our thinking on the role of governance in relation to the determination of language policy.

The Language and Literature Committee of the Board of Celtic Studies have sponsored this publication. We are grateful to Professor S. Davies, chair of the Committee, and Ruth ab Ieuan, Secretary to the Board of Celtic Studies, for their generous support of our work. I wish to thank Susan Jenkins, Director of the University of Wales Press, and Ceinwen Jones, our editor at the University of Wales Press, who worked long hours with skill and grace to make the book meet exacting professional standards.

Finally, I want to express my deepest gratitude to my wife, Meryl, who has encouraged this project from its inception and who, while it was in its final stages, endured the demands of its completion without complaint.

For permission to reproduce material from copyright works, the authors and publishers gratefully acknowledge the following: Professor A. Philbrick, Department of Geography, The University of Western Ontario, for Figures 5.2, 5.3 and 5.4; Professor Mireya Folch-Serra, Department of Geography, The University of Western Ontario, for Figure 11.1; the Welsh Office for permission to reproduce the acknowledged tables and figures in Chapter 2.

# List of Contributors

COLIN BAKER is Professor in the School of Education, University of Wales, Bangor.

CEFIN CAMPBELL is Director of Mentrau Myrddin, based at Trinity College, Carmarthen.

JEREMY C. EVAS is Research Associate in the Department of Welsh, Cardiff University.

NICHOLAS GARDNER is at the Education Department, The Basque Government, Vitoria.

HEINI GRUFFUDD is Lecturer in the Department of Adult Continuing Education, University of Wales Swansea.

GLYN E. JONES is Research Professor in the Department of Welsh, Cardiff University.

HYWEL JONES is a member of the Statistical Section at the Health Department, National Assembly for Wales.

MEIRION PRYS JONES is Head of the Education Section at the Welsh Language Board, Cardiff.

STEVE MORRIS is Lecturer at the Department of Adult Continuing Education, University of Wales Swansea.

MAITE PUIGDEVALL I SERRALVO is a Ph.D. candidate at the Department of Welsh, Cardiff University.

COLIN H. WILLIAMS is Research Professor in the Department of Welsh, Cardiff University.

# On Recognition, Resolution and Revitalization

## COLIN H. WILLIAMS

Language revitalization efforts are a significant feature of contemporary Welsh planning and policy. Bilingualism in all its myriad forms is the subject of much debate and even greater expectation on behalf of many who anticipate that as Welsh government matures its deliberations will enable the Welsh language to fulfil its due role as a co-equal national language. However, we know that, despite all the political reforms and the general positive messages being circulated through official agencies and many voluntary organizations, the Welsh language is still far from being accepted as a 'normal' medium of communication in many social contexts. The purpose of this current volume is to describe, assess and criticize the various means by which official policies in a selected set of domains have sought to encourage the development of a bilingual society. The turn of the century has seen an increase in intellectually challenging analyses of the contours of bilingualism in Wales, and current work suggests a more realistic appraisal and critique of government action and inaction than hitherto. Our intention in this volume is to complement such work by adding an applied emphasis to the debate. Three outstanding contributions to our understanding of the field may be cited from the outset and the interested reader is encouraged to absorb the often conflicting messages contained within the different disciplinary analyses. In *Language Planning and Language Use: Welsh in a Global Age* (2000), Glyn Williams and Delyth Morris have provided a challenging critique of Welsh language use. Using perspectives derived from discourse analysis they expose the often muddled, sometimes sinister, treatment of minority languages within the social sciences generally and sociolinguistics in particular. Less theoretical, but equally empirically grounded, *Language, Economy and Society* (2000) by John Aitchison and Harold Carter charts the fortunes of the Welsh language in the twentieth century. Continuing in the excellent cultural geographical traditions of the University of Wales, Aitchison and Carter provide copious information and mapped spatial analysis of the changing distribution of Welsh speakers. Their volume combines sophisticated cartography with objective interpretation to present an excellent and accessible account of Welsh in the past century. A third, more ambitious undertaking has been the 'Social History of the Welsh Language' project based at the Centre for Advanced Welsh and Celtic Studies, Aberystwyth. The successive bilingual volumes (Jenkins, 1997; D. Jones, 1998; Jenkins, 1998; Parry and Williams, 1999; Jenkins, 2000) are a landmark contribution to Welsh scholarship and provide copious evidence of the nature of language change together with detailed analysis of socio-economic trends in the modern period.

## THE EUROPEAN CONTEXT

Historically, language and religion have often been treated as the critical markers of a distinct cultural identity, a useful shorthand in which to describe a complex reality. The cultural inheritance of a Catholic, Latin civilization gradually weakened in post-medieval Europe due to a series of conflicts which underpinned the emergence of the territorial bureaucratic nation-state. Language and religion were a prime focus of political activity because the past abrogation of rights and the continued refusal of states to grant social demands promoted ethnic conflict and fragmentation. Why is a common language so often seen as essential to 'nation-building' or state development and if conflict is such a predictable outcome, why not opt for linguistic and cultural pluralism as a dominant ideology? The answer is surely that language is power – it can confer privilege, deny opportunity, construct a new social order and radically modify an inherited past which is not conducive to the pursuit of hegemonic aims. Language choice is thus a battleground for contending discourses, ideologies and interpretations of the multi-ethnic experience.

The argument advanced in the introduction and conclusion of this volume is that it is both advisable – and feasible – to construct a political framework in Europe which acknowledges the positive virtues of cultural pluralism on the basis of equality as a necessary prerequisite for democracy and freedom of action in an increasingly multicultural world order. This raises issues concerned with the distribution of power in society and the encouragement of democratic participation by previously beleaguered interest groups. A *sine qua non* of their recognition is mutual respect and the establishment of minimum structures of freedom, which guarantee the conditions for cultural reproduction.

Current language revitalization efforts operate in a completely different global context from that which obtained a century or more ago when many of the original aims and demands of language movements were first articulated. The construction of Europe-wide institutions has to deal with the diversity and tensions resulting from an international political system designed to suit the vagaries of nineteenth- and early twentieth-century statecraft, and the ensuing lack of congruence between multicultural citizenries and the sense of order prescribed by national conceptions of the modern state (C. H. Williams, 1989). Although there are indications that the neo-liberal conception of the unitary state, based upon representative democracy, is yielding to the logic of the enabling state with its focus on participatory democracy, this transition is either illusionary or faltering in many parts of Europe. Consequently the management of cultural diversity as a permanent feature of the international social order is among the most taxing of political issues facing modern Europe.

The foundation of any modern democracy lies in the ability of citizens to derive maximum security and satisfaction from their contribution to the common wealth of society. Historically, several societies allowed for instrumental pluralism as a societal norm because a broad measure of freedom from state interference provided the necessary breathing space for the peaceful coexistence of citizens. Habermas (1996) argues that such space permitted citizens of widely diverging cultural identities to be simultaneously members of – and strangers in – their own country. The historical reproduction of dissenting cultures was, in part, a function of relatively weak economic-structural assimilation, often compounded by geographical distancing from the cores of the emerging nation-states. Their maintenance today in the face of much stronger pressures for inclusion is all the more difficult. Increased secularization in the West and the enforced totalitarian conformity that described Central and Eastern Europe prior to 1989 has greatly damaged the primacy of Catholicism, Protestantism and Orthodoxy. When we add the catastrophic effects of the Holocaust on Jewish community life, then it is little wonder that organized religion is a markedly less salient part of mainstream society. The only exceptions, which appear to have witnessed real growth, are the faiths of non-European migrants and their descendants, such as Sikhs and Hindus in Great Britain, together with Islamic believers throughout much of Europe (Gerholm and Lithman, 1990) and a plethora of evangelical variants of fundamentalist Protestantism. Thus, despite the absolute decline in the number of adherents, religious faith will continue to contribute to European social life and its diversity, and not just as the tabloid banner headline where Catholic is pitched against Protestant in Northern Ireland, or where members of the Muslim nation within Bosnia-Herzegovina are set against their Orthodox and Catholic neighbours (Zametica, 1992).

The lack of congruence between the formal political system and the social inheritance of its constituent citizens is rendered even more complex by the friction that exists between attempts to maintain linguistic diversity and the increasing linguistic standardization apparent throughout the world. At the global scale, it is estimated that some 6,170 living languages – exclusive of dialects – are contained within the 185 or so sovereign states (a number that rises to around 200, if dependencies and semi-autonomous polities are included) (Mackey, 1991). Less than 100 of these c.6,000 languages are 'official', since 120 states have adopted either English, French, Spanish or Arabic as their official language, while some fifty states have their own indigenous official language (15 per cent have two or more). If a further forty-five regional languages are added, it remains the case that only about 1.5 per cent of the world's total spoken languages are formally recognized. The situation is even more polarized in that only 1 per cent of the world's languages are used by more than half a million speakers and only 10 per cent by more than 100,000. Hundreds of languages have no adolescent speakers at all and thus we are continually losing parts of our global linguistic diversity (C. H. Williams, 1995).

If it is also accepted that most minority ethnic-linguistic groups are relatively underdeveloped economically and politically, it is clear that questions of language, culture and identity may constitute the very essence of a subordinated group's relationship with the state in whose name the dominant group exercises power and control. European state development was often over-centralized around national capital cores, without any corresponding attention to the interests of 'ethnic minorities', except, of course, the need to subject them to political and strategic integration. Thus, since medieval times, religious competition was regulated by a layered system of legal securities. This involved the principle of coexistence in religiously mixed imperial cities and the realization of the *cuius regio eius religio*, following the uneasy agreement between Catholics and Protestants which ensued from the Religious Peace of Augsburg in 1555. The law gave rights to overlords to determine the faith of their territories and not to the subjects, who were theoretically free to emigrate. The principle was hailed as the most important element of the rise of the secular territorial state, one that, together with the *ius reformandi* (which was also tied to territorial privileges), formed the legal-geographical basis for the structural transition from Holy Roman Empire to Enlightenment state system. Nevertheless, most dissenting remnants in the secular territorial states, whether Catholic or Protestant, did not survive intact, for 'persecution and expulsion followed immediately upon discovery' (Klein, 1978: 57).

Our present conception of the rights of subjects and citizens has evolved such that the principle of freedom from state direction or oppression in religious or linguistic matters has given way to a demand for freedom to be represented on the basis of equality within society as the determining essence of the participative state. Nowhere are these rights more fiercely conjoined and attacked than in the question of ethno-linguistic identities in the modern state. The new politics of recognition in Europe belatedly represents an attempt to compensate for the earlier systematic exclusion of many minority groups from the decision-making structures of society. This is not to deny earlier attempts to specify the rights and obligations of minority cultures, but these prerogatives were often granted on the assumption that no permanent change would result to the state from such reforms. However, the current transition from representative democracy to participatory democracy, at least within parts of the EU, requires the decoupling of the state majority from its hegemonic position. As Habermas (1996: 289) argues:

> Hidden behind such a facade of cultural homogeneity there would at best appear the oppressive maintenance of a hegemonic majority culture. If, however, different cultural, ethnic and religious subcultures are to co-exist and interact on equal terms within the same political community, the majority culture must give up its historical prerogative to define the official terms of that *generalized* political culture, which is to be shared by all citizens, regardless of where they come from and how they live. The majority culture must be decoupled from a political culture all can be expected to join.

Thus those who are constructing the new Europe must search for a binding substitute for state nationalism. This relationship is central to the analysis since democracy avers that citizens are entitled to certain minimum rights, chiefly those of participation in – and protection by – the state. The changing nature of the state, however, both as ideology and practice, has encouraged a more pluralist view of its responsibilities.

The conventional view, characteristic of many Western societies until the early post-Second-World-War period, held that the state should neither discriminate against – nor favour – particular subgroups, however these might be defined. This view – the individual rights approach – is often justified by majoritarian principles of equality of all before the law, and is implemented through policies of equal opportunity for socio-economic advancement based upon merit and application. In reality, however, in most multicultural societies, the state persistently discriminated, by law, against religious and other minorities, be they Jews, Catholics, Protestants, Romany or a whole host of beleaguered ethno-linguistic groups. However, the admittedly patchy improvement in the treatment of minorities, and the resultant constructive dialogue between representatives of the various interest groups and governmental agencies at all levels in the political hierarchy of contemporary Europe, obviously bodes well for the medium-term future enactment of minority rights.

## THE ETHNIC REVIVAL

Four types of explanations may be offered for the so-called ethnic revival in the post-war period (C. H. Williams, 1994). First is the ethnic continuity model, which posits that ethnic regional awareness in advanced industrial states is part of a global resurgence in ethnic identification that is challenging social class and other bases for group membership and political behaviour. Second, the salience of ethnicity is a reaction against the increasing scale of human organization and anomie felt by those who are socially excluded from mainstream economic and technological developments. Third, the internal colonial thesis posits that core-periphery interaction and the uneven development of capitalism operates through a cultural division of labour to disadvantage the ethnic periphery. Subject peoples can liberate themselves from structural discrimination by adopting programmes to overthrow their hegemonic 'colonial' masters. Fourth, great play is made of the role of the ethnic intelligentsia. Through their unique vision of history and their self-defined mission-destiny, they are well placed to mobilize the populus on issues such as relative deprivation, unfulfilled aspirations and opportunism, hoping thereby to renegotiate the terms of their ethnic region's relationship with the international community.

Elsewhere, it was the turn towards an increasingly federal Europe which animated activists as they sought to harness overlapping multiple identities through the forging of political alliances with various green movements, anti-Fascist organizations, advocates of a non-nuclear economy, women's groups and representatives of the rainbow alliance. In several states, such pressure has forced more established political parties to advocate various decentralist reforms, while there have been increasing attempts by governments to manage tension and conflict through regional development programmes, through establishing regional and national assemblies and recognizing the inherent pluralism of European society in social and economic policy formulation.

In Celtic societies the collective defence of land, language and resources has dominated the relationship between the indigenous élite and the incursive, hegemonic state power. Recently, the standardization and normalization of the Celtic languages, together with their struggle to resist the incursions of English and French, have heightened the tension between attempts to protect a threatened language and to reproduce its historically conjoined culture. In Brittany and Wales, the maintenance of a separate language is judged to be crucial to the reproduction of an autonomous culture, though it is highly debatable as a foundation principle, as one can quite readily maintain an ethnic identity without reference to fluency in the indigenous language, as is the case in Cornwall, Scottish Gaeldom and Ireland.

Attempts to resist the 'folklorization' of places, the 'museumization' of communities, and the commodification and gentrification of ethno-linguistic regions through tourism and the heritage industry, focus on opportunities to empower selected communities. The sources of this power include new telecommunication networks, the mass media and linguistic intervention. Elements within this new infrastructure might include linguistic *animateurs*, local authority resource centres and sustainable local economic development agencies with a language promotion mandate.

## VARIETIES OF LANGUAGE POLICY AND PLANNING IN EUROPE

We now move on to consider the ways in which these socio-political forces are played out in linguistic terms and to assess the ensuing consequences for social policy and citizenship in the new Europe. As a mechanism for behaviour modification, language policy and planning depends largely on four attributes identified by Stewart (1968). These are the degrees of, respectively: standardization, autonomy, historicity and vitality. These characteristics of language freedom are critical in helping planners to evaluate existing language functions and to harness the dynamic cultural interactions that characterize many multilingual societies. Stewart proposes a typology of language which recognizes the multiplicity of linguistic functions that can exist even within ostensibly one-nation/one-people/one-culture states:

- official languages;
- provincial languages (such as regional languages);
- languages of wider communication (LWCs), which are used within a multilingual nation to cross ethnic boundaries;
- international languages, which are LWCs used between nations;

- capital languages (the means of communication near a national capital);
- group languages (often vernaculars);
- educational languages (used as the media of education);
- school-subject languages (those taken as second languages);
- literary languages (for example, Latin or Sanskrit);
- religious languages (such as Islamic Arabic).

Most European societies retained the language policies which were critical to the project of constructing the territorial-bureaucratic nation-state. Consequently they face severe difficulties in matching their inherited institutional agencies and organizational structures to the reality of serving the legitimate demands of increasingly multilingual populations. Historically, we can identify four types of language policy implicated in the processes of European state formation. The first and most common – as found in France, Spain and Britain – reinforced political and cultural autonomy by giving primacy to one indigenous language and thus enforcing it, and no other, as the language of government, administration, law, education and commerce. In so doing, a number of goals were achieved simultaneously. Among these was the search for national integrity, the legitimization of the new regime and its state apparatus, the re-establishment of indigenous social organization, the reduction of dependence upon external organizations and influences and the incorporation of all the citizenry in a wide range of para-public social domains. Foreign languages were reserved for the very specialized functions of higher education, international diplomacy and commerce.

A second type of language planning characterizes those situations in which the 'national' goal has been to maintain cultural pluralism, so that the state might survive through containing its inherent tensions. Under this system, language was used to define regional associations rather than state or national citizenship. It is best exemplified in Europe by Switzerland's decentralized system, which incorporates cantonal unilingualism within a multilingual federal system, and the rigidly enforced division of Belgium between its Walloon- and Flemish-speaking populations.

The third form of language planning occurred when a recognized minority was granted some degree of geographical distinction, based upon the territoriality principle of language rights. In Finland, for example, high levels of language contact along the west coast, marked religious uniformity, a strong tradition of centralized government and the unifying effects of long-term external threats, led to a recognition that the minority Swedish-speaking population should be accorded official status. Following the 1922 Language Law, all communes were classified as unilingual Finnish, unilingual Swedish, or bilingual if they contained a linguistic minority of either group of 10 per cent or more; these classifications were revised after each decennial census to take account of changing linguistic geography (McRae, 1997). In comparative terms, the Finnish system of official bilingualism is characterized by a gross disparity in numbers, asymmetry in language contact and instability over time, leading McRae to conclude that such institutional arrangements for language accommodation have been functional in terms of conflict moderation and management, but less so for language stability.

A fourth option – the 'modernization' or revitalization of an indigenous tongue – is diagnostic of societies disengaging from colonial relationships and the cultural hegemony of a dominant state. This form of language planning was a key goal of the nationalist intelligentsia in Hungary, Ireland, Finland, and Norway prior to independence, and remains critical to the political programme of nationalists and regionalists in Catalonia, Euskadi, Brittany and Wales today.

Clearly language planning in a multilingual society is not a precise instrument and is as capable of being manipulated as is any other aspect of state policy. Nevertheless, it is an essential feature of the economic and political restructuring of many states. The key issues are:

- Who decides – and on what basis – such bi- or multilingualism is to be constructed?
- Which languages are chosen?
- Who benefits by acts of state-sponsored social and identity formation?
- How is language-related conflict managed and reduced?
- How is language planning to be related to all other forms of social intervention?

Two conditions are necessary for competition to arise between language groups. First, the languages must share a common contact space. Secondly, the relationship between these two languages must become the symbolic stakes of the competition, which takes.place on the level of the shared space.

Laponce (1987: 266) has advanced the following four propositions about languages in contact:

- 'languages tend to form homogenous spatial groupings';
- 'when languages come into contact they tend either to specialize their functions or to stratify';
- 'the specialization and the stratification of languages is determined by the socially dominant group';
- 'the social dominance of a language is a function of . . . the number of its speakers and . . . the political and social stratification of the linguistic groups in contact'.

How do minority interest groups influence the state structure so that it concedes certain rights which are not requested by the majority?

Research in contact linguistics demonstrates that it is a chimera to search for a universal model for conflict reduction. On the contrary, procedures must be considered that are adaptable to each situation. Nelde et al. (1992) have argued that measures of linguistic planning, such as the personality or a territoriality principle or some expedient admixture of both, are not in themselves sufficient to avoid conflicts. However, many conflicts can be partially neutralized if the following conditions are observed.

- The territoriality principle should be limited to a few key areas like administration and education.
- The institutional multilingualism that emerges should lead to the creation of independent unilingual networks, which grant equal opportunity of communication to minority and majority speakers. These networks should also exclude linguistic discrimination connected with speakers of the prestige language.
- Measures of linguistic planning should not be based exclusively on linguistic censuses carried out by the respective governments. Rather, they must genuinely take account of the situational and contextual characteristics of the linguistic groups.
- Minority linguistic groups in a multilingual country should not be judged primarily on quantitative grounds. On the contrary, they should be awarded more rights and possibilities of development than would be due to them based on their numbers and their proportion to the majority.

Nelde et al. believe that according such equality to minorities by assuring them of more rights could result in fewer people adopting an intransigent ideological position. Unless far more attention is paid to the rights of speakers of lesser used language speakers, then more conflict will ensue. Language erosion also involves the potential loss of creativity and spontaneity mediated through one's own language(s), thus contributing to a quenching of the human spirit, and a reduction in what some have termed the ecology of 'linguodiversity' (C. H. Williams, 1991a; Skutnabb-Kangas, 1997). This reason alone may prove convincing to many. But need linguistic decline sound the death-knell for particular ethnic identities in Europe? As Edwards (1994) and G. Williams (1991) have argued, no necessary correspondence exists between linguistic reproduction and ethnic identity. Indeed, cultural activities and symbolic manifestations of ethnicity often continue long after a group's language declines. None the less, increased interdependence at the European level implies more harmonization for the already advantaged groups. In making multiculturalism more accessible, long-quiescent minorities will be rebuffed as they seek to institutionalize their cultures. It is not necessarily a tale of decline and rejection, however, for opportunities do exist to influence state and provincial legislatures and metropolitan political systems.

The project of European unity, combined with other macro-processes such as globalization, poses a threat to conventional territorial relationships and simultaneously opens up new forms of inter-regional interaction such as cable television and global multi-service networks. However, deciding between the promotion of one or many languages in the educational domain and public agencies is becoming less of a 'free choice'. The increasing burdens of economic, social and cultural development crowd in on the limited resources available for language planning and its implementation. There is also the counter-trend of regional diversity, which emphasizes the value of cultural diversity and the worth of each specific language, not least as a primary marker of identity. Ethno-linguistic minorities have reacted to these twin impulses by searching for

European-wide economies of scale in broadcasting, information networking, education and public administration, meanwhile establishing their own EU networks and entering into new alliances to influence decision-making bodies. They believe that by appealing to the superstructural organizations of the EU for legitimacy and equality of group rights, they will force individual states and the Community to recognize their claims for political/social autonomy within clearly identifiable territorial/social domains.

The EU has harmonized state and community policies so as to strengthen its majority-language regimes. But the wider question of the relative standing of official languages makes political representatives wary of further complicating administrative politics by addressing the needs of approximately fifty-five million citizens who have a mother tongue that is not the main official language of the state which they inhabit. Historically, the recognition of linguistic minority demands is a very recent phenomenon. Since 1983, the European Commission has supported action to protect and promote regional and minority languages and cultures within the EU. In 1996 some four million ECUs was allocated to European socio-cultural schemes. Equally significant is a raft of recent legislation and declarations upholding the rights of minorities to use their languages in several domains (C. H. Williams, 1993b; *Declaració de Barcelona*, 1996).

The most recent expansion of the EU in 1995 and its imminent further enlargement has increased the difficulties in translating multicultural communication and guaranteeing access to information and hence power for all groups. At the heart of the debate on European identity lies a consideration of the role of hegemonic languages as both symbol and instrument of integration. English – the premier language for international commerce and discourse – is used by over 1,500 million people world-wide as an official language, of whom some 320 million have it as a home language (Gunnermark and Kenrick, 1985; Crystal, 1987). Should English be encouraged as the official language, enabling most Europeans to communicate with each other? Or is it desirable to attempt to slow down its inevitable global spread? Critics claim that the spread of English perpetuates an unequal relationship between 'developed' and 'developing' societies. While access to information and power demands fluency, it also requires institutional structures, economic resources and power relationships.

The functions of English are nearly always described in positive terms. Language, and the ideology it conveys, is thus part of the legitimization of positions within the global division of labour. However, attempts to separate English as a European bridge language or from its British and North American value systems are misguided, for English should not be interpreted as if it were primarily a *tabula rasa*. Any claim that English is now a neutral, pragmatic tool for global development is disingenuous, being

> part of the rationalization process whereby the unequal power relations between English and other languages are explained and legitimated. It fits into the familiar linguistic pattern of the dominant language creating an external image of itself, other

languages being devalued and the relationship between the two rationalised in favour of the dominant language. This applies to each type of argument, whether persuasion, bargaining, or threats are used, all of which serve to reproduce English linguistic hegemony. (Phillipson, 1992: 288)

Such points emphasize that conflict is inherent in language issues and help explain why bilingual and multicultural education – far from encouraging the positive aspects of cultural pluralism – has hitherto been characterized by mutual antagonism, begrudging reforms and ghettoization. Attempts to overturn pejorative judgements about the normalcy of bilingual education or the promotion of minority languages as normal and as essential elements in society come up against powerful hegemonic discourses which negate the salience of such languages for general developmental issues and social intercourse. There are signs that such discourses are being challenged all over Europe and beyond (Phillipson, 1992; Skutnabb-Kangas, 1999), especially in relation to the urgent need to bring together basic human rights and economic rights within a more participative democratic process. The dilemma is encapsulated in this prescient quotation from the outstanding analyst in this field, Tove Skutnabb-Kangas:

> Globalising access to information has enabled counterhegemonic forces to ensure that there is growing sensitivity to human rights. But at the same time there is also a growing inability to secure them by progressive forces in civil society. The gap between rhetoric and implementation is growing, with all the growing inequalities. Behind this lies the collapse of institutions of democratic political control of trade and capital. In this light, it is completely predictable that states commit linguistic genocide; it is part of the support to the homogenizing global market forces . . . At present, though we can hope that some of the positive developments might have some effect, overall there is not much cause for optimism . . . we still have to work for education through the medium of the mother tongue to be recognized by states as a human right. And if this right is not granted, and implemented, it seems likely that the present pessimistic prognoses of over 90% of the world's oral languages not being around anymore in the year 2100, are too optimistic. (Skutnabb-Kangas, 1999: 56 and 63)

Modernized indigenous languages, such as Irish or Catalan are capable of expansion but struggle to displace hegemonic languages, especially within the civil service, or technological and commercial sectors. Renewed languages such as Welsh, Frisian or Basque have penetrated into new domains, such as local administration, education and the media, but even here the impression given is that much of this activity is tokenistic or reaches only the superficial structures of society. In contrast, threatened minority languages such as Romany or Skolt Lapp will be further marginalized. Because of their high fertility rates, some groups are experiencing linguistic reproduction rates greater than one, and their prospects for survival look promising, especially in constructing an infrastructure for domain extension in education, government and broadcasting. Conversely, however, some autochthonous language speakers are rapidly loosing their control in traditional core areas as a result of out-migration, capital-intensive economic development and increased mobility. The fact that lesser used language speakers have become highly politicized in the last twenty years should not divert attention from their fears of cultural attrition.

Perhaps the greatest challenge facing framers of European identity comes from non-European migrants and their descendants, especially as globalizing perspectives will reinforce the need for link languages other than English in this realm. Initially, this will result from private and commercial-oriented demands, but as the total size and significance of link languages – especially Islamic-related variants – grows, then there will be pressure to reform public agencies and the educational system, particularly in France, the UK, Germany, Belgium and the Netherlands. The increased presence of non-nationals within European states will add to the alienated feelings of many recent migrants that they do not belong by right to any particular state.

There is a growing demand for a pan-European educational policy in which 'isolated instruction in separate foreign languages should be replaced by instruction for multilingual communication' (Posner, 1991: 134). Does advocacy of a common educational approach imply that ultimately the EU will become the first post-modern, post-sovereign multicultural political system of the twenty-first century? For the optimist, this emphasis on accommodation, openness and diversity is an expression of a highly developed pluralist society, which demands mutual respect and tolerance of its constituent cultures. To the pessimist, however, such openness is a recipe for continued strife, inter-regional dislocation, inefficient government and the artificial reproduction of often misleading cultural identities.

Clearly the state is deeply implicated in the direction of change with regard to multicultural policy. As society becomes more plural, and social mobility increases, greater tensions occur between the functional provision of bilingual public services and the formal organization of territorial-based authorities charged with such provision. These conflicts are exacerbated by immigration into fragile language areas, which leads to the public contestation of language-related issues as each new domain is penetrated by the intrusive language group. Such sentiments are hard to gainsay. The difficulty lies in determining what proportion of the public purse is to be expended upon satisfying the legit-imate demands of this policy. Issues of principle, ideology and policy are frequently no more than thinly disguised disputes over levels of resource expen-diture. One arm of government is involved in extending the remit of pluralism whilst another is reining in the fiscal obligations of so doing. Either way, depend-ent cultures are tied inexorably to the largesse of the state. Governments are obliged to maintain their support for many multicultural projects, albeit simul-taneously signalling their intent to withdraw public finances and welcome private-sector funding. Either way, the languages and cultures of visible minori-ties are in danger of being expropriated by external forces, while cultural dependency is being increased. As they become better organized, however, astute minority groups will press for greater recognition of their cultural rights, seeking the individual choice and empowerment to decide their lifestyle and future prospects as participative citizens. From this perspective, multicultural-ism is a set of institutional opportunities for individual and group advancement in a competitive environment. In other words, it becomes a platform for social progress.

The politics of mutual respect presuppose a historically well-entrenched democratic order. The watchwords of the open society are redistributive social justice, participatory democracy and mutual tolerance. This in turn presup-poses a political-juridical framework adequate to ensuring that increased cultural contact will not lead to escalating conflict. Cultural communities are best represented when the state guarantees individual freedom of association and protection.

## THE EXTREME DELICACY OF LANGUAGE REVITALIZATION

Language revitalization is concerned with infusing additional energy into endangered language communities. Historically, vital energy inputs were normally derived from committed individuals whose sense of injustice was so profound that outstanding, even heroic, efforts were made to advance the cause of the disaffected minority. Many of these individuals were drawn to nationalist or ethno-regionalist movements, one of whose prime goals was the restitution of the threatened language within the broader process of ethnic revival. The best known description of this process, known as Reversing Language Shift, is asso-ciated with the work of Joshua Fishman (1991).

Fishman's key ideas have influenced the development of the sociology of language, sociolinguistics, bilingual education and language planning. He has focused on three themes: the preservation of Yiddish language and interpreta-tion of Jewish culture; language as a continuum reflected in the diversity of linguistic repertoires of American cultural pluralism; and the more pressing socio-political question of the role of ethnic consciousness in society. These issues have been explored on a comparative international basis, especially the issue of language revitalization within lesser used language communities. His early concerns with language and nationalism, ethnic identity and group conflict and public policy analysis have inspired two generations of scholars as they have grappled with the question of linguistic rights and socio-political development of states. An abiding concern has been to act as a bridge between sociologist and linguistic, for he argues that each is the poorer for ignoring the claims of sociol-ogy and the language sciences. He is particularly scathing about the neglect of theory within sociolinguistics. His most influential works are *The Rise and Fall of the Ethnic Revival* (1985), and especially his *Reversing Language Shift* (1991b: 87), which distinguishes between two sets of related environments in stages 8 to 1 of his Graded Intergenerational Disruption Scale (GIDS). The first basic set, which seeks to achieve diglossia so as to promote the intergenerational transmission of a language (X) within the community (stage 6, home–family–neighbourhood), covers levels 8 to 5. The second set (covering stages 4 to 1) seeks to achieve the normalization of a language within domains such as the workplace, the private sector and the civil service.

When implementing this GIDS, Fishman insists that language élites have to be realistic, so that they neither raise false expectations nor undervalue the potential power they may mobilize within the target group. This is sound advice, but his ideas and models for language revitalization are not without their critics. In Wales, the sociologist Glyn Williams (1999) has demonstrated that much of Fishman's programmatic, evolutionary prescription for social change is inherently consensual and conservative. He avers that Fishman's work does not take enough account of the power relations inherent in any language-related competitive context. Williams has sought to tease out the often contradictory and conflictual tendencies which masquerade as language tension and group conflict, and his most recent collaborative volume (Williams and Morris, 2000) is an excellent critique of the Welsh case from a theoretical sociological perspective.

For most interpreters of language contact situations the real difficulty is in using an LWC such as English or Spanish as the benchmark. In a recent interview (Erize, 2000) Fishman cautions the Basques about the impossible task of modernization and keeping up with the technological power of English. It is no accident that former imperial languages retain hegemonic control over key aspects of life such as science, technology, higher education and commerce. The response of Basque and Welsh language policy makers should be to identify their priorities and invest heavily in what is practical, realizable and of most utility to the promotion of the target language within the community and workplace. Rather than seek to satisfy every supplicant, or every pet project of a vested interest group, policy makers should always be conscious that the hegemonic context within which they are constrained to operate necessarily strengthens the power-base of the languages of wider communication. This is not a recipe for pessimism; rather it is a realization that the wider forces of westernization and globalization ranged against the lesser used languages are not linguistically driven. They involve linguistic considerations certainly, but their genesis is political and economic, information driven and related to the power calculations of major international actors. In contrast, the defensive response of beleaguered minorities is nearly always couched in terms of language competition and conspiracy theory, rather than in a functional delineation of boundaries.

In discussing an advanced model of diglossia, Fishman asks whether it is appropriate for Basque activists to imitate all aspects of Spanish or English, whether both high and low varieties and uses of language should necessarily shadow each other. He also asks 'What are the defensible boundaries for Spanish and for Basque at the H level?', which we could repeat as 'What are the defensible boundaries for English and for Welsh at the H level?' In similar vein he questions whether we should be operating in terms of an ethnic or a civil basis for our increasingly plural societies in Western Europe. Strengthening the social networks and community empowerment elements of participative democracy would also strengthen the popular legitimacy and relevance of holistic language policy from the bottom up and not just the top down. As discussed later in this volume, both the growth of *mentrau iaith* (language enterprise agencies) and the establishment of the National Assembly augur well for revitalization efforts in Wales. This concern with building up intimate networks and spaces for interaction is a timely reminder that we neglect the base of community language and cultural reproduction at our peril. It is a sensitive and delicate operation with which we should engage in a humble and modest manner. Consider the following typical method of engagement:

> Is talk of minor, endangered languages (who have a meagre chance of surviving and even less chance of spreading) a fitting way to start off a conference on the unlimited horizons for language spread and language policy? Indeed it is, for just as illness teaches about health, and just as psychopathology teaches us about what is normal in everyday mental life, so the problems of endangered languages teach us about the extreme delicacy of language policy and the extreme complexity of language spread. And while it behoves us to help these languages because they need our help most, because by so doing so we become more human, we should also note that our involvement with them will also benefit by making us more sensitive, more humble and more cautious language policy implementers as well, researchers and implementers more likely to realise that for every gain there is a loss, for every self-satisfied smile, a despondent tear, for every glorious triumph a tragic defeat. (Fishman, 1987)

Today the energy invested in language revitalization is more normally described in terms of a three-way partnership between a committed set of interest groups, government language planning and a responsive civil society. However, this neat formulation masks a number of different tensions and conflicts which need to be understood before adequate language policies can be implemented. This volume is about policy and planning. It recognizes that all too often there is a disjuncture between the two. Furthermore, it argues that impressive gains were made in Wales long before any consideration was given to self-conscious planning, as is described in the next section.

## THE STRUGGLE FOR WELSH IN HISTORICAL CONTEXT

Long after the Edwardian conquest of Wales (1282), English colonial control turned to a form of shared power with the accession of the Welsh nobleman, Henry VII, in 1485. His heir, Henry VIII, enacted the Acts of Union 1536 and 1542, which formally incorporated Wales into the legal and political realm of England. The Acts' most significant clause in terms of the future of the language was to exclude Welsh from official life and require all public officialdom that was transacted in the 'principality' to be in English. State policy sought to develop an indigenous, anglicized ruling class, which built upon the established practice of the Welsh gentry being incorporated within an English hierarchical stratification system. The practice of sending sons of the Welsh gentry to English public schools and of encouraging intermarriage between landed families either side of the border accelerated this assimilation process. However, as Janet Davies has reminded us,

> the process took at least 250 years and was virtually complete by the late eighteenth century. It had profound consequences. Linguistic differences reinforced class differences. Welsh culture, which had been essentially aristocratic, came into the guardianship of the peasantry and the 'middling sort of people' – craftsmen, artisans and the lower clergy. As the inhabitants of the gentry houses ceased to speak Welsh, the system of patronage which had maintained the Welsh poets over the centuries collapsed, and the standardised Welsh they had jealously defended came into peril of deteriorating into an assortment of mutually unintelligible dialects. (Davies, 1993: 23)

Some degree of autonomous cultural reproduction was encouraged in the seventeenth century by the emergence of new religious movements, such as the Independents (*Yr Annibynwyr*) and the Baptists (*Y Bedyddwyr*), which paved the way for non-established religious affiliations with their own social organizations, networks and denominational presses. Calvinistic Methodism dominated the next century, with its emphasis on order, sobriety, piety and learning. The Methodist Church soon became established as the dominant religious force in large parts of the country. In the succeeding centuries, despite discrimination and persecution, dissenting religious groups flourished and encouraged a trans-Atlantic, Welsh-medium network of correspondents, journalists, teachers, social and spiritual interpreters that culminated in a period of late nineteenth-century liberal radicalism during which the lasting values of modern Wales were formed. During the latter part of the nineteenth century rapid anglicization occurred as a result of industrialization and urbanization. For the first time in Welsh history bilingualism became a mass phenomenon, creating a new, if relatively unstable sociolinguistic pattern.

Wales's huge population growth in the mid-nineteenth century, following industrialization and urbanization, a growth based on mineral exploitation of iron and coal together with steel and engineering production, meant that bilingualism became a mass phenomenon. It was reflected in new codes of worship, of work, leisure and political beliefs, which were transmitted to an increasingly literate workforce by the mass media created by print capitalism. The Welsh language was undoubtedly saved, according to Brinley Thomas (1959), by the redistribution of a growing population consequent to industrial expansion. Glanville Williams (1971) supported this thesis, arguing that, as industrialization generated internal migration, the Welsh, unlike the Scots or the Irish, did not have to abandon their language and homeland for employment abroad, particularly by emigrating to the New World. Consequently the large-scale rural–urban shift which took place within Wales was capable of sustaining a new set of Welsh institutions, which gave a fresh impetus to the indigenous language and culture, institutionalizing them within new, modernizing industrial domains.

This may be the principal reason why modern Welsh identity is more closely linked to the maintenance of language than any other Celtic case. Welsh culture is less reliant on institutions and is reflected more through popular involvement in chapel-based social activities, choral festivals, eisteddfodau competitions in music, drama and poetry, a brass band tradition, miners' libraries and early national sporting federations. These manifestations were as much a redefinition of indigenous Welsh culture as they were the sharpening of a distinctly Anglo-Welsh identity and tradition best represented in the literary work of Dylan Thomas, Gwyn Thomas and R. S. Thomas. However, this mutually dependent Welsh and Anglo-Welsh popular culture has heavily influenced the nature of urban Welsh-medium culture, for, unlike rural Wales, such changes were operative within a set of formal, English-medium public sector and commercial domains.

## A LONG CENTURY OF DECLINE

At the beginning of the twentieth century English had emerged as the dominant language in Wales, primarily as a result of in-migration and state policy. Imperial economic advances and state intervention following the Education Act of 1870 and the Welsh Intermediate Education Act of 1889, bred a new awareness of English values, culture and employment prospects and gave a powerful institutional fillip to the process of anglicization, which encouraged the normality of transmitting Welsh identity through the medium of English.

Closer economic and administrative association with the rest of the UK followed the standardization of education and local government. Modernization reinforced English and denigrated Welsh. Refusal to speak Welsh with one's children was a common enough reaction to the status differential which developed between the languages. How the masses welcomed this 'liberation' from traditionalism and conservatism is best evidenced by the wholesale generational language shift in the period 1914–45 (Pryce and Williams, 1988). English was perceived (and still is to a large extent) as the language of progress, of equality, of prosperity, of commerce, of mass entertainment and pleasure. Wider experience of empire-building, understandably, made acquisition of English a most compelling instrumental motivation, and the key to participation in the burgeoning British-influenced world economy. Added to this was the failure to use Welsh in the wide range of newer speech domains which developed in all aspects of the formal and social life of the nation. Whether by policy choice or the habit of neglect, Welsh became increasingly marginalized. It lost ground among groups most exposed to the opportunities of an improved standard of living in the urban culture of the south and north-east.

A prime vehicle of modernization was the rapidly expanding communication network, which intensified in the late nineteenth century. Social communication theorists stress the importance of physical and social communication in the development of self-conscious nations and in the process of cultural reproduction and replacement. In Wales, geographic isolation had provided some basis

for cultural differentiation both within and between the sociolinguistic communities. However, the development of an externally derived transport and
communication system served to reduce that isolation. Technology promised to
overcome the friction of distance. The critical factors influencing the development of the transport system were defence and commerce, in that it was
designed to facilitate through traffic from England to Ireland via Wales. The
main railway routes ran east–west through the centre and along the northern
and southern coasts respectively, with branch lines penetrating the resource-rich
hinterland to allow the exportation of slate, coal and iron and steel products.
This had the effect of integrating south Wales economically with the Bristol
region, the Midlands and London, and north Wales with Chester together with
the Lancashire conurbations focused on Manchester and Liverpool. Wales's
poorly developed internal road and rail system was not conducive to the
creation of a nationally shared space and territorial identification and led to post-
war economic initiatives either being located in better-served British regions or
attracted to Wales largely as a result of government subsidies and regional development grants.

As a consequence of both industrialization and modernization, political life in
Wales reflected the radicalism of a working-class mass struggling for representation, equality of opportunity and decent working and living conditions for
themselves and their dependants. At the turn of the twentieth century the majority of voting males supported the Liberal Party. It was dedicated to social justice,
to educational and health improvements under statutory regulation, to the disestablishment of the Church of England in Wales, and to Home Rule all round for
the Celtic nations, particularly in Ireland. In the Welsh-speaking parts of Wales
Liberalism was a vehicle for cultural nationalism and for the development of a
Nonconformist-influenced moral and social order. More prosaically, it was a
mass movement within which ordinary people could achieve some degree of
upward social mobility. Its strength lay in its ability to represent marginalized
people and places, particularly those drawn from the Celtic periphery and from
the burgeoning urban settlements that were under-represented in the Tory-
dominated shire counties and long-established market towns.

During the early part of the twentieth century, under its charismatic Welsh-
speaking Prime Minister, David Lloyd George, the Liberal Party was arguably
the most influential political party on the world stage, reflecting British imperial
power and interests. It was simultaneously the national party of Wales, advocating self-government at home, whilst enslaving more and more indigenous
people abroad in the name of God, King and Country. At the local level, the main
conduit for spreading the Liberals' message of social reform and democratic
representation was the Free Church or Nonconformist Chapel System which
pervaded almost every settlement in Wales. The spectacular growth of the
Nonconformist denominations following on from the Great Religious Revival of
1905 not only made Wales an outwardly more Christian society than hitherto but
also influenced nearly every aspect of public behaviour and private life. In both

literary and scholarly terms, Welsh popular culture owes a great deal to the opportunities for self-expression and publication afforded by the various denominations. Despite the ravages of secularization, the church and chapel system has long been a pillar of support for Welsh cultural maintenance and its impact even today should not be underestimated.

A minority resisted anglicization and developed counter-movements dedicated to the promotion of Welsh, inspired by intellectuals such as the Reverend Michael D. Jones, who led the small exodus to Patagonia (in Argentina) to establish a wholly Welsh migrant community (G. Williams, 1992). The Reverend Emrys ap Iwan was the first minister of religion to appear before a court of law and insist on the primacy of the Welsh language in legal proceedings in Wales. Dan Isaac Davies, HMI (Her Majesty's Inspector) for schools, advocated a greater use of Welsh-medium education. Thomas Gee, the publisher of such ambitious multi-volume encyclopaedias as *Gwyddoniadur* was an advocate of mass-circulation periodicals in Welsh. The most influential family of all was headed by O. M. Edwards, the university teacher, writer, publisher and first Chief HMI for schools in Wales, who tried to establish a more tolerant approach to bilingualism by attacking the injustice associated with the 'Welsh NOT' within the school system (the practice, common in the nineteenth century, whereby teachers, at the request of parents and governors, punished pupils for using Welsh within the school). His son, Sir Ifan ab Owen Edwards, established Urdd Gobaith Cymru (the Welsh League of Youth) in 1922; it has become the largest mass movement in Wales, encouraging children and young adults to develop skills, competence and leadership qualities in a variety of contexts, principally community work, eisteddfodau and sporting achievements.

In the Liberal heyday, Wales established a set of national institutions that paralleled those in Scotland and Ireland. These include the federal University of Wales (established 1883), the National Library of Wales at Aberystwyth and the National Museum of Wales at Cardiff (established in 1907), and the Church in Wales, which was created following the Act of Disestablishment in 1920. A variety of cultural movements flourished, such as Undeb Cenedlaethol Y Cymdeithasau Cymraeg (the National Union of Welsh Societies, formed in 1913), and Urdd Gobaith Cymru in 1922.

However, this impressive political-cultural infrastructure was still largely dependent upon external factors and it was soon concluded that the forces which militated against the reproduction of a Welsh culture could only be mediated by a form of genuine self-government or Home Rule. For the intellectual figures in the early language movement, culture, history and education were constant reference points. Their search for identity was predicated on a platform of struggle, recognition and legitimacy, as realized in a plethora of social reforms and cultural initiatives. In 1925 Plaid Genedlaethol Cymru (the Welsh National Party) was formed in Pwllheli by a small group of bourgeois intellectuals which included Saunders Lewis, a university lecturer and playwright, the Reverend Lewis Valentine, a Baptist minister, and D. J. Davies, an economist. Their initial concerns were the preservation of Welsh cultural and spiritual values primarily through the maintenance of a small-scale, predominantly rural, communitarian lifestyle. The nationalist movement sought to differentiate itself from political movements based upon imperialist or social-class appeals. It sought to do so primarily through a series of prescient policy initiatives mostly related to the restitution of Welsh as the national language. It is no exaggeration to claim that much of the language-related activity since the 1920s has been a playing out of the agenda set by early Plaid Cymru leaders.

Cultural nationalism was profoundly influenced by Nonconformist principles, yet not exclusively so, for at a critical early juncture, nationalism's moral philosophy was deeply imbued by the Catholicism of several of its original leaders. Yet in contrast to Catholic Ireland between 1880 and 1921 Wales did not succumb to the power of the gun in the name of national freedom, despite several attempts to use the Irish example as an inspiration.[1] Both the constitutional and 'physical force' traditions contributed to the ideology that in order to be reborn the Irish nation had to demand the sacrifice of martyrs for the cause. This common thread in romantic nationalism emphasized land, language, race, a common past and the necessity for open conflict in the struggle against the oppressors. In Wales there was an overriding commitment to non-violent principles in nationalism's thought and deed.[2] In contradistinction to most other political movements in the second phase of 1921–39, pacifism and non-violent resistance characterized Welsh nationalism.[3] It articulated a popular belief in community-orientated consensus politics as advocated by the two most influential presidents of Plaid Cymru, Saunders Lewis, who was leader from 1926 to 1939, and advocated a combination of constitutional and unconstitutional direct action, and Gwynfor Evans, leader from 1945 to 1981, who was a committed pacifist and moved the party in the direction of total opposition to violence and war as a means of achieving self-government.[4]

The principal concerns of the original nationalist movements were the Welsh language, national identity and Christianity. The three aims of Plaid Genedlaethol Cymru in 1925 were all related to the promotion of Welsh.[5] It was only after 1932 that self-government was adopted as party policy as a means of achieving national self-respect and some semblance of autonomy.

Although preoccupied with questions of language defence, the nationalist intelligentsia did not adopt a narrow conception of their predicament.[6] They were well aware of, and contributed in part to, the dominant European paradigms which focused on liberalism with its insistence on individual freedom and mutual tolerance as a means of overcoming the lack of social justice and on socialism with its materialistic explanation of inequality.[7] Control of the state apparatus so as to make it more accountable and more reformist was the principal goal. Early Welsh nationalists sought a redefinition of the evolving European order in moral not in materialistic terms. However, although in the main the intelligentsia turned to the Celtic realm for moral inspiration and to post-Civil-War Ireland as an example of a successful national struggle, Saunders

Lewis sought his authenticity in the larger context of a European, Catholic and Latin civilization.[8]

Saunders Lewis believed that medieval Europe possessed a unity of spirit and of law, which protected and nurtured small nations because diversity could only be accommodated within a universal European civilization. In his seminal lecture 'Egwyddorion Cenedlaetholdeb'[9] he outlined his conception of Welsh national history, which was to be influential in subsequent justification both of the language struggle and party strategy.

He argued, perhaps ironically, that it was nationalism which had destroyed the civilization of Wales, and of other small countries in Europe. In medieval Europe individual cultures were nurtured and protected because their rulers deferred to a higher authority.[10] Having usurped the moral Christian order from the sixteenth century onwards state nationalism inaugurated a programme of state–nation congruence in the name of the people, covering a systematic extirpation of minorities under a veil of democratic rhetoric which in time emphasized the principles of liberty and equality, if not always brotherhood, within the state's aegis.

In order that his compatriots deliver themselves from the false consciousness of British imperialism and state nationalism, Lewis advocated that they promulgate a genuine nationalism as a necessary means by which Welsh culture would be nurtured within its own political institutions. Lewis justified the selection of Welsh as the critical battleground for political action because its continuance, despite centuries of state-inspired anglicization, was proof of the Welsh having kept faith with the universal values of a pre-existent Europeanness. Wales should 'demand a seat in the League of Nations, so that she may act as Europe's interpreter in Britain, and as a link to bind England and the Empire to Christendom and to the League itself' (quoted in D. G. Jones, 1973: 33).

In this redirection of Welsh politics, away from the empire and towards contemporary Europe, Lewis set the tone for a long-standing debate within nationalism, the strains of which echoed until his death in 1985. It concerned his drawing upon Catholic Europe for inspiration and his personal advocacy of Catholic social and political policy, for Lewis had converted to Catholicism and been received into the Roman Catholic Church on 16 February 1932. Ostensibly radical, dissenting and Nonconformist, the Welsh populace did not approve of his political convictions and personal style. The Nationalist Party was criticized for being élitist, intellectual, and unpatriotic because some members appeared to support quasi-Fascist movements in Europe.[11]

These conflicting interpretations are summarized in the exchange which took place in the pages of *Y Llenor* in 1927. In responding to criticism of the rise of a 'Neo-Catholic Movement in Wales', Lewis distanced himself from other nationalists, such as Ambrose Bebb, who were charged with admiring the ideas of Barres and Maurras and advocating the adoption in Wales of the ideas trumpeted by L'Action Française (D. G. Jones, 1973: 45). W. J. Gruffydd's reply has been described as 'an eloquent statement of that radical liberal individualism which had been Wales's main political tradition in the second half of the nine-teenth century' (D. G. Jones, 1973: 45). Whereas Lewis's ideas are based on a pristine conception of what Wales could and should be, Gruffydd and those he represented portrayed Wales as it was, and wanted to advance Wales into a co-equal, fully recognized partnership within the British state, wherein Welsh distinctiveness might be secured (C. H. Williams, 2000).

## NON-VIOLENT POLITICAL RESISTANCE

In the post-war period a large number of capital-intensive projects initiated by the state so as to provide water, hydro-electric power, etc., resulted in some Welsh communities being transformed and several Welsh valleys being drowned to provide water for English cities.[12] This was after unsuccessful non-violent protests, in which Gwynfor Evans, president of Plaid Cymru, played a prominent role. There followed a sporadic and largely symbolic bombing campaign directed against symbolic targets and state property.

When Gwynfor Evans became president of Plaid Cymru in 1945 he reflected a more typical stratum of Welsh nationalism, although his background was far from typical.[13] His Christian commitment to pacifism marked him out as a prin-cipled leader of his party (Evans, 1986: 16) who refused to advocate the use of violence, citing the Irish experience where the trappings of an independent state had singularly failed to institute an indigenous national culture which was both popular and geographically widespread. The accurate, if pessimistic, accounts by Fennell (1977) and Hindley (1990) of the slow death of Irish confirms this fact. Gwynfor Evans acknowledged that

> if I thought violence could ever be justified in the pursuit of any social objective it would be to secure freedom and full nationhood for Wales, the cause in which most of my life has been spent. But even this noble cause, on which the survival of the Welsh nation depends, does not in my view justify the use of violence. (1986: 15)

How the national movement, especially Plaid Cymru, developed these princi-ples has been the subject of much debate and analysis (J. Davies, 1981, 1985; C. H. Williams, 1982, 1994; McAllister, 1995). Since the early 1970s Plaid Cymru's justification for advancing the cause of independence has widened considerably from the over-dominant language issue of the inter-war years to a more balanced and holistic view of Welsh problems in a broader British and European context (Williams, 1982, 1991b). It currently returns four MPs to the Westminster Parliament, all representing heartland constituencies, and usually claims the political affiliation of about 10 per cent of the Welsh electorate. Within the National Assembly it is the second largest party, with seventeen of the sixty seats available. Plaid Cymru's leadership role has been diffused and lessened some-what as a co-ordinating body and fulcrum of resistance to anglicization and centralism.

The most significant popular manifestation of the language struggle was the formation of Cymdeithas yr Iaith Gymraeg (the Welsh Language Society) in 1963 following Saunders Lewis's radio lecture, 'Tynged yr Iaith' (The Fate of the Language). Initially concerned with single-issue campaigning in favour of reforms such as the production of official bilingual forms, tax and television licences, a separate Welsh-medium television channel and greater equality between Welsh and English in judicial affairs, Cymdeithas yr Iaith Gymraeg has developed into a real force for sustained change in Wales (Williams, 1986; Phillips, 1998). Cymdeithas yr Iaith Gymraeg is both a direct-action pressure group and an unofficial language think-tank. Its key contribution is awareness-raising within civil society. It can draw upon the active involvement of a number of independent individuals and organizations, which is another source of its collective strength. Many of the language reforms now enjoyed in Wales are largely, with the addition of other influences, the result of the persistent campaigning of Cymdeithas yr Iaith Gymraeg as a spearhead for the wider language movement, even if in many cases it is recognized that key decisions are often taken despite, not because of, the tactics which it employs.

Today the majority accepts that bilingualism is an established feature within society. Many applaud the availability of bilingual provision, especially in terms of advancing their children's education and social prospects. A minority of parents agitated for Welsh-medium education, which the Labour Party developed through its the pioneering bilingual educational policies in anglicized Wales, especially Flint and Glamorgan. In part this was a response to Nationalist pressure and also to Labour's commitment to satisfying the desires of parental pressure groups, and the increased self-esteem of Welsh speakers. Even so, it would be less than honest not to report also that the greatest opposition to the development of Welsh-medium education and of language issues generally came from within Labour-affiliated ranks. The Labour Party was rooted in a British sense of identity, predicated upon social class divisions not ethnic antagonism, and saw any increase in the development of Welsh-medium education as necessarily weakening this British base in favour of a more focused Welsh national (if not necessarily nationalist) identification.

THE GEOGRAPHY AND DEMOGRAPHY OF LANGUAGE CONTACT

As Chapter 2 details, despite many problems, the decennial census returns are still the most comprehensive data source relating to language ability in Wales. The first language census in Wales was conducted in 1891 and it recorded that 898,914 spoke Welsh (54.4 per cent). Ten years later, in 1901, 929,824 (49.9 per cent) were so recorded. At its census peak in 1911, the Welsh-speaking population numbered 977,366 (43.5 per cent) of whom 190,300 were monoglot Welsh. Continuous decline throughout the century resulted in a 1981 population of 503,549 speakers, of whom 21,283 recorded themselves as monoglot. This figure should be regarded with caution for it is highly unlikely that many individuals aged five and over are unable to speak English in Wales (Williams, 1982). By 1991 the Welsh-speaking population had declined to 496,530, a fall of some 1.4 per cent (Aitchison and Carter, 1993). Care has to be taken in the recent decennial comparison 1981–91 because the definition and treatment of absent households has changed in the intervening period. If the population base used in the 1991 census is adopted, the Welsh-speaking population of Wales is 508,549 some 18.7 per cent of the total population (aged three and over) of 2,723,623. In crude terms this suggests a proportional loss of 25 per cent, down from 44 per cent in 1911. It bodes well in that the long trend of decline has slowed, compared with the acute fall of 17.3 per cent between 1961 and 1971, and the fall of 6.3 per cent for the period 1971–81.

The contemporary Welsh-speaking population is predominantly aged and is concentrated in proportional terms in the north and west; it is showing encouraging signs of growth amongst the younger age groups, particularly in the industrial south and east; this growth can be largely attributed to the development of Welsh-medium education in such areas, in combination with the wider scale revival of interest in the language and its institutionalization in many aspects of public life. Welsh has become increasingly identified with government support and targeted for an increase in use within the economy. However, many find it difficult to secure adequate employment within predominantly Welsh-speaking regions, which atrophy because of the out-migration of the young, fecund and well-educated and the in-migration of non-Welsh-speaking residents, who are attracted by a variety of factors. Thus a central issue is whether or not a viable Welsh culture can survive without its own heartland communities serving as a resource-base for language transmission.

A second trend of the 1991 census is the substantial increase in the numbers of Welsh speakers aged between three and fifteen. Encouraging though these figures are, especially for anglicized regions, one should not forget that many factors could reduce their impact on Welsh language reproduction in the next century. The development of mass tourism, seasonal employment patterns, out-migration, economic change and language of marriage partner will still influence rates of language loss and gain but as each decennial census records higher and higher proportions in the younger age categories then the demographic future for Welsh seems brighter than at any other time since 1911. In raw statistical terms, the trends of the past two decades allow us to say that the imminent death of the Welsh language was wildly exaggerated.

Language census figures at the end of the twentieth century revealed a welcome arrest of the sharp pattern of decline and should be interpreted as a significant boost to halting language shift. Nevertheless, the 1991 census figures underestimate the total population of Welsh speakers in the UK on two counts. First, they exclude from the analysis the many thousands of Welsh speakers who reside outside Wales. Secondly, many Welsh speakers interpret their self-assessed inadequacy to communicate effectively in 'standard Welsh' as sufficient reason not to claim an ability to speak, read and write Welsh. Conversely, as with any self-administered questionnaire, there are also those who undoubtedly exaggerate their linguistic abilities. The true figure is probably nearer to 25 per cent of the population, but as the census asks for ability not use, it must be interpreted with care as reflecting potential not reality.

Historically, the hearth, the farm, the chapel and community have been the traditional domains which sustained a Welsh-medium network of agencies of language reproduction. With the secularization of society and the breakdown of the relative homogeneity of rural communities, an alternative, urban, formal set of domains have been constructed in the urban industrial environments where the Welsh-medium school system has done more than any other agency to reproduce the language and introduce it, and its related culture, to hitherto non-Welsh-speaking families. The 1991 census reported that 16.1 per cent of three to four year olds spoke Welsh, compared with 13.3 per cent in 1981 and 11.3 per cent in 1971. However, other data sources suggest that the mother-tongue figure is closer to 4.6 per cent. Higher percentages of Welsh speakers amongst five to nine year olds (24.7 per cent) and ten to fourteen year olds (26.9 per cent) as compared to the three to four year old cohort in 1981 (13.3 per cent) suggests a value-added effect of primary and secondary education, as schools are the primary extra-familial agency for language transmission. A partial explanation for this discrepancy is that the public's interpretation of the census questions has changed because Welsh has been included in the National Curriculum since 1988. Nevertheless, the school system's influence is crucial and likely to increase following the 1988 Education Act which insisted that Welsh be a core subject in the National Curriculum. It is now possible to teach a wide range of subjects including maths and science, design and computing through the medium of Welsh. After 1994, all save a few opt-out schools in the secondary sector were obliged to teach Welsh to the pupils in the lower forms. This, in turn, has exposed a far greater section of Welsh youth to the language and culture of their homeland but will also require a continued significant investment in teachers and resources if it is to be successful. In higher education circles there is a modest range of vocational and non-vocational courses available to full- and part-time students, but it must be emphasized that in all such developments the numbers involved within any particular course are small. Even so the trend and direction of change is significant for it extends both the domain use and practical utility of bilingualism in society. However, there remains a crucial sociolinguistic question. If provision is increasing apace in most domains, what of the actual usage, status and application of bilingual skills in the market-place?

The development of a lively and innovative publishing sector has also contributed greatly to the enjoyment of written and read Welsh. By comparison with English, the range and overall quality leaves much to be desired, although, given the constraints which face any lesser used language, the output is remarkable. A third of all books are school texts or children's books, initially dealing with Welsh themes by Welsh authors, but increasingly translating the more popular English-medium stories, reference books and visually stunning discovery and factual/documentary guide books. Adult books are dominated by literary conventions which prize verse, prose, eisteddfodic competition winners and the like, reflecting the niche market of Welsh-medium publishing. Contemporary drama, rather than the novel, is more likely to be translated because it is related to performance and to the probability of having been commissioned for television or radio. Broadcasting is one acid test of the social use and adaptability of Welsh culture. Radio paved the way with a limited range of Welsh-medium transmissions in the 1950s and 1960s, largely devoted to religious, children or daily-life issues. In 1977–9 as a result of the development of VHF wavebands, an English-medium Radio Wales and a predominantly Welsh-medium Radio Cymru service was launched. The latter provides some 127 hours per week, ninety of which are in Welsh and are of a reasonable quality. Radio Cymru might be said to act like a national network for it encourages audience participation to a far greater extent than do its far more diverse and hence specialist English counterparts.

The greatest boost to the popular and technical use of Welsh was the inauguration of Sianel Pedwar Cymru (S4C, a Welsh-language television channel) on 1 November 1982. For thirty years there had been a gradually expanding television output in Welsh, such that by 1982 some 10 per cent of programmes were broadcast in Welsh. The 1974 Crawford Committee recommended the establishment of a Welsh-medium channel, as did the Conservative manifesto pledge of 1979. However, within a few months of taking office the new administration withdrew its commitment, preferring to improve the existing broadcasting arrangements. This policy change engendered the largest mass protests witnessed in post-war Wales. The pivotal act of this campaign was the 5 May 1980 decision of Gwynfor Evans to fast to death unless the government announced the creation of S4C. On 17 September 1980 the government reversed its decision, and today some thirty-four out of 145 hours per week are transmitted in Welsh, mainly at peak time. They reach a relatively high percentage of their target audience and are facing the future with more confidence now. S4C's digital service includes twelve hours of Welsh-medium programmes per day. S4C is a commissioning rather than a production body, and in consequence has spawned a network of independent film-makers, animators, creative designers, writers, who can turn their original Welsh-language programmes into English or 'foreign' languages for sale in the international media market-place. Cardiff ranks second to London as a media-production centre in the UK, with all the technical, economic and post-production implications of a growing infrastructure in such a specialist industry. Four issues dominate the current Welsh-broadcasting debate: (1) financial self-sufficiency versus subsidy; (2) the relaxation of boundaries inside programmes between the use of Welsh and English; (3) the multicultural nature of S4C, which transmits European soccer and sport, repackaged documentaries, soaps, quizzes and a host of other material all dubbed into Welsh (in part this is to attract new viewers to the channel and in part it reflects S4C's participation in the European Broadcasting Union and commercial marketing of international television material); (4) the channel's response to the challenge of digital television and its search for additional opportunities and new partners. Media and technological developments are a major feature of language use and it is anticipated that a companion volume to the present will deal with the issue of language planning and technological advances in communication.

At a voluntary level there is an active network of eisteddfodau (competitive cultural festivals) which nurture school and community performances of Welsh plays, or plays in translation, of musical items, poetry, craft work, art and design and scientific projects. More recently, the Urdd (the Welsh League of Youth) has reinterpreted conventional Welsh mass culture by adding go-carting, tenpin bowling, discos and surfing 'in Welsh'. An additional voluntaristic element is the adult learning of Welsh through Wlpan and related schemes which are geographically widespread and well attended. These in turn often feed Welsh clubs and social centres, which may have sport, folk dancing or music as their focus but offer a wider entry into the indigenous culture. Capping all this is the healthy and vibrant Welsh popular music scene, which has emerged since the 1970s. It reflects a fusion of three trends: indigenous Welsh music, a revitalized Celtic music industry and the international popularity of Welsh bands, such as Catatonia, the Manic Street Preachers and Gorky's Zygotic Mynci who perform in both Welsh and English. For the first time in living memory, major British newspapers are hailing the Welsh film industry, youth scene and most of its associated activities as 'energized', 'sexy' and 'cool'.

Most of the financing for this burgeoning cultural revival has come from community support and Welsh Office funding for Welsh-language education, together with many social activities, for example, Mudiad Ysgolion Meithrin (the Welsh Nursery Schools Movement, founded in 1971), Eisteddfod Genedlaethol Cymru (the National Eisteddfod of Wales), Cyngor Llyfrau Cymraeg (the Welsh Books Council) and some economic activities such as Menter a Busnes (Business and Enterprise), which promotes enterprise in Welsh-speaking networks and communities.

## REGIONAL PLANNING AND LANGUAGE VITALITY

The language movement has rediscovered its 'ecological' heritage, and has repackaged what were deemed to be rural community issues in the 1920s and 1930s as issues of 'cultural species' survival and as a local response to globalization. Having fought for language recognition in the post-war period, the current challenge is to address questions of economic development, environmental protection and conservation and holistic planning. Processes such as the in-migration of non-Welsh speakers, mixed marriages, language shift, the revolution in telecommunications and journey-to-work patterns have all contributed to the fragmentation of 'Y Fro Gymraeg' (The Welsh Heartland) which has three consequences. First, it reduces the territorial dominance of Welsh as the unquestioned, 'normal' language of the north and west. Secondly, it reduces the cogency of territorial language planning schemes at the meso-scale. Thirdly, it throws into doubt the ability of local authorities to continue to advance ad hoc and reactive policies to promote Welsh anywhere within the country. Is fragmentation and collapse the inevitable future for these areas? And if so, should we be far less concerned with notions of domination, of territorial control and of resistance to externally induced change?

James and Williams (1997) argue for a closer integration of language considerations within structure planning. The first structure plans were approved by the Secretary of State for Wales in the 1970s. In the late 1980s and early 1990s new plans were based on the post-1974 counties and reflected the strength of Welsh speakers and the planning philosophies of the eight county council planning authorities. James and Williams recommend consideration of three elements within any development plan:

1. Does the plan examine the role of the language within the fabric of society and community in the plan area?
2. Are there specific policies relating to the language?
3. Do the combined package of policies assist the survival and continuation of distinct language communities?

The wide variations in the priority given to the language issue may be illustrated by comparing Gwynedd CC's Structure Plan (1993) which includes, as the fifth of its six strategic policies,

> to recognise that the Welsh language is a material consideration in assessing the implications of development in Gwynedd. This will be implemented in a manner which ensures that the aim of safeguarding and nurturing the use of the Welsh language in Gwynedd is achieved.

In the Clwyd CC plan (1991) the fourth, and last, objective is 'to have specific regard to the aspirations of local communities and local needs' and continues under 'social considerations' when discussing 'the scale of housing development' that 'at the local level also, many small, often predominantly Welsh-speaking communities do not want to see an influx of outsiders'. By contrast the very last of the forty-nine strategic aims of the Powys CC plan (1994) is 'to support and encourage the development of the Welsh language in communities'.

In the Gwynedd plan (1993) there is no further policy relating specifically to Welsh because its continued well-being is an integral part of the plan, especially of the housing policies. The plan, as submitted to the Secretary of State, was to restrict new housing provision to proven local need and employment-related movement. In modifying the plan before approving it, the Secretary rewrote the housing policies and removed all reference to differentiation in the housing market and so supported the lobby of the Land Authority for Wales and House

Builders Federation and overruled the support of the Campaign for the Protection of Rural Wales, the Welsh Language Society, the Countryside Council for Wales and the Welsh Language Board. A concession was the policy on affordable housing for local need. However, the 'needs and interests of the Welsh language' remains the third of ten factors to be considered when assessing the scale and phasing of new housing development. What is evident from comparing the submitted plan and modifications is the different interpretation as to how the plan can best 'take the needs and interests of the language into account' (Welsh Office, 1988).

More typical is the Powys plan (1994) which states that:

> The needs and interests of the Welsh language will be a material consideration when development proposals are being determined in areas which are significantly Welsh speaking. Developments that safeguard and facilitate the use of the Welsh language will be permitted providing that there are no unacceptable planning, access, service and amenities problems.

The main policy considerations are:

- the relevance of the Welsh language as a material consideration;
- the very strong connection between land use/development and community/language issues;
- the Welsh language was not a major issue during plan preparation;
- all physical development takes place within a policy framework that has social implications;
- social factors include community, cultural and traditional issues and language is implicit in all of these, whether it be English, Welsh, or a particular dialect of either;
- to facilitate the continued use and growth of usage of Welsh;
- the connection between housing for local needs and the emphasis on community need and local circumstances and the interaction between social communication and land use planning;
- the need to encourage the right type of economic, residential and social developments that would bring benefits.

Policies in Clwyd, Dyfed and Powys emphasize employment, housing, transport, tourism, recreation, conservation and community development in Welsh-speaking areas. They advocate positive measures on the maintenance and enhancement of balanced communities which are as important as, if not more than, a simplistic policy 'to save the Welsh language'.

Despite not being a priority within the structure plans of the anglicized counties of the industrial south-east and north-east, it is here that the most promising signs of language growth are recorded. Here Welsh speakers constitute a different type of communication network from the more conventional rural communities. Community without propinquity is a better characterization of such networks in anglicized towns. The declining significance of territorial strongholds means that conventional Welsh-language communities will become increasingly fragmented and reconstituted as nodes within a more plural sociolinguistic context. This will require a greater dependence on factors such as the mass media to integrate Welsh speakers within a communication network. Yet, no matter how comprehensive may be the new social communication system, Welsh speakers will still need a region or a set of spaces wherein their language is dominant, or at the very least, co-equal with English. This is because the routinization of culture and economy can best be accomplished within familiar spaces. We thus need to identify new ways of adopting a spatial planning perspective to serve an ever-changing reality. One of the determining factors influencing this choice will be the infrastructure currently being developed to support bilingual services. Absolute population increases and percentage and absolute increases of Welsh speakers in Cardiff, Llandrindod, Mold, Caernarfon, Llangefni, Aberystwyth and Carmarthen all point to a relocation of linguistic strength from villages in traditional heartland areas to new urban centres. These changes pose fresh planning challenges, as new nodal cores in urban networks become the centres for bilingual educational establishments and foci of bilingual service provision.

Throughout Europe we are beginning to chart the relationship between the planning profession and indigenous and exogenous cultures. The human capital of minority language groups is slowly being incorporated into both economic policy and the planning policy review process. It is inconceivable that future regional and local plans will not take full account of the statutory obligations laid upon local authorities by, for example, the provisions of the Welsh Language Act and their implementation through the Welsh Language Board. The planning system will continue to reflect a society in which the exact implications of exercising language rights in specific domains are still being realized. In that respect it remains one of the most critical, if contested, instruments of our democracy.

## THE DEVELOPMENT OF LANGUAGE POLICY

Agencies of the state and of the Established Church employed Welsh in a wide range of domains even though there has not been a statutory obligation to recognize Welsh as an official language within Wales since the sixteenth century. It was not until the passing of the Welsh Courts Act of 1942 that the provisions prohibiting the use of Welsh by the Acts of Union were rescinded. Further legal recognition in the Welsh Language Act of 1967 offered an initial and inadequate definition of the equal validity of English and Welsh in Wales. This related to the provision of Welsh in the Courts of Law and in legal proceedings generally, but did not extend into the wider sphere of public administration and formal bilingual rights.

During the 1960s and 1970s a number of statutory and non-statutory bodies called for greater state support for the language. One initial response by the Welsh Office was the establishment in 1977 of the short-lived Cyngor yr Iaith Gymraeg (the Welsh Language Council). Under section 21 of the 1980 Education

Act, government provided grants to support specific activities in schools and colleges, such as the provision of additional staff and Welsh-medium teaching resources. As a result of the increased demand, section 21 expenditure increased fourfold from £1 million in 1981 to £4 million in 1991. However, as Williams and Raybould (1991: 13) have noted, such figures compare poorly with the level of support for teaching English as a second language in England and Wales. One LEA in England, for example, received £14 million in one year under section 11 of the 1980 Act.

A more purposeful educational planning body was established in February 1986 as a result of long-term political pressure. Pwyllgor Datblygu Addysg Gymraeg (PDAG, the Welsh Language Education Development Committee) was created by the authority of the Welsh Office, but it specified that it should function within the purview of the Welsh Joint Education Committee (CBAC, Cyd-Bwyllgor Addysg Cymru) as a local authority directed but Welsh Office and County Council funded agency. Its brief was to chart the anticipated needs of Welsh-medium education in the statutory sector, but it quickly enlarged this brief by tackling both the nursery and post-school provision. A pioneering body, it helped shape the priorities in the medium term, collated valuable experience and information, distributed government finances to support resource and learning development and generally acted as a mouthpiece for educational issues in Wales. As such, despite its small staff and budget, it was an effective forerunner for what could become a more comprehensive national educational institute (C. H. Williams, 1989).

Within twelve months, calls for a stronger Welsh Language Act led to the establishment in July 1988 of a wholly government-appointed, non-statutory Welsh Language Board (Bwrdd yr Iaith Gymraeg). In its short, if controversial, lifespan, the board sought to raise the profile of Welsh in both public sector and formerly state-owned, now privately owned, corporations. It persuaded gas, electricity, telephone and water companies to adopt bilingual advertising, customer service and billing facilities, information packs and bilingual service points. These reforms enabled the language to be chosen and used in a larger number of formal settings than hitherto. The first board also advised on needs, priorities and strategies for private industry to encourage bilingual practices and consumer relations, such that in most Welsh towns and cities it was possible to identify far more bilingual service and information signs than ever, particularly in banks, large departmental stores and offices.

## LEGISLATION AND LANGUAGE PLANNING AGENCIES

The Welsh Language Act 1993 provided a statutory framework for the treatment of English and Welsh on the basis of equality and inaugurated a new era in language planning. Its chief policy instrument is the refashioned and strengthened Welsh Language Board, established on 21 December 1993, as a non-departmental statutory organization. It is funded by an annual grant from the National Assembly (for details see Chapter 3). The board has five core functions or main duties, namely: (i) promoting and facilitating the use of the Welsh language; (ii) advising on and influencing matters related to the Welsh language; (iii) stimulating and overseeing the process of preparing and implementing language schemes; (iv) distributing grants to promote and facilitate the use of Welsh; (v) maintaining a strategic overview of Welsh-medium education.

The Welsh Language Act 1993 details key steps to be taken by the Welsh Language Board and by public-sector bodies in the preparation of Welsh-language schemes. These schemes are designed to implement the central principle of the Act, namely to treat Welsh and English on the basis of equality. Since 1995 a total of sixty-seven language schemes have been approved including all twenty-two local authorities. In 1998 notices had been issued to a further fifty-nine bodies to prepare schemes. As is detailed in Chapters 3 and 8, the Welsh Language Board's primary goal is to enable the language to become self-sustaining and secure as a medium of communication in Wales. It has set itself four priorities: (1) to increase the numbers of Welsh speakers; (2) to provide more opportunities to use the language; (3) to change the habits of language use and encourage people to take advantage of the opportunities provided; and (4) to strengthen Welsh as a community language.

The Welsh Language Board has a wide-ranging remit which includes promoting the formal acceptance of bilingualism as a societal norm in the public sector, to oversee the provision of Welsh-medium education in all sectors from the cradle to the grave, to oversee the language policy of major media institutions such as the BBC and S4C, to audit the financing and subscription levels of Welsh journals, to require local authorities to submit language plans detailing their policy and provision for meeting the needs of bilinguals in their authorities. These responsibilities form part of the statutory, hence binding, remit of the Welsh Language Board. Its role in the private sector has been to encourage the voluntaristic adoption of bilingual practices through Welsh Language Board joint ventures and initiatives such as marketing the language, devising language courses for employees, preparing commercial documents and terminology to smooth the transition from English-only to bilingual working practices in some industries and regions.

Less than a decade on, we may conclude that the establishment of the Welsh Language Board, and its associated legal, research, educational and general language status divisions, represents the single most important act of formal language planning ever experienced in Wales. However, as we shall also see throughout this volume, the board has not been without its critics and detractors.

## THE GOVERNMENT OF WALES ACT 1998

The high point of the language struggle towards normalization was the establishment of the National Assembly for Wales in May 1999 which signalled a new era in the development of a bilingual society. The aim of devolution supporters was to establish a form of self-government, as a response to the democratic deficit in Wales. Significantly, from day one the Assembly operated as a bilingual chamber. This is unique within the UK but is fairly normal within the Commonwealth, European regional legislatures, such as in Catalonia and Euskadi, within the organs of the European Union, or within other supranational organizations, such as the Council of Europe, NATO and the United Nations.[14] The Assembly is committed to developing a substantive bilingual policy within a multicultural context and is likely to seek to adopt a stronger multilingual line in keeping with the demands of a rapidly evolving European Union.

Assembly deliberations on language policy will focus on three important aspects (C. H. Williams, 1999). First, there is language policy in relation to education and public administration, equal rights and the socialization of citizens within civil society. This would involve, *inter alia*, issues such as the development of bilingual education, bilingual service provision in local government, health and social services, and at a more strategic level, interaction between the British state and its unwritten constitution, the European Convention on Human Rights, and the implementation of EU language policies. Secondly, the Assembly is expected to formulate economic policies and regional development initiatives which will seek to stabilize predominantly Welsh-speaking communities, to create employment and to promote bilingual working opportunities. Thirdly, consideration of the interests of Welsh language and culture as they are impacted upon by town and country/structure planning and improvements to the transport system will be a significant feature of regional planning policies. In addition the pressing housing, property control and rural service issues highlighted by various bodies including Jigso and Cymdeithas yr Iaith are likely be addressed, though it is unlikely that they will be a priority. Even so it is probable that Assembly policies on bilingualism will be complemented by the promotion of positive attitudes to Welsh culture and heritage.

A prime issue in the normalization of Welsh will be the extent to which it can become a cross-cutting medium of governance and administration and not limited to its own committee for Welsh language and culture, that is, not become commodified and separated out as a 'problem area'. A second issue is the degree to which the bilingual Assembly will influence the language-choice behaviour of the public. Critics sympathetic to the promotion of Welsh observe that local authorities have invested heavily in statutory language schemes which in reality are of little interest to all but a handful of Welsh speakers. It would be regrettable if the Assembly's commitment were not matched by the public's adoption of Welsh as a language of interaction with national government. In turn the

Assembly may use its position as an exemplar, a testing ground, as an educator and a significant actor to influence behaviour in this regard. A third issue for political debate is how the Assembly will respond to calls for a revised Welsh Language Act to influence developments within the private sector. This is the acid test of the political commitment of the Assembly to constructing a bilingual society. There are many variants on how such an Act could be implemented, but at present the government has shown little interest in sponsoring inquiries, whether they be commercial, linguistic or legalistic in nature, as to the probable effects of implementing a far more comprehensive Language Act.

An additional issue is the supply of specialists to operate the Assembly. Critics have warned that just as the development of a bilingual media (*c.* 1985–97) drew on talented professionals from within Welsh-medium religious and educational circles, so opportunities afforded by the Assembly and its associated domains will pose a second threat to the staffing levels of the education system. This is a major challenge to the university sector which, as a matter of urgency, should provide training courses and bilingual specialist diplomas in matters related to a range of functions which fall under the remit of the Assembly. The Assembly has the potential to be a major fillip to the fortunes of Welsh but it should not be viewed either as the 'saviour of the language' or the sole agency for language promotion. Other voices should be encouraged.

## THE PRESENT COLLECTION

The eleven chapters which follow have been assembled for two major purposes. The first is to provide an up-to-date assessment of language revitalization efforts in Wales. The second is to present arguments concerning the fundamental issues which underlie language policy and planning matters. Bilingual and multicultural education, identity change, political reform, regional economic promotion, community development, European Union expansion – all of these are relevant in Wales and across contexts. Four areas are given special attention: (1) the role of strategic planning best represented by the activities of the Welsh Language Board; (2) the historical development and increasing salience of Welsh-medium or bilingual education, both within the school system and in terms of adult education provision; (3) the impact of language intervention measures on community, social and economic development; (4) the European comparative context, which is essential if current efforts at language revitalization are to be harmonized within other programmes of structural and economic change.

In Chapter 2, Hywel Jones and I demonstrate the complexity of data relating to the social systems in which language policies and practices are embedded. We examine both census and non-census sources, drawing out both the inconsistencies and implications which underpin the interpretation of behavioural trends within the family, education and the economy. Encouraging though census and educational data are for anglicized regions in particular, a number of factors could reduce the vitality of Welsh language reproduction in the future. These would include the failure of Welsh language transmission within the family, the relatively high numbers of Welsh speakers who are linguistically isolated within the home context and the difficulty of maintaining comprehensive Welsh-medium social networks. However, the worrying trend is what may be described as the weakening of the contribution of 'natural' speakers both in raw numerical terms and in terms of the uses to which the language is put. Clearly whether the quality/standard of spoken Welsh or the particular forms of Welsh expression, syntax and grammar are quite what the post-war cultural activists expected is quite another matter. This volume does not address issues of corpus language planning, but quite naturally they are directly related to all the other issues we do discuss. Indeed many of our policy recommendations will not succeed unless there is substantial investment in terminological development and diffusion.

Chapter 3 presents the Welsh Language Board's current strategy for language revitalization. Having made numerous forays into interventionist language planning, the current thinking seeks to present a more integrated, holistic overview of policy. It recognizes that long-term achievements will come only through a series of constructive partnerships with the various agencies already engaged in determining policy and delivering bilingual services. However, it would be disingenuous not to recognize that the Welsh Language Board is itself the dominant actor in such partnerships, as it exercises its statutory mandate to plan and to finance a broadening range of Welsh-language activities. Consequently the chapter also details the means by which the implementation of policy is to be evaluated through performance indicators, target dates and the medium-term monitoring of its agreed language schemes with public and voluntary organizations. Both the role and direction of the Language Board in the past have been the subject of intense criticism. The major lines of attack have been that it was an unelected quango; it failed to engage in purposive language planning; it overly occupied itself with distributing government grants and by so doing determined the priorities of Welsh cultural life; it engaged in a campaign whereby the language issue was depoliticized and its former chair, Lord Dafydd Elis-Thomas (currently President of the National Assembly for Wales) was a prominent advocate of the position that the language struggle was over. By this he meant that Wales enjoyed sufficient political and legislative autonomy to determine the construction of a fully functional bilingual society if it so willed. It was argued that slogans and battle cries, derived from a position of dependency and subservience, did not square with the current reality of a democratically elected Assembly within which issues of language policy would be decided as a normal part of governance. This is a slightly disingenuous position, for in the absence of a sustained political debate it is only by raising the matter through the campaigning activities of Cymdeithas yr Iaith Gymraeg and Cefn that periodic attention is given to the issue of enlarging the range of citizen rights as a matter of equal opportunity for the employment of Welsh, particularly in the economy.

A partial response by the National Assembly in the spring of 2000 was to ask the board to submit a report based on their corporate plan and strategy document. The report would include progress on the board's work so far, its views on the present situation and future prospects of the Welsh language, together with an account of priority actions for the advancement of the Welsh language along with the financial implications of this. The main text of this paper is included in Chapter 3. It demonstrates a clear commitment to formal language planning as a vital factor in the process of revitalizing Welsh and represents a more thorough approach to defining its wide-ranging remit. It has been accepted by the Assembly as 'a major contribution to the task of drawing up a strategy for the continued revitalization of the Welsh language and the creation of a bilingual Wales'.

In Chapter 4, Colin Baker and Meirion Prys Jones examine the role of bilingual education in language maintenance and revitalization. Having celebrated the growth of the bilingual education system, where one in five primary-school children are taught bilingually, their analysis shows the disconcerting discontinuity that exists in secondary and tertiary education. The chapter tackles the three challenges that face bilingual education planners: continuity; establishing a continuum of second language to first speaker; and a concurrent dual-language curriculum methodology. Underlying all these, they argue, is the harder challenge, to clarify the aims of bilingual education, for only when the aims are clear can the route to these destinations be firmly mapped.

The difficulties of establishing an adequate bilingual education provision without clear aims, political backing, sufficient resources and an appropriate set of school locations are clearly evidenced in the growth of Cardiff's Welsh schools, examined by Glyn Jones and myself in Chapter 5. This detailed case-study represents a fascinating illustration of the determination of an well-organized parental pressure group to develop a separate but equal Welsh-medium school system in the face of an intransigent local education authority. In common with many other anglicized locales there are significant implications of the growth of the bilingual sector both for the future of young Welsh speakers in and around Cardiff, and for the English-medium school sector which we examine. We conclude the case-study with a series of as-yet-unresolved issues which face Cardiff's educational planners.

As Heini Gruffudd in Chapter 6 notes, popular action in mobilizing support for endangered languages is a critical element, but one which has changed markedly in recent times. No longer able to muster widespread support on a range of issues dealing with fundamental injustices, language campaigners have to deal with more professional and sophisticated elements of language policy. In part this is due to the institutionalization of Welsh, in part the transfer of responsibilities from London to Cardiff and in part as a result of the changed nature of the challenges facing endangered languages as a result of globalization and the new world order (Williams, 1993a). The central focus of his chapter is the use of Welsh by young speakers both in schools and once they leave the confines of the bilingual classroom. How are they integrated into the community and to what extent can or should language planning target the needs of young people?

Gruffudd suggests that language planners should pay particular attention to strengthening the role of the community, not only in terms of supporting local initiatives, but also in terms of a national marketing campaign to raise awareness of the critical nature of community structures in maintaining endangered languages. Young people have created a vibrant set of networks which owe much to spontaneity and anti-establishment principles. It is a paradox that such spontaneity is in danger of being suffocated by attempts to formalize language planning for young people. He also avers that language choice in the case of bilingual youngsters will probably provide a more accurate guide to the state of vitality of the endangered language than statistics on language ability.

A number of contributors to this volume make the point that the type of school environment makes a significant differences to the resultant local language practices. Thus in Gruffudd's study of high schools in West Glamorgan and eastern Dyfed it was found that mixed-language schools found it more difficult to establish positive language practices than the official bilingual schools. This finding has profound implications for educational policy and should be investigated as a matter of urgency. Similarly, Jones and Williams noted that Cardiff faced a range of bilingual educational options, with different emphases between Welsh and English as a medium of instruction likely to produce quite critical differences in terms of the learning outcomes of the pupils. The contributors argue that there is a correlation between changes in language spoken and the linguistic environment of education. It is clear that introducing subjects such as science through the medium of Welsh would have a beneficial effect on the use of Welsh, and that the establishments which succeeded in fostering the use of Welsh most across the curriculum were the sixth forms of official bilingual high schools.

A further salutary caution is that success in one domain, education for example, does not automatically permeate into other domains. The leap of faith that is often mistakenly made by teachers is that their success in the classroom can influence the language used generally by young people in anglicized domains. Thus in their respective chapters Evas, Gruffudd, Morris and Williams have identified various language patterns which demonstrate inconsistencies and discrepancies between the formalized interactions which take place within the education system and the less formalized interactions of other social situations. The only way to change the language of informal conversation, and thus the language of relationships and courtships, is to change the dominant language of other pertinent domains, according to Gruffudd.

The contributors are aware of the need to prioritize. Attention must be given to ways of providing the necessary linguistic background in the domains where young people in particular spend their time and which influence their linguistic choices. Gruffudd warns that care should be taken in prioritizing appropriate targets, which could vary from place to place, and in selecting between high and low level use of the endangered language

In Chapter 7, Steve Morris tackles the issue of adult teaching of Welsh. After tracing the patchy development of the adult teaching sector he examines the range of motivations which characterize new speakers, chief of which is that they desire to support the development of their childrens' communicative competence in Welsh. The chapter also provides convincing evidence that teaching Welsh to adults can be an effective tool in the process of language revival. However, many learners face a fragmented and linguistically lonely life, because they possess the ability to discuss their particular area of interest of expertise through the medium of Welsh, but all too often lack the support and additional speakers to bring about a more permanent change of language within selected domains. As education and the economy are so intimately interlinked, the development of bilingual skills for the workplace should be a *sine qua non* of any holistic language and educational planning programme. But beyond the basic provision of training opportunities there should also be a much more integrative and mutually supportive relationship between educational establishments, employers federations, trade unions and central and local government. Such a relationship hardly exists at present and, despite the best intentions of the National Assembly, seems unlikely to develop soon unless there is a concerted campaign by both consumer groups and educational funding councils which control finance, and hence the structure of bilingual educational provision.

In Chapter 8, I describe the main findings of the Community Research Scheme (Williams and Evas, 1998) which sought to investigate the health of the language in four contrasting locales. The general attitude towards Welsh in the survey is very positive. However, the core functions which Fishman (1991b: 5) identifies as 'intimacy, family and community' remain a cause for concern. Particular attention is paid to the effectiveness of interventionist language agencies such as Menter Cwm Gwendraeth, Menter Aman Tawe and Antur Teifi. The chapter outlines the potential for developing such agencies, together with novel actors such as linguistic *animateurs*, and infrastructural support in the shape of national and county-level resource centres. The chapter concludes with a range of recommendations, several of which have been adopted by the Welsh Language Board, the respective county councils or voluntary organizations. The most significant perhaps are: a national network linking all *mentrau iaith*, including staff training and problem-solving; the development of interactive software programmes to enable bilingual versions of forms and information systems to be employed in the provision of services; the training of key personnel, such as midwives and other medical staff, to encourage Welsh as an added element of their promotion of an enhanced quality of life; the refashioning of the relationship between the Language Board and its principal partners; and the development of closer links with Catalan and Basque language planning agencies. The key recommendation was the need to invest heavily in professional staff development if the general public were to be offered a genuine free choice in the language of service provision.

The details of Welsh Language Board targets as set out in Chapter 3 suggest that planning agencies recognize this deficit, but questions have been raised as to how effective will be the immediate impact, given the relatively small budgets allocated to various facets of the bilingual training programmes. Such criticisms are well made and should be extended to cover most formal language planning activities and training provision in Wales.

Its first director Cefin Campbell in Chapter 9 describes the pioneering contribution of Menter Cwm Gwendraeth. Cwm Gwendraeth is characterized by a declining industrial base which yet manages to achieve a high level of language transmission. A clear statement of the aims, methods and resources required to implement the strategic plan of this *menter iaith* is accompanied by a detailed evaluation of the specific programmes which it launched. The *menter iaith* is faced with the spectre of community fragmentation and individual anomie as described in the Community Research Project. Its personnel and supporters have coped remarkably well, so much so that I believe that this authoritative and comprehensive account forms the core of current community language revitalization experience. This chapter is the most comprehensive account we have of the 'nuts and bolts' approach to local language planning, and as such will doubtless be a major source of inspiration for many others considering emulating this form of community language and socio-economic development.

In Chapter 10 Jeremy Evas offers another detailed language contact case-study, drawn this time from the rural Teifi Valley deep within the heartland region. Despite high percentage levels of Welsh speakers, a vibrant indigenous culture and a set of time-honoured social networks, Welsh faces a difficult future as the dominant language of the community. Evas combines intensive fieldwork analysis with his own prescient insights to interpret the contours of a fast-changing linguistic landscape. Education again features as a critical socializing and integrating agency of group identity. Several barriers to the normalization of Welsh are examined and the chapter concludes with a series of recommendations aimed primarily at local language planners, but which have relevance throughout the heartland region.

In the penultimate chapter, Gardner, Puigdevall i Serralvo and Williams focus our attention on Ireland, the Basque Country and Catalonia. After describing the main features of language policy and the respective language planning agencies, the authors discuss lessons which may be drawn from placing the Welsh experience in a comparative European context. The most significant lessons are the following:

- The critical nature of the state and the state system, both in history and today, in influencing the conditions of possibility which enable some languages to survive and flourish and others to be threatened.
- The recognition that power relationships between the groups represented by language varieties are a central feature of all language planning programmes and should not be treated as if they were an unanticipated element in the inter-group

negotiation process. There is an obvious political as well a policy element to language planning.

- The essential nature of a strong legislative framework in support of the minority language.
- The general priority given to developing new opportunities within the education system.
- A failure to tackle head on the difficult issue of creating bilingual/multilingual opportunities and skills training in the workplace and in the economy more generally.
- The need to integrate language planning within other forms of planning, particularly regional economic development planning: easy to aspire to, so very hard to implement.
- The need to understand the role of historcial discourse in structuring the way in which current conceptions of a language planning and policy are framed.
- The need to have a thorough understanding of the economic imperatives which structure language choice at both an individual and the collective level.
- The need to understand, without necessarily yielding to, the various positions adopted by sections within the unilingual majority who may be lukewarm or hostile to the normalization of the minority language.
- The willingness of many government departments to leave language planning implementation to those specifically charged with carrying it out suggests a lack of ownership of the whole process on the part of government outside the language planning élite.
- Universities too often fail to provide the intellectual resources necessary to tackle Reversing Language Shift issues which demand a syncretic, holistic approach. Multidisciplinary practitioners are scarce in comparison with the single-discipline specialists within linguistics, literature, education or history.

A final pair of contentious issues is the relationship between economic development and language revitalization and that between the National Assembly and the Welsh Language Board (C. H. Williams, 1999). In Chapter 12 I rehearse the failure of language policy to take due account of regional economic development and to interact in any meaningful way with the power of the private sector of the economy. Gruffudd, Morris and Williams all call into question the sufficiency of current arrangements regarding both the strategy and funding of Welsh language policy. In Chapter 6 Gruffudd argues that if the Welsh Language Board is to continue, its terms of reference need to be greatly expanded, with the support of a new, more far-reaching Language Act. Gruffudd's preferred option would be to replace the Language Board with a governmental Culture Authority, closer in style to current Catalan and Basque language planning authorities as described in Chapter 11. This would be closer to the perspectives offered by a number of the contributors and many other critics who, whilst being supportive of the practical assistance offered to various Welsh-language organizations by the current governmental arrangements, nevertheless are dubious as to their capacity to generate sustainable development. This is because the premiss on which they intervene is rooted in a compensation analysis derived from the deficiencies of the current power relations between various factions within society. It also derives from the limitations of the Welsh Language Act 1993 itself, and its consequent deployment of an interventionist language policy agency, the Welsh Language Board, to regulate behaviour and to transfer some of the responsibility for language reproduction back to the community. However, as officers and members of the Language Board will readily acknowledge, such a strategy is bound to lead to difficulties, because it is based on a partial view of the role of language within the relations of production and because there is insufficient direct public investment both to allow the Language Board to implement its recommendations and to enable the local community to generate self-sustaining socio-economic networks. Other critics, such as Williams and Morris (2000: 248), would go further and argue that only when language planning efforts are based upon a thorough understanding of the social construction of meaning and its relationship to discursive processes as social practice will the current opposition between the market and planning be reduced. They argue that 'variety of meaning practices linked with the relationship between linguistic form and discursive practice' could become the 'cornerstone of innovative capacity'. But this is unlikely to happen, for, in a trenchant critique of the whole thrust of contemporary language planning, they accuse the Language Board of being unable and unwilling to recognize their role in perpetuating many of the deficiencies noted in their theoretical interpretation of the malaise of current language policy. As noted earlier, the twin deficiencies are not making the appropriate links between regional development policy and language production, reproduction and use in society and, secondly, the Language Board's adherence to the dictates of a neo-liberal discourse which appears to empower community language projects, but which in reality makes them structurally dependent upon state interventionist agencies established to overcome the influence of market forces on the ability of a language group to reproduce itself. Speaking generally Williams and Morris (2000: 248) aver that:

> such issues are beyond both the capacity and the conception of the Welsh Language Board. They relate to much more than language and, as things now stand, there is no evidence that language is being constructed as an object that has relevance beyond that which it has for subjects who speak it. It begs the question of where we now stand concerning language planning.

## Acknowledgements

The themes of this chapter draw upon and update earlier analyses reported in Williams, 1998, 1999 and 2000.

## Notes

[1] Maurice Goldring, 1993; see also Brown, 1985; P. O. Riagáin, 1997: esp. 8–15. Individual groups which subsequently merged with Plaid Cymru were more heavily

influenced by the Irish direct-action methods, the best known of these were the Arfon slate quarry workers.

[2] The very same religious press and élite had earlier condemned the use of violence against fledgling Afrikaner nationalism in the Boer Wars.

[3] Again the exception would be the calculated symbolic use of destruction of state property in the burning of the bombing school in Penyberth, for details see D. H. Davies, 1983: 154–66.

[4] At the 1938 Plaid Cymru conference held in Swansea, delegates adopted, by an overwhelming majority, Gwynfor Evans's motion that 'as a party we completely reject war as a means of achieving self-government'. In contrast Lewis had been disappointed by the performance of the Party since the Bombing School incident and took consolation from the pacifist supporters recognition of the tactical utility of adopting civil disobedience on the Gandhian pattern. In arguing that sacrifice and suffering should characterize the struggle ahead, Lewis anticipated the actions of the language movement some thirty years later when he asserted that 'One path alone leads to the gateway of the Welsh Parliament. That path runs directly through the prisons of England.' Y Ddraig Goch (Sept. 1938) quoted in the detailed discussion of the conference in D. H. Davies, 1983: 167–8.

[5] The original aim of Plaid Genedlaethol Cymru was 'to keep Wales Welsh-speaking. That is, to include (a) making the Welsh language the only official language of Wales and thus a language required for all local authority transactions and mandatory for every official and servant of every local authority in Wales; (b) making the Welsh language a medium of education in Wales from the elementary school through to the University.' Quoted in Butt Philip, 1975: 14; see also D. H. Davies, 1983.

[6] Nationalism is not an autonomous force, and we should be careful not to interpret individual nationalist activists as agents of a transcendent ideology, but rather as part of practical politics, providing a context within which one could measure the success of the national programme for the survival of a distinct Welsh identity.

[7] Particularly significant in this respect was the work of D. J. Davies who admired Scandinavian social credit policies, economic co-operation and decentralization of power (1931; and with Noëlle Davies, 1939). For a critique of the class versus nationalist appeals see J. Davies, 1980.

[8] There are many parallels to be explored between idealists such as Saunders Lewis and Sabino de Arana, Valenti Almirall, Yann Foueré, E. MacNeill and Éamon de Valera.

[9] 'The principles of nationalism', delivered at Plaid Cymru's first Summer School in 1926. For development of his ideas see the collections Lewis, 1985, 1986.

[10] See Lewis, 1975: 7. For a variant on the same theme see also R. M. Jones, 1994.

[11] For a discussion of these allegations see D. H. Davies, 1983: 109–16. For a recent brief re-examination of the relationship between Fascism, anti-Semitism and the views of Saunders Lewis and his colleagues see R. M. Jones, 1998: 324–35.

[12] Of course, several valleys in the Peak District and in the Pennines were also converted into reservoirs, but that did not figure prominently in Welsh discourse.

[13] His father, Daniel Evans, was a department store owner and a deacon at Tabernacl Independent Chapel, Barry, Glamorgan, then one of the most anglicized, thriving towns in Wales. Never fully conscious of his nationality until he went up to Oxford, and re-learned Welsh, he was always something of an enigma, simultaneously embodying and standing apart from mainstream Welsh culture. In protest at the jingoistic justification of the Second World War, he preached pacifism in his home-town main square among other places and shunned the armed forces for a life as a market gardener in Llangadog, then steeped in Welsh rural culture. For details see Evans, 1986.

[14] Catalonia is the best European example of linguistic normalization which is charac-

terized by four elements. At the political administrative level a new language regime was ushered in by the Autonomy Statute of 1979, which established by decree 115 in 1980 the Direcció General de Política Lingüística, and by decree 220, 1980, within DGPL the Servei de Normalització de l'Ús Oficial de la Llengua Catalana and the Servei d'Assessorament Lingüístic. Subsequent laws included the Llei 7/1983 de Normalizació Lingüística de Catalunya, and Llei 20/1987, which created Institució de les Lletres Catalanes. Second, there is a very active marketing and promotional campaign using popular slogans denoting the role of Catalan in education, *La Premsa a l'Escola, Català a l'Escola, Contes a cau d'orella*, and in civil society, *La Norma, català cosa de tots, El català depèn de vostè, Es nota prou que som a Catalunya?* Third, wide-ranging reforms within education provided for the socialization of Catalan youth and of migrants from regions of Spain and North Africa: Convocatòria Oposicions BUP, FP (which involved the testing of oral and written comprehension of Catalan from 1981 onwards), and the decree 18/1986 whereby all teachers contracted to teach for public education must demonstrate their knowledge of Catalan comprehension and expression. Fourth, the media blossomed both in terms of Catalan editions of Spanish newspapers such as *El País*, from 1982 onwards and the establishment of an autonomous third channel TV3 which broadcast regularly from January 1984 and which was supplemented after the Telecommunications Act of April 1988 by a wider range of broadcasters.

## References

Aitchison, J. W. (1995). 'Language, family structure and social class, 1991 census data', presentation to the Social History of the Welsh Language Conference, Aberystwyth, 16 Sept.

Aitchison, J. W. and Carter, H. (1993). 'The Welsh language in 1991: a broken heart and a new beginning?', *Planet*, 97, 3–10.

Aitchison, J. W. and Carter, H. (2000). *Language, Economy and Society: The Changing Fortunes of the Welsh Language in the Twentieth Century*, Cardiff: University of Wales Press.

Ambrose, J. A. and Williams, C. H. (1981). 'On the spatial definition of minority: scale as an influence on the geolinguistic analysis of Welsh', in Haugen, E., McClure, J. D. and Thompson, D. (eds.), *Minority Languages Today*, Edinburgh: Edinburgh University Press, pp. 53–71.

Assembly of Welsh Counties (1993a). *Strategic Planning Guidance in Wales: Overview Report*, Cardiff: Assembly of Welsh Counties.

Assembly of Welsh Counties (1993b). *Strategic Planning Guidance in Wales: Topic Report*, Cardiff: Assembly of Welsh Counties.

Baker, C. (1996). *Foundations of Bilingual Education and Bilingualism*, 2nd edn., Clevedon, Avon: Multilingual Matters.

Baker, C. and Prys Jones, S. (1998). *Encyclopedia of Bilingualism and Bilingual Education*, Clevedon, Avon: Multilingual Matters.

Brown, T. (1985). *Ireland: A Social and Cultural History, 1922–1985*, London: Fontana.

Butt Philip, A. (1975). *The Welsh Question*, Cardiff: University of Wales Press.

Close, P. (1995). *Citizenship, Europe and Change*, Basingstoke: Macmillan.

Clwyd CC (1991). *Clwyd Structure Plan: Policies and Memorandum*, Mold: Clwyd County Council.

Colwyn Bay Council (1985). *Land Use Planning and the Welsh Language: Local Plan Topic Report*, Colwyn Bay: Colwyn Bay Council.

Coupland, N., ed. (1990). *English in Wales*, Clevedon, Avon: Multilingual Matters.

Crystal, D. (1987). *The Cambridge Encyclopedia of Language*, Cambridge: Cambridge University Press.

Cymdeithas yr Iaith Gymraeg (1985). *Planning a Future for the Welsh Language in Ceredigion*, Aberystwyth: Cymdeithas yr Iaith Gymraeg.

Cymdeithas yr Iaith Gymraeg (1986). *Cynllunio Dyfodol i'r Iaith*, Aberystwyth: Cymdeithas yr Iaith Gymraeg.

Dafis, Ll., ed. (1992). *Yr Ieithoedd Llai: Cymathu Newydd-Ddyfodiaid*, Caerfyrddin: Cydweithgor Dwyieithrwydd yn Nyfed.

Davies, D. H. (1983). *The Welsh Nationalist Party 1925–1945*, Cardiff: University of Wales Press.

Davies, D. J. (1931). *The Economics of Welsh Self-Government*, Caernarfon: Plaid Cymru.

Davies, D. J. and Davies, Nöelle (1939). *Can Wales Afford Self-Government?* Caernarfon: Plaid Cymru.

Davies, J. (1980). *The Green and the Red: Nationalism and Ideology in Twentieth Century Wales*, Aberystwyth: Plaid Cymru.

Davies, J. (1981). *Cymru'n Deffro*, Talybont: Y Lolfa.

Davies, J. (1985). 'Plaid Cymru in Transition', in Osmond, J. (ed.), *The National Question Again*, Llandysul: Gomer Press.

Davies, J. (1993). *The Welsh Language*, Cardiff: University of Wales Press.

*Declaració de Barcelona* (1996). *Declaració universal de drets lingüístics*, Barcelona: International PEN and CIEMEN.

Dyfed CC (1986a). *Dyfed County S. P. Review: Proposals for Alteration. Consultation Report*, Dyfed County Council: Carmarthen.

Dyfed CC (1986b). *Structure Plan Review: The Welsh Language as a Structure Plan Issue*, Dyfed County Council: Carmarthen.

Dyfed CC (1990). *Dyfed S. P. (including Alterations No. 1)*, Carmarthen: Dyfed County Council.

Edwards, J. (1994). *Multilingualism*, London: Longman.

Erize, X. (2000). 'Making good boundaries: an interview with Joshua Fishman', *Planet*, 140, 66–75.

Evans, G. (1986). *For the Sake of Wales*, Bridgend: Academic Press.

Fennell, D. (1977). 'Where it went wrong: the Irish language movement', *Planet*, 36.

Fforwm Ddwyieithrwydd Gwynedd (1995). *Tuag at Strategaeth Iaith i Ogledd-Orllewin Cymru*, Caernarfon: Fforwm Ddwyieithrwydd Gwynedd.

Fforwm Iaith Genedlaethol (1991). *Strategaeth Iaith, 1991–2001*, Aberystwyth: Fforwm yr Iaith Gymraeg.

Fishman, J. (1985). *The Rise and Fall of the Ethnic Revival*, Berlin: Mouton.

Fishman, J. (1987). 'Opening Address', Georgetown University Round Table on Language and Linguistics, Georgetown University Press, Washington.

Fishman, J. A. (1989). *Language and Ethnicity in Minority Sociolinguistic Perspective*, Clevedon, Avon: Multilingual Matters.

Fishman, J. A. (1991a). 'My life through my work: my work through my life', in Koerner, K. (ed.), *First Person Singular*, Amsterdam: John Benjamin.

Fishman, J. A. (1991b). *Reversing Language Shift*, Clevedon, Avon: Multilingual Matters.

Gerholm, T. and Lithman, Y. G. (1990). *The New Islamic Presence in Western Europe*, London: Mansell.

Goldring, M. (1993). *Pleasant the Scholar's Life*, London: Serif.

Gunnermark, E. and Kenrick, D. (1985). *A Geolinguistic Handbook*, Gothenburg: Gunnermark.

Gwynedd CC (1977). *Caernarvonshire S.P.: Written Statement*, Caernarfon: Gwynedd County Council.

Gwynedd CC (1993). *Gwynedd Structure Plan: Written Statement*, Caernarfon: Gwynedd County Council.

Habermas, J. (1996). 'The European nation-state – its achievements and its limits', in Balakrishnan, G. and Anderson, B. (eds.), *Mapping the Nation*, London: Verso, pp. 281–94.

Hindley, R. (1990). *The Death of the Irish Language*, London: Routledge.

James, C. and Williams, C. H. (1996). 'Language and planning in Scotland and Wales', in Macdonald, R. and Thomas, H. (eds.), *Planning in Scotland and Wales*, Cardiff: University of Wales Press, pp. 264–302.

Jenkins, G. H., ed. (1997). *The Welsh Language before the Industrial Revolution*, Cardiff: University of Wales Press.

Jenkins, G. H., ed. (1998). *Language and Community in Nineteenth Century Wales*, Cardiff: University of Wales Press.

Jenkins, G. H., ed. (2000). *Welsh and its Social Domains*, Cardiff: University of Wales Press.

Jones, D. (1998). *Statistical Evidence Relating to the Welsh Language 1801–1911*, Cardiff: University of Wales Press.

Jones, D. G. (1973). 'His politics', in Jones, J. R. and Thomas, G. (eds.), *Presenting Saunders Lewis*, Cardiff: University of Wales Press.

Jones, J. W. (1989). 'Bwrdd yr Iaith Gymraeg a chynllunio', *Cymru Wledig* (Summer), 14.

Jones, R. M. (1994). *Crist a Chenedlaetholdeb*, Pen-y-bont ar Ogwr: Gwasg Efengylaidd Cymru.

Jones, R. M. (1998). *Ysbryd y Cwlwm: Delwedd y Genedl yn ein Llenyddiaeth*, Cardiff: University of Wales Press.

Kaplan, R. B. and Baldauf, R. B. (1997). *Language Planning from Practice to Theory*, Clevedon, Avon: Multilingual Matters.

Klein, T. (1978). 'Minorities in Central Europe', in Hepburn, A. C. (ed.), *Minorities in History*, London: Edward Arnold, pp. 31–50.

Kukathas, C. (1995). 'Are there any cultural rights?', in Kymlicka, W. (ed.), *The Rights of Minority Cultures*, Oxford: Oxford University Press, pp. 228–55.

Laponce, J. A. (1987). *Languages and their Territories*, Toronto: University of Toronto Press.

Lewis, S. (1975). *Egwyddorion Cenedlaetholdeb*, Cardiff: Plaid Cymru.

Lewis, S. (1985). *Canlyn Arthur*, Llandysul: Gomer.

Lewis, S. (1986). *Ati, Wŷr Ifainc*, Cardiff: University of Wales Press.

McAllister, L. (1995). 'Community in ideology: the political philosophy of Plaid Cymru', Ph.D. thesis, University of Wales.

Mackey, W. (1991). 'Language diversity, language policy and the sovereign state', *History of European Ideas*, 13, 51–61.

McRae, K. (1997). 'Language policy and language contact: reflections on Finland', in Wölck, W. and de Houwer, A. (eds.), *Recent Studies in Contact Linguistics*, Plurilingua 17; Bonn: Dümmler, pp. 218–26.

Marshall, D., ed. (1991). *Language Planning: Focusschrift in Honor of Joshua A. Fishman*, 3 vols., Amsterdam: John Benjamin.

Menter a Busnes (1994). *A Quiet Revolution: The Framework of the Academic Report*, Aberystwyth: Menter a Busnes.

Nelde, P. (1997). 'On the evaluation of language policy', in Generalitat de Catalunya (ed.), *Proceedings of the European Conference on Language Planning*, Barcelona: Department de Cultura, pp. 285–92.

Nelde, P., Labrie, N. and Williams, C. H. (1992). 'The principles of territoriality and personality in the solution of linguistic conflicts', *Journal of Multilingual and Multicultural Development*, 13, 387–406.

Ó Riagáin, P. (1997). *Language Policy and Social Reproduction, Ireland 1893–1993*, Oxford: Oxford University Press.

Parry, G. and Williams, M. A. (1999). *The Welsh Language and the 1891 Census*, Cardiff: University of Wales Press.

Phillips, D. (1998). *Trwy Ddulliau Chwyldro*, Llandysul: Gomer Press.

Phillipson, R. (1992). *Linguistic Imperialism*, Oxford: Oxford University Press.

Posner, R. (1991). 'Society, civilization, mentality: prolegomena to a language policy for Europe', in Coulmas, F. (ed.), *A Language Policy for the European Community*, Berlin: Mouton, pp. 121–37.

Powys CC (1994). *Powys County Structure Plan* (draft replacement). Deposit Version. Written Statement, Explanatory Memorandum and Consultation Statement, Llandrindod: Powys County Council.

Price, G., ed. (1992). *The Celtic Connection*, Gerrards Cross: Colin Smyth.

Pryce, W. T. R. and Williams, C. H. (1988). 'Sources and methods in the study of language areas: a case study of Wales', in C. H. Williams (ed.), *Language in Geographic Context*, Clevedon, Avon: Multilingual Matters.

Skutnabb-Kangas, T. (1997). 'Language rights as conflict prevention', in Wölck, W. and de Houwer, A. (eds.), *Recent Studies in Contact Linguistics*, Plurilingua 17; Bonn: Dümmler, pp. 312–24.

Skutnabb-Kangas, T. (1999). 'Language, power and lingusitic human rights: the role of the state', in *Proceedings of the International Conference on Language Legislation*, Dublin: Comhdáil Náisiúnta na Gaeilge, Feb., pp. 50–68.

Stewart, W. A. (1968). 'A sociolinguistic typology for describing national multilingualism', in Fishman, J. A. (ed.), *Language Problems of Developing Nations*, London: John Wiley, pp. 503–53.

Thomas, B. (1959). 'Wales and the Atlantic economy', *Scottish Journal of Political Economy*, 6, 169–92.

Tollefson, J. W. (1990). *Planning Language: Planning Inequality*. London: Longman.

Welsh Office (1981). *The Welsh Language in Wales*, Cardiff: HMSO.

Welsh Office (1988). *Circular 53/88. The Welsh Language: Development Plans and Planning Control*, Cardiff: Welsh Office.

Welsh Office (1991). *Circular 31/91. Planning and Housing*, Cardiff: Welsh Office.

Welsh Office (1993). *Welsh Social Survey*, Cardiff: Welsh Office Statistical Section.

Welsh Office (1995a). *Planning Policy Guidance (Wales) Consultation Draft*, Cardiff: Welsh Office.

Welsh Office (1995b). *Planning Guidance (Wales): Unitary Development Plans in Wales*, Cardiff: Welsh Office.

Williams, C. H., ed. (1981). *National Separatism*, Cardiff: University of Wales Press.

Williams, C. H. (1986). 'Bilingual education as an agent of cultural reproduction', *Cambria*, 13, 1, 111–29.

Williams, C. H. (1987). 'Location and context in Welsh language reproduction', in Williams, G. (ed), *The Sociology of Welsh, International Journal of the Sociology of Language*, 66, 61–8.

Williams, C. H (1989). 'The question of national congruence', in Johnston, R. J. and Taylor, P. (eds.), *A World in Crisis?*, Oxford: Blackwell, pp. 229–65.

Williams, C. H. (1991a). 'Language planning and social change: ecological speculations', in Marshall, D. (ed.), *Language Planning: Focusschrift in Honor of Joshua A. Fishman*, 3 vols., Amsterdam: John Benjamin, pp. 53–74.

Williams, C. H., ed. (1991b). *Linguistic Minorities, Society and Territory*, Clevedon, Avon: Multilingual Matters.

Williams, C. H. (1992). 'Identity, autonomy and the ambiguity of technological development', in Mlinar, Z. (ed.), *Globalization and Territorial Identities*, Aldershot: Avebury.

Williams, C. H., ed. (1993a). *The Political Geography of the New World Order*, London: Belhaven and John Wiley.

Williams, C. H. (1993b). 'The European Community's lesser used languages', *Rivista Geografica Italiana*, 100, 531–64.

Williams, C. H. (1994). *Called unto Liberty: On Language and Nationalism*, Clevedon, Avon: Multilingual Matters.

Williams, C. H. (1995). 'Global language divisions', in Unwin, T. (ed.), *Atlas of World Development*, Chichester: John Wiley.

Williams, C. H. (1997). '132 English-Welsh', in Goebl, H., Nelde, P. H., Stary, Z. and Wölck, W. (eds.), *Kontaktlinguistik: Ein internationales Handbuch seitgenossischer Forschung*, Berlin: Walter de Gruyter, pp. 1075–87.

Williams, C. H. (1998). 'Room to talk in a house of faith: on language and religion', in Graham, B. (ed.), *Modern Europe: Place, Culture, Identity*, London: Arnold, pp. 186–209.

Williams, C. H. (1999). 'The Celtic world', in Fishman, J. A. (ed.), *Handbook of Language and Ethnic Identity*, Oxford and New York: Oxford University Press, pp. 267–85.

Williams. C. H. (2000). 'Restoration of the language', in Jenkins, G. (ed.), *Welsh and its Social Domains*, Cardiff: University of Wales Press.

Williams, C. H. and Evas, J. C. (1998). *The Community Research Scheme*, Cardiff: Welsh Language Board, http://www.caerdydd.ac.uk/cymraeg/ymchwil.

Williams, C. H. and Raybould W. (1991). *Welsh Language Planning: Opportunities and Constraints*, Cardiff: Pwyllgor Datblygu Addysg Gymraeg.

Williams, G. (1971). 'Language, literacy and nationality in Wales', *History*, 56, 1–16.

Williams, G., ed. (1987). 'The sociology of Welsh', *International Journal of the Sociology of Language*, 66, 1–127.

Williams, G. (1991). *The Desert and the Dream: The Welsh in Patagonia*, Cardiff: University of Wales Press.

Williams, G. (1992). *Sociolinguistics*, London: Routledge.

Williams, G. (1999). 'Language and ethnicity: the sociological approach', in Fishman, J. A. (ed.), *Language and Ethnicity*, Oxford: Oxford University Press, pp. 164–81.

Williams, G. and Morris, D. (2000). *Language Planning and Language Use: Welsh in a Global Age*, Cardiff: University of Wales Press.

Zametica, J. (1992). *The Yugoslav Conflict*, London: Brassey's.

# 2

## *The Statistical Basis for Welsh Language Planning: Data Trends, Patterns, Processes*

### HYWEL JONES* AND COLIN H. WILLIAMS

INTRODUCTION

Language revitalization efforts normally turn on an unstinting commitment to reversing language shift. Pioneers in bilingual education, community voluntary organizations or political movements were motivated by a strong sense of urgency to act so as to demonstrate their convictions regarding the discriminatory treatment of the Welsh language within the British state. Little of this commitment was informed by a rational analysis of the facts, or by any elegant theorizing of the necessity for maintaining a Welsh-medium culture. Early language activists employed impassioned appeals to the right to be recognized as being different, informed as much by a particular reading of history and literary interpretation as by any political doctrine of linguistic self-determination or political autonomy. Poetry and pamphlets, rather than policy and planning, were able to stir the imagination and commit generations of Welsh youth to engage in a struggle for collective identity. Directly or indirectly, such appeals motivated the construction of the rudimentary bilingual society we inhabit today.

Contemporary language policy is predicated less on emotion and more on analysis. However, the statistical basis for sound language planning and imaginative policy proposals is sadly lacking. Too often our decision-making is based on a collection of superficial official data surveys, together with an admixture of idiosyncratic opinion polls, inspired but ephemeral academic investigations and a great deal of wish fulfilment. Put simply, we do not invest sufficiently in time-series data analysis to enable us to plan, let alone predict, the vicissitudes of language-related change. Consequently this chapter aims to chart the essential features of official data sources, the geolinguistic distribution of Welsh, significant demographic trends, together with changes in the socio-economic position of bilinguals in the workforce.

Welsh society is characterized by a unilingual majority, a bilingual minority and a range of linguistically diverse home languages. We have little systematic data on our multilingual residents, and inadequate data on the structural characteristics of the bilingual English–Welsh population. In the medium term this situation may change as the Welsh language is gradually benefiting from insti-tutionalized recognition by the state. Historically the hearth, the farm and the chapel have been the domains which sustained a Welsh-medium network of agencies of language reproduction. This support structure reached its zenith in the late nineteenth century when the institutions of Welsh Nonconformity created a parallel 'social totality' which enabled Wales to cope with the huge upheaval of industrialization and urbanization, without necessarily losing its language or culture. Much of current planning and policy is based upon fairly conventional interpretations of Welsh language use and networking. This reflects both the lack of time-series analysis of sociolinguistic issues and a presumption by decision-makers that they intuitively understand the policy implications of serving a bilingual population.

## DEMOGRAPHIC TRENDS AND STRUCTURE

The mainstay of sociolinguistic analysis has been the decennial census, despite the fact that it asks only a limited number of questions relating to self-ascribed language abilities (for details and cartographic analysis see Pryce and Williams, 1988; Aitchison and Carter, 2000). At the beginning of the twentieth century (1901) the census recorded 929,824 of the population as able to speak Welsh and 1,577,141 as able to speak English. In addition there were 928,222 monoglot English-speaking residents, and 280,905 monoglot Welsh-speaking residents together with 648,919 bilingual Welsh–English speakers. By 1901 English had become pervasive and advantageous in most spheres of life. The majority of bilingual residents were descendants of unilingual Welsh speakers, but among the bilingual population were many English and other in-migrants who had learned Welsh. Some were the children of non-Welsh migrants who had been attracted to the resource-rich coalfields, and had been socialized within the multilingual *mélange* of the industrial crucible and had learned Welsh *en passant*. Others were the children of slate quarry workers in north Wales, part of an immi-gration flow from the Midlands and north of England who integrated into Gwynedd's predominantly Welsh-medium socio-cultural environment.

Successive inter-censal decline has been the marked feature of census evidence on Welsh speaking ever since 1911, when 977,400 persons were returned as able to speak Welsh, 190,300 of whom were monoglots. Since this peak figure of language intensity the number of Welsh speakers has consistently declined, to reach its present low of 590,800, hardly any of whom are adult monoglots. In proportional terms this represents a decline from 43.5 per cent of the total Welsh population in 1911 to only 18.7 per cent in 1991, a reduction by 24.8 percentage points. The various explanations for the absolute and relative rate of decline focus on the inter-war period when stigmatization, a collapse in confidence and Depression-induced population out-migration encouraged widespread language shift. The period 1921–39 was the crisis turning-point for Welsh, for a generation was denied the opportunity to learn Welsh. This reflected parental rejection of the language and an unresponsive education system. This powerful combination of forces mirrored the convictions of British imperial values and attitudes that deemed that Welsh was irrelevant in a modernizing world order. Such convictions have waned in the more modern period and since the early 1950s the rate of decline has been more moderate, reflecting a reversal in the language's fortunes from the already low levels of Welsh fluency.

A significant feature of language decline has been the collapse of the monolingual population. The fact that all Welsh speakers are bilingual changes the social-psychological context of language production and reproduction and, unlike many other examples of diglossic societies, individual and societal bilingualism in Wales does not vary tremendously. Pending the publication of the 2001 census results we have to rely on charting the changes between 1981 and 1991 which were fairly minimal. The bilingual population appears fairly stable, predictable and, if it should grow, will do so in very limited terms. If we disaggregate the data by age groups, the 1991 census reveals that there have been significant increases in the three to fifteen age group (Table 2.2), a consolidation of the sixteen to forty-four age group and an expected decline in the two older age groups. These trends are likely to be maintained in successive decades, which suggests that the demographic future of Welsh is brighter than at any other time in recent history. Much will depend upon how social agencies and the National Assembly implement current sociolinguistics reforms and how strong the functional motivation of future generations is to exercise their language choice and social power.

Today bilingualism represents a real social choice for *c*.590,800 individuals, who switch language by domain, by interlocutor and by whim, as the opportunity allows. However, the chief problem facing those who wish to use Welsh as their primary means of communication is to optimize the conditions wherein a

**Table 2.1. Proportion of population speaking Welsh, by county, 1921–1991**

| | % of all persons speaking Welsh | | | | | | | % of all persons speaking Welsh only | | | | | |
|---|------|------|------|------|------|------|------|------|------|------|------|------|------|
| | 1921 | 1931 | 1951 | 1961 | 1971 | 1981 | 1991 | 1921 | 1931 | 1951 | 1961 | 1971 | 1981 |
| Wales | 37.1 | 36.8 | 28.9 | 26.0 | 20.8 | 18.9 | 18.7 | 6.3 | 4.0 | 1.7 | 1.0 | 1.3 | 0.8 |
| Clwyd | 41.7 | 41.3 | 30.2 | 27.3 | 21.4 | 18.7 | 18.2 | 5.8 | 3.4 | 1.3 | 0.8 | 1.4 | 0.8 |
| Dyfed | 67.8 | 69.1 | 63.3 | 60.1 | 52.5 | 46.3 | 43.7 | 15.3 | 9.6 | 4.1 | 2.4 | 2.4 | 1.6 |
| Gwent | 5.0 | 4.7 | 2.8 | 2.9 | 1.9 | 2.5 | 2.4 | 0.2 | 0.1 | 0.1 | 0.2 | 0.1 | 0.1 |
| Gwynedd | 78.7 | 82.5 | 74.2 | 71.4 | 64.7 | 61.2 | 61.0 | 28.1 | 22.1 | 9.1 | 5.2 | 4.9 | 6.2 |
| Mid Glamorgan | 38.4 | 37.1 | 22.8 | 18.5 | 10.5 | 8.4 | 8.5 | 2.3 | 0.8 | 0.3 | 0.4 | 0.8 | 0.5 |
| Powys | 35.1 | 34.6 | 29.6 | 27.8 | 23.7 | 20.2 | 20.2 | 6.1 | 3.9 | 1.6 | 0.9 | 1.0 | 0.9 |
| S. Glamorgan | 6.3 | 6.1 | 4.7 | 5.2 | 5.0 | 5.8 | 6.5 | 0.2 | 0.1 | 0.1 | 0.1 | 0.4 | 0.2 |
| W. Glamorgan | 41.3 | 40.5 | 31.6 | 27.5 | 20.3 | 16.4 | 15.0 | 3.6 | 1.3 | 0.5 | 0.5 | 1.0 | 0.8 |

*Source*: Census 1981 *Welsh Language in Wales*, table 4, p. 50.

### Table 2.2. Welsh speakers, 3–15 years

| | % of age group able to speak Welsh | | Nos. able to to speak Welsh | | % change |
|---|---|---|---|---|---|
| | 1981 | 1991 | 1981 | 1991 | 1981–1991 |
| Clwyd | 18.6 | 27.9 | 13,796 | 18,167 | 31.7 |
| Dyfed | 40.3 | 47.7 | 23,163 | 25,811 | 11.4 |
| Gwent | 2.3 | 4.8 | 1,921 | 3,490 | 81.1 |
| Gwynedd | 69.3 | 77.6 | 28,785 | 27,889 | –3.1 |
| Mid Glamorgan | 8.6 | 16.1 | 8,906 | 14,604 | 64.0 |
| Powys | 16.7 | 30.0 | 3,284 | 5,463 | 66.4 |
| S. Glamorgan | 7.4 | 11.9 | 5,152 | 7,690 | 49.3 |
| W. Glamorgan | 9.3 | 15.0 | 6,064 | 8,719 | 43.8 |

*Source*: Aitchinson and Carter, 1993.

genuine free choice of languages may be exercised in all domains of social life, a feature which is examined in detail in relation to the Teifi Valley in Chapter 10.

### Sociolinguistic contexts and language reproduction

In its *Strategy for the Welsh Language* (1999b) the Welsh Language Board summarized recent language planning achievements and current concerns in the following manner.

> The Welsh Language Act of 1993, the *mentrau iaith*, the spread of bilingual education at primary and secondary level, Welsh as a compulsory subject in the National Curriculum, the vitality of movements such as *Mudiad Ysgolion Meithrin, Urdd Gobaith Cymru*, local and national eisteddfodau, Welsh language schemes, increasing use of bilingualism in business and the economy are just a few of the many examples where language planning has successful bucked the trend of downward shift.

Nevertheless there is still cause for concern because:

1. In many families where only one parent can speak Welsh, the children are unable to speak it.
2. A small but significant proportion of children who complete primary education as first-language Welsh speakers commence their secondary education as second-language Welsh speakers and take their curriculum through the medium of English.
3. The Welsh Language Board's commissioned surveys show that more than 40 per cent of Welsh-speaking adults lack confidence in using the language, and therefore use it infrequently.
4. During adolescence, many bilingual teenagers use the language less frequently as they grow older (though this trend may be reversed in later life).
5. Geographically, the Welsh language has tended to decline by a westward movement, with many communities lessening in their everyday use of the Welsh language.

These five areas of concern are each addressed in this volume. However, in none of these areas do we have sufficient data to be able to plan accurately the anticipated needs of our bilingual society.

### Non-census sources

Although the census is the single most comprehensive data set available it does not probe very deeply into the social context or use of bilingualism. Thus we need to supplement its findings by non-census analysis, best represented by the Welsh Office's *1992 Welsh Social Survey* (1995a), which is the largest non-census-based social survey ever to have inquired into the acquisition and use of Welsh. This contains details of 27,720 individuals surveyed between September and December 1992. The survey revealed that Welsh speakers represent 21.5 per cent of the total population (Table 2.3). If we disaggregate this ability factor we find that the highest incidence is in the youngest age range, 3–15, with 32.4 per cent of the population fluent in Welsh. The proportion drops dramatically in the age range of 16–29, at 17.8 per cent, and for the next age range 30–44, falls further to 16.7 per cent. For the age range 45–64 the figure rises to 18.7 per cent and reaches 24.2 per cent for those aged 65 and over. Clearly this bodes well for the future, but in- and out-migration, marriage patterns and a host of other reasons preclude any firm prediction that the youngest cohort will necessarily maintain their reasonable levels of fluency into adulthood. We need to know far more about the details of first and second language patterns and in this respect the survey revealed that 55.3 per cent of Welsh speakers considered it to be their mother tongue. They represent 12 per cent of the national population.

The balance between first- and second-language speakers is a delicate issue. Very often one hears about the need to encourage language reproduction within predominantly Welsh-speaking families and communities. However, language production through the education system rather than language reproduction through local community socialization seems to characterize the younger elements of the population. This is revealed clearly in Table 2.3. Here the school factor is very evident, for only 27 per cent of the total Welsh speakers in the three to fifteen age range considered Welsh to be their mother tongue. Presumably the majority consider their Welsh fluency to be a school-acquired skill, which does not invalidate any of their abilities to use the language, but nor does it assume that for such children Welsh is the first, instinctive language of daily life. Interesting trends are revealed in Table 2.3, for each successive age cohort recorded higher proportions of mother-tongue speakers, reaching a peak of 79.3 per cent for the sixty-five and over group. The conventional explanation would be that the older age groups learned Welsh at home within the family and for some linguists this is a significant feature, for their use of Welsh is likely to be natural, richer, more idiomatic and colloquial than the rather formal, English-influenced style and patterning of younger Welsh speakers. This raises difficult questions of interpretation, for in terms of vocabulary and domain confidence the quality of Welsh spoken by the youngest group may be superior to that of the eldest group, even if it is less idiomatic. Also for the younger age groups their language loyalty/affiliation may not prove to be as resolute in the future, if Welsh represents for them a predominantly second language: a useful means of communication rather than an automatic first-choice language of expression.

Further evidence on self-assessed language ability is provided by the Social Survey which indicates that 368,000 (13.4 per cent) are fluent in Welsh. A further 94,900 (3.5 per cent) described themselves as able to speak quite a lot of Welsh, and 467,300 (17.0 per cent) described themselves as speaking only a small amount of Welsh. Thus 930,200 (33.9 per cent) were able to speak a little Welsh and 462,900 (16.9 per cent) were capable of speaking a considerable amount of Welsh. These figures are far higher than the normally cited Welsh-speaking population of *c*.590,800 people and should prove useful as a rough guide to the potential Welsh-speaking mass available to use government services or consumer/audience opportunities. Of those who claimed to be fluent, 80.5 per cent came from families where both parents spoke Welsh, 7.2 per cent from where the mother was fluent, 4.6 per cent from where the father was fluent and 7.7 per cent from families where neither parent was fluent.

Welsh speakers were asked to describe one statement which best represented their current use of Welsh (Table 2.4). Interesting county variations are revealed, with the former counties of Gwynedd and Dyfed, as might be expected, recording the highest usage of Welsh at 79 per cent and 71.1 per cent respectively. Lower proportions are recorded for Powys and Clwyd at 51.1 per cent and 40.9 per cent, while West Glamorgan and the amalgamated category of the three counties of the south-east record 32.8 per cent and 33.1 per cent respectively. Significantly, while only 6.9 per cent of fluent Welsh speakers in West Glamorgan claim that they rarely use the language, as many as 15.3 per cent in the industrial south-east found little reason or opportunity to use Welsh (Table 2.4).

Table 2.3. **Welsh speakers by age, 1992**

| Age | Sample size (1000's) | Population base (aged 3+) (1000's) | No. of Welsh speakers (1000's) | Welsh speakers as % of population | Mother-tongue speakers as % of Welsh speakers | Welsh speakers as % of population, 1991 census |
|------|------|------|------|------|------|------|
| 3–15 | 5.1 | 486.2 | 157.4 | 32.4 | 27.0 | 24.3 |
| 16–29 | 4.8 | 517.0 | 91.8 | 17.8 | 48.9 | 15.9 |
| 30–44 | 5.8 | 585.2 | 97.5 | 16.7 | 60.8 | 14.8 |
| 45–65 | 6.7 | 664.4 | 123.7 | 18.7 | 70.7 | 17.4 |
| 65+ | 5.3 | 498.0 | 120.4 | 24.2 | 79.3 | 22.6 |
| Total | 27.7 | 2750.7 | 590.8 | 21.5 | 55.7 | 18.7 |

*Source*: Welsh Social Survey, 1992, Welsh Office, Cardiff.

**Table 2.4. Welsh speakers' current use of Welsh, 1992 (%)**

| Welsh ability | Wales | Clwyd | Dyfed | Gwynedd | Powys | West Glam. | Gwent, Mid & South Glam. |
|---|---|---|---|---|---|---|---|
| Rarely speak Welsh | 4.5 | 8.9 | 1.9 | 1.3 | 5.7 | 6.9 | 15.3 |
| Occasionally | 12.0 | 21.7 | 7.4 | 5.5 | 17.9 | 26.8 | 21.8 |
| Half and half | 21.2 | 28.5 | 19.6 | 14.3 | 25.3 | 33.6 | 29.7 |
| Most or all of the time | 62.3 | 40.9 | 71.1 | 79.0 | 51.1 | 32.8 | 33.1 |

*Source*: Welsh Social Survey, 1992, Welsh Office, Cardiff.

All Welsh-language survey data suggest that social context, family language transmission and exposure to formal bilingual education are key factors in language reproduction. However, both the community and the family seem to be less powerful as agents of language reproduction than was true in the past. This implies that bilingual education, for both children and adults, will be a more significant agency of language production and reproduction than hitherto. Thus we need to specify with more precision just what the relationships are between these three elements and then move on to a consideration of how formal language planning can translate the undoubted potential inherent within bilingual education into the reality of employing either Welsh or English as languages of choice in the widest possible range of social domains.

### Family/household composition

Analysis of family/household composition patterns by Aitchison and Carter (1997) reveal significant and possibly damaging trends. Their analysis of Standardized Anonymous Returns (SARs) data shows that an extremely high proportion of Welsh speakers is linguistically isolated within the home environment. Table 2.5 describes a nested hierarchy of four types of households based on the language ability of household members. A basic distinction was drawn by Aitchison and Carter between Type 1(i), those households that have at least one Welsh speaker (defined as 'Welsh-speaking households'), and Type 1(ii), those that have no Welsh speakers. Of all households 26 per cent belong to the first of these two types, but over half (51 per cent) of the households contain only one Welsh speaker within them and many of these are elderly persons living alone. This does not bode well for the future.

A second distinction is that between households which are wholly or partly Welsh speaking, Types 2(i) and 2(ii). Just over half of Welsh-speaking households are wholly Welsh speaking (54 per cent) but they represent only 14 per cent of all households in Wales. Wholly Welsh-speaking households can be further subdivided into those with and those without children (aged three to seventeen years), Types 3a(i) and 3a(ii). Aitchison and Carter (1997) aver that such a pattern is worrying for Welsh, as the data show a very high proportion of such households with no children; furthermore almost half are single-person households,

### Table 2.5.  Language attributes and household type

| Household types | % of households |
|---|---|
| Type 1 All households | |
| (i)   Households without Welsh speakers | 73.6 |
| (ii)  Households with Welsh speakers | 26.4 |
| | |
| Type 2 Households with Welsh speakers | |
| (i)   Households wholly Welsh-speaking | 53.6 |
| (ii)  Households partly Welsh-speaking | 46.4 |
| | |
| Type 3 Household composition and Welsh speech | |
| a      Households wholly Welsh-speaking | |
| (i)   With children | 10.9 |
| (ii)  Without children | 42.7 |
| b      Households partly Welsh-speaking | |
| (i)   With Welsh-speaking children | 18.9 |
| (ii)  With non-Welsh-speaking children | 5.8 |
| (iii) With no children | 21.7 |
| | |
| Type 4 Household size, composition and Welsh speech | |
| a      Households wholly Welsh-speaking | |
| (i)   With children | 10.9 |
| (ii)  Single-person households | 21.3 |
| (iii) Without children | 21.5 |
| b      Households partly Welsh-speaking | |
| (i)   Households with Welsh-speaking children – single speaker | 6.2 |
| (ii)  Households with Welsh-speaking children – more than one Welsh speaker | 12.7 |
| c      Households partly Welsh-speaking but with non-Welsh-speaking children | |
| (i)   Single Welsh speaker | 4.9 |
| (ii)  More than one Welsh speaker | 0.9 |
| d      Households partly Welsh-speaking without children | |
| (i)   Single Welsh speaker | 18.6 |
| (ii)  More than one Welsh speaker | 3.1 |

*Source*: Aitchison and Carter, 1997: 362. Each type is a successive division of the previous type. Thus Type 2 is a subdivision of Type 3. Each type (1 to 4) therefore sums to 100.

Type 4a(ii). Similarly, of partly Welsh-speaking households, nearly two-thirds (64 per cent) have just a single Welsh speaker, Types 4b(i) and 4c(i), the majority of whom are in households which have no children. Encouragingly, 41 per cent of the households that are partly Welsh-speaking have one or more children who are able to speak Welsh. More sobering is the realization that some 70 per cent of the Welsh-speaking households have no Welsh-speaking children within them. Welsh households are, in the main, linguistically fractured and structurally diverse in composition. The Welsh Office's 1997 Welsh Household Interview

Survey of 40,000 households reported that 28 per cent of households contained Welsh speakers (cf. 1991 census figure of 26.4 per cent). Only 46 per cent of those households were entirely Welsh speaking (cf. 1991 census figure of 53.6 per cent).

### Education and the structure of bilingual Wales

Following the secularization of society and the breakdown of the relative homogeneity of rural communities, an alternative, urban, formal set of domains has been constructed mainly in the south and east. The Welsh-medium school system has done more than any other agency to promote the language and introduce it, and its related culture, to hitherto non-Welsh-speaking families. The nationwide network of primary and secondary Welsh-medium institutions are actively socializing a younger generation into participating in a fully functional bilingual society.

The school's role in promoting a bilingual society has increased, following the reforms of the 1988 Education Act which made Welsh a foundation subject in the National Curriculum. It is now possible to teach a wide range of subjects including maths and science, design and computing through the medium of Welsh. After 1994, all save a few opt-out schools in the secondary sector were obliged to teach Welsh to the pupils in the lower forms. This, in turn, has exposed a far greater number of Welsh young people to the language and culture of their homeland and requires a significant investment in teachers and resources to be successful. In higher education circles also there is a wide range of vocational and non-vocational courses available to full- and part-time students, but again it must be emphasized that in such developments the numbers involved within particular courses are small. Even so the trend and direction of change is significant for it extends both the domain use and practical utility of bilingualism in society.

### THE CONTEMPORARY STRUCTURE OF WELSH-MEDIUM EDUCATION

During the period 1990–7 the proportion and number of pupils in Welsh-medium primary and secondary schools grew, albeit slowly. It is within the dominant, conventional English-medium sector that the greatest impact of educational reforms may be charted and analysed by reference to the following suite of tables. Tables 2.6 and 2.13, for example, chart the trends in maintained primary schools teaching through the medium of Welsh, 1990–7. Of the 1,718 schools in 1990, schools where Welsh was the sole or main medium of instruction accounted for 25.9 per cent (445) of the total. By 1999 the percentage in this category had risen slightly to 26.8 per cent, and further gradual growth can be expected over the next decade.

However, it is in the non-conventional Welsh-medium sector that significant changes have been recorded. In 1990, 50.7 per cent (870) of schools had classes where Welsh was taught as a second language only. By 1999 this proportion had risen to 68.3 per cent (1,133). Most of the increase was due to the curriculum impact of the 1988 Education Act and the social effects of the Welsh Language Act 1993, which in effect abolished Category D schools (Table 2.6). While in 1990 14.2 per cent (244) of primary schools were not teaching any Welsh, by 1999 all were meeting what was by then the statutory requirement to teach Welsh.

An alternative method of measuring the impact of the reformed curriculum is to analyse changes in the numbers of children able to speak Welsh as a direct result of being exposed to the school influence in addition to any home or parental fluency in Welsh. Tables 2.7 and 2.11 suggest that, during the 1990s,

**Table 2.6. Maintained primary schools teaching through the medium of Welsh**

|  | 1990/1 | 1993/4 | 1994/5* | | 1995/6 | 1996/7 |
|---|---|---|---|---|---|---|
| Schools having classes where Welsh is sole or main medium of instruction | 445 | 460 | 465 | 453 | 455 | 449 |
| % of schools | 25.9 | 27.1 | 27.5 | 26.8 | 27.1 | 26.7 |
| Schools having classes where Welsh is a medium of teaching for part of the curriculum | – | 116 | 108 | 120 | 106 | 95 |
| % of schools | – | 6.8 | 6.4 | 7.1 | 6.3 | 5.7 |
| Schools having classes of 1st- and 2nd-language pupils where some of the teaching is through medium of Welsh | 36 | – | – | – | – | – |
| % of schools | 2.1 | – | – | – | – | – |
| Schools having classes of 2nd-language pupils where some of the teaching is through medium of Welsh | 122 | – | – | – | – | – |
| % of schools | 7.1 | – | – | – | – | – |
| Schools having classes where Welsh is taught as a second language only | 870 | 1,068 | 1,091 | 1,091 | 1,109 | 1,136 |
| % of schools | 50.7 | 62.9 | 64.5 | 64.5 | 66.0 | 67.6 |
| Schools where no Welsh is taught | 244 | 54 | 27 | 27 | 11 | 1 |
| % of schools | 14.2 | 3.2 | 1.6 | 1.6 | 0.7 | 0.1 |
| Total schools | 1,718 | 1,698 | 1,691 | 1,691 | 1,681 | 1,681 |

Figures at January each year (September prior to 1993/4). Includes grant-maintained schools. The mode of instruction in primary schools varies widely according to linguistic background and a school may have classes in more than one category. However, each school appears once only in this table, under an appropriate heading. Figures from 1991/2 onwards are not directly comparable with previous years because of a change in classification.
* The method of classification changed in 1994/5: the first column indicates the schools under the old classification and the second schools under the new classification.

Table 2.7. **Maintained primary-school pupils, aged 5 years and over,
by ability to speak Welsh**

|  | 1990/1 | 1993/4 | 1994/5 | 1995/6 | 1996/7 |
|---|---|---|---|---|---|
| No. of pupils who: |  |  |  |  |  |
| Speak Welsh at home | 14,827 | 14,328 | 14,632 | 14,343 | 14,656 |
| Do not speak Welsh at home but who can speak it with fluency | 15,181 | 18,647 | 19,608 | 18,300 | 21,221 |
| Speak Welsh but not fluently | 30,573 | 64,631 | 60,907 | 63,356 | 67,666 |
| Cannot speak Welsh at all | 155,796 | 124,197 | 128,837 | 131,003 | 124,682 |
| Total | 216,377 | 221,803 | 223,984 | 227,002 | 228,225 |
| % of pupils who: |  |  |  |  |  |
| Speak Welsh at home | 6.9 | 6.5 | 6.5 | 6.3 | 6.4 |
| Do not speak Welsh at home but who can speak it with fluency | 7.0 | 8.4 | 8.8 | 8.1 | 9.3 |
| Speak Welsh but not fluently | 14.1 | 29.1 | 27.2 | 27.9 | 29.6 |
| Cannot speak Welsh at all | 72.0 | 56.0 | 57.5 | 57.7 | 54.6 |
| Total | 100.0 | 100.0 | 100.0 | 100.0 | 100.0 |

Figures at January each year (September prior to 1993/4). Includes grant-maintained schools. These figures are derived from assessments made by headteachers.

about the same number of children aged five to eleven (*c.*14,500) spoke Welsh at home. But throughout this period there is a steady increase in the number of children who could speak Welsh fluently but who did not speak it at home, from 15,181 to 22,154. Again, there is a doubling of the numbers who could speak Welsh but were not completely fluent, from 30,573 in 1990 to 73,365 in 1999, and therefore a corresponding drop in the numbers who could not speak Welsh at all from 155,796 to 117,846. Alternative evidence of the same structural change may be presented in relation to the organization of teaching through the medium of Welsh in maintained primary schools, by class distribution (Table 2.8) and by pupil distribution (Table 2.9). Note that there has been a general increase in the range and number of classes taught through the medium of Welsh and a corresponding absolute drop of four-fifths in those classes in which Welsh is not used, down from 2,455 in 1990 to only 263 in 1999. Similarly there has been a significant growth in the number of pupils in classes where Welsh was the sole or main medium of instruction from 38,404 in 1990 to 51,600 in 1999. Conversely there has been a sharp decline in the numbers of pupils in classes being taught no Welsh, from 62,245 in 1990 to 6,293 in 1999.

At the secondary level a similar picture obtains but we may trace the trend over a longer time period: 1980–99. Table 2.10 reveals that there has been a more structured and linguistically differentiated pattern of school type. The composite school category, where Welsh was taught as both a first and second language, has shrunk, while there has been a corresponding increase in the number of schools where Welsh is taught as a first language only, from the five pioneering

Table 2.8. **Organization of teaching through the medium of Welsh in maintained primary schools, by type of class**

|  | 1990/1 | 1993/4 | 1994/5 | 1995/6 | 1996/7 |
|---|---|---|---|---|---|
| Classes where Welsh is sole or main medium of instruction | 1,736 | 2,065 | 2,147 | 2,170 | 2,192 |
| Classes where Welsh is used as a teaching medium for part of the curriculum | – | 503 | 411 | 421 | 309 |
| Classes of 1st- and 2nd-language pupils where some of the teaching is through medium of Welsh | 188 | – | – | – | – |
| Classes of 2nd-language pupils where some of the teaching is through the medium of Welsh | 764 | – | – | – | – |
| Classes where Welsh is taught as a 2nd language | 5,804 | 7,318 | 7,591 | 7,876 | 8,262 |
| Classes being taught no Welsh | 2,455 | 1,280 | 1,032 | 804 | 550 |
| All classes | 10,947 | 11,166 | 11,181 | 11,271 | 11,313 |

Figures at January each year (September prior to 1993/4). Includes grant-maintained schools. Classes as organized for teaching. Figures from 1991/2 onwards are not directly comparable with previous years because of a change in classification.

Table 2.9. **Pupils by use of Welsh in class, in maintained primary schools**

|  | 1990/1 | 1993/4 | 1994/5 | 1995/6 | 1996/7 |
|---|---|---|---|---|---|
| Pupils in classes where Welsh is sole or main medium of instruction | 38,404 | 46,950 | 49,382 | 50,327 | 50,392 |
| Pupils in classes where Welsh is used as a medium of teaching for part of the curriculum | – | 12,062 | 10,303 | 10,906 | 7,649 |
| 1st- and 2nd-language pupils in classes where some of the teaching is through medium of Welsh | 17,308 | – | – | – | – |
| Pupils in classes where Welsh is taught as a 2nd language | 151,037 | 192,839 | 201,148 | 209,103 | 220,136 |
| Pupils in classes being taught no Welsh | 62,245 | 33,843 | 28,203 | 21,870 | 14,553 |
| All pupils | 272,774 | 285,694 | 289,036 | 292,206 | 292,730 |

Figures at January each year (September prior to 1993/4). Includes grant-maintained schools. Pupils as organized for teaching. Figures from 1991/2 onwards are not directly comparable with previous years because of a change in classification.

Table 2.10. **Maintained secondary schools teaching Welsh**

|  | 1980/1 | 1990/1 | 1994/5 | 1995/6 | 1996/7 | 1997/8 | 1998/9 |
|---|---|---|---|---|---|---|---|
| Schools where Welsh is taught as both a 1st and 2nd language | 82 | 68 | 48 | 50 | 50 | 54 | 51 |
| % of schools | 34.5 | 29.6 | 21.1 | 21.9 | 21.8 | 23.7 | 22.3 |
| Schools where Welsh is taught as a 1st language only | 5 | 11 | 18 | 17 | 18 | 20 | 20 |
| % of schools | 2.1 | 4.8 | 7.9 | 7.5 | 7.9 | 8.8 | 8.7 |
| Schools where Welsh is taught as a 2nd language only | 116 | 129 | 158 | 159 | 161 | 154 | 158 |
| % of schools | 48.7 | 56.1 | 69.6 | 69.7 | 70.3 | 67.5 | 69.0 |
| Schools where no Welsh is taught | 35 | 22 | 3 | 2 | – | – | – |
| % of schools | 14.7 | 9.5 | 1.3 | 0.9 | – | – | – |
| Total | 238 | 230 | 227 | 228 | 229 | 228 | 229 |

From 1993/4 at January each year; prior to that, at September each year; includes grant-maintained schools.

schools which existed in 1980 to the twenty such schools by 1999. A larger number of secondary schools are now classified as equipped to teach Welsh as a second language, up from 116 in 1980 to 158 in 1999. As a consequence, the final category of schools ($N = 35$) where no Welsh was taught in 1980 had been eliminated from the classification by 1999. Most of these thirty-five schools were either state-funded Catholic schools or secondary schools located within long-anglicized areas of Wales, mostly in the border counties abutting England.

## WELSH IN SCHOOLS AT THE END OF THE TWENTIETH CENTURY: KEY POINTS

The percentage of primary pupils who can speak Welsh fluently is increasing, though the percentage that speaks Welsh as a home language is decreasing.

About 2 per cent of those pupils assessed as fluent Welsh speakers at the end of their primary education do not study Welsh as a first language when they start in secondary school. In the primary sector, the percentage of pupils assessed in Welsh as a first language in National Curriculum assessments is higher than the percentage fluent in the language.

### Pupils

In January 1999, 16.0 per cent of primary-school children were fluent Welsh speakers, which included 6.3 per cent who spoke Welsh at home (Table 2.11); 13.3

**Table 2.11. Maintained primary-school pupils, aged 5 years and over, by ability to speak Welsh**

| School year | Speak Welsh at home | | Do not speak Welsh at home but can speak it with fluency | | Speak Welsh but not fluently | | Cannot speak Welsh at all | | Total | | Fluent | |
|---|---|---|---|---|---|---|---|---|---|---|---|---|
| | No. | % | No. | % | No. | % | No. | % | No. | % | No. | % |
| 1977/8 | 20,747 | 8.1 | – | – | – | – | – | – | – | – | – | – |
| 1978/9 | 20,486 | 8.2 | – | – | – | – | – | – | – | – | – | – |
| 1979/80 | 19,470 | 8.0 | – | – | – | – | – | – | – | – | – | – |
| 1980/1 | 18,824 | 8.1 | – | – | – | – | – | – | – | – | – | – |
| 1981/2 | 18,058 | 8.1 | – | – | – | – | – | – | – | – | – | – |
| 1982/3 | 16,577 | 7.8 | – | – | – | – | – | – | – | – | – | – |
| 1983/4 | 15,852 | 7.8 | – | – | – | – | – | – | – | – | – | – |
| 1984/5 | 15,110 | 7.6 | – | – | – | – | – | – | – | – | – | – |
| 1985/6* | 14,520 | 7.2 | – | – | – | – | – | – | – | – | – | – |
| 1986/7 | 14,720 | 7.3 | 11,800 | 5.8 | 20,049 | 9.9 | 153,479 | 76.7 | 202,048 | – | 26,520 | 13.1 |
| 1987/8 | 14,572 | 7.1 | 12,374 | 6.0 | 23,531 | 11.5 | 154,303 | 75.4 | 204,780 | – | 26,946 | 13.2 |
| 1988/9 | 14,857 | 7.1 | 13,449 | 6.4 | 26,514 | 12.6 | 155,831 | 74.0 | 210,651 | – | 28,306 | 13.4 |
| 1989/90 | 15,101 | 7.0 | 14,248 | 6.6 | 28,295 | 13.2 | 157,020 | 73.1 | 214,664 | – | 29,349 | 13.7 |
| 1990/1 | 14,827 | 6.9 | 15,181 | 7.0 | 30,573 | 14.1 | 155,796 | 72.0 | 216,377 | – | 30,008 | 13.9 |
| 1991/2 | 14,830 | 6.9 | 15,833 | 7.3 | 34,669 | 16.0 | 151,083 | 69.8 | 216,415 | – | 30,663 | 14.2 |
| 1992/3 | 14,859 | 6.8 | 16,824 | 7.7 | 42,008 | 19.3 | 144,401 | 66.2 | 218,092 | – | 31,683 | 14.5 |
| 1993/4 | 14,328 | 6.5 | 18,647 | 8.4 | 64,631 | 29.1 | 124,197 | 56.0 | 221,803 | – | 32,975 | 14.9 |
| 1994/5 | 14,632 | 6.5 | 19,608 | 8.8 | 60,907 | 27.2 | 128,837 | 57.5 | 223,984 | – | 34,240 | 15.3 |
| 1995/6 | 14,343 | 6.3 | 18,300 | 8.1 | 63,356 | 27.9 | 131,003 | 57.7 | 227,002 | – | 32,643 | 14.4 |
| 1996/7 | 14,656 | 6.4 | 21,221 | 9.3 | 67,666 | 29.6 | 124,682 | 54.6 | 228,225 | – | 35,877 | 15.7 |
| 1997/8 | 14,575 | 6.3 | 22,105 | 9.6 | 68,783 | 30.0 | 124,097 | 54.1 | 229,560 | – | 36,680 | 16.0 |
| 1998/9 | 14,320 | 6.3 | 22,154 | 9.7 | 73,365 | 32.2 | 117,846 | 51.8 | 227,685 | – | 36,474 | 16.0 |

*Source:* Schools' Census

Figures at September until 1993/4; at January in 1993/4 and thereafter.

* Figures for the years preceding 1986 are not comparable with later years. From September 1986 the wording and format of the question on Welsh-speaking ability was changed to permit a better analysis of the progress of Welsh-medium education. Before 1986, headteachers were asked to distinguish only 3 categories: First (home) language – Welsh, Second language – Welsh but less than fluently described as 'fluent' and the less fluent remainder; so leading to a drop in the former category, but allowing a better perception of the educational position.

per cent of pupils in year groups 7–11 (compulsory school age) in maintained secondary schools were taught Welsh as a first language (Table 2.16). The percentage of primary-school children speaking Welsh fluently increased from 13.1 per cent in 1986/7 to 16.0 per cent in 1998/9. The percentage of primary-school children speaking Welsh at home fell over the same period from 7.3 per cent to 6.3 per cent while the percentage speaking Welsh fluently but not as a home language rose from 5.8 per cent to 9.7 per cent (Figure 2.1 and Table 2.11). 19.8 per cent of primary-school pupils are taught in classes where Welsh is used as a medium of teaching to some degree (Table 2.12).

At the end of Key Stage 1 in 1999, 18.2 per cent of pupils were assessed in Welsh although of that age group (seven-year-olds), headteachers thought only 16.1 per cent spoke Welsh fluently (Table 2.14). On average over the period 1996–9 the percentage assessed in Welsh at the end of Key Stage 1 was just over 2 per cent higher than the percentage considered by headteachers to be fluent in the language. At the end of Key Stage 2 in 1999, 17.6 per cent of pupils were assessed in Welsh although of that age group (eleven-year-olds), headteachers thought only 16.2 per cent spoke Welsh fluently (Table 2.15). On average over the period 1996–9 the percentage assessed in Welsh at the end of Key Stage 2 was just over 1 per cent higher than the percentage considered by headteachers to be fluent in the language.

At January 1999 13.3 per cent of secondary-school pupils in Years 7 to 11 were taught Welsh as a first language; the percentage has increased virtually every year since 1977/8, when the comparable figure was 9.3 per cent (Figure 2.2). By 1999, 14.6 per cent of pupils in Year 7 were being taught Welsh as a first language (Table 2.18).

Each year the percentage taught Welsh as a first language upon transfer to secondary school is lower than the percentage assessed as fluent while at primary school. In 1999, around 10 per cent of those considered fluent Welsh speakers in primary school were taught Welsh as a second language when they transferred to secondary school (Tables 2.15 and 2.18).

At January 1999, 13.0 per cent of pupils in Year 9 studied Welsh as a first language and in the summer term of 1998/9 a similar percentage was assessed in Welsh first language at the end of Key Stage 3 (Table 2.17).

At January 1999, 67.8 per cent of secondary-school pupils in Years 7 to 11 were taught Welsh as a second language. A major growth has occurred since 1987/8 when the comparable figure was only 42 per cent (Table 2.16).

### Schools

Of all primary schools 27 per cent (445 schools) are mainly Welsh-medium schools. A further eighty-two schools, 5 per cent of the total, use Welsh as a teaching medium to some extent. In the remaining 1,133 schools, 68 per cent of all primary schools, Welsh is taught as a second language only (Table 2.13).

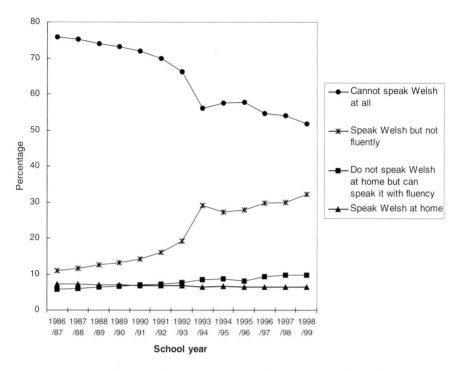

Figure 2.1. Fluency in Welsh of primary-school pupils aged 5 and over
(*Source*: Table 2.11)

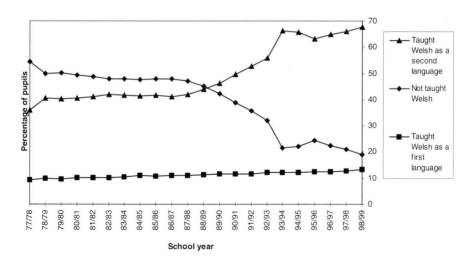

Figure 2.2. Welsh teaching in secondary schools: year groups 7–11
(*Source*: Table 2.16)

**Table 2.12. Teaching through the medium of Welsh in maintained primary schools, by type of class**

|  | 1994/5 | 1995/6 | 1996/7 | 1997/8 | 1998/9 |
|---|---|---|---|---|---|
| Classes where Welsh is sole or main medium of instruction |  |  |  |  |  |
| no. of classes | 2,147 | 2,170 | 2,192 | 2,168 | 2,206 |
| no. of pupils | 49,382 | 50,327 | 50,392 | 51,853 | 51,600 |
| Classes where Welsh is used as a teaching medium for less than half of the curriculum |  |  |  |  |  |
| no. of classes | 411 | 421 | 309 | 260 | 246 |
| no. of pupils | 10,303 | 10,906 | 7,649 | 6,535 | 6,146 |
| Classes where Welsh is taught as a second language |  |  |  |  |  |
| no. of classes | 7,591 | 7,876 | 8,262 | 8,226 | 8,639 |
| no. of pupils | 201,148 | 209,103 | 220,136 | 224,775 | 227,648 |
| Classes being taught no Welsh |  |  |  |  |  |
| no. of classes | 1,032 | 804 | 550 | 409 | 263 |
| no. of pupils | 28,203 | 21,870 | 14,553 | 10,528 | 6,293 |
| Total classes | 11,181 | 11,271 | 11,313 | 11,063 | 11,354 |
| Total pupils | 289,036 | 292,206 | 292,730 | 293,691 | 291,687 |
| Classes where Welsh is the sole or main medium of instruction |  |  |  |  |  |
| % of classes | 19.2 | 19.3 | 19.4 | 19.6 | 19.4 |
| % of pupils | 17.1 | 17.2 | 17.2 | 17.7 | 17.7 |
| Classes where Welsh is used as a teaching medium for part of the curriculum |  |  |  |  |  |
| % of classes | 3.7 | 3.7 | 2.7 | 2.4 | 2.2 |
| % of pupils | 3.6 | 3.7 | 2.6 | 2.2 | 2.1 |
| Classes where Welsh is taught as a second language |  |  |  |  |  |
| % of classes | 67.9 | 69.9 | 73.0 | 74.4 | 76.1 |
| % of pupils | 69.6 | 71.6 | 75.2 | 76.5 | 78.0 |
| Classes being taught no Welsh |  |  |  |  |  |
| % of classes | 9.2 | 7.1 | 4.9 | 3.7 | 2.3 |
| % of pupils | 9.8 | 7.5 | 5.0 | 3.6 | 2.2 |

*Source*: Schools' Census
Figures at January each year; includes grant-maintained schools.

The percentage, and number, of primary schools where Welsh is used as a medium to teach only a minority of pupils, or to teach less than half of the curriculum, has been falling in recent years (Table 2.13).

The number of 'Welsh-speaking' secondary schools increased from forty-four in 1990/91 to fifty-two in 1998/9 (Table 2.19).

**Table 2.13. Primary schools, by the use of Welsh as a teaching medium**

|  | 1994/5 | 1995/6 | 1996/7 | 1997/8 | 1998/9 |
|---|---|---|---|---|---|
| A: Welsh is the sole or main medium of instruction | 453 | 455 | 449 | 446 | 445 |
| % of schools | 26.8 | 27.1 | 26.7 | 26.7 | 26.8 |
| B: Welsh is used as a medium of teaching for less than half of the curriculum | 120 | 106 | 95 | 94 | 82 |
| % of schools | 7.1 | 6.3 | 5.7 | 5.6 | 4.9 |
| C: Welsh is taught as a second language only | 1,091 | 1,109 | 1,136 | 1,133 | 1,133 |
| % of schools | 64.5 | 66.0 | 67.6 | 67.8 | 68.3 |
| D: No Welsh is taught | 27 | 11 | 1 | – | – |
| % of schools | 1.6 | 0.7 | 0.1 | 0 | 0 |
| Total schools | 1,691 | 1,681 | 1,681 | 1,673 | 1,660 |

*Source*: Schools' census.
Figures at January each year; includes grant-maintained schools. The mode of instruction in primary schools varies widely according to linguistic background and a school may have classes in more than one category. However, each school appears once only in this table, under an appropriate heading.

**Table 2.14. Key Stage 1 assessments in Welsh**

|  | 1996 | 1997 | 1998 | 1999 |
|---|---|---|---|---|
| End of Key Stage 1 teacher assessments in the subject of Welsh (1st language) as a % of all assessment in the subjects of English and Welsh | 18.2 | 18.0 | 18.1 | 18.2 |
| % of 7-year-old pupils who are Welsh home-language speakers | 6.4 | 6.3 | 6.3 | 6.2 |
| % of 7-year-old pupils who are fluent Welsh speakers | 15.5 | 15.8 | 15.8 | 16.1 |

*Source*: National Curriculum assessments; Schools' census.
In Key Stage 1, pupils are assessed either in the subject of Welsh or in the subject of English.

**Table 2.15. Key Stage 2 assessments in Welsh**

|  | 1996 | 1997 | 1998 | 1999 |
|---|---|---|---|---|
| End of Key Stage 2 teacher assessments in the subject of Welsh (1st language) as a % of all assessments | 17.0 | 17.2 | 17.5 | 17.6 |
| % of 11-year-old pupils who are Welsh home-language speakers | 6.5 | 6.3 | 6.5 | 6.3 |
| % of 11-year-old pupils who are fluent Welsh speakers | 15.9 | 15.7 | 16.3 | 16.2 |

*Source*: National Curriculum assessments; Schools' census.

Table 2.16. **Welsh in maintained secondary schools in year groups 7–11,**
**by type of course**

| School year | Taught Welsh as a 1st language | | Taught Welsh as a 2nd language | | Not taught Welsh at all | | Total no. of pupils |
|---|---|---|---|---|---|---|---|
| | No. of pupils | % | No. of pupils | % | No. of pupils | % | |
| 1977/78 | 22,644 | 9.3 | 87,550 | 36.1 | 132,257 | 54.6 | 242,451 |
| 1978/79 | 21,730 | 9.8 | 89,612 | 40.4 | 110,523 | 49.8 | 221,865 |
| 1979/80 | 21,458 | 9.7 | 88,951 | 40.2 | 110,756 | 50.1 | 221,165 |
| 1980/81 | 22,075 | 10.1 | 88,392 | 40.5 | 107,996 | 49.4 | 218,463 |
| 1981/82 | 21,762 | 10.1 | 88,179 | 41.1 | 104,538 | 48.7 | 214,479 |
| 1982/83 | 21,669 | 10.2 | 88,963 | 41.8 | 102,108 | 48.0 | 212,740 |
| 1983/84 | 21,896 | 10.4 | 87,367 | 41.7 | 100,357 | 47.9 | 209,620 |
| 1984/85 | 22,699 | 11.1 | 84,384 | 41.3 | 97,220 | 47.6 | 204,303 |
| 1985/86 | 20,938 | 10.7 | 81,751 | 41.6 | 93,883 | 47.7 | 196,572 |
| 1986/87 | 20,911 | 11.1 | 77,630 | 41.0 | 90,602 | 47.9 | 189,143 |
| 1987/88 | 19,914 | 11.1 | 74,975 | 42.0 | 83,868 | 46.9 | 178,757 |
| 1988/89 | 19,224 | 11.3 | 74,657 | 43.8 | 76,586 | 44.9 | 170,467 |
| 1989/90 | 19,026 | 11.5 | 75,987 | 46.2 | 69,572 | 42.3 | 164,585 |
| 1990/91 | 19,242 | 11.7 | 81,109 | 49.5 | 63,592 | 38.8 | 163,943 |
| 1991/92 | 19,416 | 11.7 | 87,545 | 52.6 | 59,429 | 35.7 | 166,390 |
| 1992/93 | 20,552 | 12.1 | 94,663 | 55.9 | 54,195 | 32.0 | 169,410 |
| 1993/94 | 20,962 | 12.1 | 114,883 | 66.3 | 37,418 | 21.6 | 173,263 |
| 1994/95 | 21,658 | 12.2 | 116,268 | 65.8 | 38,892 | 22.0 | 176,818 |
| 1995/96 | 21,845 | 12.4 | 111,647 | 63.2 | 43,132 | 24.4 | 176,624 |
| 1996/97 | 22,248 | 12.6 | 114,908 | 65.0 | 39,639 | 22.4 | 176,795 |
| 1997/98 | 22,857 | 12.8 | 117,625 | 66.1 | 37,455 | 21.0 | 177,937 |
| 1998/99 | 24,013 | 13.3 | 122,112 | 67.8 | 34,111 | 18.9 | 180,236 |

*Source*: Schools' census.
Figures at September until 1993/4, in January from 1993/4 onwards; includes grant-maintained schools.

Table 2.17. **Key Stage 3 assessments in Welsh**

| | 1996 | 1997 | 1998 | 1999 |
|---|---|---|---|---|
| End of Key Stage 3 teacher assessments in the subject of Welsh (1st language) as a % of all assessments | 12.2 | 12.1 | 12.4 | 12.8 |
| % of Year 9 pupils studying Welsh as a 1st language | 12.4 | 12.5 | 12.5 | 13.0 |

*Source*: National Curriculum assessments; Schools' census.

## *Policy implications*

That the position of Welsh-medium education has been strengthened is a significant development in its own right. However, there has been a corresponding shift in the proportions of all pupils now exposed to the indigenous language, literature and culture of Wales. Some of these go on to be very active participants

**Table 2.18. Pupils taught Welsh as a first language in maintained secondary schools in year groups 7–11, by year group (%)**

| January | 7 | 8 | 9 | 10 | 11 | Total |
|---|---|---|---|---|---|---|
| 1995 | 12.8 | 12.6 | 12.1 | 12.0 | 11.8 | 12.2 |
| 1996 | 12.9 | 12.7 | 12.4 | 11.9 | 12.0 | 12.4 |
| 1997 | 13.3 | 12.8 | 12.5 | 12.2 | 12.1 | 12.6 |
| 1998 | 13.7 | 13.3 | 12.5 | 12.4 | 12.3 | 12.8 |
| 1999 | 14.6 | 13.6 | 13.0 | 12.7 | 12.6 | 13.3 |

*Source*: Schools' census.

**Table 2.19. Welsh-speaking secondary schools**

| | 1990/1 | 1994/5 | 1995/6 | 1996/7 | 1997/8 | 1998/9 |
|---|---|---|---|---|---|---|
| No. of schools | 44 | 48 | 47 | 49 | 50 | 52 |
| No. of pupils | 27,897 | 33,204 | 32,973 | 33,371 | 34,566 | 36,289 |

*Source*: Schools' census.
Figures at January each year (September prior to 1993/4); includes grant-maintained schools. Welsh-speaking secondary schools as defined in section 354(b) of the Education Act 1996. A Welsh-speaking secondary school is one where more than one half of the foundation subjects other than English and Welsh and including religious education, are taught wholly or partly in Welsh.

within Welsh-medium networks and public life. The vast majority do not, but having had such a long-term exposure to formal education through Welsh, the previous generation's suspicion and tension which surrounded the use of Welsh as a language of the minority has been reduced significantly. The general effect of this is recorded in much more positive attitudes towards bilingualism and the construction of a bilingual society *per se*. However, beneath this positive trend there remains for many a grumbling doubt as to the real worth of bilingualism. It is argued that, once pupils have left school, there is little socio-economic opportunity and instrumental justification for maintaining their fluency in Welsh, apart from some limited opportunities within the para-public sector. The commercial, private sector has been very slow to recognize the value of bilingualism. Attempts to ameliorate this situation often focus on the nature of service provision or the lack of demand on behalf of Welsh speakers, rather than interpreting it as a reflection of the lack of institutionalization. Time will tell as to whether this judgement can still be made after the current period of institutional bilingualism has had its full impact.

Two issues of direct importance for educational policy will be the wider exposure of all children in Wales to bilingual instruction and the introduction of new software and terminological data-bases which will enable students to shift back and forth between information generated in English and that generated in Welsh.

A second consideration is the creation of new bilingual opportunities for specialist use of Welsh and English within the democratic institutions and in related socio-economic agencies. How will this impact on the education system and a whole host of other activities? At present, due to the lack of systematic research we know virtually nothing as to how aspects of the education system will influence these issues. Nor do we know very much in detail about the formative influences on conceptions of national identity in Wales nor of the appropriate use of Welsh or English within selected specialist domains. Much of public policy is based on very broad assumptions and generalizations about the relevance of bilingual education in the service of society but very few research projects have sought to document the bilingual educational experience *vis-à-vis* a monolingual English educational experience. Two recent exceptions are Bellin, Higgs and Farrell (1997), which attempted to investigate the language shift process by a socio-spatial analysis of census and non-census data within selected communities, and Reynolds, Bellin and ab Ieuan (1998), which sought to assess whether or not the Welsh-medium school sector in the Rhondda Valleys was characterized by several structural advantages which enabled its pupils to outperform pupils of very similar socio-economic backgrounds who attended English-medium or Church in Wales schools.

Outside the educational system many other pillars of Welsh culture are entering a more dynamic phase which also leads to increased language reproduction. Political change at both the domestic and European levels has encouraged the recognition of pluralism in Wales. The language struggle is by no means over. However, attempts to honour the equality of Welsh and English are now taken seriously and both government planning and popular initiatives are focused on seizing the opportunities which are currently available. The keywords used by opinion-formers to describe the relationship between English and Welsh speakers are partnership, mutual respect and recognition. The key phrase describing the situation of their relationship with immigrant minority languages in Wales is *terra incognita,* not only in the profound sense that we do not know much about the context of such speakers, but more that we have yet to decide what role such languages and their speakers will be encouraged to play within our new public policy initiatives based upon our apparently characteristic features of openness, transparency and citizen diversity.


## THE COMMUNITY AND COMMUNITY INITIATIVES

Clearly by 1991 the monolingual reservoir had disappeared and the family as a pillar of Welsh cultural reproduction was under strain. There is current concern that a second pillar, the communities of the northern and western heartland, will also fragment irretrievably. Fragmentation and decline is all too pressing a description of many Welsh-speaking communities, as is demonstrated in the comprehensive spatial analyses offered by Aitchison and Carter (1994, 2000). If this cultural resource base atrophies, what then for the production and reproduction of the identity transmitted through the Welsh language?

Clearly one would be naïve to deny the rapid advancements made in technologically induced cultural change. The whole premiss of an integrated Europe depends in large part on the technical ability to realize a European Union without internal borders and trade barriers. But strident attempts are being made to counter some of the deleterious tendencies of globalization and enlargement. Those which seek to strengthen the community element in language reproduction pin their hopes on innovative reforms, such as the *mentrau iaith* (which are described in detail in Chapters 8, 9 and 10 below; Williams, 1999; Williams and Evas, 1997). Here we wish to draw attention to the need for specific data-gathering procedures to enable the *mentrau iaith* to fulfil their roles as communitiy development agencies. To do this we also need to examine the socio-spatial context within which the *mentrau* operate.

## COMMUNITY REVITALIZATION: *MENTRAU IAITH*

The original *mentrau iaith* (language enterprise agencies), dating from 1991–3, were established in Cwm Gwendraeth and Aman Tawe, both predominantly Welsh-speaking communities. There are now twenty *mentrau iaith* and several more in the process of being established. Their aim is to stimulate the development of Welsh within a wide social context, and one might almost define them as community regeneration movements with a linguistic cutting edge. They are funded mainly by the National Assembly through the Welsh Language Board, together with some ancillary funding by local authorities, which currently totals £310,384 per annum. Two compelling reasons for supporting *mentrau iaith* are that they offer a significant socio-psychological fillip for Welsh maintenance in contexts which would otherwise lead to fragmentation and they can function as a focus to create a new set of partnerships between the National Assembly, the Welsh Language Board, local government, statutory public bodies, health trusts and a variety of other voluntary agencies and private companies, so as to extend the domains within which it is possible to use Welsh.

A basic question facing all *mentrau iaith* personnel is: what is the sociolinguistic and socio-economic character of the community they wish to serve? In most cases the community does not necessarily correspond with a local government area, nor may it be fully comprehended with reference to decennial census analysis. Very few detailed local community surveys have been attempted, but those that exist reveal significant micro-level variations from the aggregate census-based studies. A significant initiative, which demonstrates what can be achieved with existing data sets, occurred in 1995 when the Welsh Office's Statistical Directorate was asked to prepare a statistical brief on the community characteristics of Welsh in the Gwendraeth Valley as a contextual basis for the 'Community Research Project' (Williams and Evas, 1997). In this chapter we demonstrate how a great deal can be gleaned about language contexts from existing data sources that are not fully utilized. It is our conviction that similar preparatory statistical investigation should also be undertaken in advance of any intensive community-based language intervention efforts.


CASE-STUDY ILLUSTRATION: CWM GWENDRAETH

Cwm Gwendraeth is situated at the western-most extension of the south Wales coalfield. It is comprised of a large number of small industrial settlements located within a prosperous peri-rural landscape. Given its high proportion of Welsh speakers it has been deemed as a significant indicator of the health of the language within a rapidly changing post-industrial context.

According to the Welsh Social Survey of 1992:[1]

- 74 per cent of the population spoke Welsh;
- 52 per cent spoke Welsh as a mother tongue, that is, they spoke more Welsh than English at home when growing up;
- 54 per cent are fluent Welsh speakers;
- 86 per cent of the Welsh speakers are able to read Welsh, which is the same level of literacy recorded for Dyfed as a whole, and slightly higher than that for the national average (84.7 per cent);
- 46 per cent of the Welsh speakers regularly watch S4C, which is a higher incidence than the national average (36 per cent).

Cwm Gwendraeth's Welsh speakers aged sixteen and over:[2]

- *were more likely* than their counterparts in other regions of Wales to speak Welsh the majority or most of the time *with the family* (76 per cent in Cwm Gwendraeth, 65 per cent across Wales) and *in a social context with their friends* (67 per cent as opposed to 56), but
- *were less likely* to speak Welsh all or most of the time in the workplace (35 per cent in Cwm Gwendraeth, 54 per cent in Wales). Welsh was used in the chapel or the church almost as much in Cwm Gwendraeth as across the nation.
- *were as likely* to use Welsh as fluent speakers across the nation when conducting their business in a bank, the Post Office, in local shops or when using the local health services;
- *were less likely* to use Welsh than the national average when dealing with the local authority (26 per cent use Welsh in this context in Cwm Gwendraeth as opposed to 48 per cent nationally).

According to the Welsh Social Survey, the area had a population of 31,000 in 1992 (see Table 2.20). Cwm Gwendraeth's 23,000 fluent Welsh speakers represent about 4 per cent of all Welsh speakers in Wales. Conventional patterns are demonstrated[3] similar to those outlined by the population census, namely:

- a decline in the proportion of Welsh speakers in the younger age groups in comparison with the older age groups;

- a higher proportion of Welsh speakers in the youngest age group, compared with older age groups, *but*
- within the youngest age group there is a significant difference between the Welsh speaking proportion in general and those categorized as mother tongue, or speaking Welsh fluently.


### *Cwm Gwendraeth's primary schools*

Menter Cwm Gwendraeth calculate that there are twenty-four primary schools in the area which they serve.[4] The following section reports on data pertaining to these schools.

### *School structure*

By comparison with 1993, the position of Welsh in the schools in 1995 was somewhat stronger. The number of classes where Welsh was used as the primary means of instruction had remained the same, yet their share as a proportion of the total had risen and they contained a larger number of pupils (Table 2.22). Between 1993 and 1995 the proportion of pupils who received their education in classes where Welsh was the principal medium of instruction rose from 70 to 76 per cent.

For statistical purposes only, the National Assembly categorizes school classes into four categories.[5] Schools representing three of these classes were present in

**Table 2.20. Chief characteristics of Cwm Gwendraeth population:**
**Welsh Social Survey, 1992**

| Cwm Gwendraeth | Age group | | | | | |
|---|---|---|---|---|---|---|
|  | 3–15 | 16–29 | 30–44 | 45–64 | 65+ | 3+ |
| Sample size | 45 | 43 | 52 | 74 | 50 | 264 |
| Population estimate | 5,300 | 5,300 | 6,400 | 8,700 | 5,800 | 31,400 |
| Welsh-speaking (%) |  |  |  |  |  |  |
|   yes | 82 | 66 | 68 | 70 | 86 | 74 |
|   no | 18 | 34 | 32 | 30 | 14 | 26 |
| Mother tongue (%) | 27 | 51 | 46 | 57 | 76 | 52 |
| Fluent speakers (%) | 38 | 52 | 45 | 57 | 74 | 54 |

**Table 2.21. 95% confidence intervals for Welsh speakers**

|  | Age group | | | | | |
|---|---|---|---|---|---|---|
|  | 3–15 | 16–29 | 30–44 | 45–64 | 65+ | 3+ |
| Upper limit | 95.7 | 80.4 | 81.0 | 80.7 | 95.7 | 80.7 |
| Lower limit | 68.3 | 52.2 | 56.0 | 60.1 | 76.5 | 67.5 |

*Note*: Estimates with allowances for design effect.

Table 2.22. **Number of classes and pupils, by principal language of instruction and year**

| Year | Mainly Welsh | | Partly Welsh | | Welsh 2nd-language | | No Welsh | |
|------|---------|--------|---------|--------|---------|--------|---------|--------|
| | Classes | Pupils | Classes | Pupils | Classes | Pupils | Classes | Pupils |
| 1993 | 81 | 1,646 | 17 | 331 | 16 | 338 | 1 | 13 |
| 1994 | 81 | 1,792 | 13 | 219 | 15 | 342 | 0 | 0 |
| 1995 | 81 | 1,815 | 12 | 208 | 15 | 348 | 0 | 0 |

Cwm Gwendraeth. Category A includes schools where the majority of classes are taught through the medium of Welsh. Category B includes schools where there are substantial numbers of Welsh-medium or partly Welsh-medium classes, but the majority of pupils are not taught through the medium of Welsh. Category C schools teach Welsh as a second language. Table 2.23 reveals that three-quarters of the area's schools belong to the first category.

*Pupils' linguistic ability*

Although three-quarters of pupils are taught in classes where Welsh is the dominant medium of instruction, Figure 2.4 demonstrates that the headteachers' returns suggest that only 70 per cent of pupils are considered to be fluent in Welsh. Between 1993 and 1994 there was a 6 per cent increase in those whom the headteacher judged to be fluent in Welsh but who did not speak the language at home. Just under 40 per cent are considered to be both fluent and to speak the language at home. As a shorthand we will describe these as mother-tongue speakers. These figures are not directly comparable with those derived from the Welsh Social Survey. In part this is because we are not comparing the exact same physical space (see notes) and in part the figures derived from the schools census are based upon primary-age pupils only. Even so, it is still worth noting that the

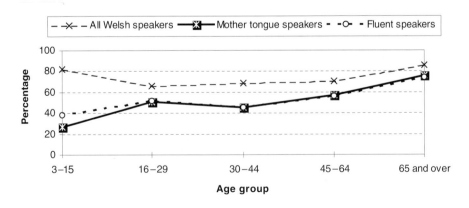

Figure 2.3. **Welsh speakers**

**Table 2.23. Number of pupils, by language of instruction and school category, 1995**

| Category of school | No. of schools | Primarily Welsh | Partly Welsh | Welsh 2nd language | No Welsh |
|---|---|---|---|---|---|
| A | 18 | 1,538 | 8 | 0 | 0 |
| B | 5 | 277 | 200 | 127 | 0 |
| C | 1 | 0 | 0 | 221 | 0 |
| Total | 24 | 1,815 | 208 | 348 | 0 |

estimates derived from the Welsh Social Survey regarding the proportions speaking Welsh aged three to fifteen are lower than those derived from the schools census pertaining to primary-aged children.

*Pupils' linguistic abilities by age*
Table 2.24 reveals higher proportions of fluent speakers in the higher age groups than in the younger age groups. Whilst one in eight of pupils aged four and over are fluent, even if they do not speak it at home, this rises to one in three among

**Table 2.24. Number of pupils, by linguistic ability and age, 1995**

| Age at 31 Aug. 1994 | No. | Mother-tongue | Fluent not mother-tongue | Not fluent | No Welsh | % fluent |
|---|---|---|---|---|---|---|
| 10 to 11 | 288 | 37.2 | 32.6 | 23.6 | 6.6 | 69.8 |
| 9 to 10 | 320 | 34.4 | 40.6 | 16.6 | 8.4 | 75.0 |
| 8 to 9 | 299 | 45.8 | 29.4 | 17.1 | 7.7 | 75.3 |
| 7 to 8 | 338 | 42.0 | 35.8 | 12.4 | 9.8 | 77.8 |
| 6 to 7 | 356 | 37.9 | 33.1 | 21.6 | 7.3 | 71.1 |
| 5 to 6 | 274 | 37.6 | 25.5 | 24.5 | 12.4 | 63.1 |
| 4 to 5 | 283 | 40.3 | 12.7 | 17.3 | 29.7 | 53.0 |
| Total 4+ | 2,158 | 39.3 | 30.4 | 18.9 | 11.4 | 69.7 |

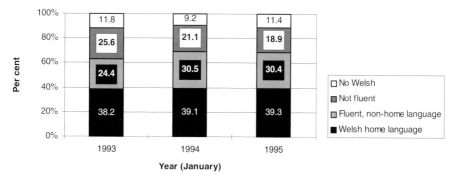

**Figure 2.4. Language of primary pupils over 4 years old in Cwm Gwendraeth**

the older pupils. Data derived from both the schools' census and the Social Survey demonstrates that the proportion of fluent children is higher than the proportion of mother-tongue. According to the survey, this feature is not seen in the older age groups.

It is quite possible that the age group differences recorded in Table 2.24 are a reflection of the varying abilities of the children as they started in the schools system. In order to ascertain the effect of formal education on language ability we need to measure the changes by each age cohort, that is, by comparing the same group of children in successive years.

Figure 2.5 reveals the experience of four different cohorts. For example, of those children who were aged four to five in 1993, 8 per cent were fluent (but did not speak the language at home). By the next year, 30 per cent of the same cohort were fluent and within another year 33 per cent of them were fluent. Figure 2.6 reveals that the proportion of mother-tongue speakers varies significantly between the schools in the area. There is some suggestion that an element of concentration in the distribution of mother-tongue speakers is occurring, as in 1995 there were more schools where mother-tongue speakers comprised more than 70 per cent of the school's total, but also more schools where the percentage of mother-tongue are speakers was less than 35 per cent.

Similar analyses in other regions where active language intervention is currently being undertaken would surely pay dividends. It is inconceivable how long-term language revitalization efforts can be expected to succeed unless a thorough knowledge of the statistical profile and aggregate nature of the community in question is obtained as an ongoing exercise in data collection and monitoring.

The current revised *Strategy* of the Welsh Language Board (1999b) gives a prominent place to the extension of the *mentrau iaith* but additional work is needed on a range of factors which influence the transmission and use of Welsh

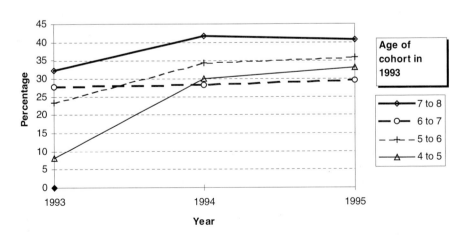

Figure 2.5. Fluent second-language speakers in age cohorts

**Number of schools by percentage of mother-tongue speakers**

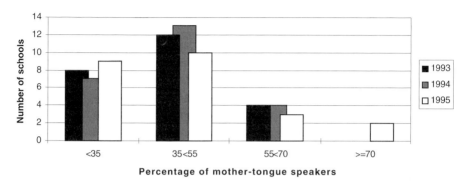

Figure 2.6. Numbers of schools by percentage of mother-tongue speakers

in the community and regional economy. Following Williams (1999), we argue that it is vital that data on each of the following elements is collected:

- demographic trends and age/sex differences by language acquisition and maintenance;
- occupational structures and local economic development;
- unorthodox social networks, especially in urban contexts;
- research on the implications of telematic networks and the digital economy;
- a lucid understanding of rural community changes which may be independent of, though contribute to, those conditions which maintain Welsh as a dynamic element in society;
- consideration of the available methods whereby the linguistic abilities of Welsh speakers could be improved;
- research on how the *mentrau* may evolve as agencies in the field of social development;
- research on how the *mentrau* may become language centres catering for other languages used within Wales.

A National Language Resource Centre could include within its responsibilities a role as a national data-base for language planning. Were a central data-base to be established it would reduce the amount of duplicated work and would promote research and facilitate the diffusion of information on applied bilingualism and the effectiveness of local language policies. There is a need for a permanent institution equipped with a staff of professionals able to train others in survey fieldwork and to analyse factors specific to particular domains. We can no longer rest content with a growth in the numbers able to speak Welsh, nor indeed with the development of new domain usage, rather we need to see Welsh being used effectively in all public spheres, such as the health services, the business sector, the voluntary sector and throughout the community.

## ENTERPRISE, EMPLOYMENT AND INFRASTRUCTURAL SUPPORT

The struggle for the development of a fully functional bilingual society has dominated the post-war agenda. Hitherto our understanding of the role of Welsh in society has been based on extensive analysis of the education system and to a lesser extent public administration and the voluntary sector. We know far less than we ought to about the role of Welsh in the economy and within particular workplace situations. What accounts for this information gap between our knowledge of cultural or educational patterns and economic realities? Conventionally it has been argued that, as many Welsh speakers believe that they are engaged in a national struggle for cultural survival, they often choose employment which in some way is both community-oriented and socially responsible, such as education or the health services. The real challenge is to determine the relationship between individual motivation and social agencies. This is the issue of holist versus individualist explanations of culturally influenced actions and beliefs. Is Welsh cultural reproduction an autonomous process or are we in danger of reifying both the process and patterns of contemporary social life by labelling them as essentially 'cultural' and 'linguistic' rather than as everyday socio-economic occurrences? There is a real difficulty in relating individual perceptions and actions to aggregate structural features of a socio-economic nature. Are many Welsh speakers in the public sector because it is one of the limited domains available to them to function in a developing bilingual environment? If so, does this small yet critical mass of employment opportunities unduly influence others to follow in their footsteps? The context of Welsh employment is critical for we need to ascertain the impact of a wide range of features, including the physical and social communication system, which structure material cultural reproduction. In rural heartland areas, employment has been heavily dependent upon farming and extractive industries which are shedding labour. In declining industrial regions the atrophying of long-established heavy industries such as coal mining, iron and steel and tin-plate working has not only caused a transformation of conventional patterns of economic activity, it has also isolated the female as the main 'bread-winner' in many families where males constitute part of the long-term unemployed. New gender-related roles impact both upon parenting and language transmission processes. What effect does this have on community involvement, the viability of scattered rural settlements, labour training and skill acquisition? Also, the size of companies in Welsh-speaking areas is limited, leading to narrow regional economic diversity, and an undeveloped urban network wherein alternative sources of employment in the service sectors could be provided.

In the Equal Opportunities Commission Report on Gender and the Welsh Language, Katherine Jones and Delyth Morris (1997) offer a systematic description of the socio-economic characteristics of the Welsh-speaking population, in which they argue that:

- Welsh-speaking women and men have similar proportions active in the labour market as their non-Welsh-speaking counterparts. However, in Wales, women at 68 per cent and men at 78 per cent have notably lower economic rates than those for GB as a whole.
- Unemployment is more prevalent amongst non-Welsh speakers than Welsh speakers for both sexes. Nevertheless, Welsh-speaking women have markedly higher levels of unemployment than non-Welsh born women.
- Of those in work, Welsh-speaking women have markedly higher proportions who work full-time than non-Welsh-speaking women (63 per cent compared to 53 per cent) whereas men have similar rates of full-time work (93 per cent and 91 per cent respectively).
- The main industrial sectors where Welsh speakers are employed are education, services, distribution and agriculture. Education and the services are usually linked with female employment, while a higher proportion of males is employed in distribution and agriculture.
- The key difference in terms of job segregation is that higher proportions of Welsh-speaking women are to be found in professional posts, and higher proportions of Welsh-speaking men are in managerial jobs. As much as a quarter of Welsh-speaking women are in professional and associated professional jobs compared to 17 per cent of Welsh-speaking men and only 15 per cent of non-Welsh-speaking women. The vast majority (83 per cent) of Welsh-speaking women professionals are teachers.
- One of the key reasons behind the over-representation of Welsh-speaking women in professional occupations is that they are comparatively well qualified. The Welsh Office Social Survey 1992 showed that over a quarter (27 per cent) of Welsh-speaking women have qualifications at A-level and above compared with 19 per cent of Welsh-speaking men, 15 per cent of non-Welsh-speaking women and 17 per cent of non-Welsh-speaking men. Clearly this gender gap in qualifications is considerably wider for Welsh speakers than for non-Welsh speakers.
- In addition to qualifications, knowledge of Welsh could assist social mobility in Wales, and therefore partly explains the over-representation of Welsh speakers in higher level occupations. There appears to be a 'niche' in the labour market for suitably qualified Welsh-speaking women which reflects the segmented nature of the local labour markets, and the needs of the Welsh-speaking population for specific Welsh language services in education and personal services.
- Despite their over-representation in professional jobs, Welsh-speaking women's apparent 'success' in terms of qualifications does not appear to be translated into substantive opportunities in the labour market. Their advantageous qualifications profile is not commensurate with their labour market situation. This may be due to the influence of other pertinent factors such as family ties, area, social class, the time females spend out of the labour market, and part-time work. (Jones and Morris, 1997: iv–v).

Within the private sector the limited research suggests that Welsh speakers favour self-employment. Census evidence for 1981 suggests that 15.8 per cent of the Welsh-speaking population were self-employed, as opposed to 9.2 per cent of the non-Welsh-speaking population (Chapman et al., 1990: 5, table 2), and that the differential was greatest in Clwyd and Dyfed, which may reflect its greater availability in rural areas. In contrast non-Welsh speakers constituted a greater proportion of the self-employed in Gwynedd and Powys. Negative attitudes which tend to denigrate the ability of Welsh speakers to innovate and to show enterprise were identified by Gahan (1989). Success in business was projected as occurring outside Wales, and there was a lack of entrepreneurial Welsh-speaking role models in business, together with a reluctance to take risks, and a higher incidence of insecurity and fear of failure (Beaufort Research, 1991). Welsh-speaking parents were unlikely to encourage their children to consider a career in business and assumed that one needed an unduly large amount of capital to start a business. Student attitudes were generally more favourable to business activities, including self-employed ventures, attending Welsh-medium post-graduate business courses and supporting services designed to integrate Welsh speakers more effectively into the world of business and commerce.

The real difficulty for interpretation is 'whether the relative lack of enterprises created and owned by the Welsh people, and Welsh-speakers in particular, owes more to the in-built social and psychological propensities of the Welsh, or should be explained instead in terms of the structural nature of the Welsh economy and society?' (Carr, 1992: 14). Though culture is significant we must also consider class differences, for middle-class Welsh speakers are differentially concentrated in the bilingual public sector, particularly in Gwynedd, while English incomers are over-represented in the private-sector managerial classes (Morris, 1989). This reflects a dependency culture which ties Welsh speakers into the local state and interventionist employment-generation agencies such as _Menter a Busnes_ seek to reduce this over-dependence (Williams, 1986, 1989). It has also been argued that the Welsh express collectivist community values rather than individualistic ones. Whether these derive from ancient Celtic, tribal patterns, from a deep affinity with Calvinism from the mid-eighteenth century or merely reflect the population settlement geography of the country is a complex issue. However, if one merely celebrates the private profit syndrome, and ignores the social responsibility of capital, this will lead to inter-group tension and exacerbate indigenous–exogenous divides. Because of Wales's radical political heritage, it is claimed that any attempt to instil a general enterprise culture will be interpreted as reproducing Conservative ideology. This is slightly ironic, for many Welsh speakers are perceived as inherently conservative and resistant to change.

The logic of uneven development too often ignores peripheral collectivities and/or renders their categorization as a separate social grouping within the state as irrelevant to the real materialist explanation for structured inequality. We need to relate macro-level theorizing to specific examples of those who least benefit from the development processes, and incorporate conceptions of struggle, conflict and dissonance into an explanation which does not assume that social cohesion and state integration are a necessary consequence of the maturing of capitalism. This would involve examining the ideological basis of Welsh culture to ascertain how messages relating to business, enterprise, political representation, regional development and planning are constructed and diffused.

The central question which revisionist economists ask is: what socialization processes predispose individuals and cultures to gravitate towards or away from entrepreneurial business skills and acumen? However, a more pluralist post-modern perspective seeks to reduce the interpretative power of structure and agency by focusing on key questions such as whether belonging to an additional language group or maintaining a high level of fluency in two or more languages is going to return an extra value in the market-place? Additional issues concern the adaptation of lesser used language speakers to the opportunities afforded by changes in global–local networks, the growth of specialized economic segments or services and of information networks which are accessed by language-related skills. Accessibility to or denial of these opportunities is the virtual expression of real power in society which must be taken on board in any discussion of the politics of cultural representation. The general pattern is expressed thus by M. Castells (1997: 476).

> Cultural expressions are abstracted from history and geography, and become predominantly mediated by electronic communication networks that interact with an audience and by the audience in a diversity of codes and values, ultimately subsumed in a digitised, audio-visual hypertext. Because information and communication circulate primarily through the diversified, yet comprehensive media system, politics becomes increasingly played out in the space of the media ... The fact that politics has to be framed in the language of electronically based media has profound consequences on the characteristics, organisation and goals of political processes, political actors, and political institutions. Ultimately, the powers that are in the media networks take second place to the power of flows embodied in the structure and language of these networks.

Systematic analysis of these insights is needed before we can be entirely confident that the current policies directed toward encouraging greater use of bi- and multilingual skills in the Welsh economy are likely to succeed.

## CONCLUSION

This chapter has demonstrated that much is known in aggregate terms about the social, educational and community context of the use of Welsh and English. However, it has drawn attention to the paucity of useful data on the use of Welsh in the workplace, in training and skills enhancement and in the economy generally. There is an urgent need for long-term, consistent data collection by a variety of agencies, whose collective work could be synthesized and made known to the informed decision-makers and policy advisers. Without such data we are frankly following our own restrictive prejudices or assuming as given the very sociolinguistic phenomena we should be investigating. A promising development is that both the National Assembly and the Welsh Language Board have recognized the need for an information data-bank, akin to systems which currently operate at the federal level in Canada, and within Euskadi and

Catalonia. However, as Chapter 11 will demonstrate, even in Euskadi and Catalonia, the statistical evidence so assiduously garnered is always subject to diverse interpretations as contested realities vie with each other for dominance in the official discourse.

### *Acknowledgements*

Tables 2.6–2.10 are reproduced with permission from Welsh Office (1998). Tables 2.11–2.19 are derived from Statistical Brief, 'Welsh in Schools', SDB, 3, 2000, Cardiff: National Assembly.

### *Notes*

\* Hywel Jones writes in a personal capacity. The data analysis offered here should not be interpreted as official National Assembly policy.

[1] These figures are derived from the Welsh Social Survey, 1992, which was conducted between September and December 1992. The sample was a stratified random sample. Some 28,000 respondents were included, representing just over 1 per cent of the population. For further information see Welsh Social Survey: *Arolwg Cymdeithasol Cymru 1992: Adroddiad ar yr Iaith Gymraeg, 1992,* Cardiff: The Welsh Office/Y Swyddfa Gymreig, 1995. For the purposes of this current analysis, Cwm Gwendraeth was defined as including the following communities: Gorslas, Llanarthne, Llanddarog, Llangyndeyrn, Llandybie, Llanfihangel Aberbythych, Cydweli, Llannon, Pontyberem, Trimsaran. Answers were received from 264 individuals within this area.

[2] These population estimates were based on a sample of 127 fluent speakers aged over sixteen. The differences noted in these summary bullet points are statistically significant with a 95 per cent confidence level.

[3] The age group differences are not statistically significant. Estimated 95 per cent confidence intervals are shown in Table 2.21.

[4] It is not possible to confirm that all the schools are located in exactly the same communities as were used for the analysis of the Welsh Social Survey, 1992, nor that the school catchment areas define precisely the same region as that covered by Menter Cwm Gwendraeth. The statistics are derived from the schools' census. This census includes all schools in Wales. The answers are prepared by the headteacher. For a more complete picture see Welsh Office, *Statistics of Education and Training in Wales,* 3 (1995).

[5] Note that this classification is for Welsh Office purposes. It should not be confused with the then extant Dyfed Education Authority's school classification.

### *References*

Aitchison, J. and Carter, H. (1994). *A Geography of the Welsh Language 1961–1991,* Cardiff: University of Wales Press.

Aitchison, J. and Carter, H. (1997). 'Language reproduction: reflections on the Welsh example', *Area,* 29, 4, 357–66.

Aitchison, J. and Carter, H. (2000). *Language, Economy and Society: The Changing Fortunes of the Welsh Language in the Twentieth Century,* Cardiff: University of Wales Press.

Beaufort Research (1991). *Agweddau tuag at Fusnes: Adroddiad Ymchwil,* Cardiff: Beaufort Research Cyf.

Bellin, W., Higgs, G. and Farrell, S. (1997). *Halting or Reversing Language Shift: A Social and Spatial Analysis of South East Wales*, Final Report for ESRC grant no. R000236330.

Carr, R. (1992). *Explaining 'Enterprise': An Examination of the Impact of the Welsh Language on Economic and Business Activities in Wales*, Bangor: UCNW.

Castells, M. (1997). *The Rise of the Network Society*, Oxford: Blackwell.

Chapman, N. D. H. et al. (1990). *Dadansoddiad o Gyfrifiad 1981 ar Weithgaredd Economaidd a'r Iaith Gymraeg*, Aberystwyth: Coleg Prifysgol Cymru.

Gahan, C. (1989). *Arolwg o Agweddau at Fenter a Busnes ymysg Siaradwyr Cymraeg*, Aberystwyth: Menter a Busnes.

Higgs, G., Bellin, W., Farrell, S. and White, S. (1998). 'Educational attainment and social disadvantage: contextualising school league tables', *Regional Studies*, 31(8), 779–93.

James, C. and Williams, C. H. (1998). 'Language and planning in Scotland and Wales', in R. MacDonald and H. Thomas (eds.), *Nationality and Planning in Scotland and Wales*, Cardiff: University of Wales Press, pp. 264–302.

Jones, K. and Morris, D. (1997). *Gender and the Welsh Language*, Manchester: Equal Opportunities Commission.

Morris, D. (1989). 'A study of language contact and social networks in Ynys Môn', *Contemporary Wales*, Vol. 3, 99–117.

Morris Jones, R. and Ghuman Singh, P. A., eds. (1995). *Bilingualism, Education and Identity*, Cardiff: University of Wales Press.

National Assembly (1997). *Statistics of Education and Training in Wales: Schools 1993–1999* (7 publications), Cardiff: National Assembly.

National Assembly (1999). *1998 Welsh House Condition Survey, Statistical Report SDB 94/99*, Cardiff: National Assembly.

Pryce, W. T. R. and Williams, C. H. (1988). 'Sources and methods in the study of language areas: a case study of Wales', in C. H. Williams (ed.), *Language in Geographic Context*, Clevedon, Avon: Multilingual Matters, pp. 167–237.

PDAG (1988). *Interim Report of the Secondary Working Committee*, Cardiff: PDAG, unpublished (mimeo).

PDAG (1992). *Response to the White Paper on Education, Diversity and Choice: A New Framework for Schools*, Cardiff: PDAG, unpublished (mimeo).

Reynolds, D., Bellin, W. and ab Ieuan, R. (1998). *A Competitive Edge: Why Welsh Medium Schools Perform Better*, Cardiff: Institute of Welsh Affairs.

Welsh Language Board (1999a). *Continuity in Welsh Language Education*, Cardiff: Welsh Language Board.

Welsh Language Board (1999b). *A Strategy for the Welsh Language*, Cardiff: Welsh Language Board.

Welsh Office (1976). *Statistics of Education in Wales: No. 11976–No. 11*, Cardiff: Welsh Office.

Welsh Office (1991). *Statistics of Education in Wales: Schools No. 11987–No. 5*, Cardiff: Welsh Office.

Welsh Office (1995a). *1992 Welsh Social Survey: Report on the Welsh Language*, Cardiff: Welsh Office.

Welsh Office (1995b). *The Welsh Language: Children and Education*, Statistical Brief SDB 14/95, April, Cardiff: Welsh Office.

Welsh Office (1996). *The Teaching of Welsh in Secondary Schools*, Statistical Brief SDB 33/96, August, Cardiff: Welsh Office.

Welsh Office (1998). *Statistics of Education and Training in Wales: Schools, 1998*, Cardiff: Welsh Office.

Williams, C. H. (1986). 'Language planning and minority group rights', in I. Hume and W. T. R. Pryce, (eds.), *The Welsh and their Country*, Llandysul: Gomer Press, pp. 253–72.

Williams, C. H. (1989). 'New domains of the Welsh language: education, planning and the law', *Contemporary Wales*, Vol. 3, 41–76.

Williams, C. H. (1994). *Called unto Liberty: On Language and Nationalism*, Clevedon, Avon: Multilingual Matters.

Williams, C. H. (1998). 'Operating through two languages', in Osmond, J. (ed.), *The National Assembly Agenda*, Cardiff: Institute of Welsh Affairs, pp. 101–16.

Williams, C. H. (1999). 'Legislation and empowerment: a Welsh drama in three acts', in *International Conference on Language Legislation*, Dublin: Comhdháil Náisiúnta na Gaeilge, pp. 126–59.

Williams, C. H. (2000). 'A language policy for the National Assembly of Wales', in ECTARC (ed.), *Culture, Nation and Region in Europe*, Llangollen: ECTARC.

Williams, C. H. and Evas, J. (1997). *The Community Research Project*, Cardiff: Welsh Language Board and Cardiff University.

# 3

# Language Revitalization: The Role of the Welsh Language Board

## THE WELSH LANGUAGE BOARD

### INTRODUCTION

The purpose of this chapter is to describe the Welsh Language Board's work in planning for the revitalization of the Welsh language. It will seek to demonstrate that the significant developments in bilingualism seen in Wales since the establishment of the board as a statutory body in 1993 have, in the main, come about as the result of strategic direction, and are not due to random events or unconnected policy implementation. Although it is too early as yet to measure the ultimate effectiveness of these strategies, and while admitting that significant progress remains to be made, the chapter argues that the strategic frameworks prepared by the board since its establishment in 1993 offer a firm foundation on which to plan for the future.

It begins with a brief description of the general historical background to the linguistic situation in Wales, leading up to the enactment of the Welsh Language Act in 1993 and the establishment of the Welsh Language Board. It outlines the role and responsibilities of the statutory Welsh Language Board as specified by the Act (with special emphasis on those elements of the board's work which relate to policy and planning), and goes on to describe the main elements of the board's strategy for the long term (as set out in the document *A Strategy for the Welsh Language*), and for the medium term (as proposed in the document, 'The Welsh Language: A Vision and Mission for 2000–2005', the main text of which is given as Appendix A below).

As we saw in Chapter 1, at the beginning of the twentieth century there were more people able to speak Welsh than ever before: roughly half of Wales's population of almost 2 million people spoke Welsh. However, the proportion of the population who spoke Welsh was beginning to decrease. The census of 1901 reported that nearly 49 per cent of the population of Wales claimed to be able to speak Welsh. By 1911 this had fallen to 43 per cent, even though the same year saw the highest number of Welsh speakers ever, with 977,366 claiming to be able to speak Welsh. From this point until 1981, the numbers speaking Welsh declined apace, as did the proportion of the population able to speak the language: by 1981, the proportion of the population able to speak Welsh had decreased to 18.9 per cent.

Immigration and emigration (especially from rural areas to the industrial centres) were key factors, especially when linked to the rise of socialism in the industrial areas which arguably contributed much to a decline in the traditional values of chapel and liberalism to which the Welsh language was closely linked at the time. The Depression of the 1920s had severe consequences for the use of the language in north and west Wales – the traditional strongholds of the language which have continued to decline and be pushed back. Rural depopulation was at its worst during this period as unemployed land workers migrated in search of work, and has continued in parallel with the decline in the agriculture industry in Wales over the past fifty years. At the 1991 census, 18.7 per cent of the population – just over half a million people – said that they spoke Welsh. When viewed from the perspective of earlier censuses, the 1991 results were in many ways encouraging, as the steady decline evident since 1901 appeared to have been arrested. What is more, there was a significant increase in the number and percentage of young people speaking Welsh.

A number of key developments have played a major part in this turnaround. Certainly, legislation has been a factor, and we can list among the milestones prior to the Welsh Language Act 1993, the Welsh Courts Act of 1942, the Education Act of 1944, the Welsh Language Act of 1967 and the 1988 Education Reform Act, under which the Welsh language became a compulsory subject in the National Curriculum in Wales. As a result, every child in Wales now has to study Welsh, either as a first or second language, in school up to the age of sixteen.

The 1980s saw the introduction by central government of specific grants to support the language which provided a more secure future for organizations such as the Royal National Eisteddfod, Urdd Gobaith Cymru (the Welsh League of Youth), Mudiad Ysgolion Meithrin (the Welsh nursery schools movement) and the Welsh Books Council. Broadcasting media have also been a factor in the improved fortunes of the language (another example of direct government support for the language). S4C, the Welsh-language television channel, has now been broadcasting for nearly twenty years and is gaining an increasing international reputation for the quality of its Welsh-medium programmes, especially in the field of animation. In addition, the BBC continues to provide Welsh-language programmes in both radio and television, and has recently launched a Welsh-medium daily news service on the Internet.

The 1980s also saw increasing pressure from a number of directions for new legislation to protect the language. In response, the government established an advisory board to consider whether there was indeed a need for a new Act, and to advise it on the issues with which the Act should deal. The report and findings of the advisory Welsh Language Board which were presented to the Secretary of State for Wales in 1992 were a major factor in convincing the government that new legislation was justified, and started a process which culminated in the enactment in 1993 of the Welsh Language Act.

## THE WELSH LANGUAGE ACT 1993

The Act's title gives a reasonable summary of what it sought to achieve:

> An Act to establish a Board having the function of promoting and facilitating the use of the Welsh language, to provide for the preparation by public bodies of schemes giving effect to the principle that in the conduct of public business and the administration of justice in Wales the English and Welsh languages should be treated on a basis of equality, to make further provision relating to the Welsh language, to repeal certain enactments relating to Wales, and for connected purposes.

The Act is a unique piece of legislation. Among its key provisions are that it places a duty on the public sector providing services to the public in Wales to treat Welsh and English on an equal basis. It also it ensured that Welsh speakers have an absolute right to speak Welsh in court and, perhaps most importantly, it established the Welsh Language Board with a key role in the Act's implementation. It should be noted that there was much that the Act did not do, certainly in comparison with the recommendations of the advisory Welsh Language Board. The Act did not amend employment law to allow employers to designate posts as requiring the ability to speak Welsh. Nor did the Act place any demands on organizations outside the public sector, nor include a statement which gave official status to the language.

Nonetheless, however one views the 1993 Act, no one can realistically deny the fact that the language now enjoys a higher status than ever before in modern times. After decades of decline, Welsh is becoming revitalized. More and more people – young and old – are learning the language and are appreciating its value. Bilingualism is increasingly becoming accepted as a completely natural and normal part of everyday life in Wales. Support for the use of the language – as evidenced by research commissioned by the board – is widespread, and the overwhelming majority of those questioned felt that the language was something to be proud of and supported its use. It is no coincidence that this change has, in the main, come about since 1993.

### The Welsh Language Board

It is important to note that the authority of the Welsh Language Board in all that it does is derived from legislation. The board is an Assembly-sponsored public body whose funds are voted by the Assembly: it is answerable to the Assembly for the way in which its resources are used. The members of the Welsh Language Board are appointed by the Assembly Secretary (formerly by the Secretary of State for Wales) in open competition. Their responsibility is to provide direction to the board and to guide and oversee its work. A new board was appointed at the end of March 2000. It is made up of eleven people, including the chairman, from across the political spectrum, from different backgrounds, all bringing to the work of the board experience relevant to its fields of interest: education and training; the media and broadcasting; business and economic development; the legal system; and language planning.

Although they are separate from the civil service, the officials of the board (the staff) are public servants whose duty is to implement legislation. Although it has a wide-ranging remit, the board is a small organization: at 31 March 2000 the board employed thirty staff. The organization chart in Figure 3.1 describes the board's structure and outlines the range of activities covered by each department. In practical terms, the board's work is aimed at making it easier for people to use Welsh in all walks of life. In this context, the board provides advice and information to central government, organizations from all sectors and, of course, to the public, on all aspects relating to the language; it seeks to ensure that providers of public services – including education and training – treat Welsh and English equally; it provides funding for Welsh-medium activities and projects; and it develops products and services which make it easier for people to use Welsh.

The board has five core functions or main duties, namely: (i) promoting and facilitating the use of the Welsh language; (ii) advising on and influencing matters related to the Welsh language; (iii) stimulating and overseeing the process of preparing and implementing language schemes; (iv) distributing grants to promote and facilitate the use of Welsh; (v) maintaining a strategic overview of Welsh-medium education. It is clear that the board's remit is very wide ranging, in effect extending to cover anything to do with the Welsh language. However, it should be noted that direct responsibility for policy formulation and service delivery for the vast majority of Welsh-language matters does not lie with the board, but with other organizations. This has forced the board to adopt the role of a facilitator and adviser, working in co-operation and partnership with organizations rather than seeking to dictate. Indeed, this has given increased importance to planning as a means of sharing our vision and mission with our partners, and of formulating an agreed and co-ordinated approach to language issues.

*Welsh-language schemes*

Welsh-language schemes are at the core of the Welsh Language Act, and are the main vehicle for implementing the principle of equality on which the Act is founded. One of the board's first tasks following its establishment was to prepare guidelines on the form and content of language schemes. The board's draft guidelines were presented to Parliament in March 1995 and approved in July 1995, with further guidance as to the form and content of schemes following in March 1996. Taken together, they clearly illustrate the close links between planning and policy in the context of scheme preparation. The text of the statutory guidelines is included at Appendix B. It goes without saying that it is not possible to implement or operate a scheme without proper emphasis on planning. Indeed, the requirement to plan is an intrinsic part of the administrative process of preparing a scheme.

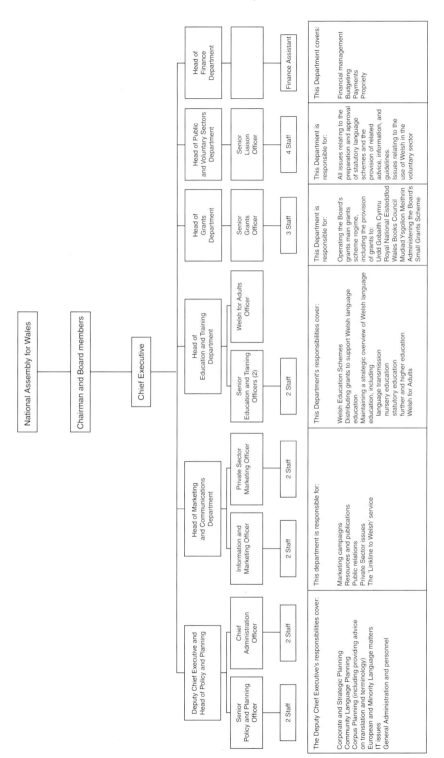

**Figure 3.1. Organization chart for the Welsh Language Board**

The chart contains the following boxes and text:

National Assembly for Wales

Chairman and Board members

Chief Executive

**Deputy Chief Executive and Head of Policy and Planning**
- Senior Policy and Planning Officer
  - 2 Staff
- Chief Administration Officer
  - 2 Staff

The Deputy Chief Executive's responsibilities cover:

Corporate and Strategic Planning
Community Language Planning
Corpus Planning (including providing advice on translation and terminology)
European and Minority Language matters
IT issues
General Administration and personnel

**Head of Marketing and Communications Department**
- Information and Marketing Officer
  - 2 Staff
- Private Sector Marketing Officer
  - 2 Staff

This department is responsible for:

Marketing campaigns
Resources and publications
Public relations
Private Sector issues
The 'Linkline to Welsh' service

**Head of Education and Training Department**
- Senior Education and Training Officers (2)
  - 2 Staff
- Welsh for Adults Officer

This Department's responsibilities cover:

Welsh Education Schemes
Distributing grants to support Welsh language education
Maintaining a strategic overview of Welsh language education, including
language transmission
nursery education
statutory education
further and higher education
Welsh for Adults

**Head of Grants Department**
- Senior Grants Officer
  - 3 Staff

This Department is responsible for:

Operating the Board's grants main grants scheme regime,
including the provision of grants to:
Urdd Gobaith Cymru
Royal National Eisteddfod
Wales Books Council
Mudiad Ysgolion Meithrin
Administering the Board's Small Grants Scheme

**Head of Public and Voluntary Sectors Department**
- Senior Liaison Officer
  - 4 Staff

This Department is responsible for:

All issues relating to the preparation and approval of statutory language schemes and the provision of related advice, information, and guidelines.
Issues relating to the use of Welsh in the voluntary sector

**Head of Finance Department**
- Finance Assistant

This Department covers:

Financial management
Budgeting
Payments
Propriety

The first statutory notices to public bodies informing them of the requirement prepare language schemes were sent in the autumn of 1995. Since then, the language has been on the public-sector agenda throughout Wales. Up to 31 March 2000, 134 schemes had been agreed, with over 120 others at various stages of preparation covering a wide range of areas of public-service provision, including local government, health, education, police, magistrates' courts, central government executive agencies and, most notably, government departments.

It should also be emphasized that this is very much a planned process. The board, from the first, has targeted organizations on the basis of a schedule it prepared, giving precedence to agreeing schemes with bodies which have contact with a substantial number of Welsh speakers, or which provide services which give rise to the greatest demand for Welsh-medium provision, or which have a high profile in Wales or are influential because of their status or responsibilities. Of the 350 organizations identified initially as priorities, over two-thirds have either prepared a language scheme or are in the process of doing so. As a result, the board is now giving greater priority to monitoring and reviewing existing schemes (as opposed to agreeing new schemes) in order to ensure that those already in place operate effectively and continue to develop to meet the needs of their bilingual customers.

## A Strategy for the Welsh Language

It has already been mentioned that partnerships are at the heart of nearly everything the board seeks to achieve. It has also been mentioned that responsibility for policy formulation and service delivery for the vast majority of Welsh-language matters does not lie with the board, but with other organizations. Indeed, the board would not have any hope in fulfilling its remit and succeeding in its work without the co-operation of others.

*A Strategy for the Welsh Language* was published by the Welsh Language Board in December 1996. The purpose of the document – which covers the period up to the publication of the results of the 2001 census – was to present a comprehensive consensus-based strategy to ensure a prosperous future for the Welsh language. The document reflects a thorough consultation exercise, which is outlined in the text of the document, and seeks to draw people together for the overall good of the language, in the knowledge that there is wide-ranging agreement and conformity on how to address the main issues which affect it.

The main aim of the strategy is 'to enable the Welsh language to become self-sustaining and secure as a medium of communication in Wales'. This ambitious aim is fully compatible with the board's duty to promote and facilitate the language, and points towards the need to achieve linguistic self-sufficiency. It could be argued that this aim will have been achieved when the position of the language becomes secure enough for a specific body to carry out this function no longer to be required. In other words, the board ultimately plans to make itself redundant.

The strategy identifies four main challenges which, in the board's vie
the Welsh language. These are (i) increasing the number of people who are able
to speak Welsh; (ii) providing opportunities to use the language; (iii) changing
habits of language use, and encouraging people to take advantage of the opportunities provided; and (iv) strengthening Welsh as a community language. In the
context of these challenges, the board identified specific areas which warrant
particular attention. First, under 'increasing the number of people who can
speak Welsh' we identify (i) children and young people; (ii) parents and the
extended family; (iii) adults learning Welsh; and (iv) support systems. It is under
this section that issues are addressed which relate to education and training at
all levels and at all stages, and the importance of intergenerational language
transmission is highlighted.

Meeting the second challenge involves 'providing opportunities to use the
language': (i) in the public sector; (ii) in the voluntary and private sectors; (iii)
socially and in the workplace; and (iv) in the context of information technology
and other supporting assistance. This section deals mainly with ensuring that
people who deal with all the above sectors are provided with opportunities to
use Welsh, and where issues involving the provision of new technologies are
concerned, translation facilities to support this aim are considered. Language
schemes play a key part in this in providing opportunities to use the language
where few might have existed before.

The third element of the strategy will be achieved by: (i) promoting the use of
the language by young people; (ii) using the language when receiving or in
providing services; and (iii) developing the role of the media. Marketing is
recognized as a valuable tool in changing attitudes. The board has consistently
sought to make the most of the opportunities available to us to encourage people
of all ages to use the language and to make use of the services provided, and to
ensure that the image and public perception of Welsh as a viable means of
communication continues to improve.

Finally, specific attention is given to (i) strengthening the position of the Welsh
language within the community, (ii) creating new networks and (iii) developments beyond Wales. The main emphasis in this area is towards developing
social aspects of language use and in addressing the factors which affect the
community foundation of the language. To quote from paragraph 8.1 of the strategy, 'It is essential that the language has a firm community foundation . . . it will
not prosper if there is a decline in its use at home and in the community, even if
the number of new speakers produced by our schools increases.'

Listed under these challenges are a total of twenty objectives, along with an
outline of the board's role and responsibilities in relation to achieving each of
them. However, one major factor which the strategy was unable to foresee when
it was published was the change in the Welsh political landscape brought about
by devolution and the establishment of the National Assembly for Wales.

It is important to note that the National Assembly for Wales is now responsible for safeguarding the Welsh language, and is given quite wide-ranging

powers to do so. Section 32 of the 1998 Government of Wales Act states that 'the Assembly may do anything it considers appropriate to support the Welsh language'. In order to highlight this remit, the board in May 1999 sent a short paper to the newly elected members of the Assembly, drawing attention to the key issues relating to the Welsh language. The paper concluded by stating that the Welsh language is one of our main national characteristics:

> Only by the goodwill of the people and the investment of our national institutions can we maintain it as part of an inclusive society. The future of the language is also dependent on functional holistic planning. In order to bear fruit any plan must ensure that everyone who has an interest in the success of the language comes together to work in partnership. The Board will continue to provide a lead in this process.

Without doubt, therefore, the advent of devolved government has brought with it significant opportunities for the Welsh language. And with these opportunities has come a new set of challenges which has required the board to reassess its priorities in the medium term. As part of this reassessment, the board conducted a review in June 1999 of its achievements against the roles and responsibilities described in the strategy. It is true to say that progress has been made against each of them since it was published, and taken together, they go a significant way to explaining the change in the profile of the language today, as compared with the situation in 1993.

The strategy forms the basis for all the board's activities. These activities are described in more detail in the board's Corporate and Operational Plans which are prepared and submitted annually to the Assembly for consideration. They are the mechanism by which funds are allocated to the board, and the framework in which targets are set and performance is monitored.

The document 'The Welsh Language: A Vision and Mission for 2000–2005' grew out of this planning process. The document was prepared at the request of the Assembly's Committee for Post-16 Education and Training, the committee that oversees the work of the board. The following is an extract from the minutes of the committee's proceedings from July 1999.

> The Chair suggested that before the Committee met with the Board in November that the Board submit a report based on their corporate plan and strategy document. The report would include progress on the Board's work so far, its views on the present situation and future prospects of the Welsh language, together with an account of priority actions for the advancement of the Welsh language along with the financial implications of this.

'A Vision and Mission' was presented to the committee in November 1999. The document clearly sets out the board's approach to holistic language planning, and includes targets for key areas and activities, along with a description of the resources required to achieve them. The document was well received by the committee. In a motion passed on 16 February 2000, the committee announced:

The Committee welcomes the Welsh Language Board's document 'The Welsh Language: A Vision and Mission for 2000–2005' as a major contribution to the task of drawing up a strategy for the continued revitalisation of the Welsh language and the creation of a bilingual Wales. The Committee agrees that the four main challenges are those noted [in the *Strategy for the Welsh Language*] and strongly supports the emphasis on Welsh-medium education as the basis for growth.

The Committee notes that achieving such an ambitious task as the creation of a bilingual Wales must involve a co-ordinated strategy, with targets of the kind described in the Board's document.

The Committee strongly supports the aim of creating a bilingual Wales as an achievable national aim, and wishes to see the implementation of an effective strategy to ensure that this aim is achieved.

The Committee welcomes the fact that the Executive accepts the Board's document as an important contribution and guide to determining priorities for the future work of the Board within the resources voted by the Assembly.

This is clearly an important development. The reference to a 'bilingual Wales' is particularly worth highlighting as it indicates that bilingualism is now part of the vision of the National Assembly for Wales (albeit a committee of the Assembly). It is conceivable that we will begin to see an increasingly positive change in attitudes among policy-makers in the public sector towards implementing the policies demanded by holistic language planning, and so see progress towards the board's ultimate goal (as set out in 'Vision and Mission'), which is 'making Wales an increasingly bilingual and multilingual society in which all its citizens may use the Welsh and English languages with equal facility in all aspects of their lives and where every language community can live together in harmony and prosper'.

However, the statement also includes the phrase 'within the resources voted by the Assembly'. Resources are a vital consideration: it is self-evident that the ambitious goal set out in 'Vision and Mission' will not be achieved without significant public investment. Unfortunately, we now know that the Assembly will only make available to the board a small proportion of the overall resources it sought in order to achieve the targets set out in 'Vision and Mission' (£200,000 a year between 2000–1 and 2002–3 as opposed to the £3.4 million, £4.7 million and £5.5 million requested in the original Corporate Plan). As such, many of the targets set out in the document are now, to all practical purposes, unachievable.

Nonetheless, the document is still useful because it exemplifies the board's approach to language planning and provides a framework to consider holistically all matters relating to the future of the language. In March 2000, the board staged two conferences to bring together partner organizations and other interested parties to discuss the document and to consider priorities in the light of the Assembly's funding decisions. Briefly, there was a clear consensus supporting the main themes of the document; most of the contributions either upheld the board's point of view, or simply sought greater emphasis on certain aspects of the document. The results of the conferences will be used to inform the preparation of the board's Corporate Plan (which for 2001–4 will be cast purely on the basis of the resources available to the board) and in making the case for additional resources in the future. Before presenting the main text of the document, it is worth looking briefly at two issues raised during the conferences which will be of great importance in the future, namely the European dimension to the board's work, and the potential offered by the development and adoption of new technologies.

First, substantial progress has been achieved in the situation of the Welsh language in Wales since the Welsh Language Act came into force in 1993. A review of achievement against the twenty objectives listed in the strategy (undertaken as part of the process of preparing the 'Vision and Mission' document) showed that progress has been made against each of them. This success goes some way to explaining the change in the situation of the language today. This in turn has created a large amount of interest in the work of the board from other parts of Europe (and other parts of the world) as other language communities seek emulate its success in preserving their own languages in the face of pressure from stronger tongues. The board has seen tremendous interest in its work in the fields of language transmission and particularly community language planning. This was the theme of a European conference held by the board with the financial assistance of the European Commission in June 1998, leading to the launch of a website in May 1999 (*www.cymuned.org.uk*), which offers models, guidelines and assistance on the subject. The board is aware that organizations in other European countries have a wealth of experience and expertise in other areas of language promotion and preservation, and is keen to strengthen ties with them to our mutual benefit. Such ties could become increasingly important in the context of the expansion of the European Union, as the issue of languages and official communication is revisited and as the European Charter for Regional or Minority Languages gains more signatories and is implemented in an increasing number of countries. Greater interaction between the board and European organizations may provide a stronger base from which to argue the case for greater recognition of regional languages within mainstream European policies, as well as strengthening the learning process of all involved within language planning and promotion. The board will actively seek to develop this aspect of its work.

Secondly, there is the issue of new technologies and their potential impact on languages generally. The World-Wide Web, the Internet, and other information and communication technology (ICT) developments offer both threats and opportunities to any language other than English. This is only to be expected because English is the main language of development in the medium and it is now arguably impossible for any other language to compete on a level playing field. Nonetheless, new technologies offer significant opportunities to languages such as Welsh to adopt and develop new, exciting and contemporary domains, especially among key age groups such as young people. The board is very aware – from the position of status planning as much as anything else – of the need to ensure that the language becomes recognized as a feasible and vibrant medium of electronic communication. There has been significant growth in this area with a proliferation of web sites with a Welsh language content and the board will seek to ensure that this trend continues, covering all aspects of ICT development. The board will seek to develop its role in this field to provide advice and encouragement, and to facilitate the participation of others in the communications revolution through the medium of Welsh.

# *Appendix A*

## THE WELSH LANGUAGE: A VISION AND MISSION FOR 2000–2005

### *1. Introduction*

**1.1**   For the majority of the world's population, bilingualism is a natural and normal phenomenon. It is estimated that between 60 and 65% of people globally use at least two languages in their everyday lives. Bilingualism and multilingualism have a prominent place in the European Union as well, where around 50 million people use a language which is different from the official language of the country in which they live.

**1.2**   Wales is a bilingual nation. It has two official languages, Welsh and English. In addition, there are smaller communities in Wales who use languages besides these in their everyday lives. The Welsh language has a special place in our history because it is one of the major factors which has made us what we are. It is not the only factor by any means, but few would deny that Welsh has played an important part in the formation of our national identity. As such, it is a part of the heritage of every citizen of Wales, whether they speak Welsh or not: it is something in which we can all take pride.

**1.3**   For most of the world's 6,000 or so languages, the future is not bright: indeed it is predicted that the majority will die or become moribund during the next century. Welsh, on the other hand, is one of the very few minority languages that is expected to buck this trend. One of the main reasons for this is well-focused language planning.

**1.4**   Through such language planning, Welsh has moved from a sharp decline this century to 'level maintenance'. At its best, language planning has led to Welsh becoming revitalised, to its being used more, more Welsh medium education, more status within institutions, and to its becoming increasingly connected with the economy, especially in the context of sustainable development. There is now a general acceptance in Wales that bilingualism is beneficial for individuals and communities. For individuals, bilingualism provides wider communication opportunities, giving access to two windows on the world by being bicultural, enabling access to two literacies, raising self-esteem, enabling a secure sense of identity, and widening employment opportunities. For communities, bilingualism provides continuity with the past, cohesiveness for the present, and a source of collaborative endeavour for building the future.

**1.5** We can all be proud of the many successes in the work of promoting Welsh in recent times. We should also be fully aware that there is no assurance that Welsh will survive as a living language without continued and purposeful effort by all those who have an interest in the language's future. And we can all learn from world-wide trends. The reasons why so many of the world's languages are predicted to die are many and varied: industrialisation, urbanisation, economic and industrial development, immigration, emigration, new trends in communication, mass media, increasing travel, affluence and the rise of the global village, amongst others.

**1.6** There are, however, two simple and primary reasons why languages die, and these are both important for the future of the Welsh language. First, languages die when parents who are able to speak the minority language speak the majority language in the home. When minority language transmission does not occur at family level, then there is little hope of future generations speaking that minority language. Second, minority languages die when education is through the majority language. When minority language production does not occur at school, again there can be little expectation that the minority language will survive.

## 2. The Achievements of the Welsh Language Board

**2.1** No minority language in the world will survive unless there is deliberate language planning. One reason that the Welsh language has bucked the world trend is due to considerable efforts by various organisations and individuals to plan for language maintenance and increased Welsh language vitality. The Welsh Language Board has been a vital institution in revival efforts – both the advisory Board which was set up in 1988, and the statutory Board which took its place.

**2.2** Since it was established in December 1993 on a statutory basis, with the principal function of promoting and facilitating the use of the Welsh language, the Welsh Language Board has been involved in a wide range of projects. These encompass not only those which the Board has itself initiated, but also those on which the Board has worked directly in partnership, and also those which it has assisted through grants. Full details of these and of all the Board's past activities are contained in its Annual Reports, and work in progress is detailed in its current Operational Plan (1999–2000).

**2.3** But what about the broader picture? Since its inception, the Board has continually stressed the importance of everyone who has an interest in the prosperity of the Welsh language working together in partnership. This is the central theme of the *Strategy for the Welsh Language* which the Board published in 1996, the first comprehensive strategy produced to secure a prosperous future for Welsh. The emphasis on partnership is essential when one calls to mind that it is the Board's partners who are the main suppliers of Welsh-medium provision. To a great extent, therefore, the Board's achievements cannot be dissociated from those of its partners. Nevertheless, it should also be noted that the Board has not shirked from taking the practical initiative itself, particularly in pioneering linguistic areas, for example the development of *CySill*, the Welsh language spelling and grammar checking software; producing guidance on *bilingual design*; and the development of Welsh language *CD-ROMs* (in conjunction with the Welsh Books Council).

**2.4**   The Board has been at the forefront in establishing a large number of partnerships, particularly in the process of preparing language schemes in the public sector, by virtue of its grant schemes in the voluntary sector and of its work with the private sector, and as a result of its function to maintain a strategic overview of Welsh language education and training. Many partnerships have been established voluntarily, particularly in the fields of business and commerce, at the instigation of the bodies themselves.

**2.5**   All this has led to more extensive opportunities to use the Welsh language in all aspects of life, and the Board has co-ordinated and facilitated the processes that have led to this. The Welsh language also commands a higher status in Wales than ever before in modern times. The Board can take credit for helping to influence the change in public attitudes that has occurred over the past decade. This has led to a situation in which the vast majority of Welsh people now take pride in the language, and regard learning two languages as a valuable skill. The extensive measure of cross-party support which the language enjoys is also indicative of the Board's diplomatic influence in revitalising the language.

**2.6.**   The Board continues to emphasise that the future of the language is dependent above all on three components:

* public goodwill;
* investment by our institutions; and
* purposeful language planning.

**2.7**   The task ahead should never be underestimated, but it will be considerably facilitated by the fact that the Board has established itself as a body able to:

* offer impartial and professional advice;
* work effectively in partnership with others; and
* provide a strategic overview over the whole Welsh language field.

### 3. *The Future of the Welsh Language*

**3.1**   The Welsh Language Board has engaged in the four different types of language planning that are needed for language survival:

- acquisition planning;
- usage planning;
- status planning; and
- corpus planning.

**3.2**   These four areas will be addressed in turn, with strategic proposals for the revitalisation of the Welsh language. For the moment, it is important to emphasise why all four approaches to language planning are vital.

**3.3**   In the field of minority languages generally, it is important to recognise that there are no fail-safe remedies and no guaranteed solutions. If a minority language is to survive in the world, there has to be permanent endeavour. There is a need to:

- market the language continuously and repetitively;
- commence new initiatives;
- set new targets;
- monitor the state and spread of the language;
- evaluate interventions; and
- constantly try to raise the language's status.

**3.4**   The time lag in terms of policy implementation in the field of language is however much longer than in other policy areas. The quick fix is a rarity. One has to be patient!

**3.5**   In international terms, the Welsh language is currently regarded as one of the most effective models of how to plan, intervene, engineer change and reverse (downward) language shift. Here are a few of many examples where language planning has successfully bucked the trend of downward shift.

- the Welsh Language Act of 1993;
- the *mentrau iaith*;
- the spread of *bilingual education* at primary and secondary level;
- Welsh as a compulsory subject in the *National Curriculum*;
- the vitality of movements such as *Mudiad Ysgolion Meithrin, Urdd Gobaith Cymru*, local and national *eisteddfodau*;
- Welsh language schemes;
- increasing use of *bilingualism* in *business* and the *economy*.

**3.6**   Nevertheless, there is still cause for concern. Here are some salient facts which illustrate the point.

- In half the families where only one parent can speak Welsh, the children are unable to speak it.
- 40% of children who complete primary education as first language Welsh speakers commence their secondary education as second language Welsh speakers and take their curriculum through the medium of English.
- The Welsh Language Board's commissioned surveys show that more than 40% of Welsh-speaking adults lack confidence in using the language, and therefore use it infrequently.

- During adolescence, many bilingual teenagers use the language less frequently as they grow older (though this trend may be reversed in later life).
- Geographically, the Welsh language has tended to decline by a westwards movement, with many communities lessening in their everyday use of the Welsh language.

**3.7** Overcoming these tendencies presents a considerable challenge, and it would be unrealistic, in the coming decades, to expect a large Welsh language revival. Maintenance at current levels would be a considerable achievement. But maintenance must not become the target: it is too limiting a vision and mission. Building on the recent successes and growing maturity of the Welsh Language Board and its partners, it is possible to plan:

- for growth where there is decline;
- to increase confidence in usage where there is doubt; and
- to market the language among parents and schools, which are so crucial in producing new generations of Welsh speakers.

Such plans must include all four language planning areas.

**3.8** At this turning point in the history of Wales, new projects and initiatives, new targets and priorities are needed for the Welsh language to flourish, revive and avoid world-wide trends in the demise of linguistic and cultural diversity. Therefore, this paper now outlines where new initiatives and targets are needed for each of the four language planning areas. These initiatives reflect a full and wide consultation by the Board with its partners over the last two years and are an evolution of its previous Corporate Plans. Drafts of this paper were reviewed and developed by a panel of experts from Wales along with an expert on language planning from the Basque Country.

**3.9** These initiatives are a selection from a large list of possibilities, and reflect the considered and agreed prioritisation of the Welsh Language Board. *The overall emphasis is on increasing language usage, by means of a comprehensive marketing strategy, with the aim of making Wales an increasingly bilingual and multilingual society:*

- in which all its citizens may use the Welsh and English languages with equal facility in all aspects of their lives; and
- where every language community can live together in harmony and prosper.

**3.10** Our vision must be considered both in the context of the new political structure of Wales, and in the wider context of the British Isles and Europe. The role of the National Assembly and of local government must not be underestimated in formulating and guiding the socio-economic processes which determine whether or not our communities prosper. If a community is in a state of economic decline, it is less able to ensure the language prospers within it. There is often a direct correlation between economic and linguistic prosperity.

**3.11** The National Assembly has undoubtedly given a new sense of identity to being Welsh, but political autonomy and linguistic prosperity do not necessarily go hand in hand. Throughout Europe, one can point to both successes and failures, and Wales needs to draw on the experiences of other countries. The National Assembly itself will need to address these issues as it determines its own responsibilities, both statutory and otherwise, with regard to the Welsh language.

## 4. Language Planning

### 4.1 Language Acquisition Planning

**4.1.1** There are two components to language acquisition planning:

a) *language transmission in the family* and
b) *Welsh medium and bilingual education.*

Important initiatives in these two areas are quintessential to ensure continuing growth.

*Language transmission in the family*

**4.1.2** For any minority language to have a future, parents need to speak the language with their children. According to Census data, we know that only 92% of families where both parents speak Welsh raise their children to speak Welsh. Where one parent is bilingual and the other parent speaks only English, only one in every two families speaks Welsh to their children. It is clear therefore that we have a significant task in persuading more parents to pass on the language to their children. Such persuasion is always going to be difficult. It is not easy to reach parents, nor is it easy to persuade them. However, it is vital to raise awareness of language issues among parents.

**4.1.3** Therefore, the Welsh Language Board has recently engaged in two highly innovative language-marketing projects to overcome such difficulties. Effective intervention has occurred by:

- providing crucial information in Bounty Packs (packs of free samples and information given via hospitals to new and expectant mothers) across Wales; and
- training midwives and health visitors to provide information about bilingualism to parents.

**4.1.4** This second project is currently operating in Carmarthenshire, with early signs of success. The Welsh Language Board will shortly be objectively evaluating this project. However, such is the importance of language transmission in the family that such language marketing is expected to become a permanent feature of the Board's work. The Board will also be working with schools and organisations dealing with young people to encourage young people to discuss the advantages of raising children bilingually.

## TARGET 1

– to provide information, advice, guidance and support to new parents on the advantages of early bilingualism. This will include extending the training of midwives and health visitors to all areas of Wales (working in harmony and sympathy with local geographical variations); relevant targets are:

*1. by March 2003*
40% of relevant health visitors and midwives to be provided with information packs and to have attended a training session;

*2. by March 2006*
100% of relevant health visitors and midwives to be provided with information packs and to have attended a training session;

*3. by March 2002*
materials for parents of pre-school children supporting the use of Welsh in the home and providing information about the benefits of early bilingualism to be produced and distributed; such materials will focus on mixed language families and homes where the medium is mostly English.

## TARGET 2

– by the results of the 2006 intercensal survey, an increase in Welsh language transmission:

1. in homes where both parents speak Welsh from a 1991 baseline of 92% to 95%; and
2. in homes where one parent speaks Welsh from a 1991 baseline of 48% to 60%.

*Welsh-medium and bilingual education*
**4.1.5**  Such is the importance of this subject that as well as forming a core part of this paper, it merits detailed consideration in its own right. Detailed reports on developing bilingual education have been prepared by the Board. Rather than reproduce these reports here in their entirety, they are appended to this document. Nonetheless, for the sake of clarity and continuity, the main themes are outlined below; detailed targets relating to these themes are set out in the appended reports (NB not included in this version, but available on request from the Welsh Language Board).

*Welsh-medium pre-school provision*
**4.1.6**  The fact is that only 6.3% of children aged 3 speak Welsh: nearly all of these will have acquired the language at home. So, in order to increase numbers, early years education has a vital part to play. In early childhood, a language is acquired easily and naturally, spontaneously and almost subconsciously. It is acquired rather than learnt. Therefore, State

provision and *Mudiad Ysgolion Meithrin* have a crucial role in Welsh language acquisition in young children, from both Welsh and English speaking homes.

**4.1.7** Due to a variety of external factors, the number of *cylchoedd meithrin* and *Ti a Fi groups* has dropped from 1041 in 1995 to 956 in 1999. Therefore, the following are needed:

- new initiatives by *Mudiad Ysgolion Meithrin*;
- a strong and effective marketing campaign to promote the advantages of acquiring Welsh through this organisation; and
- the development of language targets to measure the organisation's impact on language production.

**4.1.8** The Welsh Language Board will have agreed by March 2000 a comprehensive strategy with *Mudiad Ysgolion Meithrin* which will set out a detailed timetable for:

- developing a detailed marketing strategy;
- establishing by March 2001 a system of monitoring language outcomes in *cylchoedd meithrin*;
- increasing the provision and take-up rate of places in Welsh-medium/ bilingual provision.

*Continuity and progression*

**4.1.9** There has been a marked increase in the numbers of pupils receiving Welsh-medium and bilingual education in Wales over the past twenty years. However, a recent report by the Welsh Language Board on continuity in Welsh language education showed the decreasing use of the language:

- from primary to secondary school; and
- from secondary school to further and higher education.

**4.1.10** The Welsh Language Board has set a target that by March 2002 it will have produced in relation to the:

- individual,
- family,
- school,
- local education authority, and
- other institutions,

a report detailing the reasons for the sizeable drop in the number of children taking Welsh-medium education from primary to secondary school, and from secondary school to further and higher education. The identification of underlying reasons for discontinuity must lead to a set of actionable recommendations.

**4.1.11**  A report will also be published detailing by district the percentage of pupils who move from Welsh-medium nursery education to Welsh-medium primary education. Targets will also be set in terms of increasing the numbers of children in bilingual education at primary and secondary levels. In order to encourage pupils to follow a Welsh-medium or bilingual course, a detailed report on the nature and the implementation of the language continuum, including its relationship to assessment, will be published.

*Teaching and learning in a bilingual context*

**4.1.12**  In order to improve the bilingual capabilities of pupils in Wales, bilingual resources and teaching methodology packs will be produced which will support teachers and lecturers in bilingual classrooms. Bilingual methodology courses will be available at all training colleges by September 2004. This methodology will be used in an increasing percentage of classrooms and lecture theatres in Wales from September 2005 onwards. In order to increase bilingual opportunities, primary and secondary schools that teach Welsh as a second language will be encouraged to teach at least one curriculum area bilingually.

*Further and higher education*

**4.1.13**  At further and higher education levels, the emphasis will be on increasing the provision of bilingual courses and the numbers of students taking:

- some of their courses,
- most of their courses, or
- all of their courses,

through the medium of Welsh or bilingually.

*Multilingual skills*

**4.1.14**  In order to improve the multilingual skills of pupils, a target will be set in order to increase the percentage of trilingual children in Wales.

*Lifelong learning*

**4.1.15**  In order to enhance the opportunities to learn Welsh and to learn through the medium of Welsh and bilingually, the availability of Welsh-medium and bilingual courses for adult learners will be increased. In terms of Welsh for Adults courses, the main emphasis will be on increasing the numbers of adults who enrol in classes and who become fluent in Welsh.

## 4.2 Usage Planning

**4.2.1** Planning the use of Welsh needs to occur in two major areas:

a) *the instrumental use of Welsh* (e.g. economic use), and
b) *the integrative use of Welsh* (that is, in all fields e.g. social, cultural, leisure and community use).

*The instrumental use of Welsh*

**4.2.2** There have to be convincing reasons for parents to bring up their children in Welsh, and persuasive motivations for children to become fluent in speaking Welsh and literate in the language whilst at school. Whilst this is not the only reason, nevertheless the economic carrot has increasingly become important and needs to be captivatingly marketed.

**4.2.3** The more the Welsh language has economic and employment value, the more it is likely to be attractive to parents to transmit the language to their children, and the more it is likely to be attractive to children to learn Welsh thoroughly at school.

**4.2.4** Through the work of the Welsh Language Board and its partners, much has already been achieved in this area, in promoting the value of bilingualism among the private, voluntary and public sectors. The following are some of the things that have contributed to the process:

- Welsh language schemes;
- grants;
- the production of state of the art materials on language in business and on signage;
- marketing bilingualism to increase businesses' customer satisfaction and client base.

**4.2.5** We need to do two things so that awareness of the relationship between the local/national economy and the Welsh language is both prominent and permanent:

- to disseminate current ideas and material as widely as possible; and
- to constantly repeat and revitalise messages.

**4.2.6** Marketing the economic value of the language is increasingly essential, targeting:

- individuals (particularly in the younger age-groups);
- small and medium sized enterprises; and
- all larger public and private institutions.

This needs to operate in terms of both the local and national economy.

**TARGET 3**

– to develop and expand the use of Welsh in the private sector:

*1. by March 2003*
to have developed, produced and distributed marketing materials to increase the profile of the language in the private sector, with such materials being specific for different business sectors and sizes of organisation;

*2. by March 2005*
100 national companies providing goods and/or services to the public in Wales to have a member of staff responsible for increasing the companies' use of Welsh, in partnership with the Board;

*3. by March 2005*
100 local companies, in each area served by a *menter iaith*, and which provide goods and/or services to the public, to have a member of staff responsible for increasing the companies' use of Welsh, in partnership with the *menter iaith*;

*4. by March 2005*
to raise awareness about the use of Welsh in business within the business community generally, and specifically in 3000 companies providing goods and/or services to the public in Wales.

**TARGET 4**

– to market and develop vocational training and the use of Welsh in the workplace:

*1. by March 2003*
to have produced and distributed marketing materials to raise awareness of the importance of bilingual vocational training among:

- colleges,
- small and medium sized businesses, and
- post 16 year olds;

*2. by March 2006*
the numbers of students in Welsh-medium vocational training to have quadrupled against a 1999 baseline;

*3. by March 2006*
to have increased by 10% against the 2002 survey baseline the number of workplaces operating bilingually.

**TARGET 5**

– to monitor the instrumental use of the language:

*1. by March 2005*
to have surveyed the use made by the public of bilingual services and activities;

*2. by March 2001*
to have comprehensively surveyed the use of Welsh in the workplace (and specifically among managers), to assess the most effective modes of stimulating activity in this field, and to have produced an actionable set of targets for an increase is such use.

*The integrative use of Welsh*

4.2.7    While the economic and employment value of the Welsh language is a strong motivation for learning, retaining and using Welsh, its danger is that it can be short term, pragmatic and occasionally 'doing the right thing for the wrong reason'. Therefore, more long-term, deep-seated motivations are also needed for making Welsh a long-term living language.

4.2.8    The theory of minority language maintenance implies that a minority language requires reserved functions and usage. For example, when in times past Welsh had a reserved place in chapels and churches, maintenance occurred. Recently, the Welsh language has moved away from being reserved for particular domains into trying to capture language use into as many domains as possible. In doing this, the Welsh language is always going to be in competition against an all-pervading and powerful majority language (e.g. television, newspapers, Internet). Nevertheless, there is little choice except to try to maintain and increase Welsh language usage in as many areas of culture and leisure – in social and community relationships – as is possible, if we are to attract people to use the language.

4.2.9    It is in this context that we have seen arguably the most exciting of recent language planning developments, namely the *mentrau iaith* – community language initiatives. They are becoming a highly effective means of engineering bespoke language planning, tailored to the needs of the communities they serve. They are achieving much in terms of:

- marketing the use of the language;
- providing social opportunities to use the language; and
- revitalising the use of the language in communities.

We regard the development and expansion of the work and role of *mentrau iaith* to be a priority.

**4.2.10** This raises another key issue. With the Welsh Language Board's limited resources and the difficulty of socially engineering patterns of language usage, a clear prioritisation in terms of impact in both its allocation of grants and marketing strategy is required. The Welsh Language Board will therefore conduct a cost-benefit analysis to evaluate its current allocation of grants and project monies, to ensure they are effective:

- in relation to cost;
- from the perspective of language maintenance; and
- from the perspective of Welsh language spread.

## TARGET 6

– to extend and develop community based language activity:

*1. by March 2001*
to have produced and distributed marketing materials to raise awareness of the importance of community based language activity among community leaders, business leaders, decision makers and such like in both the private and voluntary sectors;

*2. by March 2003*
to have produced and distributed marketing materials to raise awareness of the importance of Welsh language use targeted at subgroups in the 14-19 and 20-30 age groups;

*3. by March 2003*
to ensure that all areas of Wales have access to the kind of services provided by *mentrau iaith*.

## TARGET 7

– to increase the cost effectiveness of resources:

*1. by March 2002*
an independent analysis to be received of cost-effectiveness in grant allocation and project monies against clear given criteria for increasing the use of the Welsh language;

*2. by April 2003*
resource allocation to reflect the findings of the cost-effectiveness analysis.

**TARGET 8**

– to monitor the integrative use of the language:

*1. by March 2002*
to have comprehensively surveyed the use of Welsh in the key areas of everyday communication (e.g. social, cultural and leisure activities) and produced an actionable set of targets for an increase in such use;

*2. by March 2003*
a survey of the degree of confidence of Welsh speakers in using the language in different domains to be completed, with clear recommendations for a prioritised strategy for improving confidence levels, and clear targets for the increased use of Welsh in specific domains.

### 4.3    Status Planning

**4.3.1**    Every aspect of Welsh language use is important to the status of the language – this holds for every event and for every occasion on which Welsh is used by institutions and individuals. The factors which confer status on the language are many and complex, and span the whole range of language use, from speaking Welsh in the National Assembly to listening to Welsh language pop music. Passions and prejudices, vested interests and deep-seated values affect judgements and prioritisation about 'what gives the Welsh language status'.

**4.3.2**    Parents are influenced by a variety of factors when deciding to raise their children in English or in Welsh or bilingually. The value which children attribute to the Welsh language in education will be much affected by such status effects. Whether children use Welsh:

- in the playground,
- the street,
- with friends,

and whether teenagers go on to use Welsh in their twenties and thirties, will be much affected by status factors. The choice by parents and children of bilingual or English-medium education will often be much influenced by the status factors attached to Welsh and English (and bilingualism). Status components affect the take-up of Welsh medium education.

**4.3.3**    An argument can be made for preserving (and increasing) everything that affects the status of the Welsh language. Nothing becomes unimportant. Such components of language status exist in delicate interactions and combinations and not as separate, isolatable influences. Remove a few bricks and the public may believe that the castle is beginning to crumble.

**4.3.4**  International language planning literature supports the view that *supporting key 'status' institutions* and ensuring the language has a *modern status* (e.g. in Information and Communications Technology) are two key criteria for judging the relative importance of different components that make up the status of the language. The:

- status of Welsh in the National Assembly,
- comments about the Welsh language in the committees of the Assembly, and
- the attention of the Regional Committees and unitary authorities to Welsh

can greatly influence the current and future status of the language. Indeed, there is a unique opportunity for Regional Committees to have particular regard to language issues when considering wider matters such as regional housing and planning developments.

**4.3.5**  Language schemes play a major role here, and will continue to do so. These are a specific statutory responsibility for the Board, and have become an area demonstrating a consistently high degree of expertise and effectiveness, stimulating further development in the delivery of a bilingual service. They are active right across the public and Crown sectors, and are also influencing service planning and delivery in the voluntary and private sectors. They have stimulated much of the increase in the use of Welsh that can clearly be seen in our everyday lives, and providing a bilingual service has become a mark of quality service in Wales. The Board's task over the next 5 years in this area of our work will increasingly focus on ensuring the present momentum is maintained, and that organisations are honouring their commitments. Good practice will be elevated, as we strive to continually improve the quality and efficiency of bilingual services.

**4.3.6**  The Board will also continue to seek to influence new policies and practices developed by:

- the National Assembly,
- Whitehall,
- public bodies, and
- other Crown bodies,

in order that they appropriately reflect and respect the bilingual nature of Wales and the needs of Welsh speakers. As well as the field of education and training, this will include being proactive in fields such as:

- health and social care;
- justice;
- the statutory planning process;
- the arts and culture; and
- tourism and the economy.

**4.3.7**   The targets below therefore relate specifically to areas discussed in this section which can have a direct bearing on the status of the language. It should, however, be noted that the targets in each of the other sections of this paper are also intrinsically concerned with raising the status of the language.

- Raising awareness in families,
- further developing bilingual education, and
- increasing usage in social, cultural and economic domains,

all aim to raise the status of the language.

**4.3.8**   Funding and the level of institutional support for the language also affects the status of the language. While the Board has provided institutional support financially, it is important to re-evaluate the spend based on clear criteria of cost-effectiveness. Thus Target 7(1) above also has a key place in this section.

## TARGET 9

– to promote the language on the Internet:

*1. by March 2002*
the Welsh Language Board to become a principal server for the delivery of, and links to, Welsh language Internet material;

*2. by March 2003*
the Welsh Language Board to be regularly marketing the language through bilingual Internet material aimed particularly at consumers inside Wales, but also for use by a world-wide audience.

## TARGET 10

– to develop language planning links:

*1. by March 2002*
the Welsh Language Board to have formally established mutually co-operative links with four government minority language planning institutions in Europe (to include the Basque Country and Ireland);

*2. by March 2003*
the Welsh Language Board to continually monitor best practice in language planning in minority language communities to see what lessons can be learnt for Wales.

**TARGET 11**

– to oversee the implementation and monitoring of Welsh language schemes and bilingual service provision:

*1. by March 2005*
350 statutory and 70 voluntary Welsh language schemes to have been submitted to the Board for approval;

*2. by March 2005*
the number of performance reports on the implementation of Welsh language schemes received annually by the Board to increase to 260 (from 97 in 2000): 50% of those received will be scrutinised and investigated annually over the period;

*3. between March 2000 and March 2005*
3 independent snapshot surveys into scheme implementation to be commissioned annually;

*4. by March 2004*
a report to be produced and published which analyses general progress, good practice and weaknesses in bilingual service planning and provision.

**4.4     Corpus Planning**

**4.4.1**   Corpus planning centres around two areas:

- the need for linguistic standardisation, and
- the need to develop a form of Welsh that is popular, used and useful.

**4.4.2**   The first need has often been met by producing specialised dictionaries (e.g. for nursing, education, and the law). However, one should also have regard to 'popular' standardisation which often occurs through the mass media such as S4C and radio programmes in Welsh. The second need has been addressed, so far as forms and related material are concerned, by *Cymraeg Clir*, which seeks to do for written Welsh what the *Plain English Campaign* does for English. There is certainly a case for extending this initiative to cover the spoken Welsh which is used in more formal situations.

**4.4.3**   All languages must develop and change, evolve new terminology and forms of expression that reflect changes in:

- culture,
- ideology,
- relationships, and
- means of communication.

**4.4.4**    A language that sticks rigidly to past usage becomes a moribund language. To its credit, the Welsh language has developed to reflect changes in, for example, technology and science, as well as developing terminology so that Welsh can be used in an increasing number of professions, institutions and activities. Welsh must continue to adapt, continue to spread its new terminology, and continue to gain acceptance for forms of Welsh that will make it a living language for new generations. Therefore, further initiatives and developments are needed in Welsh language corpus planning.

**TARGET 12**

– to develop and standardise terminology and translation:

*1. by March 2001*
the Welsh Language Board to have created within its own organisation a national centre for corpus planning concerned with standardisation, translation and translators, and the use of Welsh in software and the World Wide Web;

*2. by March 2004*
specialised terminology dictionaries to be available free on the World Wide Web from a Welsh Language Board server;

*3. by March 2004*
multimedia modules on *Cymraeg Clir* to be available to all institutions, public and private, and deliverable through the Internet.

*5. Monitoring*

**5.1**    It is intended that, at the end of each financial year, there will be a specific report that:

- evaluates whether the targets for the previous year have been reached;
- provides a commentary on reasons for relative success; and
- provides plans for the implementation of targets for the following years.

**5.2**    Discussions of these reports are expected to lead to new targets being set. Such flexibility and evolution in target setting is regarded as essential so that the Board can adapt quickly to political, economic and cultural developments. It is important not to become trapped within a five year framework of targets, but to continually develop and seek ever-higher achievements.

**5.3**    It is also intended to use three benchmarks as an overall evaluation of progress.

contribution to the workings of the British–Irish Council. The initiatives will enable increased co-operation with our Irish and Scottish neighbours in revitalising our Celtic languages. We will also be leading Europe in a task that faces the many communities across Europe with minority languages, and we envisage our European partners benefiting from the practical policies that will be tested in Wales.

**7.3**    It is appropriate to end with a reference to the National Assembly's responsibilities.

- Firstly, there is the European dimension. One of the most important aspects is the Assembly's duty to implement the European Charter for Regional or Minority Languages in the United Kingdom.
- Secondly, there are the statutory references to Welsh in the Government of Wales Act 1998, the most open-ended of which is contained in section 32, which states that 'the Assembly may do anything it considers appropriate to support . . . the Welsh language'.

**7.4**    This will clearly need to be defined more precisely as the Assembly develops its own policies to promote a bilingual Wales. Since the Board now has a statutory responsibility to advise the Assembly on matters relating to the Welsh language, we look forward to playing a key part in the development and in the implementation of these policies.

# *Appendix B*

### *Preparing Language Schemes*

In what follows 'organisation' means a public body preparing a scheme under Part II of the Act or a person acting as the servant or agent of the Crown preparing a Welsh language scheme, and 'scheme' means a scheme prepared by a public body under Part II of the Act or a Welsh language scheme prepared by a person acting as the servant or agent of the Crown. An organisation preparing a scheme shall have regard to the following guidelines as to the form and content of schemes:

A 'scheme' should be more than a policy. It should be a strategy or action plan which includes 'measures' which:

- are policy statements;
- are descriptions of the services available in Welsh;
- are practical arrangements;
- put in place an implementation and monitoring framework for the 'scheme';
- include a definite timetable for implementing the 'scheme' measure by measure.

*Guidelines as to the Form and Content of Schemes*

1. The scheme should be presented in Welsh and in English and in a form which is suitable for publication to the members of the public with whom the organisation has dealings.

*Guidelines as to the Content of Schemes*

### General

2. The scheme should specify the measures an organisation proposes to take in order to give effect to the principle of equality set out in section 5 of the Act, and how the organisation proposes to implement each measure.

### Service planning and delivery

3. The scheme should specify the measures an organisation proposes to take when assessing the impact of new policies and initiatives and when implementing them;
4. The scheme should specify what steps the organisation will take to deliver services through the medium of Welsh;
5. The scheme should specify what standards of quality are to be achieved in the delivery of services in Welsh, including having regard to the principles of the Citizen's Charter presented to Parliament on 22 July 1991.

### Dealing with the Welsh-speaking public

6. The scheme should specify the measures to be taken in order to give effect to the principle of equality set out in the Act in relation to:

   (i)     corresponding with the public;
   (ii)    telephone communication with the public;
   (iii)   public meetings (including hearings, inquiries and other legal proceedings);
   (iv)    other meetings with the public;
   (v)     other dealings with the public.

### The organization's public face

7. The scheme should specify the measures to be taken in order to give effect to the principle of equality set out in the Act in relation to:

   (i)     the corporate identity of the organisation in Wales;
   (ii)    information signs within the curtilage of property in Wales owned or occupied by the organisation, including internal areas to which the public has access;
   (iii)   other public information signs located in Wales, and for which an organisation is responsible;

(iv)   publishing and printing material directed at the public in Wales;

(v)    all forms and associated explanatory material for use by the public in Wales;

(vi)   press notices for distribution in Wales;

(vii)  publicity material for distribution in Wales;

(viii) advertising campaigns and exhibition material directed at the public in Wales;

(ix)   material used for direct marketing campaigns in Wales;

(x)    response mechanisms linked to publicity activities in Wales;

(xi)   official notices, public notices and staff recruitment advertising in Wales.

### Implementing and monitoring the scheme

8. The scheme should specify:

(i)    measures to ensure that workplaces which have contact with the public in Wales seek access to sufficient and appropriately skilled Welsh speakers to enable those workplaces to deliver a full service through the medium of Welsh;

(ii)   measures to identify those staff posts where the ability to speak Welsh is considered to be essential and those where it is considered to be desirable in order to deliver a full service through the medium of Welsh;

(iii)  measures to assess the need for specific vocational training through the medium of Welsh and measures for meeting that need;

(iv)   the administrative arrangements the organisation will make to facilitate its scheme;

(v)    the steps to be taken to ensure that any agreements or arrangements made with third parties which relate to the provision of services to the public in Wales are consistent with the terms of the scheme. This includes (without limitation) services which are contracted out;

(vi)   the steps to be taken to monitor implementation of the scheme;

(vii)  targets against which implementation of the scheme can be measured;

(viii) the steps to be taken to publish information comparing the organisation's performance with the standards set out in the scheme.

# 4

# Welsh Language Education: A Strategy for Revitalization

## COLIN BAKER AND MEIRION PRYS JONES

### INTRODUCTION

The aim of this chapter is to examine, both historically and with a future perspective, the role of bilingual education in Wales in language maintenance and revitalization. It begins, through evidence and then explanation, by revealing the quiet revolution that has taken place in education in Wales since 1939. From a system before the Second World War that virtually excluded Welsh, we now have a system where, for example, one in five primary-school children are taught bilingually.

Having celebrated the growth of bilingual education in Wales, the chapter then paradoxically shows the disconcerting discontinuity that exists in such education. After primary schooling, considerably fewer pupils take their secondary, further and higher education bilingually. The chapter provides the evidence for this dysfunction in the educational system of Wales. Explanations are not offered because, as yet, there is no empirical evidence to explain the causes of discontinuity.

The chapter closes by presenting briefly the challenges that face bilingual education in Wales in a new century: continuity, establishing a continuum of second-language to first-language speaker, and a concurrent dual-language curriculum methodology. At the end it is suggested that, however, the initial challenge is to clarify the aims of bilingual education. Only when there is clarity in desired destinations can the route to those destinations be firmly established.

### A HISTORICAL PERSPECTIVE

In the last hundred years, the Welsh language has declined in numerical terms from a million speakers at the turn of the century to a current total of around half a million. According to census and recent survey data, in the last three decades, the Welsh language would appear to have reached a relatively stabilized numerical state. Such stabilization has been partly if not mainly due to Welsh-medium education which has recently grown and flourished. The stabilization in the numbers of Welsh speakers and the rise of bilingual schools need to be under-stood historically as a quiet revolution in education in Wales that has been a central plank in revitalization efforts.

There was a very limited amount of bilingual education in Wales before the middle of the twentieth century. In the first half of the twentieth century, the greater economic potential of the English language, with increased chances of employment and affluence, status and security for speaking and working in English, often militated against the Welsh language in education. This was reflected in schools, where policy-makers were joined by Welsh-speaking parents who were keen for their children to be educated exclusively in English to escape slate quarries and coal-mining areas, for example, and relative material deprivation. Parents were typically enthusiastic for their children to join the professional classes – as teachers, doctors, lawyers, ministers. Thus, before the middle of the twentieth century, schools in Wales tended only to foster the English language and culture. In most schools, there was very little or no use of the Welsh language in the classroom until the last four decades of the twentieth century.

## THE GROWTH OF BILINGUAL EDUCATION IN WALES

Bilingual education in Wales developed from a small acorn planted in 1939 to, by the turn of the century, a sturdy and mature oak tree. In 1939, the first bilin-gual Welsh school was opened in Aberystwyth by a group of enthusiastic parents. Following this development, the Butler Education Act of 1944 allowed Local Education Authorities (LEAs) to consider opening Welsh-medium schools. Parental pressure resulted in the establishment of the first officially designated Welsh-medium primary school run by an LEA in Llanelli, Carmarthenshire, in 1947, and by 1950 there were another six Welsh-medium schools in south Wales and five in north-east Wales. Initially the provision was for children for whom Welsh was their first language, but by the 1960s increasing numbers of pupils came from non-Welsh-speaking homes. This dramatic growth of Welsh-medium primary schools in anglicized areas aided the establishment of Welsh-medium secondary schools, initially Ysgol Glan Clwyd in Flintshire in 1956, followed by schools in Denbighshire and in Glamorgan.

Between the 1950s and 1990s, there was a growth in bilingual education in the primary sector, to a lesser extent in the secondary sector, but only minimally in further education and university education. From Welsh being excluded from the curriculum in the early decades of the twentieth century, it has now become compulsory in primary and secondary schools throughout Wales.

One significant development during the 1990s was the introduction of Welsh as a subject within the curriculum for every child in Wales. By the year 2001, every child in Wales will have been taught Welsh between the ages of five and sixteen for eleven years. Other 'performance indicators' of the rapid rise of bilingual education in Wales are, first, that Welsh has spread throughout the curriculum such that all subjects in the curriculum can now be taught through the medium of Welsh. There has, secondly, been an exponential rise in the number of examination subjects offered and entered through the medium of Welsh. This revitalization is apparent from Figures 4.1–4.3.

There are variations across Wales and different models of bilingual education both within and across districts. The bilingual education system in Wales must not be seen as uniform. For example, there are some primary schools that use Welsh almost solely as the medium of education. English tends to be taught only as a second language and not used to teach the curriculum. Other schools have a mixture of language-medium teaching, for example, with Welsh being used for humanities and physical education while English is used for sciences and mathematics. Also, within some bilingual schools, particularly at secondary-school level, there can be a variety of provision such that children can elect to take more or less of their education through the medium of Welsh.

This variety of provision within a school is also due to varying community language profiles. In north-west Wales, for example, some communities are thoroughly Welsh-speaking and thus the children attending are Welsh-speaking in the main and take most of their education through the medium of Welsh. In other schools, there is a mixture of first-language Welsh and first-language English children such that a classroom contains both a 'Developmental Maintenance Programme' as well as an 'Immersion Programme' (see Baker and Prys Jones,

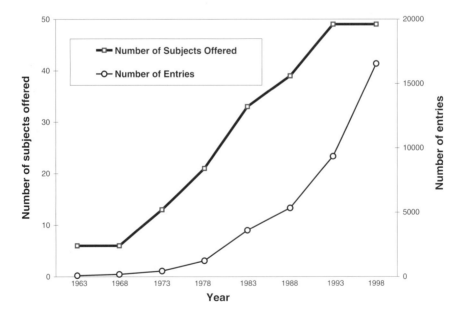

**Figure 4.1. Examinations through the medium of Welsh**

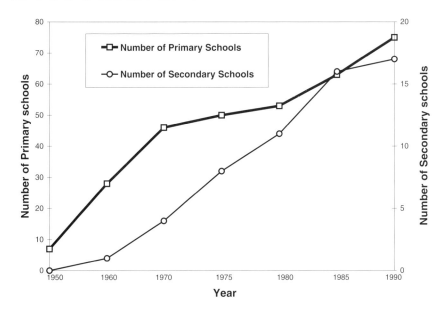

Figure 4.2. The growth of designated bilingual schools

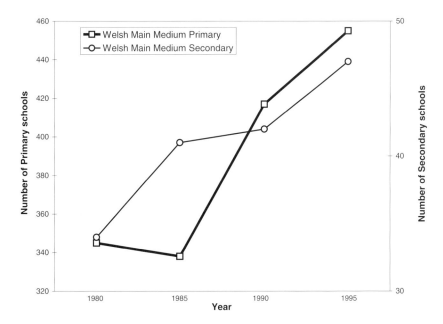

Figure 4.3. The growth of schools where Welsh is used as the main medium of instruction

1998, for an explanation of these international terms to describe different models
of bilingual education).

## EXPLANATIONS OF THE GROWTH IN BILINGUAL EDUCATION IN WALES

Sixty years of growth in bilingual education in Wales, and its current strength and
stability, are due to a complex set of interacting and debated causes. At one level,
language activists working mostly through protests and non-violent action pres-
sured LEAs to institute bilingual schooling. Behind such campaigns there has
been widespread and growing support from parents. The motivation of some
parents was integrative, concerning the production and reproduction of Welsh
language and culture in their young. For six decades, many Welsh-speaking
parents have been enthusiastic that their heritage language be recreated in their
children with considerable help from bilingual education. The pressure for such
bilingual education has also come from non-Welsh-speaking parents. Part of such
parental motivation is integrative, wanting children to belong to a Welsh Wales,
to have the flexibility of speaking two languages and sharing in two cultures.

However, economic motivation and other instrumental motives have been a
major part in the rise of bilingual education in Wales. Many parents perceive
bilingual education as leading to improved employment prospects, and more
chance of promotion and affluence. This reflects a growing language minority
economy. For example, in north-west Wales, most jobs in bureaucracy and
increasingly in the private sector where face-to-face contact with the public is
important (for example, supermarkets, marketing, public relations work) require
fluency in Welsh and English. In an increasing number of jobs in Wales, there is
a requirement for bilingualism and sometimes biliteracy in Welsh and English as
a prerequisite for being considered for employment. This, in turn, places importance on bilingualism attained through bilingual education.

To argue that the economic stick and the Welsh cultural carrot explain the
growth and current strength of bilingual education in Wales would be naïve. A
series of institutional support systems and public pressures have driven and
encouraged bilingual education. Part of the equation for success in bilingual
education in Wales was the quality enhancement role played by Her Majesty's
Inspectors for Education in Wales, local authority advisors and inspectors,
pioneering headteachers and teacher trainers, plus institutions such as the Welsh
Language Board, the Welsh Joint Education Committee (WJEC) and the Schools
Council in Wales and its subsequent transformations. Such institutions produced
Welsh-language curriculum resources and computer software, for example. This
has enabled Welsh-language materials to be available in every subject, for every
age group and for all ability ranges. Sometimes these curriculum resources are
translations of high-quality English language materials. Other times, there are
home-grown products that have shown originality and creativity, reflecting a
Welsh rather than a British curriculum.

Another important part of the success equation of bilingual education in Wales has been the ethos of Welsh-medium schools, both at primary and secondary school level, particularly in the early days when pioneers were enthusiastic for schools to be successful. The commitment and dedication of teachers and pupils in bilingual schools have been strong and marked. Promotion of the Welsh language and culture seemed to evoke increased motivation, commitment and sense of direction. This notion of the importance of school ethos adds an important dimension to bilingual education success. Success is not guaranteed for any form of bilingual education (Baker, 1996). Bilingual education can be ineffective as well as effective. Bilingual education is ultimately dependent for its success on grounded activity in classrooms, interactions between teachers and students, between collaborative and competitive groups of students, and the provision of stimulating and well-structured curriculum resources.

So the conclusion drawn here is that the revitalization of the Welsh language has been in strong part due to the rise of bilingual schools and the legitimization of Welsh as a first or second language in the National Curriculum for all pupils age five to sixteen. After this historical and structural background, this chapter now looks to the future and asks how the quiet revolution in bilingual education in Wales can continue. This is theoretically contextualized within language planning, particularly language acquisition planning. There are two components to language acquisition planning: language transmission in the family and bilingual education. The thesis of the chapter is that language revitalization demands important initiatives in these two areas. Indeed, language acquisition planning is an essential foundation on which status and corpus planning can build. Without language reproduction and production in families and education there is little basis for other forms of language planning.

While the home, family and neighbourhood are crucial domains for language planning, they are not easily accessible to language planners. However, it is daily, informal social interaction which is the lifeblood of a living language. It is in the family that a deep bond of language-based activities is fostered and cherished, shared and refashioned, to create deep personal, social, cultural and linguistic identity. Historically, language planning has preferred to focus on the easier to engineer 'language status' and 'language corpus' options and work with more influenceable and newsworthy institutions rather than the local home, family and neighbourhood. Yet it is the institution of the family that potentially has the highest probability of reproducing and revitalizing a minority language.

## LANGUAGE TRANSMISSION IN THE FAMILY

For any minority language to have a future, parents need to reproduce the language in their children. When analysing the 1991 census data in Wales, Baker and Jones (1999) found that: in 11.6 per cent of households in Wales, both partners speak Welsh; in 5.2 per cent of households in Wales, the husband speaks Welsh and not the wife; and in 6.0 per cent of households in Wales, the wife speaks Welsh and not the husband. This amounts to a total of 22.8 per cent of households where one or more partner potentially could speak Welsh to their children (unless they are childless).

If both parents are Welsh-speaking, there is a 92.0 per cent chance of their child becoming Welsh-speaking. Being a girl slightly increases the chances (92.9 per cent for girls; 91.3 per cent for boys). If the father and not the mother is Welsh-speaking, there is a 48.8 per cent chance of their child becoming Welsh-speaking. Where only the father is Welsh-speaking, 55 per cent of daughters and 43.0 per cent of sons become Welsh-speaking. This gender interaction is marked. If the mother is Welsh-speaking and not the father, there is a 53.5 per cent chance of their child being Welsh-speaking (at home or school). As with fathers, the percentage is much higher for daughters than sons. When only the mother is Welsh-speaking, 48.4 per cent of sons and 58.3 per cent of daughters become Welsh-speaking. When neither parent speaks Welsh, there is still a 12.1 per cent chance that the child will become Welsh-speaking, for example, at Ysgolion Meithrin (Welsh-medium nursery groups), in primary schooling or elsewhere. Again, there is a gender difference here. When neither parent speaks Welsh, 14.5 per cent of daughters become Welsh-speaking compared to 10.0 per cent of sons. However, a caution must be expressed with all the above census statistics. The census data on who is Welsh-speaking or not may be as a result of schooling rather than, or in addition to, family language patterns.

This data, particularly the shortfall in reproducing the Welsh language where both parents are Welsh-speaking, indicates that language revitalization planning needs to locate strategies to persuade more parents to pass on the language to their children. It is not easy to reach parents, nor is it easy to persuade them. However, it seems vital to raise awareness of language issues among parents. Therefore, the Welsh Language Board has recently engaged in two internation-ally innovative language marketing projects to overcome such difficulties. Effective intervention has occurred by:

- providing crucial information about Welsh-language reproduction in the family and the advantages of bilingualism in 'Bounty' packs (packs of free samples and information given via hospitals to new and expectant mothers) across Wales; and

- training midwives and health visitors to provide information about family aspects of bilingualism to parents. This second project is currently operating in Carmarthenshire, with early signs of success.

## LANGUAGE ACQUISITION PLANNING THROUGH PRE-SCHOOL BILINGUAL EDUCATION

By the age of three, only 6.3 per cent of children in Wales can speak Welsh (National Assembly, 1999). To meet a 'level maintenance' target (from 1991 census) of 18.5 per cent, bilingual education has a vital role. Through the voluntary sector (for example, Mudiad Ysgolion Meithrin), the public sector (primary, secondary, further, higher education) and through adult and distance learning, bilingual education has the language revitalization responsibility of increasing the stock of Welsh-speakers from 6.3 per cent to the maintenance target of 18.5 per cent. Not to take on this responsibility would probably leave the language in an increasing perilous state, with language decay and death not impossible.

Figures 4.1–4.3 indicate that bilingual education has structurally grown to shoulder this language revitalization responsibility. To ensure such revitalization, early years education has a vital part to play. The first educational experience outside the home for many children is often a local nursery school, a mother and toddler group or a similar venture. Mudiad Ysgolion Meithrin (the National Association of Welsh-medium Nursery Schools and Playgroups) has played a distinctive and important role in both strengthening the language abilities of children who speak Welsh at home and introducing children from non-Welsh-speaking homes to the Welsh language and enabling them to take their primary schooling through Welsh.

Mudiad Ysgolion Meithrin works with children at a linguistically pliant age. Children at the nursery stage subconsciously acquire rather than learn a language. In early childhood, a language is acquired easily and naturally, spontaneously and almost subconsciously. Without anxiety about making mistakes, young children coincidentally pick up a language while playing. The grounds for acquiring Welsh at an early age are thus sound and secure. State provision and Mudiad Ysgolion Meithrin thus have a crucial role in Welsh-language acquisition in young children, from both Welsh- and English-speaking homes.

### THE EFFECTIVENESS OF MUDIAD YSGOLION MEITHRIN

The geographical spread of Welsh-medium nursery schools can be one part of an appraisal of the effectiveness of this movement in Welsh-language production, and this is now considered. It is acknowledged that any analysis of such effectiveness also involves other dimensions (for example, numbers and frequency of child attendance, quality of learning experiences, language competence on leaving). The geographical distribution of Welsh-medium nursery schools is just one quantitative performance indicator of the effectiveness of this national movement. Other measures of quality of provision, practice and performance are also needed.

The geographical distribution of Welsh-medium nursery schools is given in

Map 4.1 and Figures 4.4–4.6 (data regarding the sites of all Welsh-medium nurs-ery units (*cylchoedd meithrin* and *cylchoedd* Ti a Fi) were kindly provided and checked by Mudiad Ysgolion Meithrin). These show a considerable spread of units with variations in density mostly consonant with (a) population spread (that is, sparsely populated areas have few 'dots' on the map) and (b) Welsh-language strength. Figure 4.4 shows that Gwynedd, Carmarthenshire and Ceredigion have the most *cylchoedd*. The second graph shows the ratio of *cylchoedd* to the general population of under fives in each county. If every child under five in a county is seen as the potential customer of the *cylchoedd*, then availability is shown to be varied in Figure 4.5. Newport stands out as having 1,314 potential children per *cylch*. In Wales as a whole, the average is one *cylch* to every potential 256 children.

Figure 4.6 shows the ratio of *cylchoedd* to the estimated Welsh-speaking popu-lation of under-fives in each district (the estimate is based on 1991 Welsh language census figures). One district, Flintshire, stands out for a possible under-provision of *cylchoedd*. For every potential 139 Welsh-speaking children in Flintshire, there is one *cylch*. This compares to an average in Wales of one *cylch* for every potential fifty Welsh-speaking children (a very favourable overall average). Overall, the figures and the map show a remarkably extensive and intensive coverage of *cylchoedd* throughout Wales. The distribution of *cylchoedd* and the relatively high ratios of *cylchoedd* to densities of population indicate a voluntary movement that makes a major contribution to language production in children of a young age.

However, due to a variety of external factors, the number of *cylchoedd meithrin* and Ti a Fi groups has dropped from 1,041 in 1995 to 956 in 1999. Therefore new initiatives by Mudiad Ysgolion Meithrin are needed, particularly a strong and effective marketing campaign to promote the advantages of acquiring Welsh through this organization, and the development of language targets to monitor the organization's impact on language production in children and therefore its contribution to language revitalization.

To call for initiatives and to make pleas for planning is not enough. To engage in Welsh language revitalization with a clear focus, the Welsh Language Board has set targets for the next five years in all areas of language planning (Welsh Language Board, 1999). A few examples of these targets, relevant to pre-school education, are shared in Table 4.1 for illustrative purposes.

Mudiad Ysgolion Meithrin's provision is limited mainly to part-time educa-tional care provision during the day. Bilingual provision needs to be extended to 'before school' and 'after school' provision and to all-day educational care provi-sion if bilingualism is to be a real choice in the context of education. Therefore, a separate target is set: by December 2002 to have increased by 25 per cent the provision of bilingual educare from a 1999 baseline.

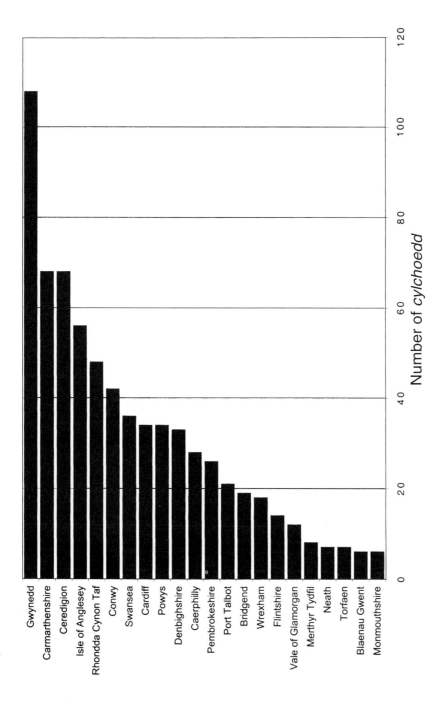

Figure 4.4. The number of *cylchoedd* in each district

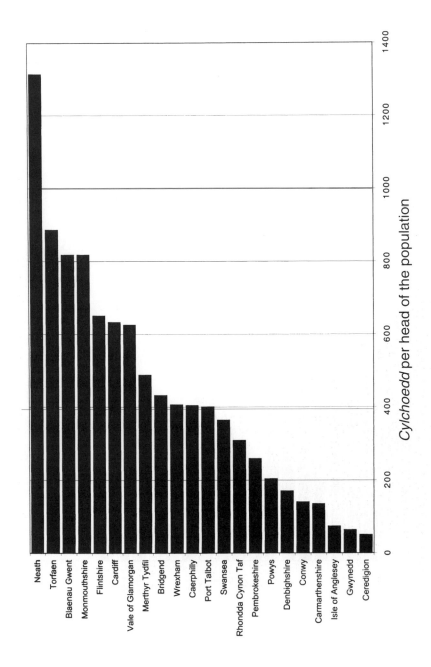

Figure 4.5. Proportion of *cylchoedd* to the size of the population (under age 5)

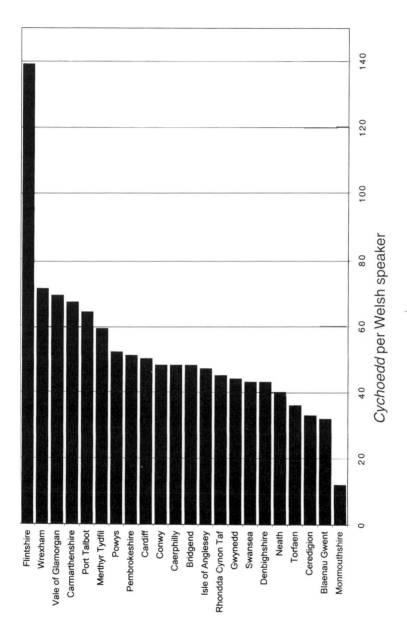

Figure 4.6. Proportion of *cylchoedd* to the size of the Welsh-speaking population (under age 5)

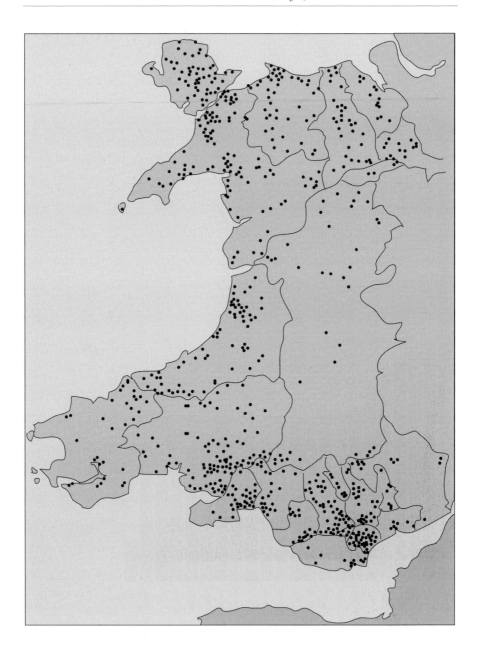

Figure 4.7. Sites of Mudiad Ysgolion Meithrin groups (*cylchoedd*) in Wales

**Table 4.1. Targets for improving Welsh-medium and bilingual pre-school provision**

**B**y March 2000   the Board to have agreed a comprehensive development strategy with Mudiad Ysgolion Meithrin;

By March 2001   to have agreed a strategy for increasing bilingual provision with other providers of pre-school education;

By March 2001   to have established a system of monitoring language growth in all Mudiad Ysgolion Meithrin *cylchoedd*, and all other bilingual providers;

By March 2002   to have increased state provision and the number of *cylchoedd* so that (a) no district has a ratio of less than 100:1 (Welsh-speaking under-5 child population: schools / units / *cylchoedd*) and (b) no district has a ratio of less than 1000:1 (under-5 child population: schools / units / *cylchoedd*);

By March 2005   to have increased the number of parents choosing state or voluntary Welsh-medium nursery education by 10 per cent against a 1999 baseline;

By March 2005   to have increased the number of schools / units / *cylchoedd* providing Welsh-medium education by 5 per cent against a 1999 baseline;

By March 2005   to have increased the number of schools / units /*cylchoedd* including a bilingual provision by 50 per cent against a 1999 baseline;

LANGUAGE ACQUISITION PLANNING THROUGH PRIMARY AND
SECONDARY SCHOOL BILINGUAL EDUCATION

There are currently 446 Welsh-medium or bilingual primary schools out of a Wales total of 1,673 schools (National Assembly, 1999). In the secondary sector, fifty out of a total of 228 schools are defined as Welsh-medium or bilingual schools. However, there is much discontinuity between the two sectors, primary and secondary, in bilingual provision.

*Primary schools*

Every year the National Assembly collects statistics about Welsh education in every primary school. For example, every primary school is required to say where each pupil has acquired Welsh (home or school) and to what degree of fluency. The current statistics (for those aged five to eleven) are as follows (National Assembly, 1999): 6.3 per cent of pupils speak Welsh at home; 9.6 per cent of pupils speak Welsh fluently but not via the home; 30.0 per cent of pupils speak Welsh but not fluently; 54.1 per cent of pupils have little or no fluency in Welsh. The figures show that 15.9 per cent of primary pupils are rated as fluent in Welsh. Of these pupils 60.4 per cent become fluent at Welsh via education (including Ysgolion Meithrin) rather than via the home. Almost one in three remaining pupils speak some Welsh, albeit not fluently.

The current National Assembly (1999) statistics show that 19.9 per cent of pupils are in primary schools where Welsh is the sole, main or part medium of teaching in the class. A further 76.5 per cent of pupils are in Welsh second-language classes. The remainder, 3.6 per cent, are classified as not being taught Welsh. The above figures accord well with pupils being designated as first language or second language at Key Stage 1 (age five to seven) and Key Stage 2 (age seven to eleven).

| Key Stage 1 | Welsh first language | 18.5% |
| Key Stage 1 | Welsh second language | 81.5% |
| Key Stage 2 | Welsh first language | 18.2% |
| Key Stage 2 | Welsh second language | 81.8% |

Generally this set of figures is promising. By the age of eleven almost one in five children in Wales is fluent in Welsh. Primary schools appear to be playing a crucial role in producing many more fluent Welsh speakers than does the home. Through the National Curriculum second-language Welsh curriculum, a large population of second-language Welsh speakers, albeit with different levels of fluency, has been produced. This would seem a firm foundation upon which secondary schools can build. Unfortunately, this turns out to be not the case.

### Secondary schools

In an educational system that is successfully supporting the Welsh language, secondary schools should be taking over from the laudable work of Mudiad Ysgolion Meithrin and Welsh primary schools and including two main Welsh language aims. First, those children fluent in Welsh by the end of primary schooling should have their Welsh extended, enriched and enlivened. Second, the 80 per cent or more pupils who come out of primary schools with second-language Welsh should be moving towards fluency during the five compulsory years of secondary schooling.

In addition to these two aims, there is a need for smooth movement between second-language and first-language Welsh speakers. Instead of having two separate groups, first-language pupils and second-language pupils, it is important to think of a continuum between second-language and first-language Welsh. Pupils should be moving from second-language Welsh to being considered fully bilingual.

As one of their central aims, secondary schools should be building on the firm foundations made in Welsh language acquisition among all pupils. In reality, there is major dysfunction between secondary and primary schooling with regard to the Welsh language. Between 18 and 19 per cent of children leave primary schooling as first-language (or fluent) Welsh speakers. Thereafter, there is decline, as the following figures reveal (National Assembly, 1999).

In Year 7 (the first year of secondary schooling) only 13.7 per cent of pupils are taught Welsh as a first language. In Year 9 (the third year of secondary schooling) only 12.5 per cent of pupils are taught Welsh as a first language. In Year 11 of secondary schooling (the fifth year, GCSE year), only 12.3 per cent of pupils are taught Welsh as a first language (and not all of these are entered for the GCSE examination – see below).

Out of every twenty children in Wales who leave the primary school capable of taking bilingual education at the secondary level, only twelve do so. That is, about 40 per cent of children do not opt for bilingual education at secondary level even though they are capable of such dual-language education. This is confirmed in second-language figures at secondary school: 85.9 per cent of children in Year 7 are taught Welsh as a second language; 85.2 per cent of children in Year 9 are taught Welsh as a second language. The Welsh Joint Education Committee (WJEC) GCSE entries in 1998 reveal an extension of the downward trend in secondary schooling: only 11.5 per cent of children were entered for first-language Welsh in GCSE; only 23.9 per cent of children were entered for Welsh second-language GCSE. In conclusion, primary schools produce more fluent Welsh language speakers than the home, and produce sufficient percentages of pupils fluent in Welsh at least to maintain the language. If children who are taught Welsh as a second language at primary school are included, then the Welsh language would seem to be moving beyond maintenance towards revitalization.

However, in the secondary school, around 40 per cent of children in Wales move from the first-language to the second-language Welsh category. Thus, the Welsh language is not being sufficiently strengthened and supported by secondary schooling. Indeed, there is evidence that the structures and systems in place (and not teachers or the curriculum) are not extending the preparatory work of Mudiad Ysgolion Meithrin and Welsh primary schools. Such discontinuity between primary and secondary schooling is present in almost all the districts of Wales, although there are some regional variations (see Welsh Language Board, 1999).

The issue of continuity highlights the need for a continuum of language rather than the simple categorization of Welsh first-language and Welsh second-language, particularly as all children in Wales are taught Welsh between the ages of five and sixteen. In between those who are fully fluent and those who are incipient bilinguals, there is a wide range of different levels of fluency. Hence, there is a need to abandon a simple first-language and second-language categorization. The idea of a continuum of proficiency in Welsh is a less static concept, fostering the idea of progression and improvement for all pupils. This idea of a continuum also makes it more rational for children who become fluent in Welsh to move to bilingual education rather than be placed in second-language Welsh classes. If the assessment of proficiency in Welsh was connected to a continuum, the movement of children from first-language Welsh classes in primary school to second-language Welsh classes in secondary school would certainly decrease.

*Further education*

Discontinuity in bilingual education extends to the further education (FE) and higher education (HE) sectors. Indeed, as this section will reveal, there is a

considerable dysfunction at the further and higher education levels where relatively minimal Welsh-medium provision occurs.

Until the mid-1980s, very little Welsh-medium/bilingual provision was
provided in the FE colleges of Wales. What provision existed was primarily
focused around the following areas: business, secretarial work and care/nursery
education, all of which were situated in Bangor, Wrexham and Ammanford. In
1986, the Manpower Services Commission established a project situated in the
WJEC with the aim of promoting bilingualism in FE until 1990.

During this period, and resulting from this project, a significant increase was
seen in the provision within colleges and a number of colleges which had not
previously offered bilingual courses began to do so. When the project ceased to
operate, no central co-ordination of colleges' work occurred, and from 1993
onwards there was a decline in bilingual provision across Wales, even though
some colleges such as Coleg Menai and Coleg Meirion-Dwyfor increased their
provision. Many colleges which had previously aimed to offer a wide range of
courses were by then only offering one or two bilingual/Welsh-medium courses.

Following the reorganization of FE in the 1992 Act, funding became dependent on the number of students enrolled on bilingual courses and more importantly the numbers being terminally assessed through the medium of Welsh.
This Welsh-medium provision was funded with a 0.3 secondary weighting over
and above the basic formula. However, such extra funding did not increase, in a
stable manner, the number of Welsh-medium courses or students taking bilingual courses.

The Welsh Language Board has placed considerable emphasis on further
education in the last few years. It has stressed that support must be awarded to
this sector in order to assist employers to operate within the 1993 Welsh
Language Act so as to offer bilingual services to customers. In order to achieve
this, an effective bilingual workforce must be secured and the board has emphasized in its discussion with FE/HE colleges the need to foster bilingual skills in
vocational education. The board has deliberately avoided over-emphasis on
solely Welsh-medium courses and stressed bilingual courses instead, since there
is a clearly acknowledged need for a bilingual workforce in Wales.

The figures in Tables 4.2 and 4.3 for further and higher education have been
accumulated from different sources and must be regarded as provisional, but
were the best available when the chapter was written. Table 4.2 indicates the
percentage of students formally assessed in Welsh in further education colleges
in Wales in 1996/7. The average in Wales is 2.31 per cent compared with 5.7 per
cent of GCSE examination entries through the medium of Welsh. Coleg Meirion-
Dwyfor (70 per cent), Coleg Llysfasi (41.56 per cent), Coleg Harlech (22.56 per
cent) and Coleg Menai (10.88 per cent) are the four colleges with over 10 per cent
of students assessed in Welsh. It is notable that the overall percentage had
dropped from 2.92 per cent in 1996/7 to 2.31 per cent in 1997/8. This represents
a drop in Welsh-medium assessments of 21 per cent.

Table 4.2. **Further education: students assessed in Welsh (1997/8)**

|  | No. of students formally assessed in Welsh | Welsh-medium assessment as % of enrolments |
|---|---|---|
| Aberdare College | 0 | 0.00 |
| Afan College | 0 | 0.00 |
| Barry College | 0 | 0.00 |
| Bridgend College | 12 | 0.15 |
| CCTA | 231 | 1.91 |
| Coleg Ceredigion | 36 | 1.65 |
| Deeside College | 66 | 0.83 |
| Coleg Glan Hafren | 0 | 0.00 |
| Gorseinon College | 0 | 0.00 |
| Gwent Tertiary College | 0 | 0.00 |
| Coleg Harlech | 6 | 22.56 |
| Coleg Llandrillo | 31 | 0.24 |
| Coleg Llysfasi | 830 | 41.56 |
| Coleg Meirion-Dwyfor | 1,697 | 70.00 |
| Coleg Menai | 1,081 | 10.88 |
| Merthyr Tydfil College | 0 | 0.00 |
| Neath College | 302 | 2.91 |
| Pembrokeshire College | 0 | 0.00 |
| Pencoed College | 0 | 0.00 |
| Pontypridd College | 13 | 0.16 |
| Coleg Powys | 30 | 0.59 |
| St David's 6th Form College | 0 | 0.00 |
| Swansea College | 0 | 0.00 |
| Welsh College of Horticulture | 30 | 1.79 |
| WEA (North) | 19 | 1.14 |
| WEA (South) | 0 | 0.00 |
| Yale College | 22 | 0.22 |
| YMCA | 8 | 1.41 |
| Ystrad Mynach College | 0 | 0.00 |
| UW Aberystwyth (FE Rural Studies) | 5 | 0.55 |
| Totals (1997/8) | 4,419 | 2.31 |
| Totals (1996/7) | 5,530 | 2.92 |

## *Higher education*

Since the 1950s, the University of Wales has been under pressure to establish a Welsh-medium college within the university. Rather than undertaking this course of action, the university decided to fund a number of lecturing posts in its colleges which would be specifically for teaching through the medium of Welsh. Over the years a total of some thirty-eight of these lecturers were appointed, mainly in Aberystwyth and Bangor, and their work was to teach subjects other

Table 4.3. Higher education: Welsh-medium provision in Wales (1996/7)

| Institution | Welsh-medium (fte) | % of students (fte) on Welsh-medium courses |
|---|---|---|
| University of Wales Institute, Cardiff | 70.6 | 1.2 |
| Trinity College, Carmarthen | 290.0 | 18.4 |
| University of Wales, Lampeter | 0.0 | 0.0 |
| University of Wales, Aberystwyth | 156.2 | 2.4 |
| University of Wales, Bangor | 410.9 | 6.2 |
| University of Wales, Cardiff | 0.1 | 0.0 |
| University of Wales, Swansea | 7.3 | 0.0 |
| University of Glamorgan | 0.0 | 0.0 |
| University of Wales, College of Medicine | 0 | 0.0 |
| University of Wales College, Newport | 0 | 0.0 |
| North East Wales Institute | 0 | 0.0 |
| Swansea Institute of Higher Education | 0 | 0.0 |
| Welsh College of Music and Drama | 0 | 0.0 |
| Totals | 935.1 | 1.6 |

The figures concern those students taking HE (and not FE) courses through the medium of Welsh and are based on HEFCW tables. (fte = full time equivalent)

than Welsh through the medium of Welsh. In 1993 a report was published by a committee chaired by Dr Brynley Roberts and this report set a new agenda in terms of funding methodologies, whilst at the same time retaining the general direction of provision.

A premium has recently been paid to HE establishments for increasing their Welsh-medium provision. In real terms, however, there has been little progress to date, since only two establishments have been able to demonstrate an increase in provision since 1995/6 (the first year in which the funding formula commenced), namely the University of Wales, Bangor and Trinity College. As well as the premium, a Development Fund was set up which earmarked £100,000 per year for five years in order to sponsor specific projects.

In 1980 the University Board for Welsh Medium Teaching was established. This board's remit was to decide how best to spend the extra funding provided for Welsh-medium teaching. When the HEFCW was founded in 1992, much of this board's power in making funding decisions discontinued. Following a period of discussion on ways to progress and regarding which colleges should be represented on the new board, it was relaunched in 1997 and now represents not only the University of Wales but also the University of Glamorgan and other HE colleges in Wales. Encouraging signs of the new board's proactive intentions are apparent (Welsh Funding Councils, 1999).

Table 4.3 indicates the percentage of students taking part or all of their courses through the medium of Welsh in higher education establishments in Wales in

1996/7 (more recent detailed figures were not available). The percentage of HE students in Wales following Welsh-medium courses (in part or in full) is 1.6 per cent. This figure includes a numerator that is based on all students, including those who come from outside Wales for their higher education. In 1995/6, 56.5 per cent of students from Wales stayed in Wales for higher education; 42.3 per cent attended universities in England; 1.2 per cent went to Scotland. Of all students in higher education in Wales in 1995/6, against a 1.5 per cent figure of students who were in Welsh-medium education: 54.3 per cent of all students were from Wales; 32.6 per cent were from England; 1.3 per cent were from the rest of the UK; 5.9 per cent came from European countries; and similarly 5.9 per cent came from non-European countries.

CONCLUSION

This chapter has portrayed a promising start to Welsh-language maintenance in nursery and primary schooling. Support for the Welsh language in secondary, further and higher education is not so strong. If the analogy will stand, Welsh-language education is like a house built on a partial foundation of a combination of home language reproduction and Mudiad Ysgolion Meithrin provision. The primary school securely reinforces and extends the foundations laid, building year by year to a first floor that is significant and substantial. The second floor is varied with some parts successfully heightening first-level provision and potential. There are also sizeable sections where second-level provision fails to build on first-level potential. The third floor is small and sparse, short and skimpy.

Since the 1950s, a reformation has occurred in education in Wales, giving equality of language opportunity to many parents and many children in many areas. The momentum of that reformation needs to be continued in affirmative action on the *continuity* issue. If the momentum in Welsh-medium education is to be maintained, the issue of continuity becomes crucial and critical. But continuity is just one issue in ensuring that language revitalization through bilingual education continues to grow in Wales. New strategies are needed, for example establishing a *continuum* from early language learning to full fluency, and to move from the current separation of Welsh first- and second-language lessons and Welsh-medium content teaching to establish a *concurrent* use of both languages in teaching and learning contexts; evolving a bilingual approach in classrooms rather than language separation.

The Welsh Language Board's document 'The Welsh Language: A Vision and Mission for 2000–2005' (1999: see above Chapter 3, Appendix A) provides a comprehensive scenario for such language revitalization to occur, through status, corpus, usage and acquisition language planning. This document regards bilingual education as having a central place in revitalization efforts. Through targets in all of these language planning areas, it seeks at policy and provision levels to set the agenda for Welsh language revival. It is important that a bilingual education and training strategy for Wales has clear targets that reflect priorities, time scales, ownership of responsibility, with well-mapped routes containing clear destinations and evidence for arrival at those destinations. The needs of employers, students and communities in Wales need to be reflected in such target setting.

Yet the quiet revolution in bilingual education also needs to revisit the roots of educational policy-making and planning. Rarely have the aims of bilingual education in Wales been discussed and agreed. The vision and mission of bilingual education has been latent, assumed and almost never centrally defined or defended. There has been local provision rather than central policy; school practice rather than political decisions. This has meant that the Welsh-medium sector has developed in an *ad hoc* manner. LEAs have developed their own policies and patterns of provision and even the terms used to describe these schools vary from district to district. The bilingual education journey in Wales has been undertaken without sight of clear or agreed destinations. There is now a need to bring bilingual education into mainstream provision and to agree a strategic plan for the development of a linguistically integrated education and training system in Wales. A National Assembly in charge of education in all sectors makes a strategic plan for bilingual education possible.

Therefore, this chapter concludes by suggesting that, at the start of a new political era in Wales, there is a need to clarify the aim of the bilingual education journey and the destination we aim to reach. The Welsh Language Board has offered the following to focus and clarify language planning via bilingual education in Wales. It issues a challenge to move towards a society in Wales where bilingualism is the norm, and this can be partly engineered through bilingual education.

For all children, the essential aims of bilingual education in Wales should be:

- to develop communicative fluency in the Welsh and English languages;
- to develop biliteracy in the Welsh and English languages;
- to become multicultural and increasingly multilingual;
- to have entitlement to an equal access to the potential economic and employment benefits of bilingualism.

For language revitalization in Wales, that is the first and immediate challenge.

## References

Baker, C. (1996). *Foundations of Bilingual Education and Bilingualism*, 2nd edn., Clevedon, Avon: Multilingual Matters.

Baker, C. and Jones, S. P. (1998). *Encyclopedia of Bilingualism and Bilingual Education*, Clevedon, Avon: Multilingual Matters.

Baker, C. and Jones, M. P. (1999). *Continuity in Welsh Language Education*, Cardiff: Welsh Language Board.

National Assembly (1999). *Statistics of Education and Training in Wales: Schools 1999*, Cardiff: Welsh Office.

Welsh Funding Councils (1999). *Further and Higher Education and Training Statistics in Wales: 1997/98*, Cardiff: Welsh Office.

Welsh Language Board (1999). *The Welsh Language: A Vision and Mission for 2000–2005*, Cardiff: Welsh Language Board.

# 5

# Reactive Policy and Piecemeal Planning: Welsh-medium Education in Cardiff

## GLYN E. JONES AND COLIN H. WILLIAMS

## INTRODUCTION

Education has long been recognized as the principal socialization agency of advanced societies within modernizing states. The right to be taught in one's mother tongue, home or preferred language is often born in struggle and realized as an expression of personal human freedom. Bilingual education is not a natural government-planned service. It is nearly always a struggle between a beleaguered minority and a hegemonic state majority. Consequently the Cardiff case-study presented here is not *sui generis*; it forms part of a much larger struggle, namely the construction of a Welsh society within a British and international context. Ostensibly driven by a concern to maintain both a unique culture and a national language, the development of bilingual education in the capital city may also be interpreted in terms of a socio-political agenda to realize a more inclusive, democratic and plural basis for society. Tension and social conflict often accompany initial attempts at establishing a bilingual educational system, especially if the rationale of the reform is to compensate for the previously discriminatory experience suffered by a particular section of society within the state educational system.

When bilingual schools were established in Wales in the post-war years they were criticized for being linguistically and educationally divisive and were accused of serving the interests of a small cultural nationalist élite. These charges were predictable on two grounds. First, such schools ran counter to the educational status quo and were an intrusive and additional element within the educational system. Secondly, the most vociferous champions of Welsh-medium schools were key figures within the Welsh-speaking intelligentsia, often, but not necessarily, adherents of Plaid Cymru.

However, as we shall see, this has also occasioned internal divisions as parents and other interest groups have sought to resist the demands of the assertive minority to have their linguistic preferences normalized within the state's educational system. Although echoes of charges of being élitist and politically partial are still heard, the success of bilingual schools and the consequent socio-political changes within the attitudes of many sections of society has been such that bilingual schools are now championed as models of good educational practice and as significant locales in preparing citizens to participate fully within a bilingual democracy and a multicultural European Union. The arguments rehearsed in the introduction to this volume suggest that social context, family language transmission and community life are less powerful agencies of language reproduction than was true in the past. This implies that bilingual education, for both children and adults, will become far more salient and if this is true for Wales in general, it is even more true for its capital, Cardiff.

## A RELEVANT CURRICULUM FOR WALES?

For the majority of the modern period Welsh education was planned in tandem with educational provision for England, but over the last thirty years a separate and distinct Welsh system has evolved. The main currents of educational reform are summarized in Figure 5.1 which charts both those features which were held in common between England and Wales and those which contributed to a separate Welsh character. The process may be divided into three periods: 1944–64 which saw the evolution of two types of curriculum; 1964–88 which saw a swing towards a teachers' informed curriculum; and the post-1988 period where both London and Cardiff sought to develop separate national curricula for England and Wales respectively.

In many respects, the new institutionalization of Welsh consequent to the recent reforms described in Chapter 1 promises to influence attitudes and behaviour patterns in a more constructive manner. The past decade has seen a more accommodating reaction on behalf of unilingual English speakers and this bodes well for the future extension of services which seek to convince them that they also may benefit from sharing a bicultural community.

The school's role in promoting a bilingual society has increased following the reforms of the 1988 Education Act, which identified Welsh as a core subject in the National Curriculum. Welsh-medium education across the curriculum now includes maths and science, technology and computing, in addition to the conventional humanities and social science subjects.

We saw in Chapters 2 and 3 that Welsh-medium education underwent a profound change in the period 1980–99. In the decade 1990–9 the proportion and number of pupils in Welsh-medium primary and secondary schools grew very slowly. Consequently, it is within the dominant, conventional English-medium sector where the greatest impact of educational reforms have been realized. For example, in 1990, 50.7 per cent (870) of schools had classes where Welsh was taught as a second language only. By 1999 this proportion had risen to 67.6 per cent (1,136). Most of the increase was due to the curriculum impact of the 1988 Education Act and the social effects of the Welsh Language Act 1993, which in effect abolished Category D schools. While in 1990 14.2 per cent (244) of primary

| England/Wales | | Wales |
|---|---|---|
| | *1944–64 Two types of curriculum* | |
| Butler Education Act | 1944 | |
| SeC Schools Exam Council | 1946 | 147 grammar/24 technical/127 secondary modern |
| | | Ysgol Gymraeg Llanelli |
| | 1948 | CBAG. Welsh Joint Education Committee |
| GCE O Level (16+) | 1950 | |
| 3.2% | 1952 | Ysgol Gymraeg Y Barri |
| | 1954 | WYEC textbook scheme |
| | 1956 | Ysgol Glan Clwyd |
| Finance Act | 1958 | |
| (extending LEA powers) | 1960 | 35% grammar/35% modern/12% comprehensive |
| Education Act | 1962 | Ysgol Uwchradd Rhydfelen |
| | *1963–86 The teacher's curriculum* | |
| School Council | 1964 | Secretary of State for Wales |
| Circular 10/65; CSE exam | 1966 | The Welsh committee of the Schools Council |
| 5% GDP | 1968 | The Gittins Report |
| Plowden Report | | |
| Black Papers | 1970 | Education transferred to Welsh Office |
| | 1972 | Mudiad Ysgolion Meithrin (Nursery) |
| APU | 1974 | Local Government Reform |
| Callaghan's Great Debate | 1976 | |
| Curriculum 11–16 (HMI) | 1978 | |
| Framework for the School | 1980 | 97% Comprehensive Schools |
| Curriculum | | Welsh grants from section 21 |
| (DES) | 1984 | Development Committee of the schools curriculum |
| SCDC; SEC | | |
| GCSE exam | 1986 | PDAG |
| | *1988–99 The centre rules – which centre?* | |
| National Curriculum; NCC, SEAC | 1988 | The Curriculum Council of Wales |
| LMS; direct grant schools | 1990 | History/Welsh Committees |
| 3.3% GDP | 1992 | Geography/Arts/Music |
| | | 6 Direct Grant Schools |
| SCAA | 1994 | Schools Examination and Assessment Authority |
| Constitutional Reform | 1997 | Government Wales Act |
| Devolution in UK | 1999 | National Assembly for Wales |
| | | Welsh core subject in all schools |

*Source*: PDAG (1992); Williams (1994) with recent revisions and additions.

**Figure 5.1. A relevant curriculum for Wales?**

schools were not obliged to teach any Welsh, by 1997 only one school was exempted from this statutory requirement.

That the position of Welsh-medium education has been strengthened is a significant development in its own right. However, there has been a corresponding shift in the proportions of all pupils now exposed to the indigenous language, literature and culture of Wales. Some of these go on to be very active participants within Welsh-medium networks and public life. The vast majority do not, but because they have had such a long-term exposure to formal education through Welsh, the suspicion and tension of previous generations, which surrounded the use of Welsh as a language of the minority, has gradually subsided. The general effect of this is recorded in much more positive attitudes towards bilingualism and the construction of a bilingual society *per se*. However, beneath this positive trend there remains for many a grumbling doubt as to the real worth of bilingualism, for it is argued that once pupils have left the confines of the school classroom there is little economic and instrumental justification for maintaining fluency in Welsh. Time will tell as to whether this judgement can still be made after the current period of institutional bilingualism has had its full impact.

A continued uncertainty is the relationship between the Schools Funding Council for Wales and the local education authorities (LEAs). It has been described as an unbalanced partnership, reflecting the emasculated role of local government during the Conservative administrations of Margaret Thatcher and John Major (1979–97). LEAs have acted increasingly as intermediate agencies, processing government initiatives in, for example, training and in dispensing formula funding to individual schools. In comparison with England, very few schools in Wales have chosen to opt out. Within the context of bilingual education this has been a positive trend, for so much of the good practice in bilingual education has its origins at the local authority level, often developing county-wide infrastructures. As we shall see in relation to the development of Cardiff's bilingual education policy, under the LEA formula an element of increased power has been transferred to individual schools and to local communities. Should the institutionalization of Welsh continue apace, then both the educational reforms, and the 'free market' philosophy which drives them, could benefit the Welsh language and culture, because of a number of complex and unpredictable trends relating to the implications of the Welsh Language Act 1993 and the establishment of the National Assembly for Wales in 1999.

As the trend towards sending children from non-Welsh-speaking homes to Welsh-medium schools is increasing, there is a real possibility that within the next generation bilingual citizens in Wales will be advantaged and monolingual citizens will feel at a relative disadvantage – the opposite of what has hitherto been the norm. Because language-related considerations have periodically been a feature of political mobilization in Wales, it is likely that in future there will be increased agitation and mobilization of the needs of the monoglot English inhabitants in terms of identity formation, educational opportunities and access to certain types of employment and representation. There is a social tension between those who claim that the Welsh language has been rendered politically neutral and therefore acceptable, and others who argue that this is a smoke screen, despite rapid advances in the status of Welsh, for the struggle between Welsh and English remains at a more subtle level and needs investigating.

The absence of national, time-series educational data, as we saw in Chapter 2, makes both inferential reasoning and educational planning very difficult and hazardous at times. We need to assess and research the concerns and involvement of second-language learners and non-Welsh speakers in a more systematic fashion, thereby extending the bicultural nature of society from both ends of the spectrum. In view of the foregoing, it is clear that there are fundamental differences between the development of Welsh-medium educational provision within various parts of Wales. As noted earlier, most of the worthwhile advances in the promotion of bilingual education were achieved in the absence of any sophisticated planning and all too often in the face of intense opposition to the very notion of normalizing Welsh within the educational system.

The history of Welsh-medium education in greater Cardiff represents a fascinating illustration of the determination of a well-organized parental pressure group to develop a separate but equal Welsh-medium school system in the face of an intransigent local education authority. We offer it as a detailed cameo of language revitalization in action where official policy evolved from practice to strategy.

## WELSH-MEDIUM EDUCATION IN CARDIFF: A CASE-STUDY 1939–1981

The last two decades of the nineteenth century saw the emergence of Cardiff as the metropolis of Wales.[1] It was a period of rapidly expanding commercial activity for it as a major world port exporting the coal and iron from the industrialized hinterland of the south Wales valleys; of a growing population – which increased from 82,761 in 1881 to 164,330 in 1901; of the founding and erecting of civic and commercial buildings such as the Central Library (1882), the Coal Exchange (1883–6), the Customs House (1898), the Pier Head Building (1896), as well as two new hospitals and two theatres. This period also saw the location in Cardiff of major national institutions such as the University of South Wales and Monmouthshire in 1883, one of the constituent colleges of the University of Wales, the Baptist College of South Wales (1874) and, in the first decade of the twentieth century, the National Museum of Wales. Nothing epitomizes the sense of well-being and civic pride better than the magnificent civic centre, built between 1901 and 1910 (Hilling, 1975a: 194–6), which includes the City Hall, the National Museum of Wales, the Law Courts and the main building of the University, all in glistening white Portland stone – in stark contrast to its industrial hinterland to which it owed its prosperity.

Cardiff was characterized by a substantial Welsh-speaking element at the turn of the nineteenth century which became more anglicized as the population grew

(Thomas, 1998: 177–8). There were considerable numbers of Welsh speakers included in the in-migration to Cardiff and the 1891 census shows that there were over 12,000 Welsh speakers within the borough of Cardiff itself and some 3,080 in the surrounding parishes (Thomas, 1998: 191–2). Many of these incoming Welsh speakers undoubtedly shared in the economic prosperity of the town, especially in the professions and in business: they were referred to by one prominent commentator of the 1930s as 'gwyr y fodrwy aur' (Jenkins, 1968: 247, 'the men with the gold ring', that is, the wealthy businessmen, the lawyers, doctors, administrators and academics – not the unskilled manual dockside labourers, shop assistants and women in service). Within this group were a number who took pride in being Welsh and in speaking Welsh and it was these who founded Cymdeithas Cymmrodorion Caerdydd (the Cardiff Cymmrodorion Society), of which more later, in 1885 (J. G. Jones, 1987). By 1909, this society had a membership of 1,250 and they were very much perceived as a Welsh intelligentsia (Evans, 1984/5: 381).

To provide for the spiritual needs of the Welsh-speaking population, numerous places of worship were being relocated/rebuilt and enlarged or newly established during the nineteenth century: Seion (1810, relocated in 1827, and in 1878 as Pembroke Terrace), Tabernacl (1821), Ebeneser (1826), Salem (1856), Bethania (1856), Libanus (1868), Jerusalem (1892), Minny Street (1884), Horeb (1884, relocated in Heol-y-Crwys, 1900) (J. G. Jones, 1984: 24–42).

However, despite the social and economic success of many of the Cardiff Welsh, they failed to make an impact as a group of Welsh speakers, as one astute commentator in the latter half of the nineteenth century noted: 'Y maent yn lluosog o ran nifer, ac yn ddylanwadol yn fynych fel personau unigol; ond nid ydynt, fel corff o bobl, yn meddu dylanwad cyfatebol i'w rhif a'u pwys personol' ('They are large in number, and frequently influential as individuals; but as a body, they possess no influence proportional to their numbers and personal weight': Dan Isaac Davies, in Thomas, 1998: 186). The Welsh language also fared less well. Despite the apparently thriving Welsh chapels there was some disquiet concerning their future from a linguistic point of view. When the matter of the relocation in 1878 of Seion, the Welsh Presbyterian Church, was discussed, some members expressed doubts as to its future survival as a Welsh church (J. G. Jones 1984: 26). In 1886, Undeb Ysgolion Sul Cymraeg Caerdydd (Association of Cardiff Welsh Sunday Schools) was established to foster the use of Welsh and parents were urged to maintain their use of Welsh in the home (Evans, 1984/5: 377; Walters, 1966/7: 21–2). By 1910, the minister of the Pembroke Terrace, alarmed at the weak grasp of Welsh among the younger members of his congregation, began to conduct language classes, a practice followed by the minister of another church (Crwys Road) in 1913, who wrote to his congregation: 'Hyderwn y bydd i holl bennau teuluoedd yr eglwys gefnogi y dosbarthiadau Cymraeg drwy anfon y plant iddynt a thrwy siarad Cymraeg gartref' ('We hope that all the heads of families of the church will support the Welsh classes by sending their children to them and by speaking Welsh at home'). The final comment in the message is significant – it indicates that one of the major features of language shift was ongoing – that is, parents were failing to pass the language on to their children. This fact is confirmed by the comment made by the minister of Ebeneser, another Welsh chapel, in 1929 that: 'mae mwyafrif mawr ein plant yn cael ei magu'n Saeson uniaith, gyda'r canlyniad eu bod yn tyfu i fyny heb ddi-ddordeb mewn pethau Cymraeg' ('the great majority of our children are being brought up as monoglot English, with the consequence that they are growing up with no interest in things Welsh': J. G. Jones, 1984: 57). The decline of Welsh in the population of Cardiff during this period is clearly reflected in the census returns: in 1901, 8.1 per cent spoke Welsh; 1911, 6.7 per cent; 1921, 5 per cent; 1931, 5.1 per cent.

In the early 1930s, Cardiff did not escape the ravages of the economic depression that afflicted the rest of Britain. As a consequence of the Depression, cuts in public spending led to cuts in education and many prospective young teachers, graduates among them, found themselves facing a period of unemployment, and those who desired to remain in Wales, and in Cardiff in particular, in the words of one of their contemporaries:

> now scrambled for posts in elementary schools if we wished to stay in Wales. Cardiff availed itself of the opportunity to recruit graduates to staff elementary schools, and particularly to its peripatetic Welsh staff. As a result the city received what was probably its greatest single infusion of Welsh life and influence since the Act of Union.[2]

Ignoring this final extravagant claim, there was undoubtedly a group of committed Welsh speakers in the city who, together with other influential individuals on the staff of institutions such as the University and the National Museum as well as the ministers of the Welsh chapels, formed a close-knit group committed to the well-being of the Welsh language. These individuals had a distinct language-dominated network centred on the Welsh chapels and on Tŷ'r Cymry, a house given as a centre for Welsh speakers to meet and to socialize. These younger Welsh speakers disassociated themselves from the Cymmrodorion Welsh whom they regarded as snobbish and anglicized (Jenkins, 1968: 250).[3] Some of them formed themselves into a group known as Cylch Dewi: 'Cwmni bychan anghyoedd a geisiai wneud rhywbeth i "ddiogelu'r diwylliant Cymraeg"' ('A small private group who sought to do something to safeguard the Welsh culture': Jenkins, 1968: 251). They published a series of pamphlets (Pamffledi Cylch Dewi) on topics relating to the teaching of Welsh in schools. It was from such a group of individuals that the impetus to establish a Welsh-medium school in Cardiff came between 1939 and 1949, when the first Welsh-medium school was eventually opened in Cardiff.

Welsh had been taught as a subject in primary schools in Cardiff since at least the 1880s. Through pressure brought upon the School Board from the Cymmrodorion Society, the teaching of Welsh was extended in the primary schools in 1888 and 1889 (J. G. Jones, 1987: 13). An 1897 survey of 6,000 parents eliciting their views as to the teaching of Welsh to their children showed that 81 per cent of them were in favour (Aitchison and Carter, 1988: 3). Two surveys of parents' views on the teaching of Welsh conducted in 1901 did show that they were mostly against compulsion, nevertheless the School Board decided in 1901 that Welsh was to be taught in every school. However, lack of teachers of Welsh and a hostile profession caused problems (Evans, 1984/5: 378). In 1905, Welsh was made compulsory in Standard 1 but pressure to make Welsh optional grew, with strong opposition from the Chamber of Commerce and from a group who called themselves the British League; their views carried the day and Welsh was made optional in 1907 (Evans, 1984/5: 379).[4] This was the status of Welsh in the educational system and instruction in the language was provided by a team of peripatetic teachers whose numbers had risen from ten in 1908 to thirty-nine by 1948.

In 1939, a small group of Welsh-speaking parents in Cardiff under the leadership of Gwyn Daniel, one of those committed Welsh speakers who was a teacher in Cardiff, decided to set up a private Welsh-medium school and locate it in Tŷ'r Cymry, the cultural centre referred to above.[5] Gwyn Daniel sought the backing of the influential cultural movement Urdd Gobaith Cymru (Welsh League of Youth, founded in 1926), and of various other influential figures in Welsh life who were asked to covenant subscriptions for a period of seven years.[6] Among those to whom the appeal was sent was the then Lord Mayor of Cardiff, a step that was to prove most effective. In his reply to Gwyn Daniel, the Mayor recommended that the matter of establishing a Welsh-medium school in the city should be put before the Cardiff Education Committee, and he provided very good reasons why:

> I think it a pity that it should not be put before the Education Committee for consideration. I should imagine that with the support of the Education Committee, the permanence of such a class or classes would be assured, and this would also avoid what would, in all probability, be a great problem for you, and that is the finding of sufficient money to maintain this class or school over a period of years. (Archive)

The Mayor was clearly very supportive of the whole idea of the Welsh school and concluded his letter with the words:

> I would be very pleased to interest myself in this matter should you decide to ask the Education Committee to help you. I feel, as a member of the Local Authority, that this step should first be taken before you come to a definite decision to undertake a class at Tŷ'r Cymry. (Archive)

The Mayor followed this reply with another letter (27 March 1940, this time in Welsh) in which he stated that he had consulted with the Director of Education. In the letter he suggested that a deputation of supporters of the campaign for a Welsh school should arrange to meet with him, the Mayor, and some members of the Education Committee to discuss the matter. The Mayor again reiterated the importance of securing the support of the Education Committee, pointing out: 'Cofiwch pe bai eich antur yn fethiant fe gollai eich apel [*sic*] lawer o'i rym yn y dyfodol' ('Remember if your venture were to fail your appeal would lose much of its power in the future': Archive).

The deputation duly met with the Director of Education and he responded that if he could have the names of thirty children, he would be prepared to set up a class for them as a unit within an existing school which would have the opportunity to develop into a Welsh-medium school. This was 1940, however: the Second World War had broken out and, due to air attacks on Cardiff, children had to be evacuated from the city and the whole matter went no further (*Braslun*).

Some three years later, however, the same group of parents set up a voluntary Welsh school to meet on Saturday mornings in Tŷ'r Cymry – Ysgol Fore Sadwrn (Saturday Morning School). The minutes (*cofnodion*) of the school are held in the UCAC archive (see Acknowledgements below) and will be referred to as *Cofnodion*. The minutes of the first formal meeting of the convenors of the school state clearly that the aim and purpose of the school was: 'i fod yn gymdeithas o Gymry bach a siaradai Gymraeg â'i gilydd ac a chwaraeai a'i [*sic*] gilydd yn Gymraeg' ('to be a society of little children who speak Welsh with one another and who play with one another in Welsh': *Cofnodion*). These words mirror exactly in sentiment those used by Fishman with his call of the need for minority speakers to create for themselves 'concentrated space where Xish can be on its own turf, predominant and unharassed' (Fishman, 1991: 58). The school did not preclude the eventual admission of children who could understand yet not speak Welsh, but initially the rule that the children admitted must be able to speak Welsh was to be rigorously applied:

> rhaid i bob plentyn ar gychwyn y sefydliad ac am gyfnod beth bynnag wedyn, fod yn medru siarad Cymraeg. Cedwir at y rheol hon hefyd nes bo'r Pwyllgor yn sicr fod aelodau cyntaf yr ysgol wedi ymgynefino digon â'i gilydd, a bod y Gymraeg yn iaith naturiol eu hymgom, y pryd hynny yn unig y gellir mentro ar dderbyn aelod neu nifer bach o aelodau a ddeall y Gymraeg, ond heb ei siarad. (*Cofnodion*)

> [at the outset and at least for a period afterwards, each child must be able to speak Welsh. This rule will also be adhered to until the Committee is certain that the first pupils of the school have become sufficiently familiar with one another and that Welsh is the natural language of their conversation, then only can one venture to admit a member or a small number of members who understand Welsh, but do not speak it.]

Two clear points emerge here. The first is that the group sought to preserve and maintain its language and identity and to resist the pressures of being absorbed into the English-speaking majority culture. Securing the intergenerational transmission of the language was clearly the purpose of one prospective parent who wrote in response to an appeal for money from the school: 'Carwn i Eryl ddod iddi nes ymlaen oblegid yr wyf yn bur awyddus iddi gadw ei Chymraeg' ('I would like Eryl to attend [the school] later on for I am very keen on her retaining her Welsh': Archive). Secondly, consideration was to be given to operating a submersion programme for children with limited Welsh. It is quite probable that the school's founders did not envisage a demand from the non-Welsh-speaking sector but, as we shall see below, there existed a hidden demand for Welsh-medium education in Cardiff. Shortly after the school had opened a mother wrote to the school enquiring for a place for her six-year-old daughter:

> She attends Minny Street Sunday School and has taken part in the children's services, and with my help has learnt several hymns and shows a keen liking for the language which I want to encourage, and I thought her attendance at this Welsh class would be of considerable help to her. (Archive)

In the mean time, a Welsh-medium school had been set up at Aberystwyth since 1939 under the auspices of the Urdd. In 1943, the Urdd wrote to the Ysgol Fore Sadwrn as follows:

> Bu'n Llywodraethwyr ni yma'n meddwl am ddatblygu'r Ysgol, a chychwyn rhai tebyg mewn trefi eraill yng Nghymru, ond hoffem wybod i ddechrau beth sydd yn cael ei wneud eisoes. (Archive)
>
> [The school governors here have been considering developing the school and starting similar ones in other towns in Wales, but we would like to know first of all what is already being undertaken.]

A further letter was sent in January 1944 (although the year is given as 1943 in the letter) stating:

> Ni synnwn i ddim gweld y Llywodraethwyr yma yn awyddus i gyfarfod rhai ohonoch chwi, a thrafod yn fanwl sut y gellid estyn dipyn ar y cortynnau a datblygu'r Ysgol Fore Sadwrn i fod yn debyg i'r ysgol sydd gennym ni yma. (Archive)
>
> [I would not be surprised if some of our governors here would like to meet with some of you, and discuss in detail how the threads might be stretched a bit and develop the Saturday Morning School to be similar to the school that we have here.]

It would seem that we have here the stirrings of an idea to form a national network of Welsh-medium schools.

Another important event was the passing of the 1944 Education Act. Section 76 of this Act gave parents the right to expect their local education authority to cater for parental choice. This was seen by many as a 'parents' charter' and it was frequently invoked in the efforts to set up Welsh-medium schools in the 1940s. In 1946, the steps that were eventually to lead to the setting up of the Welsh-medium school in Cardiff were taken. The matter of the school was taken up through the Cardiff Cymmrodorion Society which submitted a plan to the Director of Education to establish two schools, one in the east and one in the west for children aged five to eight. These schools would offer submersion in Welsh, as most of the children would be non-Welsh-speaking: special units would be required for Welsh-speaking children. The plan also recommended setting up a unit in one of the schools to teach children between eight and eleven – the scholarship class (see Walters, 1966/7: 118–19 for full details). The

Cymmrodorion believed that implementing such a plan would provide 'arweiniad nid yn unig i awdurdodau ardaloedd Cymreig a Seisnig De Cymru ond i holl wledydd dwyieithog y byd' ('leadership not only to the authorities in Welsh and anglicized districts in south Wales but to all the bilingual countries of the world': J. G. Jones, 1987: 37). At a difficult meeting held between a deputation from the Cymmrodorion and the Education Committee on 23 May 1947 the matter of costs involved in the teaching of Welsh were raised: the authority was not prepared to admit children from outwith its borders (*Braslun*). The Education Committee resolved that the Director would prepare a report for the next meeting of the Education Committee (Minute 1293). In the mean time there was some discussion and disagreement between the parents of the Ysgol Fore Sadwrn and the Director of Education as to the number of children who would attend a Welsh-medium school (*Braslun*). However, a meeting of the LEA's Schools Management Committee on 12 November 1947 resolved that the proposal to establish a Welsh-medium school was 'impracticable at the present moment' but 'decided to review this matter when there is a substantial increase in the number of parents desiring their children to be educated at such a school' (Minute 33). The *South Wales Echo* (13 November 1947) reported: 'Representations by the Cardiff Cymmrodorion Society to the local education authority for a Welsh school have failed', and added, 'There should be 100 children to begin, and until a case was substantiated by numbers nothing could be done'. Nevertheless, the Education Committee on 28 November 1948 referred the matter back to the Schools Management Committee, with the striking recommendation: 'for further consideration with the view to a survey being undertaken throughout the Primary Schools in the City to ascertain the number of parents who desired their children to be educated in a Welsh school' (Minute 255). In January 1947, Ifan ab Owen Edwards, founder of the Urdd and one of the prime movers behind the Welsh-medium school at Aberystwyth, had addressed a meeting of 500 supporters for the Welsh-medium school in Cardiff.[7] In the report of the meeting in *Y Cymro* (16 January 1948), under the heading 'Dinas Caerdydd yn arloesi'r ffordd' ('The City of Cardiff leading the way'), much praise was heaped on Cardiff for its commitment to the teaching of Welsh, to its desire to be recognized as a capital of Wales and a centre of Welsh culture, the implication being that setting up a Welsh-medium school would be of advantage to it (Walters, 1966/7: 114).[8]

On 3 May 1948, the Director of Education presented a report on the survey of primary-school parents to ascertain the demand for a Welsh-medium school to the Schools Management Committee (Minute 1278). Attendance officers had delivered 8,798 census forms to the parents of every child between the ages of five and eight. These were collected seven days later, a total of 5,991 or 67 per cent being returned, the other 2,807, according to the minutes of the committee, reported orally that they did not wish to send their children to a Welsh school.

What kind of school was being offered? According to the circular sent to the parents, the school was for the children of both Welsh-speaking and non-Welsh-speaking parents. We quote from the Director's report:

. . . a Welsh school would be conducted on the following lines:

(a) General.

The official language for the six years (5–11 years of age) would be Welsh. It would be the language used in the time-tables, terminal reports, registration, assembly, the play-ground, and in the social and corporate activities of the School.

(b) Infants' School.

Instruction in all subjects, including the teaching of number, would be given in Welsh at the Infant stage, ages 5–7 years. Materials for lessons would be drawn from Welsh traditional rhymes, Welsh folk songs, and folk-lore and stories from Welsh history, etc. The object of this early course would be to give the child a thorough grounding in the Welsh language and to relate the Welsh language to the cultural background of Wales. Two or three lessons a week would be devoted to teaching the English language when the child is 6½ years of age, as English would be the language most frequently heard outside the school. On transfer from the Infants' to Junior Schools at 7 years of age, pupils should be able to speak, read and write and count proficiently in the Welsh language.

(c) Junior School.

For children between the ages of 7 and 11 years, the official language of the School would continue to be Welsh. It would also be the language used in the teaching of Religious Knowledge, the History and Geography of Wales, and subjects relating to Welsh life and culture. English, however, would be used increasingly in the teaching of other subjects, particularly Arithmetic, so that Welsh pupils would not be handicapped when sitting for the entrance Examination to Secondary Schools.

It is clear that for the five to seven year olds, an immersion programme would be operated, whilst for the seven to eleven year olds, a partial immersion programme would be the order of the day. The final sentence of the last paragraph would seem to be based on misgivings that Welsh was not totally adequate as a medium of instruction for all subjects and could indeed be a handicap.

The outcome of the survey showed that parents of 331 children between the ages of five and eight had indicated that they would like their children to attend the Welsh school.[9] Of these, the parents of 255 children (77 per cent of the total) were non-Welsh-speaking, with seventy-six children (23 per cent) having one or both parents able to speak Welsh. Of the children themselves, 15 (4.5 per cent) were Welsh-speaking whilst the remainder, 316 (95.4 per cent) were not Welsh-speaking. Following the Director's report, 'It was decided that the Director be requested to prepare a report on the lines indicated by the Committee, with the object of setting up of a Welsh School in Cardiff, to meet the demand of parents as shewn in the report' (Minute 1278, p. 246). At the next meeting of the Education Committee, 16 July 1948, it was decided 'to convene a special meeting of the Committee immediately after the vacation to consider the report' (Minute 1807). This meeting was held on 2 November 1948. The Director outlined the various options available to accommodate the demand for the school. The final decision was 'That the Council be recommended to proceed with the formation of a Welsh School, and that the City Surveyor be instructed to prepare the necessary plans and specification as soon as possible'. The decision was not unanimous: an amendment to refer the matter back was defeated by thirty-four votes against and twenty-two for. At the 14 January 1949 meeting of the Education Committee, funds totalling £16,535 were approved for a site, six temporary classes and furniture for the Welsh School (Minute 2900). However, this was not the end of the matter. At the 8 February 1949 meeting of the Schools Management Committee it was proposed by the Director of Education that, until a new school was built, a Welsh school could be temporarily set up as a self-contained unit within an existing English school and further: 'The Director suggested that a circular be issued to the parents of the children who have already intimated that they desire their children to attend the Welsh School and he proposed to report further on the matter to the next meeting of this Committee' (Minute 2957). The results of the second survey were reported to a meeting of the Schools Management Committee on 5 April 1949. The survey revealed a substantial drop in the number of parents wishing to send their children to the Welsh school: the total was now 123. The reason for the drop would seem to be that many parents had interpreted the initial proposal as giving their children more instruction in Welsh, not providing instruction through the medium of Welsh. (Walters, 1966/7: 124). The minute of the committee relating to the matter (Minute 2957) covers nearly three A4 sheets and reveals the considerable detail gone into regarding the options considered. The outcome was that a Welsh unit should be set up within an English school and the principle that the majority of the children must be Welsh-speaking was adopted, and 'that where English-speaking children are admitted they should be of Infant Age, and, numerically, they should constitute the minority in each class'. The final resolution was

> the selected children should be drawn from the above [that is, the 123] and that the admissions to the school in September next be as follows: – 15 Welsh-Speaking children, 3 English-Speaking children with both parents Welsh-Speaking (6–7 age groups); one child in the 7–8 group with both parents Welsh-Speaking, and it should not be discounted that these 4 English-Speaking children may experience some difficulty in the early stages in adapting themselves to a curriculum in Welsh.

The wishes of the parents of the remainder of the children who had reaffirmed their desire to send their children to a Welsh school were not addressed. However, had they been admitted by the LEA it is quite likely that the Minister of Education would not have approved, for in the Ministry's assent to establishing the unit, strong reservations were expressed as to educating a child in a language other than the 'home language'. The Minister's response stated:

> the Minister attaches importance to the observance of the generally accepted policy that Infant children should be educated . . . through the medium of the home language. He would therefore depreciate the admission of monoglot English speaking children to Welsh Schools or Departments, even when both parents are Welsh speaking, more particularly in the initial stages, when the teachers involved will have to undertake a task which is entirely new to them. The Minister understands that so far only one English speaking child has been admitted to the Welsh Infants' department . . . He will

expect therefore that the progress of this child shall be carefully watched, with a view to transfer to an English-speaking Infants Class if it is found that he or she is not capable of profiting by the education provided, and no further English-speaking children will be admitted, at any rate until considerable experience of the arrangements has been gained. (Minute 1212, 8 November 1949 meeting)

The status of the campaigning parents was transformed and normalized as reflected in the way they referred to themselves. Previously, as parents of the children who attended the voluntary Ysgol Fore Sadwrn they had referred to themselves as '*hyrwyddwyr* Ysgol Gymraeg Fore Sadwrn Caerdydd' ('*promoters* of the Cardiff Saturday Morning Welsh School') but became *Pwyllgor* yr Ysgol Gymraeg (*Committee* for the Welsh School)[10] in correspondence with the LEA and, as soon as the decision to set up the Welsh School was made, became *Cymdeithas Rhieni* Ysgol Gymraeg Caerdydd (*Parents' Association* of the Cardiff Welsh School). The Parents' Association distributed a circular dated 12 March 1949 urging prospective parents to send the names of their children to the Parents' Association by 21 March, stating 'Plant a fedr siarad y Gymraeg fydd y dewis cyntaf, plant sydd ar restr Cymdeithas Rhieni yr Ysgol' ('Children who can speak Welsh will have first offers, children who are on the list of the Parents' Association': Archive).[11] Clearly in order to allay any fears parents might have as regards their children's command of English or their children's future, the same circular included the following reassurance:

Dysgir Saesneg a Rhifyddeg drwy gyfrwng y Saesneg yn drwyadl ynddi ar ôl i'r plant gyrraedd chwe blwydd a hanner oed, a pharatoir hwy ar gyfer yr Arholiad Ysgoloriaeth.

[English and Arithmetic will be taught thoroughly through the medium of English after the children reach the age of six and a half, and they will be prepared for the Scholarship Examination.]

This echoes the earlier comments of the Education Committee, and suggests there were some potential parents who may have had misgivings about the efficacy of teaching though the medium of Welsh only. The school eventually opened on Monday 5 September 1949 with eighteen children present and a staff of two female teachers (Education Committee, 6 September 1949, Minute 668).

Over the next thirty years Welsh-medium education was treated as marginal rather than as integral to the LEA's education provision. The LEA's position, as we shall see, was that Welsh-medium education had to be addressed only in response to parental pressure, or some crisis caused by external factors. Even then the response and/or solution was always of a temporary nature, for there was no forward planning.

Initially, the school was to be a unit temporarily housed in an English school and money had been earmarked for a site, building and furniture in January 1949. However, barely a year and a half after the school unit had been opened, the

Education Committee for 6 February 1951 (Minute 1929) recorded the Director of Education's report that the school was growing and that it would need a building of its own. The committee's response was that the matter would need to be discussed in the future. A letter from the Parents' Association to the Director some four months later raised the following issues (Archive) which, as the years went by, became a constant source of friction between the LEA and the parents, namely:

- the need for a permanent building for the school of sufficient size and with sufficient resources;
- the need for the school to be located at a site nearer to the children's homes;
- the matter of transport to the school;
- the attention of the authority was drawn to the existence of a Welsh-medium nursery school.[12]

The 5 June 1951 meeting of the Education Committee noted receipt of the letter and approved that steps be taken to have the Welsh school recognized as a separate school by the Ministry of Education and that it be located in the premises of the redundant Highfields school in Llandaff (Walters, 1966/7: 131). The move took place in 1952 and there the school stayed for the next sixteen years. At this site the Welsh school adopted the name Bryntaf. The building was clearly inadequate: it was described as 'sub-standard' in 1963 (Walters, 1966/7: 132). No action was taken to remedy its condition and a deputation from the Parents' Association met with the Director of Education in April 1964 to press for action, with little avail (Walters, 1966/7: 134). Again at a meeting of the authority's Primary Schools Committee of 1 November 1966, 'The Committee considered the report of Her Majesty's Inspector on Bryntaf Welsh Primary School and a letter from the Parents' Association concerning the need to improve facilities at the school' (Minute 1222). Although the Director of Education reminded the committee that the Public Works and Town Planning Committee had been requested to designate a site for the new school, the only action taken was to ask the Director to prepare a report 'on the future development of the school'.

By 1967 the question of Welsh-medium education in Cardiff assumed an additional dimension. Because of changes in the city's boundaries, a school containing a Welsh Unit now came under the authority of Cardiff Education Committee.[13] The unit was under pressure due to lack of space and a move to another school site was considered on the 14 April 1967 at a meeting of the Education Committee's Executive Committee and 'Arising from the discussion the Committee agreed that the provision of a suitable school for Welsh-speaking pupils of Primary School age be subject of consideration and report as soon as circumstances permit' (Minute 2634). This would seem to indicate a decision to open another Welsh school in Cardiff. However, at a meeting of the same Committee two months later, on the 9 June 1967, it was noted that 'The Committee were informed that there was no possibility of a new school being included in a foreseeable building programme' (Minute 323).[14] The authority 'resolved' the unit's problem by relocating it in an almost empty secondary-school building (known as Viriamu Jones School) in the Gabalfa area of the city in 1967. The remnant of the secondary school, which was being phased out, was housed on the first floor of the building, the Welsh Unit on the ground floor.

In 1968, Bryntaf was relocated within the same building, and the unit and the school were amalgamated. The Welsh school retained the name Bryntaf (Minute 377 of Primary Schools Committee of 18 June 1968). This was the Welsh school's third home and its location was determined by a combination of pressure from the parents, overcrowding at both the unit and Bryntaf, and the availability of a redundant building.

The authority's response to the accommodation needs of the Welsh School indicates that it was neither prepared to plan for, nor to satisfy, the needs of Welsh-medium education. This culture of reactive rather than purposive planning led to an unpleasant conflict. The school in Gabalfa was located in a fairly large council estate with access to it along narrow roads. As the children attending the Welsh school had to be bussed from various parts of the city, and as the school inevitably grew, the number of buses increased and the roads were seriously congested by school buses at arrival and departure times. Local people, already vocal in their opposition to the buses, protested to the authority and the parents, fearing the effects of the antagonism on their children, requested that an escort be provided to accompany the bussed children to the school. The authority refused to appoint an escort but requested that buses leave the area as soon as possible after depositing the children (Minute 1462 of meeting of Special Services Sub-committee, 4 January 1974). Things deteriorated further with the local protest turning into verbal abuse of the children. The authority in an ironic volte-face resolved 'in view of the need for the County Council to exercise is duty of care, the appointment of an escort be approved' (Minute 2103 of meeting of Special Services Sub-committee, 4 January 1975). The Education Committee meeting of 13 March 1975 added the proviso 'until a rear access to the school is provided'. The situation deteriorated further, with protesters blocking access to the school and the authority was now faced with a serious local problem. Its response was to relocate the school and once more a redundant secondary school building was used. At its meeting on 18 July 1975 the Education Committee approved 'the temporary transfer of Bryntaf School to the former Cardiff High School for Girls premises' (Minute 823). This was an empty building and whilst its suitability as a location, however temporary, for children of primary school age does not seem to have been considered, the Education Committee did instruct that 'the Environment and Planning Committee be asked to examine any traffic hazards in the Parade occasioned by the school's transfer'. Following on this crisis the Parents' Association requested the authority to set up an advisory committee composed of representatives of the parents, the authority and other interested parties to discuss the matter of a permanent home for the school. The authority rejected this but it was noted that consultation would take place as necessary (Schools Sub-committee, 11 September 1975, Minute 895).

The local confrontation over the school spurred Cardiff Education Authority to take a less opportunist and complacent attitude to the matter of Welsh-medium education, albeit as the result of an external crisis rather than the considered well-being of the Welsh school itself. At the 17 June 1976 meeting of the Schools Sub-committee a draft consultative document proposed closing the present school and replacing it with three primary schools, plus an additional fourth school should the need arise; these schools would be on the sites of existing English-medium primary schools. The first of the three schools was to be opened in September 1977 and the other two the following September.[15] The document also included a proposal to open the first Welsh-medium secondary school in Cardiff.[16] This was undoubtedly a serious attempt at addressing the needs of Welsh-medium education in the city, not only in terms of locating schools in different areas but also in making some provision for growth. The proposals would also have implications for the localities of school sites that were selected and in particular it would directly involve individual local councillors who had hitherto had little responsibility for a Welsh-medium school at ward level. As the school had previously been housed in redundant school buildings, this had occasioned little conflict of interest or demands at the local level.

Henceforth real and potential conflict was generated by four distinct, if related, issues, namely (i) the parents of the targeted English schools would have to relinquish something like half their current resources in terms of space to accommodate Welsh schools; (ii) superficially at least, the Welsh school was being set up at the expense of the local English school; (iii) several individual local councillors would find themselves directly involved and facing conflicting interests and demands; (iv) the Bryntaf parents would also find themselves facing serious local opposition to the schooling of their children.

How did the authority proceed? At the 8 October 1976 meeting of the Education Sub-committee it was decided that 'the matter of primary Welsh education be referred to a Working Party to be appointed by the Education Committee' (Minute 1254). This Working Party met ten times before presenting its proposals some twenty months later to the 10 July 1978 meeting of the Education Committee. The Working Party had based its proposals on the following guidelines:

> (a) any change should be accompanied by the minimum of disruption; (b) any child at present attending an English medium school should be able to continue to do so irrespective of proposals for the establishment of a Welsh School at the site; (c) selection of possible sites for dispersal [of the Welsh school's pupils] should be closely related to areas of demand; (d) total dispersal should not be attempted at the present but should be phased through several stages. (Minute 691)

One site had been identified which met the guidelines and it was proposed that a Welsh school be opened on this site the following September[17] This was approved by the Education Committee, which decided that 'approaches be made to the Welsh Office for additional funds to enable the need for Welsh-medium education to be met by the provision of new schools'. The Education Committee at its meeting on 20 July 1978 rejected an amendment to refer the decision back and approved the proposal, while the authority sought and was given the approval of the Welsh Office to establish the school.

The Working Party had obviously foreseen the consequences of the proposals: parents of the English-medium schools would be assured that their children would not have to move; the implementation of the plan would be phased; thirdly, and of some significance to the needs of Welsh-medium education, sites would be related to the areas of demand, that is, a form of Welsh-medium neighbourhood school might now be envisaged. The proposal explicitly stated that 'a catchment area be determined, as a guide to admissions to the new Welsh Primary School, based upon a detailed survey of the location of demand'. This was the first reference to the concept of a *catchment area* for a Welsh school and the intention to conduct a survey of the location of the demand implied a seriousness of purpose on the authority's part and a move towards the normalization of Welsh-medium education.

The proposals for the Welsh school involved splitting the site hitherto solely occupied by the English school, allocating the infants' school building to the Welsh school and housing the English school in the main primary-school building. As expected there was strong opposition from the parents of the English school: the Welsh parents were accused of linguistic apartheid; there would be discord between the children of the separate schools; there could be civil conflict and it was feared that the Welsh school would eventually take over the entire site. Petitions for and against the proposal were presented to the authority. The *Western Mail* (3 October 1978) carried a report on the matter under the headline 'A blow-up if school is split up, say parents' and with the opening paragraph 'Plans for a new Welsh school in Cardiff will cause a "blow-up" which will lead to violence between Welsh and English speaking pupils with even six- and seven-year olds fighting, parents claimed yesterday.' The matter was raised in Parliament by the area's MP, which the *Western Mail* (7 November 1978) reported under the heading 'Segregation by language row'.

Parental pressure has been the single most effective instrument for language revitalization in general and educational reform in particular. From the outset, the parents of the Welsh school, organized through the Bryntaf Parents' Association, played a prominent role in its affairs, continually lobbying the authority to improve conditions at the school.[18] Because of the scattered nature of the location of demand for Welsh-medium education, children had to be bussed to the school from all over the city, and the parents bore part of the transport costs, which was set at 40 per cent of the total costs by the Education Committee on the May 1974 (Minute 255), being reduced to 30 per cent at the 7 January 1975 meeting in response to an appeal from the Parents' Association (Minute 1788). The costs borne are testimony to the parents' commitment to the school: the Association's balance sheet for 31 March 1980 shows that their contribution to the transport costs totalled £18,699.93 for the two school years of 1978 and 1979. As a consequence of the school's third relocation in 1975, the Parents' Association established its own working party to give itself clear aims and objectives and to formulate a coherent policy. By 1979 two documents had been drawn up, one entitled *Addysg Gymraeg yng Nghaerdydd 1978–93* ('Welsh-medium Education in Cardiff 1978–93') was a development plan for Welsh-medium education based on past demand and anticipated growth up to 1993 and called for the setting up of four schools in the city. The other document was a policy statement that was adopted formally by the Association. During 1979, however, a dispute broke out between the authority and the Parents' Association when the authority's Working Party on Welsh-medium education sought to restrict entry to the Welsh schools in September 1979 to ninety children, arguing that priority should be given to children of whom at least one parent was Welsh-speaking. This was interpreted as a crude attempt to limit admission and stem the growth of demand. It also suggested that the authority was either unaware of, or chose to ignore, the increasing number of non-Welsh-speaking parents opting for Welsh-medium education for their children – it was claimed that some 60 per cent of the parents in 1979 were non-Welsh-speaking.[19] Had the authority monitored the growth of Welsh-medium education and planned accordingly it would not have attempted to impose this restriction.[20] The Parents' Association brought considerable pressure on the authority over this issue. Letters were sent to every councillor and the matter received prominent press coverage. The *Western Mail* (23 March 1979) reported, under the headline 'School for Welsh warned of boycott', that 'Three hundred irate parents warned county councillors last night that they were not prepared to accept any restrictions on entry into Cardiff's Welsh-medium primary schools'. Further, the *South Wales Echo* (16 March 1979), under the headline 'Limit-pupil move could start rush for places', reported: 'A scramble for places at Welsh-medium primary schools in Cardiff from September will face parents – if a controversial move to limit pupil numbers by "selection" wins support from South Glamorgan County Council'. Members of the Parents' Association met with the chair of the County Council and sought to convince him to accept the need for four schools strategically placed in the city.[21] The chair accepted the thrust of the parents' case and asked for a copy of the Association's development plan. Members of the authority, including the chair of the County Council and the chair of the Education Authority attended a packed and stormy meeting of the Parents' Association and the authority withdrew its attempts at selection.[22] The minutes of the Education Committee of 14 May 1979 record the decision economically with the words

> Consultation had taken place but it now appeared that the total demand for places in the coming year would not be as great as had been originally envisaged. It would not therefore be necessary to invoke any selection procedure and the normal primary school admissions policy would therefore apply. (Minute 2273)

In the *Western Mail* (15 May 1979), the Chairman of the Education Committee is quoted as saying, in respect of the growth of demand for Welsh-medium education: 'We realise there is more and more yet to come and I think it incumbent on this county council to pull out all the stops to find the extra schools.' At the same meeting it was decided that

the Welsh Working Party undertake a study of the scope for the provision for Welsh Medium Primary School places to achieve the dispersal of Ysgol Bryntaf as soon as possible and also consider the likely increase in demand for additional places in the longer term. (Minute 2273)

Events moved quickly between the end of 1979 and 1981. A crisis arising from the failure of the central heating boilers at the school which could have forced the evacuation of the school during the winter period was averted by installing mobile gas heaters (Executive Sub-committee meeting, 11 November 1979, Minute 703) – to the dismay of the parents who were concerned with the safety aspects. In December 1979, the Education Committee approved a plan (which had come from the Executive Sub-committee, 20 October 1979, Minute 1036) to open two Welsh-medium schools by either September 1980 or January 1981 and a further school by 1986 to accommodate the probable demand. The catchment area of the three schools would be demarcated following a detailed analysis of the location of the demand. This plan again affected two English-medium schools; in the one case it meant amalgamating the infants' and junior sectors and housing them in one building, and housing the Welsh-medium school in the vacated building; in the other instance it was proposed that the English-medium school, which had falling numbers on roll, become a Welsh-medium school. The split-site school was set up and opened in September 1980;[23] the second plan was abandoned (having met with severe opposition from the local parents, and from the Bryntaf parents due to its location being far removed from the areas of demand) and it was resolved to establish another as soon as possible and 'an application be made to the Welsh Office for the inclusion of a new one form entry Welsh Primary School at a site to be determined in an early school building programme' (Executive Sub-committee meeting, 11 December 1979, Minute 1327).

Thus by 1980 there were three Welsh-medium schools, one of which included the original Bryntaf awaiting final dispersal. The 19 February 1980 meeting of the Education Committee considered establishing a further Welsh-medium school on a site to be shared with the extant English-medium school (Minute 1795). At the 28 May 1980 meeting it was resolved to proceed, the English-medium school being housed in the junior building and the Welsh-medium school in the vacated infants' building. An additional nursery unit was provided for the English-medium school to compensate for the consequent loss of space. This third Welsh-medium school opened in September 1981.[24] The final, formal dispersal of Bryntaf was affirmed at the same meeting

a one-form entry Welsh-medium primary school be established in September, 1981 to serve mainly the South Cardiff area, to be located on a temporary basis in part of the premises of the former Ysgol Gymraeg Bryntaf pending the provision of permanent premises on a site to be determined . . .

These final decisions fulfilled the Parents' Association's wishes as stated in their development plan forwarded to the authority in 1979. Four schools had been established by September 1981, three of them strategically placed in the north and west of the city and the fourth's current temporary location was convenient enough for the east of the city. As a Welsh-medium secondary school had also been opened in Cardiff, Welsh-medium provision was available for each pupil's entire school life. With these developments, the relationship between the parents and the authority became far more harmonious.

## INTERIM ASSESSMENT

This case-study has outlined the long and unsteady process towards the normal-ization of Welsh-medium education in Cardiff. Success was achieved initially through the determination of committed individuals and then more formally by an equally committed Parents' Association. It is clear that the provision was peripheral to the authority's priorities. There was no coherent planning for growth, the authority acting only under pressure from parents or in response to an external crisis. As the demand grew, the school was shunted to unwanted and inadequate poorly located sites. It was only when inaction became unsustainable due to problems with the residents in the school's locality and the scope of the demand could no longer be ignored (and despite the crude, almost desperate attempt to impose selection and admission restrictions) that the authority grasped the nettle and sought to formulate and implement a coherent plan for Welsh-medium education.

The authority's unwillingness to engage in coherent planning derives from three considerations. First, Welsh-medium instruction was not considered part of its 'normal' education provision. Secondly, the demand for Welsh-medium education was scattered, and consequently had no clearly defined catchment area. Thirdly, both demographically and politically it was a minority provision. It may also be argued that there was a degree of democratic deficit facing the parents electing for Welsh-medium education; the scattered demand meant there was no concentration of need nor of petitioning parents in any given ward. Consequently, no individual councillor/group of councillors was under pres-sure at ward level to take up the parents' case nor indeed did they face any threat at local elections from disaffected parents. This contrasted with electoral influ-ence of parents of local English-medium schools. Interview evidence indicates that Welsh-medium parents found their local councillors evasive and equivocal when approached for their support for Welsh-medium schools, as evidenced by the following reply: 'Thank you for your letter . . . I can understand your concern about this important matter but I will have to balance my position about support with all the representations I have received.'

Since 1981 Welsh-medium education in Cardiff has continued to grow, with a current complement of eight Welsh-medium schools in the city – one of them opened in 1999 as a unit within an existing English-medium school pending location in a building of its own, the re-emergence of the very beginnings of this type of education in Cardiff. In addition there are two Welsh-medium units permanently located within two other English-medium schools. At the secondary level there are now two Welsh-medium schools. The Welsh Nursery Schools movement has been equally successful over the succeeding years. According to the city's 1998 Education Plan there were thirty-four Welsh-medium nursery schools containing 582 city pupils. Of the children attending the authority's Welsh-medium schools, 75 per cent come from non-Welsh-speaking homes.

Following the Education Act of 1988, which enshrined the place of Welsh in the National Curriculum, and the Welsh Language Act 1993, which obliges education authorities to submit educational provision plans to the Welsh Language Board, Cardiff published its plans in 1998. The authority has fully complied with the Act's requirements in stating its aims and in forecasting the growth in demand up to the year 2001. Additionally, the authority conventionally sends a bilingual handbook to the parents of each child entering primary education, which contains information on the options for both English-medium and Welsh-medium education. However, the crux of the matter is the implementation of the plan and two features are of fundamental significance.

The first is the question of school sites. Given the forecasted increase in demand for Welsh-medium education there will be an increasing pressure for space. The authority's stated aim is to normalize Welsh-medium provision to such an extent that there will be a Welsh school in each ward in the city; the plan states: 'The ultimate aim of the Authority is to establish catchment areas for Welsh-medium primary schools in line with other schools. This will be fully implemented when there is a Welsh-medium school in every ward' (p. 4). The most practical way of achieving this will be more English-medium and Welsh-medium schools sharing split sites. This will undoubtedly create tension, even in those instances where the numbers of pupils on roll may be decreasing in an English-medium schools, for as the chair of the County Council said, as far back as 1979, 'The trouble with half empty schools is that they are half full!' If conflict is to be avoided in the future, sensitive handling on the part of all the parties involved, not least the authority and its elected officers, will be essential.

The second issue is the authority's resolve to implement its stated policy. Under the heading 'Action to be taken', section 14.2, Primary Education, in the plan, the second of the three actions is given as: 'Annual review of the curricular needs and *accommodation of existing Welsh-medium primary schools*' (our emphasis). There are two schools, which we will call School A and School B, where the will of the authority to act on its findings are likely to be put to the test. School A opened as a one-form entry school in 1979 and School B opened as a one-form entry school in 1981. Both share split sites with English-medium schools. The numbers on roll at School A for September 1998 were as follows: Welsh school

289, English school 301; total number of pupils sharing the split site 590. School B has: Welsh school 395, English school 230; total number of pupils sharing the split site 625. In School A, the Welsh school is almost equal in size to the English school, whilst in School B, the Welsh school is larger than the English school by almost a third. Both Welsh schools have grown well beyond the normal one-form entry size. The authority's response to the needs of all the schools on these two sites will be a matter of some delicacy.

## A SPATIAL INTERFACE MODEL OF CULTURES

What general lessons can we draw from this detailed reconstruction of Cardiff's Welsh-medium provision? Allen Philbrick (1983) has suggested that it is possible to construct models of spatial contacts among cultures in a city region by permuting two cultural attitudes (active–passive and negative–passive) for each of three intercultural contact situations he describes as attachment, containment and displacement. Two separate aspects must be combined in such models: the variation in attitudes of individuals and groups on the one hand, and the varieties of spatial contact accompanying the exchange of ideas. If we confine ourselves only to discussing the attitudes of parents (and pupils) to bilingual education (and all that this implies in a Cardiff context) then we can trace the dynamism of attitude formation and change as follows.

Active/passive, positive/negative attitudes: a four-cell matrix (Figure 5.2) provides places for two variations for each of two poles of attitude. On any given issue, related to bilingual education provision, one's attitude may be active or passive and negative or positive. In a cumulative sense, therefore, Philbrick's model contains four necessary combinations:

*Active-Positive*     aggressively promoting a position in favour of something
*Active-Negative*    aggressively opposing something
*Passive-Positive*    passively agreeing with but simply accepting something
*Passive-Negative*  resignedly accepting something one disagrees with.

The arrows across the boundaries in Figure 5.2 indicate that attitudes can change.

If we also relate attitude change to physical and perceptual movement we see that it is possible to describe three ideal-type relationships as attachment, containment and replacement (see Figure 5.3). In cases of attachment the arrow indicates the dominant and subordinate groups. Containment suggests a stand-off relationship. Replacement is a resolution of pressure in favour of one group by intrusion upon the space (or domains) of the other, where one group penetrates or replaces the other in the latter's territory.

Figure 5.4 is an illustration of the spatial interface model. When one combines attitude with attachment, containment and replacement, each attitude creates

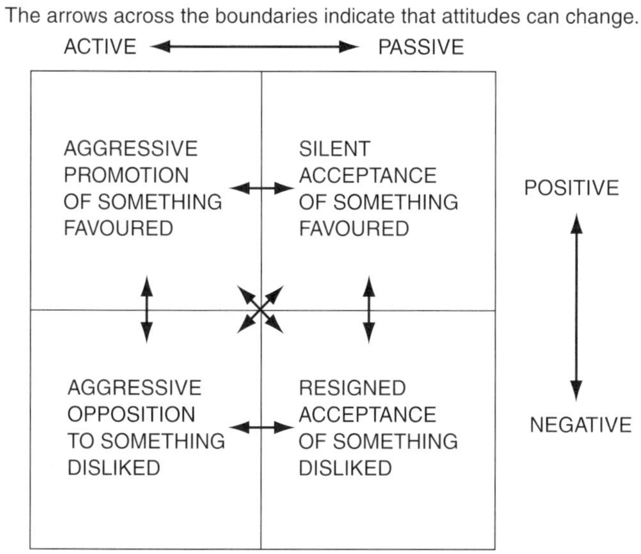

The arrows across the boundaries indicate that attitudes can change.

ACTIVE ←————————→ PASSIVE

| | | |
|---|---|---|
| AGGRESSIVE PROMOTION OF SOMETHING FAVOURED | SILENT ACCEPTANCE OF SOMETHING FAVOURED | POSITIVE |
| AGGRESSIVE OPPOSITION TO SOMETHING DISLIKED | RESIGNED ACCEPTANCE OF SOMETHING DISLIKED | NEGATIVE |

**Figure 5.2. Attitudes and connectivity**
*Source*: **Philbrick, 1983**

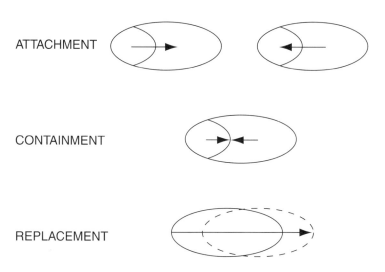

ATTACHMENT

CONTAINMENT

REPLACEMENT

**Figure 5.3. Attitudes and connectivity**
*Source*: **Philbrick, 1983**

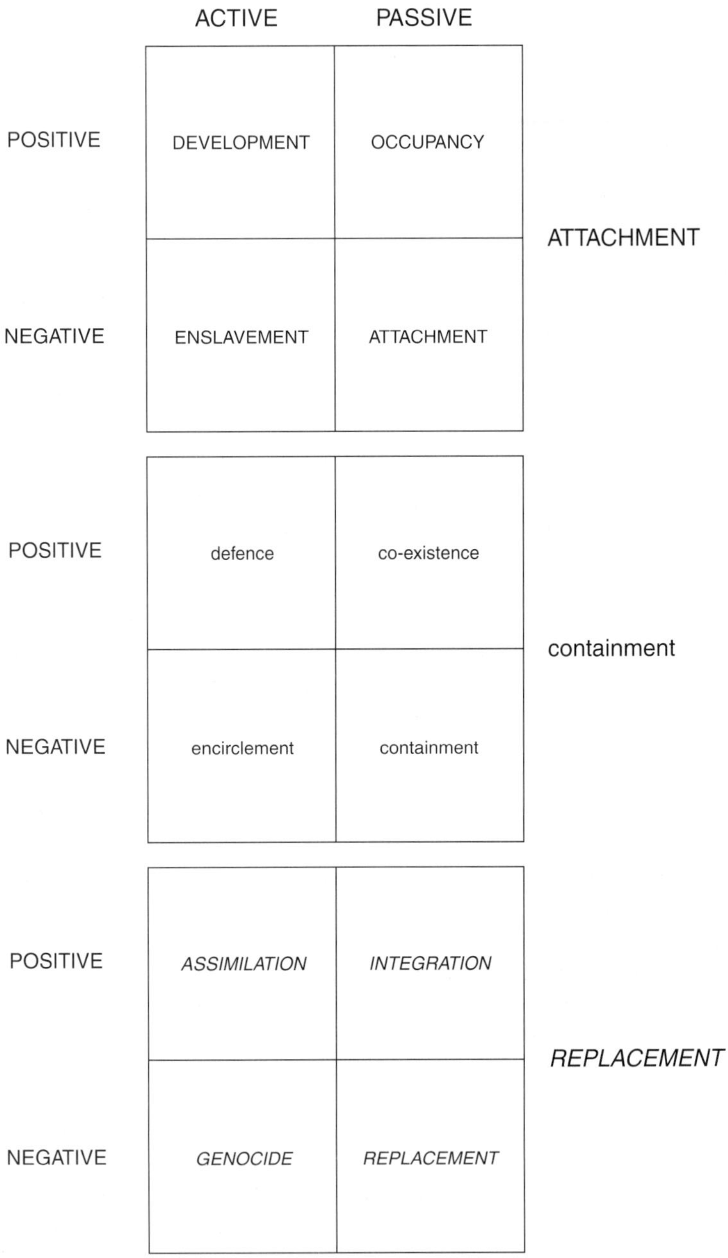

|  | ACTIVE | PASSIVE |
|---|---|---|
| POSITIVE | DEVELOPMENT | OCCUPANCY |
| NEGATIVE | ENSLAVEMENT | ATTACHMENT |

ATTACHMENT

|  | ACTIVE | PASSIVE |
|---|---|---|
| POSITIVE | defence | co-existence |
| NEGATIVE | encirclement | containment |

containment

|  | ACTIVE | PASSIVE |
|---|---|---|
| POSITIVE | *ASSIMILATION* | *INTEGRATION* |
| NEGATIVE | *GENOCIDE* | *REPLACEMENT* |

*REPLACEMENT*

**Figure 5.4. Spatial interface model**
*Source*: **Philbrick, 1983**

four different expressions of each of the three types of spatial events (Philbrick, 1983: 97). Inter-group relations are, of course, far more complex than ideal. Nevertheless, the following schemata have relevance in interpreting the shared experiences of promoters and detractors of bilingual education in Cardiff, and by extension, Wales.

Under *attachment*, which is defined as passive/negative, active-positive is *development*; passive-positive is simply *occupancy*, while active-negative is the much stronger idea of *enslavement*. Under *containment*, which is deemed passive-negative, active-positive is named *defence*, while the passive form of positive stand-off is *coexistence*. The active-negative is the stronger concept of *encirclement*. Under *replacement*, which is deemed passively negative, the active form is *assimilation*, passive-positive *integration*, while the active-negative is the most extreme position of genocide.

In our detailed account of bilingual education, most of these attitudes have been expressed, except, of course, the extreme cases of *enslavement*, *encirclement* and *genocide*. The shift has been from a majority position of defence, and a minority position of occupancy (in the post-war period), through a majority position of containment and a minority position of development (up until the mid-1980s), to a current majority position of integration and a minority position of assimilation through replacement at key locations as we shall see.

One should not expect the distribution pattern of Welsh-medium schools within the authority to reflect the pattern of Welsh speakers within Cardiff because the overwhelming majority of parents are themselves not Welsh-speaking. However, given the concentrations of Welsh speakers in wards such as Rhiwbeina, Heath, Llandaf and Whitchurch, it is not unreasonable to expect that there should be a neighbourhood effect for the clustering of Welsh-medium nodes, such as *ysgolion meithrin*, *ysgolion cynradd* and chapels (see Aitchison and Carter, 1987). That there is little direct correspondence over time between local distribution patterns and specific locational siting of school facilities is due largely to the policy of the LEA in accommodating the needs of Welsh-medium education within schools which are either surplus to capacity or in other ways, regardless of where they are located within the city. This accounts for the generally skewed western concentration of facilities, especially since as a result of local authority reform in 1974 which created the new county of South Glamorgan, high-school pupils from Penarth, Barry and the Vale are educated at one of two locations in the west of the city.

A more recent stratagem has been to advocate that both English-medium and Welsh-medium education be offered within the single split-site location. This does not necessarily satisfy either group of parents. Locational conflict is often intertwined with language antagonism and competition. This may increase if the model of split-site schools is not well managed. Alternatively, if the city's commitment to a Welsh-medium school in each ward is realized, the split-site solution may enable English-medium schools with falling rolls to remain viable.

One of the lessons to be drawn out from this experience is that bilingual education arguments based upon exceptionalism need to be recast in terms of normalization. We have seen that a changed political context has been marked by the development of a robust Welsh-medium educational system; a National Curriculum Council for Wales, 1988; The Welsh Language Act, 1993; the Statutory Welsh Language Board, 1993; the Schools Examination and Assessment Authority, 1994; the Government of Wales Act, 1998, and the National Assembly for Wales, 1999. All of these structural reforms help legitimize the normalization of Welsh.

As in Canada (Heller, 1999) bilingual schools in Wales demonstrate a vision of pluralist pragmatism, in which language becomes capital not emblem, and in which the school, as a social institution, plays a key role in producing and distributing newly valued capital. These schools are clearly situated in the transition from a struggle over and about the role of the minority language to a more instrumental justification for bilingualism as a social and economic fact. However, we have to recognize that the bilingual school system's own legitimacy is based upon a number of contradictions:

(a) between a conception of education which is Welsh-medium as opposed to essentially bilingual;
(b) between the economic value of the standard as opposed to the authenticating value of the vernacular;
(c) between a commitment to a dynamic Welsh culture and a social reality which emphasizes the multicultural pluralist, urban-social context of Cardiff;
(d) between a conventional representation of Welsh cultural life and the more innovative, intrusive and sometimes less-valued patterns of shadowing a globalized internationalist cultural system;
(e) the school is replacing the home and community as the privileged site for the production and distribution of the linguistic resource that is Welsh, and yet the school has to forge or reinterpret a sociolinguistic network which vitiates the use of Welsh outside the formal educational domains;
(f) the schools recognize the authenticating value of Welsh, it after all legitimizes their existence. However, in facing the fact that this linguistic variety is not as valued in the international market to which many of the citizens want access, the schools' strategy is to focus on the quality of both languages in a bilingual context, arguing that this is a European norm, thereby universalizing the experience;
(g) consequently the role of English within the school system is also vital, it reinforces the ideology of linguistic capital; it is probably the main medium by which the students will earn their living; it is a significant home language for a large proportion of the pupils and it is the means by which many of the contradictions noted above are resolved. From initially being seen as a threat, the role of English is now dealt with in a far more structured and holistic manner.

The Welsh-medium school system also aids the legitimization of Cardiff as a national, if not yet a bilingual capital. Language has long been used as a marker of authenticity by the city leaders and the current commitment to a comprehensive provision of Welsh-medium schools is testimony of that ambition. These are the principal considerations:

1. Educational policy is reactive rather than purposive, little attention has been paid to long-term planning.
2. Demand over a ten-year period is estimated to be growing at 6.5 per cent per annum.
3. Current Five Year Capital Programme includes significant developments, namely, the development of Ysgol Pencae costing £1.1m representing 45 per cent of the total capital funding for the Primary Sector in 1996/7; the development of Ysgol Gyfun Gymraeg Glantaf costing £1.265m represents 38 per cent of capital funding for the Secondary Sector in 1997/8; current development of Ysgol Pwll Goch to serve Canton, Riverside and Grangetown will cost £2m plus and provide 225 places including nursery provision.
4. Great attention needs to be paid to the training and resourcing of teaching Welsh in English-medium schools. This is critical in order to realize the potential of the contribution of second-language learning in the development of a bilingual citizenry.
5. It is likely that the Educational Committees of the National Assembly will initiate new policies which together with the currently reformulated Strategy of the Welsh Language Board will make educational and career-related language planning a more central plank of language policy.
6. The needs of other language groups in Cardiff, that is, South Asian, Somali, European migrants, will also figure more prominently. There is good cause for arguing that the whole reportoire of language skills within the city-region should be viewed as a continuum of cultural wealth rather than as separable and individual issues to be addressed. This is especially important if the notion of an 'Intelligent Region', able to attract substantial inward investment because of human resource skills, is to be made credible.

## FUTURE POLICY IMPLICATIONS

A central argument in the promotion of bilingual education within Cardiff and elsewhere had been that bilingual citizens become empowered to choose which language they wish to use in social and economic contexts. It is fitting then that we question how these are related to contemporary political developments by asking the following.

1. What effect will the arrangements for the bilingual servicing of the National Assembly have on the legitimization of bilingualism as a societal norm?
2. How will the experiences generated within the National Assembly impact on the bilingual character of educational and public administrative services, together with the local government and legal system?

The strengthening of the bilingual character of our national institutions should have a long-term impact, but we recognize that, even with the modest reforms to date, there are severe difficulties in using Welsh as a matter of course in public transactions. Two issues of direct importance for education will be the wider exposure of all children in Wales to bilingual instruction and the introduction of new software and terminological data-bases which will enable students to shift back and forth between information generated in English and that generated in Welsh. A second consideration is the creation of new bilingual opportunities for specialist use of Welsh and English within the democratic institutions and in related soci-economic agencies. How will this impact on the education system and a whole host of other activities? At present, due to the lack of systematic research we know virtually nothing as to how aspects of the education system will influence these issues. Nor do we know very much in detail about the form-ative influences on conceptions of national identity in Wales nor of the appro-priate use of Welsh or English within selected specialist domains. Much of public policy is based on very broad assumptions and generalizations about the relevance of bilingual education in the service of society but very few research projects have sought to document the bilingual educational experience *vis-à-vis* a monolingual English educational experience.

Three recent exceptions have produced limited information relating to the performance of bilingual schools in the industrialized south-east of Wales. The first study by Higgs, Bellin, Farrell and White (1997) investigated the process of language shift by undertaking a socio-spatial analysis of census and non-census data within selected communities. Reynolds, Bellin and ab Ieuan (1998) under-took a second, more focused, study which sought to assess whether or not the Welsh-medium school sector in the Rhondda Valleys was characterized by any structural advantages which enabled their pupils to outperform pupils of very similar socio-economic backgrounds who attended English-medium or Church in Wales schools. The results suggested that bilingual children in Welsh-medium education were distinctive because (i) their bilingualism generates an interaction effect whereby utilizing the two main languages together boosts cognitive performance and intellectual confidence; (ii) their Welsh identity gives them security in a rapidly differentiating and increasingly heterogeneous world; and (iii) they are conscious of their distinctiveness in a way which helps to boost social confidence and self-esteem. A third study by Stephen May (2000) analysed the attitudes of teacher trainees to the advantages and disadvantages of working within a bilingual state and the impact of the compulsory elements of the Welsh National Curriculum. Teacher trainees were chosen because they constitute a key group of prospective public-sector workers in Wales. As education is vital for reversing language shift, this cohort will be involved in the future delivery and development of bilingual education. The sample strongly endorsed the prin-ciple of Welsh as a public language in Wales, but there was a far more cautious reaction to the implication that the battle over bilingual education policy had been won. It would be difficult to translate a *general* support for bilingual educa-tion as a public good into *particular* policy proposals in specific domains. There was considerable support for the *opportunity* to learn Welsh, but this support was conditional on the provision of a *range* of learning options, since Welsh-medium education as the *only* option was not favoured by the cohort. May asserts that these 'contested responses indicate that the notion of individual choice with regard to language learning continues to exert significant influence, *even among a group that is largely well disposed to a formalised bilingual policy*' (2000: 26).

Four considerations derive from these academic studies and from our Cardiff case-study. First, how widespread is genuine support for bilingual education within the population at large? To what extent does this support remain dependent on an implicit voluntarism beyond the realm of the school? To what extent do non-Welsh-language speakers conceive of individual choice and language rights as a means by which to opt out of bilingual policy requirements? How should bilingual policy proceed in the light of these considerations?

The former Conservative administration in Wales, as personified by Rod Richards, Minister of Education within the Welsh Office, favoured individual choice on matters of Welsh-language teaching in state schools. The party line was that an element of compulsion was commendable up until year 9, but thereafter Welsh should not be obligatory as part of the National Curriculum in years 10 and 11. Many Welsh-speakers have agreed with this position, citing the element of Irish-language compulsion in the Irish Republic as a precedent for what could transpire in Wales, especially if the investment in Welsh-medium teacher training and resources is not increased considerably. Consequently, the normalization of Welsh as a national language remains problematic for many exactly because it requires some element of compulsion (May, 2000).

## CONCLUSION

Survey data and academic analysis suggest that even when the legitimization of Welsh has been formally achieved that there will still be specific issues which are contested. As the Spatial Interface Model (Philbrick, 1983) and May's (2000) analysis makes clear this is because minority language policies necessitate changes within a given nation-state to the balance of wider power-relations between the linguistic groups and the languages they speak. May argues that the

> policy of quiet coercion that seems apparent from the Welsh Language Act guidelines may be the best way to proceed. Certainly a gradual and graduated approach is more likely to attain the degree of 'tolerability' (Grin, 1995) needed from majority language speakers to ensure the long term success of any formal bilingual policy in Wales.

The debate over choice and compulsion will invoke opposition to the normalization of Welsh, and, though not exclusively so, this opposition derives from the wish of the majority to remain monolingual. Cardiff's LEA policy of gradual bilingual education has always taken account of the wishes of the majority for fear of incurring opposition to its incremental and pragmatic approach. In that respect it stands in marked contrast to, for example, Gwynedd County Council, where the demographic and political power of the local majority could justify a greater element of compulsion. Gradualism has served the authority well, but it has not served the best interest of Cardiff's Welsh-speaking residents.

> Education may also play an important mediating role here, since the notion of language compulsion within formal education appears to be more readily accepted by majority language speakers. The key here is a tacit recognition that minority language compulsion provides the best opportunity for all students to learn Welsh – an opportunity that would otherwise be denied to them, given the language's minority status (May, 2000: 33).

However, May's analysis reveals tensions over compulsion and voluntarism which indicates that, even within a cohort broadly committed to Welsh bilingual policy, the fears and antagonisms of majority-language speakers, and the associated discourses of individual choice and rights, continue to militate against its successful development and enactment in the longer term. As he suggests, achieving favourable attitudes to Welsh at a general level is a significant achievement and should not be underestimated. However, 'it must be regarded as only a first step, and one that can still be easily undone within the crucible of majority language speakers' attitudes'.

The delicacy of language revitalization procedures surfaces again. Nevertheless, we conclude with a positive vision. In the 1940s, when the first Welsh-medium school was opened in Cardiff, from the point of view of the future of the Welsh language, the city was seen as a bleak place. At the outset of the twenty-first century, the city is seen as one of the most promising areas in Wales, where the rejuvenation of the Welsh language is seen as the most marked and successful (Aitchison and Carter, 2000).

## *Acknowledgements*

In preparing the middle section of our discussion the authors are deeply indebted to the following individuals for valuable information, details and comments: Mrs Hilda Ethal (one of the original teachers of the 1939 Ysgol Fore Sadwrn), the late Professor A. O. H. Jarman (one of the parents of the Ysgol Fore Sadwrn and chair of the Parents' Association in 1951), Mr Tom Evans (former headmaster of Ysgol Gymraeg Bryntaf), Mrs Heulwen Jones (teacher at the Welsh Unit, Ysgol Llanisien, and afterwards at Bryntaf when the unit and Ysgol Bryntaf were amalgamated), Mrs Meriel Myers (a Bryntaf parent), Mr Huw Powel (a Bryntaf parent and committee member of the Parents' Association during the 1978–9 period), Dr W. T. R. Pryce (a Bryntaf parent and committee member of the Parents' Association during the 1978–9 period), Mr W. Alun Mathias for generous loans of books and periodicals, Mr Emyr Currie-Jones for reading the discussion and offering comments, and particularly to Mr Iorwerth Morgan for a close reading of the discussion and many valuable comments and additional points of information. We are also indebted to Iorwerth Morgan for allowing us unlimited access to the papers in the archive of Undeb Cenedlaethol Athrawon Cymru (UCAC) (see n. 5). We are also deeply indebted to Professor R. D. Thomas who generously sent us copious notes and documents based on his experience as a parent and member of the Bryntaf Parents' Association during the 1960s – information to which we would not otherwise have had access (see n. 18). We also acknowledge the gracious permission of Professor A. Philbrick to reproduce Figures 5.2–5.4 from his work.

## Notes

[1] An excellent account of the emergence of Cardiff as the major Welsh city is to be found in Evans (1984/5: 351–87).

[2] Mr Iorwerth Morgan kindly informed us that the author of this contribution (p. 19) in the Gwyn Daniel Memorial Number of *Undeb/Unity* was Victor Hampson Jones.

[3] It should be noted that some prominent Welsh figures of the period, notably Iorwerth Peate (National Museum of Wales and subsequently founder and Director of the Welsh Folk Museum) and W. J. Gruffydd (Professor of Welsh at the University), were contemptuous of attempts to cymricize Cardiff and of its desire to be the capital of Wales; see Davies 1997. Nevertheless, both Peate and Gruffydd supported the campaign to establish a Welsh school in Cardiff (see n. 7 below).

[4] N. Evans (1984/5: 377–9) gives a succinct account of the compulsion/ optional argument. A detailed account of the teaching of Welsh in Cardiff from the 1890s to 1966 is to be found in Walters (1966/7).

[5] The account of the campaign to establish the Welsh school is partly based on the materials held in the UCAC archive which has recently been deposited in the Salisbury Library in the Arts and Social Studies Library, University of Cardiff. The archive contains letters and a document of four A4 pages giving an account of the efforts to establish the Welsh school over the period 1939 to 1949 when it eventually opened. This account is headed *Braslun o'r digwyddiadau i sicrhau Ysgol Gymraeg yng Nghaerdydd* (An outline of the events to secure a Welsh school in Cardiff). The account is not dated and has no attribution. It is clearly the campaigners' account and will be referred to as *Braslun*. The archive has not been indexed yet and all references made to materials contained in it will be acknowledged as 'Archive'. In addition, we have throughout this discussion drawn heavily upon the minutes of the various committees of Cardiff Education Authority as well as reports in the press.

[6] An appeal letter was sent out to these individuals. In one version of the appeal letter it is stated that the intention was to establish a Welsh School *o dan nawdd yr Urdd* (under the patronage of the Urdd) (Archive) and this version also includes the names of some of those who had already contributed; they include a justice of the peace, an inspector of schools, a member of the staff of the National Museum and a principal of a training college.

[7] Ifan ab Owen Edwards was also a member of the deputation that had met with the Cardiff Education Committee on 23 May 1947. Other members were Iorwerth Peate (National Museum of Wales), W. J. Gruffydd (Professor of Welsh at the University), Evan J. Jones (lecturer in Education at the University), Morgan Watkins (former Professor of French at the University), Jenkin Jones (Secretary of the University of Wales Press) and Gwyn Daniel.

[8] Ironically, the fact that a Welsh school was to be established in Cardiff was used in

support of its claim to be the capital city in 1948 (Walters, 1966/67: 122–3). This may account for the decision to reconsider the matter of the school at the 28 November 1948 meeting of the Education Committtee.

[9] If the number of children between the ages of eight and eleven were included (fifty-nine) the total would be 390.

[10] They probably viewed themselves as a temporary Parents' Association in the months prior to the opening of the school. The December 1949 issue of *Y Gaer* (an inter-denominational Welsh weekly produced by the Welsh chapels in Cardiff) reported that 'Cymdeithas Rhieni yr Ysgol Gymraeg' (The Parents' Association of the Welsh School) had been formed with Mrs Alun Humphreys as secretary and 'Fe fydd hithau'n barod i helpu'r rhieni ym mhob ffordd' ('She will be prepared to help parents in every possible way').

[11] The UCAC Archive contains a list of the children who would attend the Welsh School. It is entitled 'Ysgol Gymraeg Caerdydd. Rhestr Enwau Plant (Trwy Gymdeithas y Rhieni) Sef Ymateb Cadarnhaol Rhieni mewn Ysgrifen' (Cardiff Welsh School. List of Children's Names (Through the Parents' Association) Being the Parents' Confirmation in Writing'). The list contains more names than the actual number of pupils who were present when the school was opened.

[12] Walters (1966/67: 99–109) gives a detailed account of the growth of the Welsh nursery schools in Cardiff for the period 1951–66, with three having being established by 1966, see also n. 20.

[13] This was the Welsh Unit at Ysgol Llanisien. The unit had been set up in 1964. We are grateful to Mrs Heulwen Jones for much valuable information regarding the unit.

[14] We have not been able to follow up the entire details of the matter but it had been hoped that the unit would become a second Welsh-medium school in Cardiff. However the proposal became embroiled with another proposal to build a Catholic school. The *South Wales Echo* (15 April 1967) reported: 'The city's director of education . . . was unable to say at this stage whether a Welsh primary school planned would be affected by the [Catholic school] proposal.' It is interesting to note that in the mid-1960s many in the Parents' Association wanted to set up a campaign for a second school but a majority at a meeting held in Ebeneser Chapel in 1965 opted to press for one big school believing that they would get better facilites (information provided by Professor J. D. R. Thomas).

[15] The proposed split-site development for the 1977 school was Ysgol Coed Glas, Llanisien, and for the 1978 schools Ysgol Eglwys Wen, Whitchurch and Ysgol Peter Lea.

[16] This was Ysgol Glantaf.

[17] This was Ysgol Eglwys Wen, Whitchurch.

[18] We have not been able to do justice to the involvement and commitment of the Bryntaf Parents' Association to the development of Welsh-medium education in Cardiff. This is because we have been unable to consult the minutes and papers relating to the Association: the Association's entire files were deposited in the Cardiff Central Library in the early 1980s following the final dispersal of the original Ysgol Bryntaf. Regrettably the Central Library is unable to locate them. We are deeply indebted to Professor J. D. R. Thomas who was chair of the Parents' Association, 1962–3, who provided copious notes and copies of documents relating to the Parents' Association that he had kept. It would be impossible to include here all the details of the Association's activites and it is to be hoped that a comprehensive study of the parents' role will be written in the future.

[19] According to a statement by the chair of the Parents' Association reported in *Y Cymro* (27 March 1979).

[20] We do not have the exact details of the growth of the Welsh nursery schools in Cardiff itself; but the number has increased from three in 1966 (see n. 12 above) to 34 in 1998 . For a history of the Nursery Schools Movement see Stevens (1996).

[21] The meeting with the chair of the County Council took place on 16 March 1979 and the two representatives of the Parents' Association who met with him were Glyn E. Jones (chair of the association) and Huw Powell (committee member).

[22] This meeting was held at Ysgol Bryntaf on 22 March 1979.

[23] This school became known as Ysgol Coed y Gof.

[24] This school became known as Ysgol y Wern.

## References

Abler, R., Janelle, D., Philbrick, A. and Sommer, J. (1983). *Human Geography in a Shrinking World*, North Scituate, MA: Duxbury Press.

Aitchison, J. W. and Carter, H. (1987). 'The Welsh language in Cardiff: a quiet revolution', *Transactions of the Institute of British Geographers*, pp. 482–92.

Aitchison, J. W. and Carter, H. (1988). *The Welsh Language in the Cardiff Region*, Aberystwyth: Rural Surveys Research Unit, Monograph 1.

Aitchison, J. W. and Carter, H. (2000). *Language, Economy and Society: The Changing Fortunes of the Welsh Language in the Twentieth Century*, Cardiff: University of Wales Press.

Bellin, W., Higgs, G. and Farrell, S. (1997). *Halting or Reversing Language Shift: A Social and Spatial Analysis of South-East Wales*, Final Report for ESRC grant no. R000236330.

Cardiff County Council (1998). *Welsh Education Scheme*, Cardiff: Cardiff County Council.

Davies, J. (1997). 'R. T. Jenkins a Chaerdydd', *Taliesin*, 85–98.

Evans, N. (1984/5). 'The Welsh Victorian city: the middle class, civic and national consciousness in Cardiff, 1850–1914', *The Welsh History Review*, 12, 351–87.

Fishman, J. A. (1991). *Reversing Language Shift*, Clevedon, Avon: Multilingual Matters.

Grin, F. (1995). 'Combining immigrant and autochthonous language rights: a territorial approach to multilingualism', in Skutnabb-Kangas, T. and Phillipson, R. (eds.), *Linguistic Human Rights*, Berlin: de Gruyter, pp. 31–48.

Heller, M. (1999). *Linguistic Minorities and Modernity*, London: Longman.

Higgs, G., Bellin, W., Farrell, S. and White, S. (1997). 'Educational attainment and social disadvantage: contextualising school league tables', *Regional Studies*, 31(8), 779–93.

Hilling, J. (1975a). *The Historical Architecture of Wales*, Cardiff: University of Wales Press.

Hilling, J. (1975b). 'Cardiff', in Williams, S. (ed.), *South Glamorgan: A County History*, Barry: Stewart Williams Publishers, pp. 38–115.

Jenkins, R. T. (1968). *Edrych yn Ôl*, Denbigh: Gwasg Gee.

Jones, J. G. (1984). *Cofio Yw Gobeithio: Cyfrol Dathlu Canmlwyddiant Achos Heol-Y-Crwys 1884–1984*, Cardiff: Yr Eglwys Bresbyteraidd.

Jones, J. G. (1987). *Y Ganrif Gyntaf: Hanes Cymmrodorion Caerdydd, 1885–1985*, Cardiff: Cymmrodorion Caerdydd.

Jones, J. R. (1966). *Prydeindod*, Llandybïe: Llyfrau'r Dryw.

Mackey, W. (1988). 'An introduction to geolinguistics', in Williams, C. H. (ed.), *Language in Geographic Context*, Clevedon, Avon: Multilingual Matters, pp. 20–46.

May, S. (2000). 'Accommodating and resisting minority language policy: the case of Wales', *Journal of Bilingual Education*, 3, 2, 101–28.

Morris Jones, R. and Ghuman Singh, P. A. (eds.) (1995). *Bilingualism, Education and Identity*, Cardiff: University of Wales Press.

Philbrick, A. (1983). 'Cumulative versus mutually exclusive regions in the future', in Abler, R., Janelle, D., Philbrick, A. and Sommer, J., *Human Geography in a Shrinking World*, North Scituate, MA: Duxbury Press, pp. 87–98.

PDAG (1988). *Interim Report of the Secondary Working Committee*, Cardiff: PDAG, unpublished (mimeo).

PDAG (1992). *Response to the White Paper on Education, Diversity and Choice: A New Framework for Schools*, Cardiff: PDAG, unpublished (mimeo).

Stevens, C. (1996). *Meithrin: Hanes Mudiad Ysgolion Meithrin 1971–1996*, Llandysul: Gwasg Gomer.

Reynolds, D., Bellin, W. and ab Ieuan, R. (1998). *A Competitive Edge: Why Welsh Medium Schools Perform Better*, Cardiff: The Institute of Welsh Affairs.

Thomas, O. J. (1998). 'Yr iaith Gymraeg yng Nghaerdydd c.1800–1914', in Jenkins, G. (ed.), *Iaith Carreg Fy Aelwyd*, Cardiff: University of Wales Press.

Trudgill, P. (1993). *The Ausbau Sociolinguistics of Minority Languages in Greece*, mimeo, Lucerne University.

Walters, I. M. Ll. (1966/7). 'Hanes datblygiad dysgu Cymraeg yn ysgolion cynradd Caerdydd', Traethawd BA Addysg, Aberystwyth, Prifysgol Cymru.

Welsh Office (1993). *Welsh Social Survey*, Cardiff: Welsh Office.

Welsh Office (1998). *Statistics of Education and Training in Wales: Schools, 1998*, Cardiff: Welsh Office.

Williams, C. H. (1988). *Addysg Ddwyieithog yng Nghymru ynteu Addysg ar gyfer Cymru Ddwyieithog?*, Bangor: Canolfan Astudiaethau Iaith.

Williams, C. H. (1994). *Called Unto Liberty*, Clevedon, Avon: Multilingual Matters.

Williams, C. H. (1998). 'Operating through two languages', in Osmond, J. (ed.), *The National Assembly Agenda*, Cardiff: Institute of Welsh Affairs, pp. 101–16.

Williams, C. H. (2000). 'A language policy for the National Assembly of Wales', in ECTARC (ed.), *Culture, Nation and Region in Europe*, Llangollen: ECTARC.

Williams, C. H. and Evas, J. (1998). *The Community Language Project*, Cardiff: The Welsh Language Board and Cardiff University.

# 6

# Planning for the Use of Welsh by Young People

## HEINI GRUFFUDD

Education must be at the heart of language planning in the context of reversing language shift, as acquisition of the endangered language is essential before any long-term progress can be made in furthering the use of that language in the various aspects of community life. In Wales, over the last thirty years or so, we have witnessed a substantial growth in the number of schools providing education through the medium of Welsh. Recent figures collated by the Welsh Office suggest that 25 per cent of Wales's primary schools now use Welsh as a medium of instruction. There are at present 449 bilingual primary schools and forty-nine bilingual secondary schools (Welsh Office, 1998). The remarkable success, both academic and numerical,[1] of these schools follows a long history of an anglicized education system in Wales. Although the growth is at a modest pace compared to the advances made during the last decade in the Basque Country,[2] where a broadly similar number and proportion speak the native language, it is nevertheless a solid achievement, brought about often by the determined efforts of a growing number of parents in the anglicized parts of Wales. In west and north Wales the growth has been largely achieved through the adoption of bilingual literacy as an aim by local education authorities, and it augurs well that the policies of the former counties of Gwynedd and Dyfed have been continued by the unitary local authorities which began operating in April 1996.

Nevertheless, concern has frequently been expressed regarding the possibly transient nature of the linguistic success of these schools. On the one hand, the actual number of Welsh-medium primary schools has remained fairly static during the last decade of the twentieth century, suggesting that there may be material and political barriers hindering the continued growth of these schools. On the other hand, concern has been expressed regarding the opportunities available for former Welsh school pupils to use Welsh in daily life. The Welsh Language Board, in launching its consultation exercise before formulating its strategy for Welsh, acknowledged the difficulties facing the new generation of Welsh speakers and saw the lack of use made of Welsh in certain areas of Wales and in certain domains as a cause of worry (Bwrdd yr Iaith Gymraeg, 1995: 4).

Some people, such as Dr Tim Williams,[3] take the view that the lack of opportunity to use Welsh in the society at large renders useless much of the schools' efforts. The meagre figure of around 300 children of primary-school age living in Welsh-speaking homes in the old county of Mid Glamorgan confirms that the

is in a parlous state. In Wales as a whole just 6.4 per cent of primary-
upils are brought up with Welsh as a first language, but a further 9.3 per
ak it fluently, mostly through the efforts of schools, and another 29.6 per
cent are able to speak it but without fluency. A more positive view towards
Welsh would be to investigate ways in which small- and large-scale language
planning measures could enhance the opportunities of those who have acquired
Welsh through education to use it.

It is also necessary to face squarely one of the many issues raised often and
ardently by Joshua Fishman, namely the central role of the family in language
transmission, and the need for family and community use of the endangered
language to ensure its survival. He has argued that teachers often assume a
language-rescuing role far in excess of what they can realistically achieve (1991:
368–70).


## NEED FOR A COMPREHENSIVE LANGUAGE PLAN

Most attempts at language planning in Wales have been haphazard, and largely
the result of the vision, activities and pressure of individuals and movements.
Institutions such as S4C and Welsh-medium schools, Welsh playgroups,
language centres and camps, publishing ventures and the entertainment and
cultural scene have been created more by individuals, movements and community pressure than by coherent governmental planning.

Plaid Cymru, the national party of Wales, and Cymdeithas yr Iaith Gymraeg
(the Welsh Language Society) have largely concentrated on the kind of high-
level language issues, such as radio and television services and official language
recognition. It cannot be denied that the increase in the use of Welsh by central
government, local authorities and other public bodies has probably surpassed
the wildest dreams of Saunders Lewis, the disillusioned founder of Plaid Cymru
who argued in 1962 for a campaign of unconstitutional action in the Welsh-
speaking parts of Wales to ensure official status for Welsh.

The setting up of the partly Welsh-medium television channel, S4C, in 1982,
and the passing of the 1993 Welsh Language Act, in spite of its inherent weaknesses, must be seen as monumental achievements for comparatively small pressure groups. It can be argued that a positive view of the endangered language is
fostered by these advancements. Nevertheless, these are the very fields which
Fishman warns us against regarding as an easy substitute for the transmission of
native language in the home.

Popular action and support for the endangered language is a key element in
language revival in the context of asserting ethnic identity. Nevertheless, such
action, while achieving reasonable success in recognizable and tangible objectives, can often be severely lacking in influence over more intricate and less
easily defined domains. This difficulty cannot easily be overcome by the individuals and movements which were so crucial in the development of Welsh in

the educational, entertainment and public spheres during the last third of the twentieth century. Cymdeithas yr Iaith, for example, cannot now fight campaigns for highly visual targets, as these have largely been won. Targets now have a closer relationship to the plethora of economic and societal elements which constitute modern life, often not considered as being relevant to language. Simplistic youthful campaigns are no longer so effective.

Further difficulties are caused by the increasing globalization of media on the one hand, and on the other by the continuing privatization of services which were previously provided by public bodies. The increasing dominance of Anglo-American culture and the spread of English-based electronic media are an ever-present challenge to endangered languages while governmental linguistic intrusion concentrating on public bodies, which was regarded as a main plank by the creators of the 1993 Welsh Language Act, is no longer as relevant as it was ten years ago.

How is Welsh to face these challenges? As it is now much harder for individuals and movements to influence the complex and distantly based machinery of so many aspects of life, it is now ripe for the National Assembly to shoulder responsibility for language planning. The presence of this body, which one would not have envisaged even in 1995, presents Wales with an ideal opportunity to tackle language issues in a way not previously possible. Whereas the force of language protests in the past was largely targeted towards London government, which was politically convenient for Welsh-language movements, Wales is now faced with a wholly different situation.

With the advent of the National Assembly no language campaigner can now simply blame London for shortcomings in Wales, although any necessary legal changes in language status would at present have to be made in London, and Wales could still find itself tied to London in many matters of policy. Although transnational companies wield significant influence in the economic sphere, and although the vagaries of European funding present some unfathomable peculiarities, there is now a national body which can take decisions in the field of language planning.

At the time of writing, however, the National Assembly has taken precious few steps in this field. While it has hotly disputed issues concerning bones and meat, it has yet to begin to face up to the need to put flesh on our increasingly skeletal language. The Welsh Language Board, having pleaded for extra money from the National Assembly to give as grants to various bodies which promote Welsh, has been given little extra, and has found that it has had to decrease the annual grant to the National Eisteddfod. That there may be a furore over this decrease is, however, to miss a much more basic need. The giving of grants by the Welsh Language Board, or by whichever board, be it in the guise of Arts Lottery Funding, Lottery Charity Board or any other, does not begin to deal with the many fundamental aspects which should be a part of a national language plan. Any amount of grant-giving, however important to the grant receivers, will have little effect on the multitudes who have to be won over to the language to ensure its long-term survival. A national language plan would have grant-giving as a possibly minor item compared to the many faceted spheres of every-day life which need to be cymricized if Welsh is to be given scope to breathe.

The very existence of the present Welsh Language Board, with its limited powers and funds, needs to be called into question in this context. Were it to continue, its terms of reference would have to be greatly expanded, with the support of a new, wide-ranging Welsh Language Act. It should possibly be substituted by a governmental Culture Authority and subdepartments, akin to the governmental departments of Catalonia and the Basque Country, which could administer and put into effect a cohesive and comprehensive language plan for Wales (Gruffudd, 1999).

With education as its cornerstone, a comprehensive language plan would need steps to make it possible for the newly acquired language to be used effectively in a sufficient number of domains to ensure the necessary degree of language vitality among the new generation of speakers. This responsibility of language planning seems to be in its infancy in Wales and in many European countries.

Catalonia, as detailed in Chapter 11, is one of the few countries in Europe to have prepared a comprehensive plan for extending the use of the native language in a broad spectrum of activities, including media and culture, educa-tion, sports, health and social institutions, and the socio-economic field. In this plan, specific targets have been set, as well as means of achieving them (Generalitat de Catalunya, 1995). Special attention is paid to youth culture, and the general aim includes promoting youth culture products in Catalan, and the language in a range of leisure activities. Specific targets include promoting Catalan as a 'language of relations [*sic*] among young people'; supplying 'competitive products aimed at young people (computer games, radio and tele-vision programmes)'; increasing the use of Catalan in youth programming on 'the different television channels', and 'encouraging the use of Catalan in the most common social environments for young people between the ages of 14 and 24 (pubs, discos, bars etc.)'. Government intervention, when the native language has its own autonomous government, plays a vital role in such endeavours. Only at government level can such plans be created and executed, and only a govern-ment can co-ordinate the hopefully willing co-operation of the complex network of institutions and organizations which make up much of a nation's organized life. It remains to be seen to what extent a Welsh Assembly run by London-based parties will be committed to such a plan (C. H. Williams, 1999).


## LANGUAGE ABILITY AND LANGUAGE USE

In view of the apparent dichotomy between the success of Welsh-medium schools and the use of Welsh in the community, it is essential for language plan-ners to pay particular and swift attention to this latter field, both on a national scale, by providing the appropriate linguistic and cultural background through the mass media and other means of public and commercial communication, and on a local scale, in an attempt to make it attractive, if not essential, to use the endangered language in social and familial discourse. Recent increased donations by the Welsh Language Board to the *mentrau iaith* (local language initiatives) suggest that the board's thinking is creative, but the actual amounts are derisory compared to the funding, for example, given towards the production of one television play.[4]

As has been suggested, success in reversing language shift cannot be measured by the numbers of endangered-language speakers alone. When the number of young people speaking the language increases, as the census figures of 1991 showed to be the case in Wales, there is no guarantee that the tide has turned. At the peril of sacrificing hard-earned gains would those who have campaigned for the endangered language rest on their laurels. In many parts of Wales, a comparison between children and young people claiming to speak Welsh and the numbers seen by headteachers to be fluent in the language shows a wide discrepancy.[5] According to school heads, 15.7 per cent of primary pupils spoke Welsh fluently in 1996 compared with 22.3 per cent of under-fifteens who spoke it according to the 1991 census (Aitchison and Carter, 1994: 104). Although this latter figure might include those who learnt Welsh at secondary level, it is also possible that pupils' self-confidence causes their perception of their linguistic ability to be relatively greater than that of the older generation. This suggests that the figures provided by the government censuses, based on subjective perception of language ability, do not give an accurate or a complete picture of language ability.

Recent surveys have suggested a much wider ability to speak and to understand a certain amount of Welsh, but figures showing an increase in Welsh-speaking young people, especially in areas not served by Welsh-medium schools, can be explained by the success of teaching Welsh as a second language rather than by ability to speak Welsh in social settings. This begins to mimic the language patterns of Ireland, where around 50 per cent claim to speak Irish in the ten to nineteen age group, but actual language use is minimal, as described in Chapter 11 below. The numbers claiming ability in Irish falls in each age group from secondary schooling until pension age, and the real position of Irish is probably reflected by the 5 per cent of children who speak it before school age (Hindley, 1990: 34). Census figures give no idea of actual language use, and this is the fatal flaw in measuring language vitality according to numbers of speakers.

If we accept Joshua Fishman's thesis that intergenerational language transmission is all-important, then we should pay much more attention to the numbers of pupils who speak Welsh at home, or to those who use the language as their first or equal language, rather than simply to language ability. Language use, if it could be measured, would give a truer picture of language vitality. The reverse side of the coin is that success of any language plan must eventually be measured by the numbers choosing that language as their first language rather than simply by ability in language use. The Basque Autonomous Community regularly attempts to measure this factor (Eusko Jaurlaritza, 1999).

## YOUNG PEOPLE AND LANGUAGE PLANNING

Gaining an understanding of patterns of language use by bilingual young people is a prerequisite of any attempt at language planning. Of particular interest in the attempt to map what is happening to the Welsh language among young people is that, in all the achievements and activities, a significant proportion of young people have been politically and culturally mobilized and have themselves contributed widely to the efforts to safeguard the language. Young people have developed a vibrant popular culture through the medium of Welsh which presents their generation with a choice of youth popular culture that was not available during the 1950s and early 1960s. More has been achieved through voluntary action among young people than through central planning, and this element of spontaneity, often linked to an anti-authoritarian approach, should not be lost in any attempt to formalize language planning for young people.[6] Indeed, many young people in Wales, afraid of political interference, were quite suspicious of attempts to give government money to an organization which encourages Welsh-medium rock music.

It is clear that the efforts of pressure groups involved in the education field have had significant successes in giving young people ability in Welsh and have led to opportunities for these to use the language in extra-curricular activities, thanks to the unstinting contribution of many committed teachers. RHAG (Parents for Welsh Education), MYM (Welsh Playgroup Association) and the Urdd (the Welsh League of Youth) have largely concentrated on developing Welsh in educational circles and have achieved their successes sometimes in the face of determined opposition of Labour councillors in areas such as the old county of West Glamorgan, but with the co-operation of many of their counterparts in the old Mid Glamorgan.

Politically orientated movements have given young people an opportunity to take an anti-authoritarian stance, which is a prerogative of the young. Young people have always played a major role in the activities of the militant Cymdeithas yr Iaith Gymraeg, and the assumption sometimes made that this movement would lose momentum as the first young generation grew older has not been realized. Most of the new leaders of Cymdeithas yr Iaith are around twenty-five years old or younger, and the less prominent profile of the movement in recent years is due more to the intricate issues now being tackled, the earlier headline-grabbing campaigns having been won, than to a change in age profile.

Young people have been served by the bodies that have been established by central government as a result of pressure and possibly through genuine cultural and linguistic concern. The extent to which specific issues in the field of language planning for young people have been given attention by these bodies varies. Accusations have been levelled at S4C and Radio Cymru that they have catered mainly for traditional ageing Welsh speakers, while recent attempts at programming specifically for young people have been criticized by traditional-ists. There is some evidence that the Welsh radio service has attracted more listeners[7] but competition from the enormously influential Anglo-American media continues unabated.

Although the statutory Welsh Language Board, as already mentioned, has acknowledged the importance of furthering the language among young people, concern has been expressed regarding its ability to contribute towards compre-hensive language planning.[8] The small amount of money at its disposal is in contrast to the huge programme of work it seeks to undertake. The government-financed Books Council of Wales has at various times commissioned books specifically aimed at teenagers and young people, although the bulk of its activ-ities caters for the general reader and children. Welsh still lacks youth magazines and the kind of popular fiction available in English.

The regional *mentrau iaith* in Glamorgan and eastern Dyfed have regularly held events aimed at young people in an attempt to popularize the native rock-music culture, and the success of this kind of activity, organized in other parts of Wales by voluntary groups or by the various Welsh-language social clubs, such as Clwb Ifor Bach in Cardiff, Clwb y Bont in Pontypridd, Tŷ Tawe in Swansea, is a hopeful indication. On a local level, there has been intense activity both in anglicized and in largely Welsh-speaking towns and villages in Wales over the last twenty-five years, with the specific aim of furthering the endangered language, and much of this activity is aimed at young people. This activity would include the work of the above-mentioned voluntary movements, but would also involve the parents' associations of all the bilingual schools and the work of many Welsh chapels.

## USE OF WELSH BY YOUNG PEOPLE

With this background of many successes, and with vigorous efforts having been exerted in so many activities which attempt to promote the use of Welsh among young people, a project at the University of Wales Swansea attempted to discover to what extent the knowledge of Welsh acquired by young people was used by them in their day-to-day life after the end of compulsory education (Gruffudd, 1996). The linguistic ability and patterns of language use among the young will inevitably give a basis for planning for future use of the language, as well as providing a measure of the success of any efforts made in the field of language maintenance and intergenerational language transmission. Language choice in the case of bilingual young will probably provide a more accurate guide to the state of vitality of the endangered language than statistics on language ability.

How successful has the above-mentioned activity been in furthering the use of Welsh among the new generation? It is difficult to give a specific answer, as the variables involved are so great, and it is impossible to start from a 'were it not for these activities' point of departure. Our results should, however, throw some light on three fields of interest: first, the actual use of Welsh, which includes the tendency to use the language in various domains, and the situations which seem to contribute to the use of Welsh, and those which seem to hinder it; secondly, they should highlight any discrepancy between the success of teaching an endangered language and the use made of that language by its speakers; in the third instance, as well as suggesting any increase or decrease in the use of Welsh between the generations, they should suggest whether language transmission through education is likely to produce future parents who will transmit the language at home.

We chose to investigate the use of Welsh among young people immediately after the end of compulsory schooling. This would, on the one hand, suggest any immediate change between the use of the language at school and in the community at large and in further education; on the other hand, it would add to research work already undertaken on the use of Welsh, and the attitude towards Welsh, among pupils in primary schools and in the secondary schools (Baker, 1992; Sharp et al., 1973; Jones, 1983; Williams and Thomas, 1977, 1978).

## YOUNG PEOPLE'S BACKGROUND

Our sample contained 60 per cent (329) of the sixteen- to eighteen-year-old bilingual people within a 20-mile radius of the University of Wales, Swansea, in south Wales. The sample was based on the previous year's cohort of sixteen year olds in five 'bilingual' secondary schools in the area. Four of these were designated bilingual schools, while the fifth, in the Aman Valley area, was considered a traditional bilingual school, which we will refer to as a mixed-language school, with English and partly Welsh streams. The work undertaken attempted to determine the various factors which form the linguistic background of these young people, so that these could then be correlated to language use.

The area included the largely anglicized city of Swansea, and a surrounding area including the former county of West Glamorgan and eastern Carmarthenshire, which has comparatively high percentages of Welsh speakers. This area straddles the linguistic divide between anglicized and Welsh-speaking south Wales, a line that has been shown to be moving incessantly westwards. This divide has been clearly demonstrated by C. Baker in his language map of Wales (Baker and Jones, 1999: appendix 1). Percentages of Welsh speakers in the area ranged from under 10 per cent to over 80 per cent, and were thus representative of patterns to be found throughout Wales. Almost half the sample lived in areas where Welsh is spoken by more than 70 per cent of the population, 22 per cent of the sample lived in areas where Welsh is spoken by less than 25 per cent of the population.

Our work, as will be seen, shows that this divide, among young people, has moved westward from Swansea Valley to Aman Valley, where the Welsh language is no longer the main means of communication. Most young people aged between sixteen and eighteen attended various establishments of further education: 32.9 per cent were at an English tertiary college while 52.7 per cent were at sixth forms in bilingual schools; a small proportion were in a sixth form in an English-medium school, while the remainder were in the sixth form of a mixed-language school in Ammanford; 70 per cent were receiving non-academic further education, and 30 per cent were following academic courses. The language of their present education course was also varied: 48.9 per cent were following English-medium courses; 40.7 per cent were following some courses in Welsh and others in English, while 10.4 per cent were following Welsh-medium courses. Their academic ability was gauged according to their GCSE results: 59.8 per cent were considered to be of a 'high' standard with an equivalent of six or more passes at C grade; 28.8 per cent were of 'medium standard', with at least the equivalent of five passes at D grade, and 11.3 per cent attained lower standards than this. Their ability in Welsh, according to these examinations, corresponded on the whole to their general ability: 52.9 per cent had obtained at least a C grade in the first-language examination or an A in the extended Welsh examination; 38.7 per cent were 'medium' and 7.4 per cent were weak; 53.8 per cent of the sample were girls; 46 per cent belonged broadly to working-class families, and 54 per cent to middle-class, defined according to the type of housing and type of parents' employment.

## QUESTIONS ON LANGUAGE USE AND ATTITUDE

Use of Welsh was measured according to answers given to a lengthy questionnaire, which included 180 variables. The patterns that emerged were then used to choose a sample of around twenty for partly structured interviews. The questions regarding use of Welsh involved the language used in the home context, in

Table 6.1. Location of education of the sample at age 16

| | Nos. | % of sample | % of Welsh speakers in the area |
|---|---|---|---|
| Gwendraeth Valley, Welsh 'heartland' | 80 | 24.3 | 80+ |
| Aman Valley, Welsh-medium stream | 20 | 6.1 | 65+ |
| Aman Valley, English-medium stream | 35 | 10.6 | 65+ |
| Llanelli and surrounding area | 62 | 18.8 | 45+ |
| Swansea Valley and surrounding area | 73 | 22.2 | 35+ |
| Swansea and surrounding area | 59 | 17.9 | 10+ |

the community at large, in specific domains and in the field of entertainment and mass media. The field covered included language use with parents, with siblings, with peers and with various age groups in the community. Domains relevant to the study included education establishments and various social domains which included the pub or club, sporting centres, dances and discos, youth clubs and other activities, chapel and church and the cinema. After establishing the popularity of these domains, and how often they were frequented, one could then measure the relevance to young people of the language or languages associated with them.

The mass-media inquired into included books and magazines, radio and television, as well as English and Welsh pop music. This would give in some instances an idea of the cultural background of the home, for example, whether the local monthly Welsh papers were read, but would also suggest the media which were most attractive to young people, and to what extent the languages were involved in these activities.

In order to gauge the nature of language use in various situations, and in order on the one hand to confirm the tendencies given by answers in the context of domains and on the other hand to obtain a pattern of any language shift, questions were asked regarding the tendency to use English or Welsh when discussing various topics, and the extent to which English interfered in Welsh speech when discussing these. This tendency could then be corroborated by the linguistic evidence of interviews held. Lastly, questions were asked regarding attitude towards Welsh which would reveal young people's view of Welsh both as a national language and as a language fit for everyday practical use.

PERCENTAGE OF YOUNG WELSH SPEAKERS

Generally in West Glamorgan, the percentage of young people (eleven to seventeen year olds) able to speak Welsh is higher than the average for all ages in the county as a whole, although it is lower than the percentage of Welsh speakers among people aged sixty and above. In some wards the difference between the percentages of young and old is substantial (Gorseinon 15.1/48.7; Onllwyn 7.4/52; Trebannws 36.4/73.7; Clydach 27.1/49.3 per cent; Blaendulais 18.6/47.8; Pontardawe 30.2/64.9). This change clearly shows a dramatic language shift within two generations, with lower Swansea Valley and parts of Neath and Dulais Valley quickly losing their Welshness.

On the other hand, some wards in the Welsh-speaking heartland of West Glamorgan are succeeding in keeping their Welsh character (Lower Brynaman 80.5/ 86.9; Cwmllynfell 89.1/85; Gwaun Cae Gurwen 88.2/86). This positive upkeep of language is also seen in almost all wards of the Welsh heartland of eastern Carmarthenshire (Cross Hands 89.6/88.3; Gorslas 87.3/83.8; Penygroes 85.4/81.8; Pontyberem 93.5/83.7; Tumble 80.6/84.5). The other areas where an increase between these two groups is seen are the already anglicized urban areas

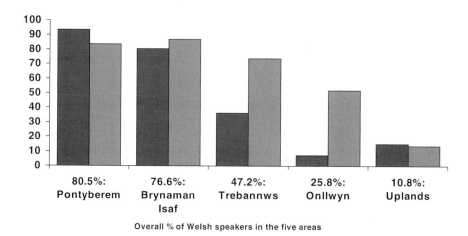

Figure 6.1. Percentages of Welsh speakers: comparison between
age 11–17 (left column) and 60+ (right column)

of Swansea, some of which now have a higher percentage of young people than
areas assumed to be traditionally Welsh (Mayals 20.4/17.2; Uplands 15.2/13.7;
Pennard 14.2/9.8).

The trend, then, is for the heartland areas to keep their Welshness, and for
largely anglicized areas to become more Welsh, but for intermediate areas to
become anglicized fairly quickly. These intermediate areas, from Llanelli to
Aman Valley, Swansea and Neath Valleys, are part of a heavily populated area
which should be at the heart of language planning strategy.

## HOME LANGUAGE

The general result of our enquiries was, however, not heartening for those who
wish to see an increase in the number of young Welsh speakers accompanied by
a corresponding increase in the use of Welsh. Scrutiny of the responses, nevertheless, will suggest many paths still open for language planners.

The young people came from a varied linguistic home background. We asked
for their perception of their parents' standard of Welsh. More than half had
parents considered to have a 'very high' standard of Welsh, whereas around 30
per cent had parents with a 'fair' knowledge of Welsh or less: 64.4 per cent of
their mothers could speak Welsh fluently, and 57.5 per cent of fathers could do
likewise; 23.7 per cent of mothers could speak little or no Welsh, while 31.7 per
cent of fathers were in this position.

A degree of shift towards English was seen among parents who were considered to have a 'strong' or 'very high' ability in Welsh. Whereas 71 per cent (236)
of pairs of parents were considered to be in these categories, just 39 per cent of
parents spoke mainly Welsh to each other. A further 7.7 per cent spoke Welsh to

` half the time. There was a large variance between Welsh-speaking
...d anglicized areas, with 65 per cent of parents in the Gwendraeth Valley
using mainly Welsh with each other, compared with 16 per cent in Swansea.
This, of course, reflected the linguistic patterns of these different areas.

There seems to be a clear need, if Welsh is to regain its dominance in the home,
for parents to be made aware of their possible linguistic contribution. This
contribution will be seen to have a strong correlation with the language used by
young people. The vast majority of young people who succeeded in using Welsh
as their main language came from Welsh-speaking homes, in both Welsh- and
English-speaking communities. Other correlations, such as between using Welsh
and social class and sex, were far weaker than this apparently crucial factor.

The decline in use of Welsh by parents was to some extent alleviated by their
use of Welsh with their children: 54 per cent of mothers spoke mainly Welsh to
their children, and 47.5 per cent of fathers did this. A score of 49 per cent for
parents in this field compared favourably to the 39 per cent of parents who spoke
Welsh to each other. This displays a tendency, also found among young people,
to view Welsh as a language more suitable for use with children than as a
language relevant to their own daily use. A regional variation was seen, with 75
per cent of parents in Gwendraeth Valley speaking mainly Welsh to children,
compared to 21 per cent in Swansea.


## LANGUAGE BETWEEN SIBLINGS

Unlike their parents, all young people in the survey could speak Welsh. Their
language use in the home, however, clearly mirrored language use by parents.
41 per cent used mainly Welsh with siblings, a percentage lower than that of
parents' use of Welsh with them, but higher than the percentage of parents
speaking Welsh to each other. Of the 41 per cent of young people who spoke
mainly Welsh to siblings, all but two had parents with at least a 'strong' ability
in Welsh, and 86 per cent of them had parents with 'very high' ability in Welsh.
In a similar pattern, all but 9 per cent of them had parents who spoke mainly
Welsh to them, and 73 per cent of them had parents who used Welsh 'to a very
high degree' with their offspring. It can safely be claimed, with a few exceptions,
that only where parents speak Welsh to children do young people use the
language when speaking to brothers and sisters.

It was seen, in families where parents' ability to speak Welsh was 'strong' or
'very high', that 20 per cent of siblings spoke mainly English to each other, but
where parents spoke mainly Welsh to their children, only 4.3 per cent of siblings
spoke mainly English to each other. The significance of this finding must not be
underestimated. The remarkable success of such homes shows that young
people do not react negatively to being spoken to in Welsh; they tend to copy the
language patterns of the home domain, and their ability to use Welsh is put into
practice by most of them where other domains give them an opportunity to use

the language. As has been suggested, a campaign to convince parents of their linguistic influence should bring swift dividends.

One feature of this language pattern was that the percentage of siblings speaking English generally corresponded to the linguistic nature of the community. Whereas 26 per cent of siblings in Gwendraeth Valley spoke mainly English to each other, this rose to 70 per cent in Swansea. A disturbing feature, however, was that young people in Aman Valley were nearer in language patterns to anglicized Swansea than to the Welsh heartland in Gwendraeth Valley. Of young people in Aman valley 61 per cent spoke mainly English to siblings.

The importance of home language in establishing language patterns among young people was confirmed in various interviews carried out. 'Most who have parents speaking Welsh speak Welsh', said a seventeen-year-old girl from an anglicized area. 'I'd say that most of the people who speak Welsh at home speak Welsh to each other', was a similar view expressed by a person from Neath Valley. But actual language patterns in the case of many individuals can be more complex. 'I'm more used to speaking English to my mother, and I speak more Welsh with my father. I speak Welsh and English, half and half . . . I speak a lot of English at home, a lot of English in the school', said a young person from Gwendraeth Valley area.[9]

## LANGUAGE SPOKEN WITH PEERS

This reduction in use of the endangered language in the home from one generation to the next is also reflected in society at large, where just 41 per cent of the young people speak mainly Welsh to Welsh-speaking peers. A further 22 per cent speak Welsh half the time to this group. It is clear that there is a relationship between home language and language used outside the home, but the effects of the linguistic patterns of educational and societal domains were now playing a stronger role. (It was seen in another comparison that there was a marked difference in language use between those who were attending a Welsh-medium or bilingual establishment of further education and those attending an English-medium establishment.)

In the Gwendraeth Valley 88 per cent of Welsh-speaking young people spoke

Table 6.2.  Use of Welsh by young bilingual adults among Welsh-speaking peers

|  | No. | % |
| --- | --- | --- |
| Never/very little | 56 | 17.0 |
| Less than half | 67 | 20.4 |
| Around half | 72 | 21.9 |
| More than half | 70 | 21.3 |
| Always/almost always | 64 | 19.5 |

Table 6.3. Use of Welsh by young adults among Welsh-speaking peers,
according to area

| Use of Welsh | % speaking Welsh in various areas | | | | |
|---|---|---|---|---|---|
| | 80%+ | 65%+ | 45%+ | 35%+ | 10%+ |
| Never | 3.8 | 29.1 | 14.5 | 15.1 | 28.8 |
| Less than half | 8.8 | 30.9 | 21.0 | 17.8 | 28.8 |
| Around half | 18.8 | 10.9 | 37.1 | 23.3 | 18.6 |
| More than half | 23.8 | 18.2 | 17.7 | 27.4 | 16.9 |
| Always | 45.0 | 10.9 | 9.7 | 16.4 | 6.8 |

Welsh to each other at least half the time. In Swansea 42 per cent did this. Once again, Aman Valley presents a disturbingly weak 40 per cent, confirming that its language patterns are more similar to anglicized areas than to the patterns of the adjacent Welsh heartland. This alarming loss of language use in the Aman Valley can be explained by several factors. These include lack of employment prospects locally, a lack of Welsh-medium entertainment opportunities for the young, an influx of English-speaking people from Swansea and further afield, and the mixed-language nature of the secondary school, which in spite of recent developments has a far stronger leaning towards English than the designated bilingual secondary schools which serve the remainder of the area studied. More than half of the bilingual pupils in Aman Valley had attended the English-medium stream of the secondary school. There is, then, clearly a discrepancy between language knowledge and language use, especially the use of Welsh as a main language, but it is important not to dismiss the fact that 83 per cent of the sample do use Welsh with each other to some degree. The retention of a Welsh heartland should clearly be a major part of any language plan, but such a plan should also aim at extending the heartland patterns into adjacent areas which display language loss at an alarming rate.

LANGUAGE SPOKEN IN SOCIETY

There was among these young people an awareness that their society had been more Welsh, and also an awareness that children should be able to speak Welsh. If this latter assumption could be translated by these young people into a greater home use of Welsh when they themselves become parents, future patterns of language use could improve markedly. At present, however, the amount of Welsh used by these young people is at its weakest when they are in contact with each other. The comparative lack of relevance of Welsh to their daily lives is observed in young people's conception of the linguistic make-up of their own society: 79 per cent (259 of the sample) would speak mainly Welsh with Welsh-

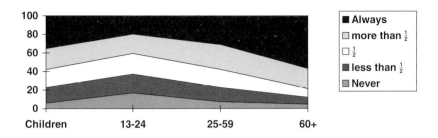

**Figure 6.2. Amount of Welsh spoken by young people to various age groups (%)**

speaking people aged sixty and over, and 58 per cent (190) would use mainly Welsh with Welsh-speaking children under twelve.

The pattern in Figure 6.2 peaks at the age group of the young people themselves. This shows a conception of a Welsh-speaking society as being an ageing one, but it also displays an awareness that children should be able to speak the language. This also reflects the decline of the use of Welsh in areas where Welsh was the *lingua franca*, and also, on the other hand, the continuing desire to safeguard the language, as testified by the growth of Welsh-medium primary schools. This latter concept was strongly confirmed by a question on the possibility of giving bilingual education to their own children in the future (see Table 6.4). Almost all the negative responses came from people who had not themselves received education in specifically designated bilingual schools. The schools, it seems, will be self-perpetuating, and they succeed in producing positive reactions. As in the case of homes, young people tended to accept the value of the schools' language policies.

**Table 6.4. Parents' desire to give bilingual education to their children**

|         | No. | %    |
|---------|-----|------|
| No      | 14  | 4.3  |
| Perhaps | 73  | 22.3 |
| Yes     | 240 | 73.4 |

USE OF WELSH IN VARIOUS DOMAINS

A cause of greater concern is the effect that various societal domains have on language use. The popular centres used for socializing exert great linguistic pressures which in turn establish language patterns between individuals at a stage in life when new friendships are formed, and when the language of courtship, which could become the language of future homes, is established. At this age young people's culture tends to be dominated by the various kinds of mass media, the provision of which is mainly in the English language.

There was an overwhelming tendency among the young people to watch English television, read English magazines and books, listen to English radio and English music, but in each instance, this overwhelming tendency reflects the availability and dominance of English in these media of entertainment (see Figure 6.3). The experience of mass media in the home displays such a pattern. In the case of television, 89 per cent would view at least an hour's Welsh television per week, but only 8 per cent would view more than ten hours of Welsh, compared to 88 per cent who would view more than ten hours of English television. A detailed study of viewing habits revealed that soap operas, comedies, films and popular music were the favourite programmes. Targets in a language plan in the media field should include increasing the total number of hours available in Welsh, and producing programmes in the above areas – not necessarily programmes especially created for young people.

S4C, supported by funding in excess of £100m, has taken the opportunity presented by digital television to offer an all-day Welsh service, but at present this is not within the technical grasp of most of the population, and when this becomes possible, the service will be open to fierce competition from countless other channels. Radio listening provided a more dismal picture: 80 per cent did not listen to Welsh radio at all, whereas only 8 per cent did not listen to English radio. Around 7 per cent would listen to more than one hour of Welsh a week, while 82 per cent would listen to this amount of English programmes. Radio Cymru has since changed its schedule to appeal to younger people.

The Anglo-American popular music scene must be one of the most powerful marketing forces aimed at young people in the whole world. Wales's misfortune is to be so closely connected to this massive and pervasive influence. It was seen that young people spent a considerable amount of time listening to a variety of tapes, cassettes and CDs, and there was, as could be expected, a large weighting towards English-language media: 87 per cent listened daily to English music, compared with 3.4 per cent who listened daily to Welsh music. While around 13 per cent could claim to listen to Welsh music weekly, 98 per cent listened to

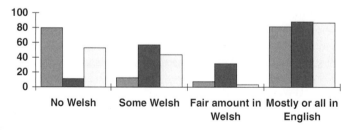

Figure 6.3. **Listening and viewing habits of young people, according to language (%)**
radio: television: CDs

English music. It may be a source of comfort to those involved in Welsh music that 47 per cent could claim to listen to it at various times. This does certainly show that the efforts made in this field have given young people committed to Welsh culture an alternative to the English scene, and that there are many who could be attracted to it if the marketing of the Welsh scene were to be given a significant impetus.

The music scene in Wales as elsewhere has always been in private hands and although broadcast royalties are a means of secondary support, it has received little direct state aid. A language plan would need to address means of supporting the youth music scene as a matter of priority. Recent successes of Wales-based groups have not necessarily meant an expansion of the Welsh music scene *per se*. Although some popular bands have released Welsh-medium albums, there is a tendency to regard language (that is, Welsh) as less important than musical expresssion. The consequent expression of Welsh identity through the medium of English could on the one hand harm efforts to promote the Welsh music scene but on the other hand it could broaden the acception of Welsh-medium music if popular groups choose to sing in Welsh in circumstances previously limited to English-medium music.

Unlike Welsh efforts in the field of popular music, Welsh book and magazine publishing has received government financial support since 1956. In 1991 the Welsh Books Council, as it was then called, published a catalogue of 2,000 books aimed at children and young people. This catalogue contained just seven thrillers in a series commissioned for young people, and a further seventy-nine titles of novels and stories written for young people. Younger children receive far more attention. It is a matter of debate, of course, whether there is a specific sixteen to twenty-five age group audience for books. Adults books are read avidly by this age group in English, and it could be patronizing for adults to produce what they regard as suitable books for this particular readership. Producing popular adult books could be more beneficial. With less than £1m support given to book production, it is very much a poor sister when compared to television, and there are consequently huge gaps in the product. Compared to the Basque example, where annual book production is around 1,000, Welsh books attain around half that figure.

Our survey asked the young people to list books read by them, apart from books read for educational courses, during a period of six months: 611 English books were read, compared to 185 Welsh books (18 per cent of the sample did not read any books). This proportion of Welsh books suggests that Welsh holds its own more successfully in this form of mass media than in the music world. Nevertheless, 64 per cent did not read Welsh books at all, while 18 per cent read at least as many Welsh books as English ones. Girls read more: 75 per cent of boys did not read Welsh books, compared to 54 per cent of girls. There was a general confidence in reading skills. Only 26 per cent of the young people thought that their ability to read Welsh was less than 'good'. Almost all those who did read Welsh books had a substantial degree of confidence in their ability to read Welsh. Nevertheless, 135 young people who had this confidence did not read any Welsh books.

There was a marked difference between the books which were most popular in English and in Welsh. In English, spine-chilling thrillers by Thomas Harris and Stephen King were the most popular, while Jackie Collins and Jeffrey Archer were also popular. Authors such as Angharad Tomos and Penri Jones were popular in Welsh. If Welsh authors copy the popular English genre, will they be seen as second class? If so, it could be argued that native Welsh authors should be encouraged to write many more novels about the Wales they know. On the other hand, it is clear that young adult readers are attracted by the world of horror thrillers, blood, adventure and sex.

The world of magazines is a different matter: 86.5 per cent of young people read English magazines at least once a month, compared to 20 per cent who read Welsh magazines and papers. Girls, probably because of the large number of magazines aimed specifically at them, were more avid readers of English magazines; 67 per cent of them read these weekly magazines. When asked to name Welsh magazines, 24 per cent could name *Golwg*, and 14 per cent claimed to read it. The subject content of Welsh magazines, and the money given to marketing them, should be a concern for all interested in this field.

The field of ITC products remains hardly touched by Welsh production. At the time of writing no word-processing packages are available in Welsh, whereas the Basque government has signed several agreements with Microsoft in order to facilitate packages in Basque. Almost no computer games are available in Welsh, nor other software which interests young people. While there is a world-wide similar difficulty for small and not so small languages, the almost total absence of Welsh from this market is potentially damaging for future use of Welsh by young people.

## CHOICE OF LANGUAGE IN CONVERSATION

Complicated patterns of language use were observed, and individuals often expressed preference of language use according to domain or the matter discussed. For Welsh to become a natural language of choice for young bilingual people, it needs to pervade many more domains and all subject-matter.

The language associated with the various fields of interest and the various domains is clearly seen to affect the language which young people most happily used when discussing these areas (see Table 6.5). In areas where Welsh has a dominant role for many, and these would include the chapel and previous or present education, the young people as a whole seem equally happy to use either language in discussion. Sports activities are often held through the medium of Welsh, and there is substantial provision of sports broadcasting through the medium of Welsh, which probably contributes to the large number who could discuss it happily in both languages.

**Table 6.5. Ease of language use in discussing various topics**

| | Better in Welsh | | No difference | | Better in English | |
| --- | --- | --- | --- | --- | --- | --- |
| | No. | % | No. | % | No. | % |
| Religion | 94 | 28.9 | 137 | 42.2 | 94 | 28.9 |
| College work | 73 | 22.2 | 159 | 48.3 | 97 | 29.5 |
| Sports | 28 | 8.5 | 202 | 61.4 | 99 | 30.1 |
| Jobs | 34 | 10.3 | 140 | 42.6 | 153 | 46.8 |
| Courtship | 27 | 8.2 | 124 | 37.7 | 178 | 54.1 |
| Television | 17 | 5.2 | 117 | 35.6 | 194 | 59.1 |
| Rock music | 16 | 4.9 | 68 | 20.7 | 244 | 74.4 |

But in fields of mass media and Anglo-American culture, English holds sway. Discussion of television and rock music had a weighting towards English which corresponded to the dominance of English in these media. These fields contribute substantially to the cultural orientation of young people, and cannot be underestimated in their influence; they are also the most problematic of all fields for language planners. It is against the background of these fields that friendships are often formed, and courtship begun. English seems to be the language of love; English is thus more likely to be the main language of homes of Welsh speakers in the future.

The encouraging element in these figures is that young people do respond to Welsh surroundings when these are provided: 70 per cent are comfortable with using Welsh when discussing education, and this is a positive indication of the way in which bilingual education is succeeding. The leap of faith that is often mistakenly made by teachers is that their success in creating a Welsh domain can influence the language used generally by young people in other anglicized domains. This is clearly not the case, although about 25 per cent of young people are comfortable with Welsh in the most anglicized of domains. The only possible answer to the task of changing the language of conversation, and thus the language of relationships and courtships, is to change the dominant language of other pertinent domains.

## LANGUAGE OF DOMAINS

At the moment, however, English seems to be the dominant language in all domains except those associated with chapel, and the traditionally Welsh domain of chapel is by no means the main attraction for young people. Other domains, some of them linked traditionally to village and town life, others more connected to the relatively new dominance of Anglo-American mass culture, form the centre of the social life of young people, and it is these domains which should attract the attention of language planners.

The movement that in Wales is seen as the main provider of Welsh activiti⸗ for young people, the Urdd, clearly has no attraction for the vast majority. ]⸗ activities are mostly concentrated in schools, and it was seen that more we drawn in rural and semi-rural areas to the activities of the Young Farmers' Clu⸗ The Urdd, because it has traditionally avoided the local pub or club as a me⸗ ing-place, has lost the active support of many young people who would ha⸗ taken part in various cultural activities in the school or at Urdd camps. The Urd⸗ would do well to consider how it can include in its activities the kind of centr⸗ of socialization which are most popular with young people.

Dances, pubs, sports and the cinema are by far the most popular centres c⸗ activity, and it is worth noting how participation in these centres compares witl the chapel and with the Urdd (see Table 6.6). Although the young people wer⸗ younger than eighteen when questioned, the pub or club was the most frequented centre of socializing, followed closely by the disco or dance, where alcohol is also provided. These two centres are probably the most important linguistically because they provide a meeting-place for both sexes, and personal interaction is at its highest. The cinema is possibly less important because of the passive nature of the entertainment, while sporting activities are often confined to one sex.

The number of monthly participants can be graphically summarized to give an idea of relative importance (see Figure 6.4). The dominant language in the most popular of these domains – the pub, disco, sports and cinema – is English. Because of the small number participating in Urdd activities in this area, the prominence given to Welsh in its activities has no effect on the language generally spoken. The chapel, on the other hand, still holds its place to a lesser, and probably diminishing, extent. Outside the world of education, which has led to an equality between both languages in ease of use, and which is the one growing domain of Welsh dominance for young Welsh speakers, Welsh does not dominate in any of the popular domains in the lives of young people. The patterns of language use in various domains and of willingness to discuss various topics connected to those domains through the medium of Welsh showed a

Table 6.6. Frequency of participation in various centres and activities

|  | Never | | Monthly | | Weekly | |
|---|---|---|---|---|---|---|
|  | No. | % | No. | % | No. | % |
| Chapel | 160 | 48.6 | 34 | 10.3 | 39 | 11.9 |
| Urdd | 221 | 67.4 | 8 | 2.4 | 1 | 0.3 |
| Disco | 16 | 4.9 | 118 | 35.9 | 91 | 27.7 |
| Sports | 51 | 15.5 | 55 | 16.8 | 117 | 35.7 |
| Pub/club | 29 | 8.8 | 77 | 23.5 | 151 | 46.0 |
| Cinema | 11 | 3.3 | 140 | 42.6 | 20 | 6.1 |

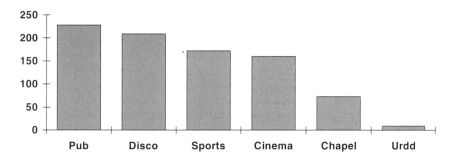

Figure 6.4. Number of young people attending various centres or activities
at least monthly

high degree of correlation, emphasizing the importance of language use in various domains (see Table 6.7).

A weighting towards English is clear and the difference between both ends of the scale suggest a weighting of around 8:1 towards English. However, in assessing the position of Welsh in the anglicized domains, one should include those who use both languages to an equal degree, and this would suggest that between 30 and 36 per cent use Welsh to a substantial degree. More than half would use at least some Welsh in these circumstances and up to 80 per cent of young people use it at various times. Nevertheless, the Welsh language, in a context of cultural domination of the greater used language, will always be at a disadvantage unless specifically targeted attempts are made to redress the linguistic balance of the popular socializing domains.

This can be best achieved in the largely Welsh-speaking areas, and a breakdown of the figures shows clearly that there is a tendency for these domains in the Welsh-speaking areas to provide a more hopeful background (see Table 6.8). The Welsh heartland is the only area where the tendency to use Welsh is approximately equal to the tendency to use English. The figures for other areas show some inconsistencies. The main surprise again is the remarkable tendency to use English in Aman Valley, a tendency which is again greater than that seen in

Table 6.7. Amount of Welsh used in activities and centres

|  | Welsh only | | More Welsh | | More English | | English only | |
|---|---|---|---|---|---|---|---|---|
|  | No. | % | No. | % | No. | % | No. | % |
| Chapel | 104 | 57.5 | 19 | 10.5 | 13 | 7.2 | 28 | 15.5 |
| Urdd | 53 | 45.7 | 32 | 27.6 | 5 | 4.3 | 14 | 12.1 |
| Disco | 17 | 5.4 | 26 | 8.3 | 80 | 25.6 | 133 | 42.6 |
| Sports | 20 | 7.3 | 36 | 13.1 | 85 | 31.0 | 89 | 32.5 |
| Pub/club | 17 | 5.8 | 40 | 13.6 | 75 | 25.5 | 113 | 38.4 |
| Cinema | 20 | 6.4 | 27 | 8.7 | 65 | 20.9 | 155 | 49.8 |

Table 6.8. Use of Welsh by young people in various domains, according to area (%)

| | % of Welsh speakers in area | | | | | | | | | |
| | 80+ | | 65+ | | 45+ | | 35+ | | 10+ | |
| | W | E | W | E | W | E | W | E | W | E |
|---|---|---|---|---|---|---|---|---|---|---|
| Disco | 29.9 | 41.6 | 0 | 90.0 | 3.4 | 79.9 | 17.4 | 62.3 | 10.6 | 80.7 |
| Sports | 43.9 | 37.8 | 9.1 | 65.5 | 8.7 | 71.7 | 23.0 | 59.0 | 7.7 | 83.0 |
| Pubs | 41.2 | 35.3 | 6.4 | 76.6 | 8.9 | 75.0 | 13.9 | 59.7 | 8.9 | 82.2 |
| Cinema | 32.9 | 40.8 | 2.0 | 92.0 | 6.4 | 83.9 | 17.4 | 72.5 | 9.3 | 75.9 |

Swansea. Other factors may be associated with the anglicized nature of the college of further education at Amanford, and with a lack of Welsh-language activity outside the traditional Welsh chapel culture. As already suggested, this area deserves urgent and immediate attention. Other more anglicized areas, such as Swansea and Neath Valleys, may present a more positive picture than an area such as Llanelli because of the way in which modern Welsh culture has been promoted by the bilingual comprehensive school at Ystalyfera, and the active role taken by influential young people in the area in establishing Welsh pop groups which have had a local following.

FURTHER CORRELATIONS

Comparative ease in using Welsh or English while discussing various topics was compared to various factors, including the type of further education establishments, academic ability, sex, area, language spoken by parents to their children, network of friends, class and the young people's own confidence in their language skills (see Table 6.9). The strength of weighting of the various factors was measured according to the difference between the percentages favouring either Welsh or English. The highest correlations were confidence or lack of confidence in linguistic skills, the use of Welsh or English with friends, and the language spoken by parents (giving a difference between percentages of between 48 and 41). Those who chose to use Welsh on one end of this scale would broadly speaking be those who had been brought up to speak Welsh at home, and who subsequently spoke mainly Welsh with friends, and who partook of various forms of Welsh mass-media culture, or who were active in local Welsh-medium cultural activities.

A slightly weaker correlation existed between ease of using Welsh and academic ability in Welsh, with a differential percentage of 31. Because most were adjudged to have a comparatively high ability, this factor could not be seen as a decisive one. Other weaker factors included living in a Welsh-speaking area, attending a Welsh-medium centre of further education, and having a high general academic ability, with a differential percentage of between 16 and 19 per

Table 6.9. **Difference between percentages who tend to use English or Welsh**

|  | Difference |
|---|---|
| Confidence/lack of confidence in language literacy | 48.1 |
| Using Welsh/using English with friends | 41.5 |
| Parents speaking Welsh/English with children | 41.0 |
| Academic ability/lack of academic ability in Welsh | 31.1 |
| Attendance at bilingual/mixed-language sixth form | 25.0 |
| Attendance at bilingual sixth form/English tertiary college | 18.7 |
| Living in a Welsh-speaking/English-speaking area | 17.4 |
| General academic/lack of academic ability | 16.2 |
| Girl/boy | 8.3 |
| Middle class/working class | 6.6 |

cent. It is a source of encouragement for those living in anglicized areas, but who speak Welsh at home, that they can be just as successful in their ease of using of Welsh as those living in the Welsh heartland. Although attending a Welsh-medium centre of further education does not seem to be a strong correlation, it could be quite significant because it is a new factor. The personal interviews, moreover, suggested a sharp decrease in ease of using Welsh, and in attitude towards Welsh, among those from English-speaking homes in anglicized areas who attended English-medium centres of further education.

Weaker still in their correlation were gender and social class, with differential factors between 6 and 8 per cent. This must surely put an end to the arguments that Welsh-medium education is in any way élitist. An almost equal number was attributed to the working class and the middle class, and this low correlation suggests that there is little difference between them.

Having said this, individual patterns of language use must vary. One significant factor, found more through the interviews than through the questionnaires, was that the tendency of many to use Welsh depended on the language spoken by less flexible peers. If a young person was known to speak almost only English, others would tend to speak English with him or her. Similarly, a determined Welsh-speaking young person would draw others to speak Welsh to him or her, and would influence the language spoken by a group. This gives individuals a significant linguistic role, whatever other circumstances tend to dictate.

## USE OF WELSH AND EDUCATION

As education remains the one domain where Welsh is increasing in use, it is worth considering for a while how young people respond to receiving their education in Welsh, and to see whether there is any backlash to the use of the endangered language by schools and colleges in a society that is becoming increasingly anglicized. Others have seen that children become less interested in the language as they progress through the school and this happens concurrently with their increasing experience of an anglicized society. Colin Baker states firmly, 'It is an established research finding that a favourable attitude to Welsh declines as age increases' (1985: 147).[10] Although differences can be found between attitude towards language and actual use, a measurement of use must be more tangible than the complexities which form attitude. We found, in a measurement of self-assessment of language use, that this apparent reaction against Welsh was not only less evident by the age of transition to sixteen-plus education, but that there was a positive change towards Welsh.

In answer to our questions, 17 per cent of our respondents replied that they used only English with pupils while they attended the last two years of primary school (Table 6.10). It was noteworthy that the lowest percentage of English-only users was in Swansea (12 per cent), where the Welsh-medium schools obviously attempt to counter their pupils' already anglicized domains. The percentage was at its highest (25 per cent) in Aman Valley. In fact, overall, the differences in self-assessed language use between ten and eleven years of age and their present language use (sixteen to seventeen years of age) was extremely small.

When asked about any change in the amount of Welsh they used when transferring to secondary education, there was a swing at both ends of the scale. A percentage of around 25 per cent said they used less Welsh, and around 30 per cent said they used more. The greatest increase was in Gwendraeth Valley (45 per cent) while the greatest decrease was in Swansea and Aman Valley (Swansea 48 per cent, Aman Valley 56 per cent). This could be coupled to the language policy of the various schools or to the impact of coming into contact with pupils from a different language background. As the Swansea bilingual secondary school has a vigorous Welsh policy, it is quite likely that general linguistic background is more influential. The Aman Valley case coincides with the depressing picture obtained throughout the survey of the language among that valley's young people, but it was the experience of half the sample in Aman Valley that teachers spoke more English to them than Welsh: a suggestion that a mixed-language school finds it more difficult to establish positive language practices than the official bilingual schools which other young people in the sample had attended. Significant swings to both directions were seen among children of both Welsh-speaking and English-speaking parents: 29 per

**Table 6.10. Language used with pupils in the last two years of primary school, in secondary school and when 16–17 years old**

|                | Age 10–11 | | Sec. school | | Age 16–17 | |
|----------------|------|------|------|------|------|------|
|                | No.  | %    | No.  | %    | No.  | %    |
| English only   | 55   | 16.7 | 57   | 17.3 | 56   | 17.0 |
| Mainly English | 68   | 20.7 | 77   | 23.4 | 67   | 20.4 |
| Equal          | 72   | 21.9 | 100  | 30.4 | 72   | 21.9 |
| Mainly Welsh   | 62   | 18.8 | 61   | 18.5 | 70   | 21.3 |
| Welsh only     | 72   | 21.9 | 34   | 10.3 | 64   | 19.5 |

cent of children from English homes used more Welsh in the secondary school, and 31 per cent of children from Welsh homes used more English.

These changes must be seen to be significant. Although they have altered little of the overall numbers of percentages who speak Welsh, a considerable switch in language use is made by individuals, with 60 per cent of the sample changing their language patterns significantly. As the period of transfer to the secondary school is a period of establishing new friendships, and as the language first used between friends tends to be the one adhered to, special attention must be given to this stage of school life.

The drop in the number speaking only Welsh when transferring to secondary school, from 22 to 10 per cent, shows the anglicizing nature of the new environment, but it is evident that by the sixteen to seventeen age group the language pattern of the primary school has been restored, with 40 per cent speaking mainly Welsh together. By the stage of sixteen-plus education, a greater proportion of the young people were receiving English-medium education: 49 per cent of the respondents were following English-medium courses, 41 per cent were following courses with some Welsh-medium teaching, while just 10 per cent were receiving all their education through the medium of Welsh. This is reflected by the 35 per cent who claimed they now spoke more English, and was counterbalanced by 25 per cent who claimed they spoke more Welsh.

There was a substantial difference between language pattern changes among young people attending different kinds of establishments. Only eight attended the sixth forms of English-medium schools, and half of these claimed they now spoke more English; none spoke more Welsh; 108 attended tertiary colleges, which tend to offer few Welsh-medium courses, and 68 per cent of these now spoke more English; 12 per cent spoke more Welsh; thirty-nine attended the traditional bilingual school serving Aman Valley, and of these 33 per cent now spoke more English, while 16 per cent spoke more Welsh; 173 attended the sixth forms of official bilingual schools. It was in these schools that the balance differed: 14 per cent spoke more English, but 35 per cent spoke more Welsh.

Although the total numbers speaking mainly Welsh or mainly English from one period to another stay fairly constant, with a dip in Welsh speakers during secondary school age, there is an obvious change in the individual linguistic patterns of pupils during this time. There is a clear correlation between changes in language spoken and the linguistic environment of education. It is clear that introducing subjects such as science through the medium of Welsh would have a beneficial effect on the use of Welsh, and that the establishments which succeed in fostering the use of Welsh are the sixth forms of official bilingual schools.

Another issue emerged. Some negative reaction to the way in which teachers urged pupils to use Welsh was seen in the individual interviews. 'The school got under my nerves actually, because the teachers were so, feeling so strongly about the language. They pushed children not to speak English', said one pupil who attended a school in the Welsh heartland. He explained the attitude of some children,

We would speak English, then she [a teacher] would walk past, hell, she'd scream, 'Speak Welsh! The official language of the school – speak it! . . . Well, we'd have a belly-ful of fright at the time, and we'd turn to Welsh, but once she'd gone past, it was back to English we'd turn.

Another pupil at the same school, who was supportive of the use of Welsh, said, 'There's no point in giving rows in the yard all the time . . . if you win some, you lose more.' Pupils inclined to speaking English at the bilingual school in Swansea spoke of a 'Pavlov reaction' to teachers who insisted that they spoke Welsh, but this did not change their language with each other.

This certainly raises the issue of a negative reaction to coercion, and the result could be for a split to be created between pupils who chose the school's English provision and those who chose the Welsh provision. The issue here is whether it would be more beneficial for the integrity of the community of the school for all subjects to be taught through the medium of Welsh. This would not incite the negative reaction to demands to speak Welsh in circumstances which are not conducive to this. Carmarthen's language policy, as accepted by the Welsh Language Board, takes positive steps in this direction.


## ATTITUDES TOWARDS WELSH

One positive factor, observed generally among most young people, and confirmed by other surveys such as that conducted by NOP (1995) for the Welsh Language Board, was a general consent that the Welsh language was an impor-tant part of Welsh identity, and that the language was also considered to be useful in a variety of everyday situations. We have already seen that there was an almost unanimous desire among those who had attended Welsh schools that future children should do likewise. The concept that the language was an inte-gral part of Welsh identity was widespread, and this could be expected in view of previous surveys of pupils of a younger age,[11] especially those who attended Welsh schools. C. H. Williams and C. H. Thomas as early as 1977/78 demon-strated that Welsh sixth-formers in English-speaking areas could often develop attitudes to Welsh which 'even surpassed the favourable attitudes expressed by the sixth formers from the Welsh-speaking core area' (Williams and Thomas, 1978: 166).

It was evident in our findings, however, that the favourable attitude towards Welsh as a national language was not translated into a determination to use it in everyday life. There was a clear difference between the young people's attitude towards the language generally in Wales and its relevance to their interpersonal relationships. This can be confirmed by their view of the linguistic make-up of their own society, as discussed above, but there is also a further difference between their still fairly positive attitude towards the use of Welsh in the family and social domains and the actual use made. A declining graph can thus be formed, from the almost unanimity regarding the importance of Welsh context of a 'national future' for Wales, its importance for a good job, its importance in family and social domains, to a view of its place in friendship relationships, and lastly to the actual use among Welsh-speaking friends (see Figure 6.5).

The positive attitude towards Welsh as a qualification for a good job must be regarded as a breakthrough for language planning in Wales. In spite of accusations of élitism sometimes levied against the comparatively new Welsh-speaking professional class concentrated in south-east Glamorgan, which is nevertheless still numerically small when compared with the size of the professional class in that part of Wales, and which is quite minute in comparison with the professional class in Wales as a whole, it has given the Welsh language a remarkably positive boost in creating an awareness that knowledge of Welsh is desirable. 'It is the literate Welsh-speakers who are now the most fortunate group,' claim Giggs and Pattie (1992: 48), who base this argument on the proportion of such people of their own linguistic group in individual counties rather than as a proportion of the professional class as a whole. They argue that it is the English speakers of the industrial valleys of south Wales who are now deprived of the opportunity of achieving a high work status. It is quite misleading, however, to assume that this is so because of the increasing desirability of Welsh for professional posts. The lot of Welsh-speaking workers in the Welsh heartland is economically quite similar to that of their English-speaking counterparts in the eastern valleys. This has surely more to do with colonialist economic exploitation patterns, which have robbed people of wealth and livelihood, and language in the south-east, than with language policies. What is relevant here, however, is that Welsh, at last, in some economic fields, is seen to achieve parity of status with English. This has resulted in an awareness of the importance of Welsh that possibly exceeds actual experience, but this can only be of benefit to Welsh, as is testified by the remarkable growth of Welsh schools in Glamorgan.

Nevertheless, highest rating attitudes towards the importance of Welsh were in situations which did not necessarily demand any action on behalf of the

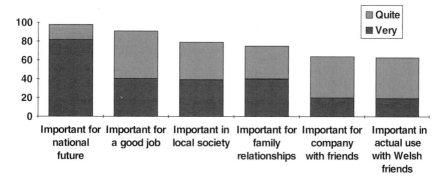

**Figure 6.5. Role of Welsh as seen by young people (%)**

responders. A belief in the importance of Welsh for safeguarding Welsh traditions was just as strong as the belief in the importance of Welsh for Wales's national future, but this is not reflected by similar beliefs on the importance of Welsh in immediate domains, where attitudes are probably influenced by actual experience: 40 per cent thought that Welsh was 'very important' in the family, compared to just 20 per cent who thought that the language was 'very important' for friendships. On the negative scale, 25 per cent thought that Welsh was not important in the family, and 36 per cent that it was not important for friendships.

The association of Welsh with Welsh identity was uniformly high throughout the area, but once again Aman Valley had the lowest percentage believing very strongly in this association (around 73 per cent with to 77 per cent in Swansea and 85 per cent in other areas). A similar degree of agreement was found in areas with regard to the importance of Welsh in the field of work. Once again, Aman Valley young people held the language to be least important: 33 per cent of Aman Valley young people believed very strongly that Welsh was an advantage, compared to 36 per cent in Gwendraeth Valley and 40 per cent in Swansea Valley and the surrounding area. A surprising 44 per cent believed this in Swansea. This difference can be explained in many ways; it could be attributed to an actual awareness in the heartland that Welsh is not as essential as it appears, or to low employment levels that make young people generally pessimistic about work opportunities, or perhaps the Swansea young people tend to belong more to the professional class.

Greater differences were seen in attitudes towards Welsh in the home and among friends. In keeping with the linguistic nature of the areas, Gwendraeth Valley displayed the strongest attitudes, with 51 per cent believing that Welsh was very important for the family, and 34 per cent for friends. The lowest percentage for the family domain was in Swansea, with 22 per cent. The importance of Welsh for friendships was seen to be very strong by just 15 per cent in Swansea, 8 per cent in the Llanelli area and 11 per cent in Aman Valley. These figures suggest that traditionally Welsh areas which are now outside the heartland display weaker attitudes among Welsh-speaking young people than the anglicized areas. Swansea Valley and the surrounding areas has a stronger 26 per cent, which is possibly due to specific cultural activities carried out in the area for young people and by them.

The general attitude towards Welsh, therefore, is positive. In all fields the percentage believing that Welsh is not important is a minority, but there must be concern that the language is seen to be least important in the very fields on which Fishman puts most weight, namely, 'intimacy, family, community' (1991: 5).

## THE CONTRIBUTION OF LOCAL EFFORTS

It is clear that vigorous local activity throughout the country has not succeeded in reversing the language shift towards the dominant language and towards the pervasive influence of Anglo-American culture, although the well-being of the endangered language would very probably be much weakened were it not for this activity. Must it be the case that the localized nature of language activities will eventually submit to the enormous linguistic, historic forces of political and administrative subjugation, and of cultural and commercial annexation?

The success of education in presenting a domain where there is no domination by the exogenous language, even in more anglicized areas, shows that it is possible to create new, successful domains, provided the parameters of the domain offer a controlled environment. Moreover, the language spoken at home is evidently still a major influence, and must be central in any attempt at reversing language shift, as the decision to change the language of this domain can be made independently of all external influences. When these positive influences are coupled with the clearly positive attitude of young people towards language survival, it should be possible to foresee a measure of success for coherent and specifically aimed language planning policies.

Although our findings can be viewed pessimistically, especially if one assumes that young people's domains will become increasingly anglicized, it is possible, on the other hand, to take heart from the low percentage of young people who seem never to use the language. These young people, around 10 per cent of the group, mostly come from English-speaking homes, and as such do not represent a loss. One could argue that there is very little backlash against the use of Welsh in education and in the home. As has been already mentioned, language planning in the area of young Welsh adults is still in its infancy, and urgent steps must be taken to counter the defeatist attitude that is promoted by certain vociferous adherents of British political parties.

The various organizations, movements and institutions which have developed in Wales in the field of education, youth work, the popular entertainment scene, publishing, and even in the world of radio and television, have never been part of a unified or comprehensive language plan. This has at various times meant a duplication of effort, a lack of cohesion and an uncertainty of aim. On the other hand, as the developments have been to some extent organic ones, based on the aspirations and efforts of individuals and communities, and as the various institutions now supporting Welsh-language activities have been established as a response to vehement demands on the part of Welsh speakers, the growth of the activities and institutions are safeguarded by the roots which they have in the community.

It could be argued that an approach which became more centralized and comprehensive might also lose the necessary ties with the community which it aims to serve. Nevertheless the complexities of socio-economic and culturo-linguistic factors which today play a role in determining the language of society and individuals mean that further attempts at language maintenance and regeneration will increasingly depend on central Welsh government support.

## A NATIONAL LANGUAGE PLAN FOR YOUNG PEOPLE

A language plan for young people cannot come about without governmental structures to formulate it and to support it. The Welsh Language Board must at some stage be replaced or reconstituted, and a Welsh cultural and language authority, possibly as a cultural secretariat, set up with sufficient funding to deal with the many fundamental issues facing the Welsh language. The urgency of addressing this must become a priority for the National Assembly, which could turn to the Basque Country or Catalonia for models. In these countries valuable partnerships are formed between the Department of Culture and other governmental departments, and also with local government and the private sector, to further positive language planning.

A primary object must be to ensure that a majority of school pupils in Wales are able to acquire Welsh to a level of fluency, and this will inevitably mean strategically converting English-medium schools to bilingual or Welsh-medium schools. Targets must be set, so that the present 20 per cent or so of Welsh-speaking young people doubles over the next generation. Apart from education, one needs to define the fields which call for urgent action, and those where appropriate action would most probably meet with success.

### The home

The first need is to encourage parents to be more linguistically aware, and to provide a Welsh-speaking home environment for children and young people. Although significant numbers of young people from Welsh-speaking homes do not use Welsh as their main language, it is almost only such homes, especially in anglicized areas, which produce young people who use mainly Welsh. How such encouragement is to be generated, whether it is orchestrated by a national language planning body and government departments, contributed to by voluntary organizations, and whether it should take the form of an overt propaganda campaign using the public media, or through projects aimed at raising awareness, possibly through the education programme, must be a matter of immediate attention.

### Domains

The trend towards use of English by young people from Welsh-speaking homes must be attributed to external influences. Attention must be given therefore to ways of providing the necessary linguistic background in the domains where young people spend their time and which tend to influence the linguistic patterns of behaviour. As the domains are quite variable, care should be taken in prioritizing appropriate targets, which could vary from one area to another, and in selecting emphasis between the high and low level use of the endangered language. Education and work are the domains connected with livelihood. The development of bilingual skills for the workplace, based on the accepted willingness of Welsh speakers to use Welsh in this sphere, should become common practice for educational establishments, and training in bilingual skills should receive support from employers. Social clubs, sporting clubs, pubs and disco and dance halls are important centres associated with domains of socialization.

One needs to determine to what extent language planning activity which could be more localized should be served by positive contributions from language laws, central and local government administrations and from language policies for public bodies and the private commercial sector. A difficulty for companies operating through the medium of Welsh in a largely Welsh-speaking area, for example, where using Welsh for interpersonal business relationships is an advantage (Morgan, 1995), is that English is almost the only language of commerce elsewhere.

Because of the widely varying linguistic nature of Wales's communities, it would be fair to assume that the unitary local authorities should be the government units most closely involved with language planning of this nature. They would be the natural bodies to collaborate with the *mentrau iaith* already in existence, and while some have already shown the political will to take on this role they must be given adequate resources to do so meaningfully.

### Youth culture

Youth culture, the third area of interest, is one which creates conflict between young people which extends beyond the domain itself. It can affect the sense of belonging to a community or an ethnic group, and the sense of ownership of language. Young people create a specific cultural environment for themselves, and respond in various ways to the culture of previous generations. This includes different responses to a culture which is linked to a code or a language which is not perceived to be the code of the young people.

The world of popular music has provided the younger generation with a particular means of self-expression, but this world has been exploited by international commercial concerns to such an extent that young people seem to be little more than passive receptors or imitators of an imposed cultural uniformity which is asserting its hold on wide areas of the globe. This cultural imperialism may be less oppressive than the military imperialism of past eras, but its effect on native languages could be just as threatening.

Does using the endangered language, however, offer young people an opportunity for genuine self-expression through this popular medium, and allow them to free themselves from the addictive effect of the dominant language? An answer to this question involves not only issues of language planning but also of societal and individual culture. It would seem that providing easy opportunities for the active participation of young people in this popular culture, to form and support their own groups and perform in the endangered language in a cohesive cultural scene, could be an important way of counterbalancing the huge commercial weight behind the dominant language's activities in this field.

Attention must be given to how resources can best serve the endangered language. There seem to be three needs. The first is to develop the traditional culture along creative lines which could be at variance with the trends of the popular anglicized youth culture. The second is to develop the endangered language's capacity to express itself in a similar vein to the world-wide popular youth culture (although the boundaries between this and traditional culture should not be precise – crossfertilization of cultures would be a creative gain). There would be a need to ensure that the evolving expressions of culture are more than weak reflections of the powerful dominant language media and efforts must include marketing as well as product. The type of cult following on which mass popular culture thrives will be very difficult to reproduce successfully. The third need is to digest the exogenous culture through the medium of the endangered language. It is to its credit that BBC's Welsh-language radio service has boldly striven to attend to these last two needs.

There will remain for some time an inherent problem for language planners in this field. While there is a need to encourage self-expression in the endangered language, there is evidence that young people, because of a social need to identify with a cultural group, tend to belong to a group where one language dominates. There is then a divide between two linguistic and cultural groups, with the smaller minority-language group seen by the larger majority-language group as being politicized, possibly with a more academic and literate culture. The task is to provide bridges across this divide, and to make it possible, in the first instance, for the larger group to enjoy its Anglo-American culture through the medium of the minority language.

Several other questions will have to be answered. To what extent should limited resources be concentrated on the comparatively passive medium of television, operating in an increasingly competitive scenario, where fierce competition from the terrestrial, digital and satellite television services of the dominant languages will increase the number of channels to several hundreds during the first part of the twenty-first century. Should more support be given to effort to change the linguistic nature of locally organized events, so that young people's personal and active experience of youth culture will become more Welsh? The present balance of spending is massively in favour of television.

The support given to the printed word does not at present give young people the number or the variety of products available in the dominant language. Welsh publishing does not compete with the number and appeal of magazines aimed at teenage girls, and the corresponding number of specialized interest magazines which are available in English. The very lack of numbers of authors, publishers and total readership, in comparison with the numbers available in the dominant languages, will always put the lesser used language at a disadvantage. There is a need for substantial support for popular youth magazines so that young people's reading matter can contain a fair proportion of the lesser used language.

## Social networks

A fourth priority is to encourage Welsh socializing networks for young people. The Welsh heartland provided the only societal background which could cause young people to use more Welsh, and as such, it is vital to strengthen its social networks. In anglicized areas this work must be a priority. An active programme, which must essentially be localized in its nature, would provide better means of social intercourse between Welsh speakers, and would serve two functions. The first would provide an awareness of the value of the language as a means of communication, and the second would provide a suitable background for social intercourse in the language. The effectiveness of voluntary organizations, and of more formalized bodies, such as *mentrau iaith*, should be monitored to ensure maximum local support for such ventures. The encouragement of social networks could become the most important field of activity for *mentrau iaith*, a sufficient number of which should be set up to cover the whole country.

## CONCLUSION

It seems that success in popularizing the endangered language in any of these individual fields will depend on success in making it the dominant language for young people generally, so that it will become natural for them to use that language at home, for social intercourse and in the field of popular entertainment. This will mean that the endangered language must be their main means of expression in important interpersonal and social domains, and this could eventually depend on having the necessary density of language use, as is the case in large parts of Catalonia.

For effective action to be taken in the field of language planning in Wales, the envisaged Welsh Language Authority must be allowed to develop an encompassing role. Any action is likely to fail if it is done in isolation, without regard to the economic and social well-being of communities, as national economic and political forces can be stronger than any well-intentioned language plan. The vitality of social networks depends on a thriving and stable local community. This will only come about through deliberate government action at local and national level aimed at economic revitalization of rural and urban communities. Whether this is produced through creative use of European Objective 1 funds remains to be seen. In the mean time, efforts in the field of language regeneration must be organized in a manner that embraces the main domains of young people, paying specific attention to the organic life of individual communities and to the mass and localized means of cultural self-expression.

*Notes*

[1] The claim that bilingual schools attain greater academic achievement compared with English monolingual schools is the subject of recent studies, and is referred to by Baker, 1995: 130–58. D. Reynolds et al. (1998) have attempted an analysis of reasons for the success. But see Gorard 2000 for a counter-argument that says bilingual schools often do not perform better in the league tables than would be expected from their intake.

[2] Reliable figures, as given by www.eustat.es (17 Dec. 1998), suggest that around 70 per cent of pupils in the Basque Autonomous Community now receive primary education through the medium of Basque.

[3] His negative interpretation of the demise of Welsh is seen in his Ph.D. thesis (1989). His numerous public pronouncements that Welsh has no future must be seen in the context of his political stance – he was an ardent anti-devolutionist during the 1997 devolution referendum. It is ironic that Pontypridd particularly has recently witnessed a resurgence in Welsh-medium schooling.

[4] In February 2000 it was announced that £44,348 would be given to Menter Maldwyn a Menter Brycheiniog, £42,000 to Menter Aman Tawe, £40,092 to Menter Iaith Rhondda Cynon Taf, £30,930 to Menter Iaith Sir y Fflint, £23,717 to Menter Caerdydd and £22,231 to Menter Bro Ogwr. Welsh Language Board, press release, 8 Feb. 2000.

[5] Statistics on fluency of children, as given by heads of schools, are included in the annual education statistics reports published by the Welsh Office. These can be very different to the statistics in the government censuses on language ability. See the detailed treatment by H. Jones and C. H. Williams in Chapter 2 above.

[6] This view has been expressed by Siôn Meredith, one-time national organizer of CYD (the movement that integrates Welsh learners with native Welsh speakers): 'dylai pobl ifainc eu hunain gymryd rhan flaenllaw wrth ddylanwadu ar eu cyfoedion a threfnu gweithgareddau ar eu cyfer, a . . . dylai unrhyw sefydliad neu gyfundrefn fod yn ddigon hyblyg i ymateb i hynny' (1992: 9), 'young people themselves should take a leading role in influencing their peers and in organizing activities for them, and . . . any institution or system should be flexible enough to react to this.')

[7] 'Mwy yn gwrando ar RC', *Y Cymro* (9 Feb. 2000), 3. Audience figures have risen to 197,000 per week, 22,000 up from the previous year.

[8] 'Let the Board forget about comprehensive language planning – it hasn't done Irish much good – and set about those practical tasks which I think it well understands' Thomas (1989: 7)

[9] All quotations are translated.

[10] Baker (1992: 41) reiterates this, 'One consistent finding from research on attitudes to the Welsh language is that attitude declines with age.' He refers to the work of W. R. Jones (1949, 1950), Sharp et al. (1973) and E. P. Jones (1983) to confirm this.

[11] This is suggested by Colin Baker (1992), who also notes the difficulties involved in obtaining satisfactory attitude measurements in view of the complexities of background, domains and other factors.

*References*

Aitchison, J. and Carter, H. (1994). *A Geography of the Welsh Language*, Cardiff: University of Wales Press.

Baker, C. (1985). *Aspects of Bilingualism in Wales*, Clevedon, Avon: Multilingual Matters.

Baker, C. (1992). *Attitudes and Language*, Clevedon, Avon: Multilingual Matters.

Baker, C. (1995). 'Bilingual education and assessment', in Morris, B. and Ghuman, P. S. (eds.), *Bilingual Education and Identity*, Cardiff: University of Wales Press, pp. 130–58.

Baker, C. and Jones, M. P. (1999). *Continuity in Welsh Language Education*, Cardiff: Welsh Language Board.

Bwrdd yr Iaith Gymraeg (1995). *Amlinelliad o Strategaeth ar Gyfer yr Iaith Gymraeg*, Cardiff: Bwrdd yr Iaith Gymraeg.

Bwrdd yr Iaith Gymraeg (2000). '£5 miliwn i'r iaith', press release, 8 February, Cardiff: Bwrdd yr Iaith Gymraeg.

Eusko Jaurlaritza (1999). *Enquête sociolinguistique au Pays Basque 1996*. www.eustat.es (17 Dec. 1998).

Fishman, J. A. (1991). *Reversing Language Shift*, Clevedon, Avon: Multilingual Matters.

Generalitat de Catalunya (1995). *General Language Normalisation Plan*, Barcelona: Generalitat de Catalunya.

Giggs, J. and Pattie, C. (1992). 'Wales as a plural society', *Contemporary Wales*, vol. 5, Cardiff: University of Wales Press, pp. 25–63.

Gorard, S. (2000). *Education and Social Justice: The Changing Composition of Schools and its Implications*, Cardiff: University of Wales Press.

Gruffudd, H. (1996). *Y Gymraeg a Phobl Ifanc*, Swansea: University of Wales Swansea.

Gruffudd, H. (1999). *Awdurdod Iaith i Gymru*, Talybont: Y Lolfa.

Hindley, R. (1990). *The Death of the Irish Language*, London and New York: Routledge.

Jones, E. P. (1983). 'A study of some of the factors which determine the degree of bilingualism of a Welsh child between 10 and 13 years of age', Ph.D. thesis, Bangor: University of Wales.

Jones, W. R. (1949). 'Attitude towards Welsh as a second language. A preliminary investigation', *British Journal of Educational Psychology*, 19, 1, 44–52.

Jones, W. R. (1952). 'Attitudes towards Welsh as a second language. A further investigation', *British Journal of Educational Psychology*, 20, 2, 117–32.

Meredith, S. (1992). 'Rhagymadrodd', in Jones, B. (ed.), *Iaith Ifanc*, Aberystwyth: CYD, pp. 8–13.

Morgan, T. (1995). 'Y Gymraeg yn y Gweithle . . . yng Nghwm Gwendraeth', M.Phil. thesis, University of Wales, Swansea.

NOP (1995). *Public Attitudes to the Welsh Language*, London: NOP, Social and Political, Nov.

Reynolds, D., Bellin, W. and ab Ieuan, R. (1998). *A Competitive Edge*, Cardiff: IWA.

Sharp, D., Thomas, B., Price, E. and Davies, I. (1973). *Attitudes to Welsh and English in the Schools of Wales*, Basingstoke and London: MacMillan and University of Wales Press.

Thomas, N. (1989). 'Sponsors and Subversives', *Planet*, 76 (August/September), 3–8.

Welsh Office (1998). *Statistics of Education and Training in Wales, Schools 1998*, Cardiff: Welsh Office.

Williams, C. H. (1999). 'Governance and the language', *Contemporary Wales*, 12, 130–54.

Williams, C. H. and Thomas, C. J. (1977, 1978). 'A behavioural approach to the study of linguistic decline and nationalist resurgence: a case study of attitudes of sixth-formers in Wales', *Cambria*, 3, 102–24, and 4, 152–73.

Williams, T. I. (1989) 'Patriots and citizens: language, identity and education in a liberal state: the anglicisation of Pontypridd 1818–1920', Ph.D. thesis, University of Wales, Cardiff.

# 7

# Adult Education, Language Revival and Language Planning

## STEVE MORRIS

In his book *Why Adults Learn*, Sean Courtney states that 'Participation in Adult Education is not a phenomenon *sui generis* but the extension of a much more significant participation in society at large, politically, economically and socially' (1992: 10). There can be no doubt that in many countries or regions with 'minoritized languages' the contribution of *adult* or *continuing* education (in its broadest sense) to the revival of these languages amongst the indigenous population (Fishman's Yish-speaking X men) or newcomers (Y men) by creating new Xish speakers has been both important and influential (Fishman, 1991). Indeed, in Wales, Professor Bobi Jones has argued that 'in the restoration of the language, the determining factor is and must be the adult-learning movement'.[1] Any contribution that adult/continuing education might have in the context of language revival and processes of language planning will naturally depend upon the actual situation of the 'minoritized language' under scrutiny: it is my intention in this chapter to look at the situation in Wales with the Welsh language as a point of reference whilst encouraging comparison with other countries and linguistic communities whose own circumstances may be reflected by those in Wales.

It was during the 1960s and early 1970s that the stark realization of the ever-decreasing number of Welsh speakers (656,002 in the 1961 census to 542,425 in 1971 or from 26 to 20.8 per cent of the population of Wales) provoked renewed interest and vigour in campaigns to arrest the decline in the number of Welsh speakers, create a fully bilingual country and, more importantly, give the language real status. One manifestation of this flourishing of interest in the language was a demand for more – and more effective – classes for adults to learn to speak Welsh (coupled with a corresponding increase in the demand for more Welsh-medium schools, especially in the more anglicized areas of Wales). There had, of course, previously existed classes for adult learners of Welsh. These, however, were predominantly short once-a-week classes, intermixed with subjects such as cookery, flower-arranging, car mechanics, etc. Williams's study (1965: 17) of adults' reasons for joining Welsh classes during that period illustrates the more culturally esoteric motivations prevalent at that time: (i) to understand the news on the radio and the television, (ii) to join in social life with friends, (iii) popular light reading and (iv) an interest in languages.

During the 1970s, however, it came to be realized that a fundamental shift was needed in the field of teaching Welsh to adults both from a curricular standpoint, including the teaching methods employed, and with regards to accessibility. It was during this period that a network of Welsh-for-adults classes was developed through the extra-mural departments of the University of Wales as well as in further education colleges, the Workers Education Association, local education authorities, numerous voluntary movements and courses on the media. One of the most significant developments at this time was that of the first 'Wlpan' courses held in the early 1970s in Cardiff and Pontypridd in south Wales and Aberystwyth in Mid Wales (Rees, 1974; James 1974). This system had been developed from intensive teaching which originated in Israel where the main aim had been to assimilate linguistically – and culturally – non-Hebrew-speaking Jewish incomers and to ensure that Hebrew would be the main language of the new state (Crowe, 1988: 17). The intensive methods of the 'Wlpan' were adapted by pioneers in the field such as Chris Rees of the Centre for Teaching Welsh to Adults in Cardiff and principles were introduced such as (i) intensive, functional-structural drilling, (ii) emphasis on oral skills, (iii) emphasis on Welsh as the principal teaching and class language, (iv) attending classes five times a week for a period of three to four months at a time. It is only after fully mastering the basic principles and patterns of the oral language that students move on to the formal written language. This development was a very important step forward in the organization of Welsh for adults in Wales, giving a better opportunity for students to *succeed* in learning to speak basic Welsh in a comparatively short period – succeed not only in being able to *speak* the language but in being able to *use* it like first-language speakers. Very strong motivation – and motives – were needed to succeed on an Wlpan course. The launch of these courses in the middle of the 1970s illustrates a corresponding fundamental change in students' reasons for learning from the period of the Williams 1965 report and those reasons noted by James (1974: 111–14). He observes motivations which are more typical of students on today's courses, namely reasons of work, assimilation, children receiving a Welsh-medium education and feelings that one should speak the language as part of one's identity.

A general provision for adults therefore evolved in Wales whereby the intensive-course provision was – on the whole – the responsibility of the departments of adult continuing education in the University of Wales and the University of Glamorgan and the once-a-week provision was located in the further education colleges, local education authorities and various other providers. This situation was to some extent formalized during the mid-1990s when the Further and Higher Education Funding Councils for Wales, having undertaken a comprehensive review of Welsh-for-adults provision, gave responsibility for planning that provision and formulating development plans to eight consortia broadly based on the county boundaries prior to local government reorganization in Wales in 1996. In general – although this has not always been the case in all parts of Wales – there is a holistic provision where the adult student can choose at what pace she/he would like to study, and at which level they should begin. Consortia have also been charged with ensuring adequate systems of educational guidance and support for those unsure of where they should 'fit in' or how to progress. A structure and system of quite specific progression routes has evolved and developed in addition to nationally recognized systems of accreditation of the various levels available. There have been, however, a number of obvious flaws with this present system. Until the release of council circular FE/CL/98/38,[2] there was little that the funding council could do should a consortium member choose to ignore the local development plan and compete for students (that is, finance). A lack of clear Welsh Office or National Assembly planning in the field of Welsh for adults and devolvement down through quangos (quasi-autonomous non-governmental organizations), such as the funding council and the Welsh Language Board, of responsibility for this area are further undermining the development of a comprehensive adult immersion programme in Wales and its location within a coherent language planning policy for the country. This is in stark contrast to the Basque system, as we shall see in Chapter 11, where HABE – the Institute for Literacy and Re-Basquization of Adults – is located with those responsible for language planning, culture, promotion of the Basque language and linguistic normalization programmes in the Department of Culture of the Basque Autonomous Community (see *Euskararen Berripapera*, 1995). Where coherent planning in the field of Welsh for Adults does exist in Wales, it is primarily at the level of those immediately responsible for the delivery of the provision, that is, the tutor/organizers at local level, who work together on an all-Wales level with the national officer for Welsh for adults who – until August 1998 – was located at the Welsh Joint Education Committee in Cardiff.

In order to understand better the potential contribution of second language acquisition (SLA) by adults to any process of language revival, it is necessary to know (i) more about the student profile, that is, which sectors of society are being reached, and (ii) why these students decide to learn the language in the first place. Their motivations also give a good indication as to the current status of language planning in the country – one would, for example, expect a greater degree of instrumental motivation in a country where the minoritized language is a necessary requirement in the field of employment. During a three-year survey of students attending preliminary meetings for Wlpan courses in the University of Wales Swansea region, a detailed picture emerged of the profile of students attracted to these courses. The region served by the university is very linguistically mixed as the figures in Table 7.1 (based on the former counties of West Glamorgan and Dyfed and their constituent district councils) illustrate.

Even within these areas, there is considerable variation at a local level, with 70 per cent or more speaking Welsh in wards in parts of the old Dinefwr, Llanelli and Lliw Valley areas. Linguistically, therefore, the region can be seen as a microcosm of the more general language situation throughout the rest of Wales, with a number of highly anglicized areas to the south and east and gradually increasing Welsh-speaking figures as one moves to the west and the north.

**Table 7.1. Region served by the University of Wales Swansea**

| | Resident population aged 3+ | % able to speak Welsh | No. able to speak Welsh |
|---|---|---|---|
| West Glamorgan | | | |
| Port Talbot | 49,178 | 8.59 | 4,222 |
| Neath | 63,051 | 12.97 | 8,177 |
| Swansea | 174,962 | 10.00 | 17,500 |
| Lliw Valley | 60,588 | 36.92 | 22,369 |
| East Dyfed | | | |
| Llanelli | 72,048 | 46.47 | 33,483 |
| Dinefwr | 37,297 | 66.52 | 24,811 |

*Source*: Aitchison and Carter 1994: 92–3. Figures refer to 1991 census.

During the three years in question (1992/3, 1993/4 and 1994/5) a question-naire was distributed to all prospective students on the university's Wlpan courses (which are held throughout the region outlined above). Before the commencement of an Wlpan course, a preliminary meeting is held to impress upon the students the need for commitment and regular attendance in order to be able to succeed on such a course. It was during these meetings that the ques-tionnaires were distributed to everybody who attended (including those who came to the meeting but subsequently failed to follow the course itself – a very small percentage of around 1 per cent). The total number of questionnaires distributed and completed during this period was: 165 (1992/3), 270 (1993/4) and 173 (1994/5). There is a tendency for more women than men to attend these courses: in 1992/3 there were 60 men (36 per cent) to 105 women (64 per cent); in 1993/4, 121 men to 149 women (45:55); and in 1994/5, 76 men to 97 women (44:56). This is lower than the average three women for every man noted in adult education language classes in the UK (Smith, 1987) but similar to the gender balance observed in other Welsh-for-adults classes in Wales.[3] Numerous reasons can be offered for this but, considering the importance given in the university's provision to holding courses close to nursery groups, coupled with heavy marketing in Welsh-medium schools, such a proportion is to a certain extent to be expected.[4]

I have already referred to Professor Bobi Jones's contention that the 'key to the revival of the language [is] to be located specifically amongst adult learners, particularly 15–30 year olds' (R. M. Jones, 1993: 11). The Swansea sample showed exactly that, namely the largest age group was those aged twenty-five to thirty-four. Yet again, these results are very similar to those found in other parts of Wales.[5] From the point of view of the future of the Welsh language and language revival, these figures bode well: (i) the language can be seen to appeal to younger age groups, thus giving it a young and vibrant image; (ii) this is the very age group in which one finds the majority of parents with young children who will

Table 7.2. Students attending Wlpan courses at University of Wales Swansea

| Age group | 1992/3 | 1993/4 | 1994/5 |
|---|---|---|---|
| 15–24 | 17 (10%) | 23 (8%) | 12 (7%) |
| **25–34** | **55 (33%)** | **95 (35%)** | **50 (29%)** |
| 35–44 | 47 (28%) | 54 (20%) | 36 (21%) |
| 45–54 | 23 (14%) | 39 (15%) | 40 (23%) |
| 55–64 | 19 (12%) | 37 (14%) | 25 (15%) |
| 65+ | 3 (2%) | 20 (7%) | 6 (3%) |
| No response | 1 (1%) | 2 (1%) | 4 (2%) |

be deciding on the medium of their education and be able positively to influence those children's attitudes towards the language – and speaking the language – in the future; (iii) the sixteen to forty-four age group is the very group which is least represented in the 1991 census figures for the Swansea region.[6] The potential for these 'new' adult speakers of Welsh to redress the linguistic deficit in this age group is obvious. There can be no doubt that *if* the potential of this process does translate itself into new Welsh-speaking parents who transmit their newly acquired language to their children, then it will have been a valuable contribution to efforts at reversing language shift in Wales, despite claims to the contrary by certain critics who were particularly vociferous in the 1990s.[7]

Nearly 50 per cent of the students who responded to the questionnaire were actually born in the former counties of West Glamorgan or eastern Dyfed – in other words, within the university's department of adult and continuing education catchment area. Of the others, 16 per cent were born in other parts of Wales and almost 28 per cent in England. This last figure is significant for two reasons: (i) it is proof that some of the people who have moved into the predominantly Welsh-speaking areas of the west are trying to assimilate and integrate into the Welsh-speaking society around them (something which is later reflected in their stated motivation for learning the language: see Morris, 1997); (ii) the students were also asked how many years they had lived in Wales and it would seem that a substantial number (almost a third) of those born in England have spent the majority of their lives in Wales, that is, having been brought up in Wales, with parents from Wales who had returned to the country to live.[8]

Mention has already been made of the fact that many English-speaking parents who have chosen a Welsh-medium education for their children subsequently decide to learn the language themselves. From the Swansea sample, 64 per cent to 70 per cent of the students actually had children, with a greater number of them attending Welsh-medium than English-medium schools. Much has been made in recent years of the fact that Welsh is a compulsory subject (for the most part) in the National Curriculum in all schools in Wales and substantial percentages of parents – 30 to 47 per cent – stated that this had also influenced their decision to learn Welsh. There can be little doubt that the education – and the language of that education – of the students' children is an important factor in their choosing to come on an intensive course. However, this is but one factor among a number of others for the majority of the students in the sample.

## STUDENTS' MOTIVATIONS

An HMI (Wales) report on the teaching of Welsh as a second language to adults published in 1984 broadly divided the students' motivations into four groups: (i) learners who were attempting to regain a language which was not transmitted to them by the older generation; (ii) newcomers who wished to become integrated into the Welsh-speaking communities around them; (iii) learning Welsh for work purposes or in order to improve one's chances of finding work; (iv) having children in Welsh-medium schools. A similar report on the county of Gwent published in 1991 suggested two primary motivations: (a) a feeling of Welshness, coupled with a desire to acquire the native language of their country; (b) a desire to assist their children who attended the county's Welsh-medium schools/units. Gardner (1985) argues that there are two kinds of motivation or orientation when acquiring a second language: an *integrative orientation* where the students learn in order to understand first-language speakers better and communicate with those parts of their communities who speak the language 'for social-emotional purposes' – and an *instrumental orientation* where the students learn in order to get a job or to advance their education, more utilitarian, practical reasons.

In a survey of learners in north-east Wales, Hughes (1989) observed that integrative reasons were the most important. In the Swansea questionnaire, the students were asked to note their reasons for learning Welsh and tick as many as they deemed to be relevant to themselves. The categories were chosen with an eye to keeping the questionnaire brief and also based on similar responses obtained from other surveys/HMI reports. In hindsight, it could be argued that more instrumental motivations should have been included for the sake of balance;[9] however, under point 6, the students were given the opportunity to note any other possible reasons for attending the course.

1. I live in Wales and feel I should speak the language.
2. I have children in a Welsh-medium school.
3. My family are Welsh-speaking.
4. I live in a Welsh-speaking area.
5. It will be advantageous for my work [including those who indicated that Welsh would be advantageous to them in finding employment].
6. Any other reason.

Students were subsequently asked to note one main reason. Reason 1 was the most popular response, with 39 to 48 per cent noting it as their main reason during the three years in question. Second came reason 2, which is once again an integrative motivation. The only instrumental motivation in the list is 5 and that came third, jointly with number 6. Numerous reasons were proffered under point 6, including some which were mainly integrative – that is, reasons of culture/patrimony, Welsh-speaking friends – however, there were also examples of instrumental motivation, for example, expanding personal knowledge/improving one's education.

It is evident that the Swansea sample conforms with those obtained in other Welsh surveys. In other words, the integrative motivation is the most prominent one amongst Welsh-for-adults students in this region. This situation is a unique one in the field of second-language teaching in Britain because people do *not* have to learn Welsh in a bilingual country in order to be able to communicate from day to day, as Trosset noted (1986: 174): 'Learners have a special significance because they represent a *reverse* trend in language acquisition. Unlike Welsh-speakers learning English (the normal pattern), Welsh learners are *not* motivated by practical intensity . . .' There exists, undoubtedly, a feeling among many adult learners of Welsh that learning and succeeding in mastering Welsh will make them somehow *more* Welsh or belong more to a Welsh-speaking community. To quote Trosset again (p. 174):

> All Welsh speakers by their very existence symbolise the Welsh struggle for linguistic survival . . . Welsh learners' voluntary acquisition of the minority language is an expression of their respect for the Welsh-speaking community and is significant of a desire to prevent the impending death of the Welsh language.

However, are strong integrative motivations and positive feelings/attitudes towards language preservation and revival enough on their own to contribute at any significant level to reversing language shift in a country like Wales, given the dearth of any structured language planning context within which these could be nurtured and developed to the good of the language?

Conversely, after the passing of the Welsh Language Act in 1993, in spite of its obvious inherent weaknesses, the demand for Welsh speakers – especially in the public domain – is likely to increase, together with a corresponding rise in the number of learners with instrumental motivations. Once again, however, as has been observed in other countries with effective systems of language planning and normalization in place, any success in training workers to use the minoritized language in a work context does not necessarily translate into success in persuading them to use the language in their family or social lives outside of the workplace. The reverse side of this equation is, of course, that the increased availability of services in the other language encourages and creates opportunities for more integrationally orientated learners to expand their use of the language outside the classroom (K. Jones, 1993: 49). The potential for successful language shift reversal in this field is evident – as is the potential for resource-draining failure unless these developments are brought about within the context of sensitive and sound language planning.

Can teaching Welsh to adults be an effective tool in the process of language revival in Wales? As previously noted, there are those in Wales who refuse to accept the possibility that the anglicized areas of Wales will ever become Welsh-speaking areas again. Figures published by the Further Education Funding

Council for Wales would seem to illustrate the depth of the problem showing that adult learners in Wales account for only 0.74 per cent of the non-Welsh-speaking population (FE/HEFCW, 1994: 37). There is, however, a huge untapped demand for the opportunity to be able to learn the language: the Welsh Office's *1992 Social Survey: Report on the Welsh Language* gives a figure of 1 in 10 of all non-Welsh-speakers who would like to learn Welsh or improve their ability in the language. In addition, it is estimated that 33.9 per cent of the population of Wales can speak at least a little Welsh and that 16.9 per cent can speak a fair amount or are almost fluent (Welsh Office, 1995: 7). This is significant as it means that the official figure (1991) of 18.65 per cent of the population of Wales as Welsh speakers is considerably lower than the potential pool of Welsh speakers with a passive knowledge of the language. These people are largely ignored by providers of continuing education in Wales and yet a properly planned network of confidence-building or literacy/*alfabetización* courses, as well as more general vocational courses through the medium of Welsh, would be a significant contribution towards boosting the number of confident and pro-active Welsh speakers in the community. A strong, well-resourced, coherent national policy to cultivate these two groups could bring the number of Welsh speakers in Wales towards the one million mark within a generation or two and would be a turning-point in the language's destiny in this new millennium.

We should not, however, assume that this kind of massive social and linguistic change can be brought about because of the positive attitudes and motivations of these potential language revivers. As Fishman warns (1995: 165–6) when discussing the case of the Basque language and the success of Basquization efforts in the workplace and amongst adults:

> Even were the numbers of the unreached to become substantially smaller, the feedback of these RLS-efforts to the home–family–neighbourhood–community nexus of inter-generational tongue transmission is far from certain, particularly given their occupational orientation and general lack of internal motivation among the adult learners to whom they were directed.

Any successful language revival policy in Wales would therefore need to harness the integrational motivations of many of our adult learners today and translate these into genuine opportunities: (i) to master the language *successfully*; (ii) to increase and encourage in anglicized areas the opportunities to use the language; (iii) to encourage positively and actively the use of the language within the context of the family and neighbourhood. Similarly, those learners who are increasingly coming to the language with instrumental motivations need to be actively encouraged in their classes to participate in the wider community and activities made available to them through the Welsh language outside of the work environment. This latter group in turn provides increased opportunities for the former to use Welsh and the former group will also reciprocate by encouraging use of the language in the wider community and family situations.

Robat Gruffudd, the well-known Welsh publisher and author, has argued in an article in the Welsh-language monthly *Barn* for a twenty-year national revival plan for the Welsh language and asks: 'if not now, when; if not here – where?' (1995). There is a substantial untapped source of new or 'reborn' Welsh speakers which could give a significant boost to such a programme here and now. The present system in Wales encourages providers to view the teaching of Welsh to adults as the teaching of any other subject – indeed, the Further Education Funding Council for Wales originally gave the subject a 0.2 weighting whereas English as a second language receives a weighting of 0.5! Until recently, institutions were not obliged to plough the money accrued from teaching Welsh to adults back into the same field and, despite the eight consortia's strategic plans and attempts at programme planning, very real problems of overlap and competition between providers can still be found. In addition, the growth of in-company provision and Welsh in the workplace has seen a plethora of providers – some who actually work on a daily basis in the field and others more 'unregulated' – and increasingly cases are being reported of poor-quality tuition and lack of structure in the courses. In other words, for some of the *non-traditional* providers the profit motive is obviously paramount. If properly and coherently conducted, the initial contact with the provider of a Welsh in the workplace course can often prove a catalyst for a more thorough audit of a particular body or business's language policy with benefits which extend beyond the field of simply providing language tuition for employees. At the other extreme, negative experiences of a badly advised business are likely to result in negative feelings towards the whole process of formulating language policy and in a less enthusiastic approach to language issues in the future.

In recent years, the Welsh Language Board has endeavoured to play a more active role in the strategic development of Welsh for adults. Initially, it was felt by the Higher and Further Education Funding Councils for Wales that they themselves did not have a planning remit within the field of Welsh for adults and that the Welsh Language Board should be given this role (FE/HEFCW, 1994). In many respects, the development of Welsh for adults in Wales prior to the funding changes initiated in 1994 had *evolved* rather than been *planned*: the planning that has occurred has to a great extent been the result of initiatives between tutor-organizers and the national officer for Welsh for adults through an all-Wales Welsh for Adults Panel, as evidenced in comprehensive and far-reaching plans such as the *The Way Forward* document published in 1992. These proposals were never allowed to come to fruition and, as so often happens in issues of attempted language planning in Wales, practitioners in the field were informed (with little consultation) by one quango – the Further Education Funding Council for Wales (FEFCW) – that another quango – the Welsh Language Board – had been given the responsibility for formulating a national strategy plan on Welsh for adults. The group which emerged, consisting mainly of representatives of the eight consortia, effectively took the place of the Welsh for Adults Panel and worked over two years to produce a comprehensive strategy for the field which was eventually endorsed by the Language Board in January 1998.

What is now needed in order to address in part the urgency expressed previously by Robat Gruffudd is an adult learning programme which is comprehensive, accessible and geared towards integrational immersion. This programme must be part of a coherent and progressive language revival plan for Wales, free of the binds of bureaucracy, administrative demands and financial formulas imposed by the funding council and the language board but properly monitored and resourced. The Language Board as presently constituted places great emphasis on promotion and advice (J. W. Jones, 1994): there will need to be a radical shift in language planning in Wales if the potential contribution of adult learners of Welsh is to be fully realized in the next twenty years. I have purposely used the term 'department of language normalization' as a label for a department in the National Assembly which could bring about this shift.[10] The word 'normalization' must loom large in the vocabulary of those who wish to plan for a language revival – a normalization of the language not only amongst those who are able to speak it but also amongst those who form the majority of the population of Wales, many of whom aspire to speak the language. If the tide is to be turned and the shift towards English to be reversed in Wales, then it is evident that the Welsh-for-adults provision *must* be seen as an important component of any language revival or revitalization plan. It is by nature an *inclusive* activity, welcoming potential students whatever their origins, backgrounds or reasons for learning the language – it is also aimed at the majority of the population of Wales who do not speak Welsh but whose attitudes are well-disposed towards the language. The *1992 Welsh Social Survey* (Welsh Office, 1995: 4) showed how learners of the language – both children and adults – constitute a growing percentage of the total Welsh-speaking population. Speakers of Welsh as a mother tongue accounted for only 26.7 per cent of Welsh speakers amongst those aged three to fifteen with the proportion increasing until sixty-five years or over where 78 per cent of Welsh speakers spoke Welsh as a mother tongue.

Not only is the age profile of these new speakers different to that of mother-tongue speakers but also their cultural, religious, ethnic and workplace experiences. This diversity of background and life experience enriches the language and holds the potential to develop and expand those domains through which Welsh can be used. It is no longer unusual to meet Welsh-speaking Catholics or Muslims, Welsh-speaking people born in other countries or members of ethnic minorities, Welsh speakers who play little or no part in 'traditional' Welsh-language domains. Our mass media have shown – when they make the effort – that it is possible to locate Welsh speakers in widely varying circles of life and experience. The Welsh-for-adults provision has the potential to increase and strengthen this diversity which, although remarkable and welcome, can also mean a fragmented and linguistically lonely life for many Welsh speakers who, although possessing the ability to discuss their particular area of interest of expertise through the medium of Welsh, very often lack the support and additional speakers to bring about a more permanent change of language within a particular domain.

Increasingly, language strategies are acknowledging the potential of adult learners of Welsh and many public bodies and companies in Wales, in attempting to formulate a coherent language policy as required under the 1993 Welsh Language Act, have launched into procuring *in situ* courses for the workforce to learn Welsh. It is imperative that this aspect of language acquisition is well-planned and executed and motivated by the needs and aspirations of the procuring bodies rather than the short-term financial gains possible for educational establishments providing these courses. When properly planned, this provision can enable organizations or bodies to provide a sound, comprehensive bilingual service to their users and through this endow their employees with new linguistic skills which might then be applied outside the workplace in their own communities. When *not* correctly planned, the resultant failure can give recalcitrant employers the excuse they need to scale down or stop such workplace-based courses, viewing them as a waste of finite staff development resources.

Once again, the above example provides further evidence of the need for Welsh for adults to be seen as an important part of language planning and highlights its potential role for language revitalization. Finally, the samples in our Swansea survey demonstrated that, whereas fifty or a hundred years ago the main focus of Welsh-speaking activity in many parts of Wales was the home and the chapel, today for those learners (and first-language speakers) in a predominantly anglicized region like the former West Glamorgan county area, the main focus is the school. Substantial numbers of adults are attracted to intensive courses because their children attend Welsh-medium primary schools. Given that intergenerational use of minoritized languages is one of the cornerstones to their continued existence, the potential for developing this aspect of language revitalization is considerable. The role that adult learners of Welsh could play in bringing about an actual *change* in the language spoken within the family is potentially huge. This needs to be harnessed and developed so that young parents, for example, are not learning when their children have already reached the age at which they can speak – wherever possible, strategies need to be devised whereby this will to learn can be harnessed and enacted *before* the children have established a language pattern with their parents.

Any policy for adult learners *must* be part of a larger comprehensive language policy for Wales which empowers its speakers and thereby enhances and encourages successful acquisition of the Welsh language by non-Welsh speakers. It seems unlikely that the present climate of *ad hoc* language evolution, promotion, advice and gentle persuasion in which we find ourselves at the moment in Wales will be able to deliver this goal in time.

## Notes

[1] R. M. Jones, 1993: 10. See also p. 11: 'All this therefore leads me to the conclusion that not only is the key to the revival of the language to be located specifically amongst adult learners, particularly 15–30 year-olds, but that this is already being realized, and

something is already being done about it, although we are still just beginning, with miles and miles to go before we sleep.'

[2] This circular released on 25 March 1998 informed consortia members that the Council has henceforth decided to: '(i) re-emphasise that all funding to institutions for Welsh for Adults provision is conditional on institutions participating and adhering to the relevant consortium strategic plan; and (ii) tie part of the programme area weighting (PAW) to consortia activity.'

[3] Welsh Office, 1991: 4. A ratio of 18:1 is noted – which is very high – although some classes were more balanced from the point of view of gender. A further study in the same area undertaken between 1994 and 1996 with adults who had already joined classes revealed a similar ratio: women 64 per cent and men 36 per cent. See Morris, 1999.

[4] Courtney (1992: 45) noted that adult education is more important to women from the point of view of raising self-confidence before returning to the workplace and it is possible that this is another element with some women who have more utilitarian motivations. See also C. Jones, 1995: 4–6.

[5] R. M. Jones, 1993: 4. 'Some classes contain a variety of age groups, but in general the majority who attend Welsh classes are in the 25–45 age group. A considerable number of learners are over 45 years of age, but there are few under 25.' See also Hughes, 1989: 16–17.

[6] The 1991 census figures give 11.3 per cent Welsh-speaking in the City and County of Swansea between ages three and fifteen falling to 6 per cent ages sixteen to forty-four and then rising to 10.1 per cent ages forty-five to sixty-four and peaking at 17.3 per cent for sixty-five and over.

[7] Tim Williams, for example, has studied the ways in which Wales became anglicized and claims that the language will never be revived in the south-east of the country. See *Western Mail* (12 July 1994), where families from the Rhondda area talk of their success in learning the language *and* speaking it with their children, making Welsh the main language of the whole family.

[8] See Aitchison and Carter, 1994: 108, table 6.10. Of the 508,098 who said that they could speak Welsh in the 1991 census, 48,919 were actually born outside Wales.

[9] The Welsh Language Act of 1993 has certainly brought about an increase in those learning Welsh through workplace-based courses (this is noted in Welsh Language Board, 1999). This particular area of Welsh-for-adults provision is an area which needs to be further researched and evaluated.

[10] Heini Gruffudd (1999) uses the term *Awdurdod Iaith* (or Language Authority) in his plea for a democratization of the work of the Welsh Language Board via the Assembly. He draws a similar conclusion on the need for such a body or department to engage in serious national language planning and end the *ad hoc* system of the past fifty years.

## References

Aitchison, J. and Carter, H. (1994). *A Geography of the Welsh Language 1961–1991*, Cardiff: University of Wales Press.

Courtney, S. (1992). *Why Adults Learn: Towards a Theory of Participation in Adult Education*, London and New York: Routledge.

Crowe, R. (1988). *Yr Wlpan yn Israel*, Aberystwyth: Canolfan Ymchwil Cymraeg i Oedolion.

European Bureau for Lesser Used Languages (1994). *Language Rights, Individual and Collective*, Dublin: EBLUL.

Euskararen Berripapera (1995). 'La Viceconsejería de Política Lingüística se incorpora al Departamento de Cultura', no. 38 (July).

Fishman, J. (1991). *Reversing Language Shift*, Clevedon, Avon: Multilingual Matters.

Further Education/Higher Education Funding Councils for Wales (1994). *Report of the Welsh for Adults Joint Review Group*, Cardiff: FE/HEFCW.

Gardner, R. C. (1985). *Social Psychology and Second Language Learning: The Role of Attitudes and Motivation*, London: Edward Arnold.

Gruffudd, H. (1999). *Awdurdod Iaith i Gymru*, Cyfres y Cynulliad, 7: Tal-y-bont: Y Lolfa.

Gruffudd, R. (1995). 'Ble mae Cymru?', *Barn*, 392 (September), 9.

HMI (Wales) (1984). *The Teaching of Welsh as a Second Language to Adults: Education Survey 12*, Cardiff: Welsh Office.

Hughes, M. (1989). *Selecting, Adapting, Creating Communicative Materials for Welsh Learners*, Wrexham: The Language Unit of the North East Wales Institute of Higher Education.

James, D. L. (1974). 'Ulpan Cymraeg Aberystwyth (1)', *Yr Athro*, 26 (December), 106–16.

Jones, C. (1995). 'Cymhelliant a rhyw – rhai sylwadau', *Y Tiwtor* (Summer ), 4–6.

Jones, J. W. (1994). 'The case of Wales: an evolving situation', in European Bureau for Lesser Used Languages, *Language Rights, Individual and Collective*, Dublin: EBLUL.

Jones, K. (1993). 'Expanding the use of Welsh', *Planet*, 101, 46–9.

Jones, R. M. (1993). *Language Regained*, Llandysul: Gomer.

Morris, S. (1996). 'The Welsh Language and its restoration: new perspectives on motivation, lifelong learning and the university', in Elliott, J., Francis, H., Humphreys, R. and Istance, D. (eds.), *Communities and their Universities: The Challenge of Lifelong Learning*, London: Lawrence and Wishart, pp. 148–63.

Morris, S. (1997). 'Ethnicity and motivation amongst adult learners of Welsh', in Synak, B. and Wicherkiewicz, T. (eds.), *Language Minorities and Minority Languages in the Changing Europe*, Gdansk: University of Gdansk Press, pp. 201–12.

Morris, S. (1999). 'Adult language learners as a force for language revitalisation: a Welsh experience', paper presented at the VII International Conference of Minority Languages, Bilbao, 1 Dec.

Rees, C. (1974). 'Wlpan', *Barn*, 145 (November/December), 563–5.

Smith, D. (1987). 'Modern languages and the adult student', in Sidwell, D. (ed.), *Teaching Languages to Adults*, London: CILT, pp. 1–15.

Trosset, C. S. (1986). 'The social identity of Welsh learners', *Language and Society*, 15, 165–91.

Welsh Language Board (1999). *Strategaeth Cymraeg i Oedolion/Welsh for Adults Strategy*, Cardiff: Bwrdd yr Iaith.

Welsh Office (1991). *Report by H.M. Inspectors on a Survey of Teaching Welsh to Adults in Gwent: Inspected during the Spring Term 1991*, Cardiff: Welsh Office.

Welsh Office (1995). *1992 Welsh Social Survey: Report on the Welsh Language*, Cardiff: Government Statistical Service.

Williams, I. T. (1965). *Oedolion yn dysgu Cymraeg (Astudiaeth o Gymhellion)*, Pamphlet 13, Aberystwyth: Education Faculty, University College of Wales.

WJEC (1992). *Welsh for Adults: The Way Forward*, Cardiff: Welsh Joint Education Committee.

# 8

# *Community Empowerment through Language Planning Intervention*

## COLIN H. WILLIAMS

Between the politics of recognition and the politics of compulsion, there is no bright line. (Appiah, 1994: 163)

Community empowerment is an attractive notion but one which citizens find increasingly difficult to realize because of the complexity, scale and pace of socio-economic development and political change. In particular the increased mobility of capital and the rise of neo-liberal ideas in economics and public administration means that state policy-making is less a matter of authoritative allocation and more a function of complex patterns of negotiation and adjustment among actors. However, in an increasingly globalized context where policies have switched from a concern with regional balance and social inclusion to the need to promote national competitiveness in global markets, there has been a corresponding shift of emphasis in the relationship between the state and agencies used to deliver a range of services. Reforms in public policy-making have produced a disjuncture between policy-making and political institutions (Keating and Loughlin, 1997: 11). Marin and Mayntz (1991) demonstrate that policy processes can better be understood through an examination of 'networks' and 'policy communities' which span tiers of government and the public and private sectors. Deconcentration and decentralization policies have also made the 'regional' level of government more central and contentious. Thus, while state-level governments adopt a neo-liberal approach and attempt to reduce their activities and expenditure, substate governments often seek to maintain a neo-Keynesian perspective and retain a number of functions abandoned at higher levels of governance. In such circumstances a complex policy-making system emerges in which policies based upon quite different logics, such as neo-liberalism and neo-Keynsianism, may coexist (Loughlin and Peeters, 1997).

There is also the difficulty of locating notions such as 'community', 'empowerment' and 'partnership' within pre-existent discourses. A key aspect of managerialism in the public sector has been the attempt to 'empower' workers and consumers. Loughlin and Peeters (1997: 57–8) reveal how the notion of 'empowerment' has its roots in quite different political traditions. The New Left critique of the repressive and over-bureaucratic state embraced empowerment principles and encouraged radical reforms in state–civil society relations based upon 'participation', 'self-government' and 'autogestion'. These have been accompanied within the Welsh context by variants on communal and economic sustainable development derived from nationalist and environmentalist discourses (Williams, 1999). On the other hand, the libertarian right remained suspicious of active state involvement and conceived of citizens as individuals governed by self-interest and relating to each other in market-type conditions. The public sector was correspondingly changed to establish internal markets so that purchasers were separated from providers and price and other market regulators were used to influence the behaviour of physicians, hospitals and patients in the provision of health care (Loughlin and Peeters, 1997). From this New Right perspective patients were consumers and service providers were managers charged with a responsibility to enagage, empower and involve clients in the decision-making processes of their organizations.

In a similar vein the notion of community has also been revised as an active component in state–civil society relations. In a comprehensive critique Williams and Morris (2000: 232) demonstrate how community has become

> the object around which a range of issues are problematized and resolutions are presented. Community becomes the focus of action in relation to economic development and social problems . . . The community is now presented in a number of different ways – as the focus of shared interests, as the embodiment of networks, as local interests, as the relay of communications, as the sum of cultural similarity. They rely upon shared identity. The rolling back of the state has shifted responsibility to the community, which becomes the focus of developmental attention.

There is now a large literature on the implications of requiring individuals to invest in their own self-governing communities and to take responsibility for the contours of local social change. However, instilling a sense of ownership within communities which have been ravaged by successive waves of deindustrialization, social fragmentation and economic collapse is a huge challenge. In terms of our concern with language planning the key question is to what extent such a challenge can, or should, be met by organizing around the issue of language decline and revitalization. Apart from the disingenuous nature of government policy, shifting responsibility without releasing sufficient resources to maintain community development, there is also the question of structural tension and mutual suspicion between the state and civil society and between fractions within society. These arise when questions of ownership of a social process are engaged and challenged, especially when languages in contact are also in competition. The issue of contact and conflict is a sensitive question because revitalization processes are seen by detractors as reflecting top–down bureaucratic interference promoting knowledge of Welsh as a privileged social identity marker, rather than as an expression also of bottom–up mobilization seeking to form a social partnership based upon a common goal.

How may endangered communities mobilize their own resources and those of external official agencies to promote language revitalization efforts? How may such communities engage in the politics of language mobilization without running the risk of alienating the very people in whose name language revitalization efforts are conducted? These are cardinal questions because all too often community-level initiatives become hijacked by the conventions of government bureaucracy, and what starts out as the politics of recognition soon becomes the politics of compulsion.

> It is a familiar thought that the bureaucratic categories of identity must come up short before the vagaries of actual people's lives. But it is equally important to bear in mind that a politics of identity can be counted upon to transform the identities on whose behalf it ostensibly labours. (Appiah, 1994: 163)

The normalization of language intervention can result in innovative strategies becoming routinized as departmental goals and a set of targets to be measured by performance indicators. Often such measurement procedures fall back on the financial accountability of grant-aided ventures rather than upon gauging the full impact of intervention on a community's sociolinguistic vitality. This is an understandable, if regrettable, state of affairs because government agencies are generally ill-equipped or ill-disposed to undertake comprehensive analyses of sociolinguistic change within particular communities.

## HOLISTIC PERSPECTIVES AND NEW DIRECTIONS

As we saw in Chapter 1 the first generation of language planners were understandably preoccupied with questions of educational curricula, the development of bilingual or multilingual public services and the interpretation of new legal requirements to promote a previously disadvantaged language. The challenge facing the current generation is to realize the fulfilment of a fully functional bi/multilingual society through creating new opportunities for language choice within the public, voluntary and private sectors of the economy. In practical terms this translates into questioning the extent to which interventionist language planning can reinvigorate beleaguered communities and establish bilingual service provision in new domains. The Welsh Language Board's goal is to enable the Welsh language to become self-sustaining and secure as a medium of communication. It does so primarily through changing the public-sector milieux in accordance with

> the main thrust of the Welsh Language Act (which) is that it makes provision for the delivery of public services through the medium of Welsh by placing a duty on public bodies which provide services to the public in Wales to prepare Welsh language schemes. As a consequence of the Act, the Welsh-speaking public in Wales can expect much more from providers of public services in terms of Welsh-language provision than ever before. (WLB, 1995: 6)

In successive strategy documents the board has set itself four priorities: (1) to increase the numbers of Welsh speakers; (2) to provide more opportunities to use the language; (3) to change habits in relation to language use and (4) to strengthen Welsh as a community language (for details on how such priorities are implemented see Chapter 3). Here we focus on the fourth objective, which is 'that Welsh-speaking communities be given the facilities, opportunities and the encouragement needed to maintain and extend the use of Welsh in those communities'. The board will

- undertake research into the linguistic make-up of Welsh-speaking communities and the social and economic factors which affect them;
- identify the main threats to the Welsh language within Welsh-speaking communities and formulate effective action plans for addressing potential problems in conjunction with key players across all sectors;
- discuss and develop with unitary authorities, especially those in the traditional strongholds, their role in terms of administering language initiatives and co-ordinating language policies;
- promote co-operation between communities to foster mutual support, encouragement and understanding;
- assess the effectiveness of existing community-based initiatives (such as *mentrau iaith*) as a means of promoting the use of Welsh and their usefulness as a model for facilitating the creation of new locally run initiatives;
- facilitate the establishment of local language fora to promote Welsh language initiatives, to create opportunities for using Welsh and to motivate and encourage people to do so;
- promote the learning of Welsh by adults (including the provision of worthwhile opportunities to use Welsh outside the classroom and other ancillary support);
- provide grants to support activities to strengthen Welsh within the community.


THE STRANDS OF COMMUNITY LANGUAGE PLANNING

In 1996 the Welsh Language Board commissioned Cardiff University to undertake a community research project. After the initial findings were reported to the Welsh Office (Williams and Evas, 1977), the Welsh Language Board hosted a series of national fora and has implemented several of the recommendations detailed at the end of this chapter, which takes developments up to 2000.

This chapter reports on those aspects of the research project which sought to identify opportunities for using Welsh and to determine what effect language planning intervention might have on strengthening Welsh as a community language. The four sites chosen were the Gwendraeth and Aman Valleys, the region served by Antur Teifi, and the town of Mold and its immediate hinterland. In the first two locations, *mentrau iaith* (community language enterprise initiatives) had been operative for a few years. By contrast, the Teifi Valley had witnessed the increasing influence of Antur Teifi, a private enterprise innovation and training agency which operated primarily through the medium of Welsh. Mold, the fourth location, is a long-anglicized service centre in north-east Wales, whose limited Welsh-medium networks had been maintained by formal religion, bilingual education and public-sector employment opportunities in the county town.

The first task was to identify the social context of the four study locations. The census data from 1991 were analysed to determine the chief characteristics of the study areas, including language data, migration trends, rates of relative deprivation and socio-economic factors. The Statistical Section of the Welsh Office was commissioned to undertake a detailed socio-economic analysis of selected sample sites (as reported in Chapter 2 above). This was supplemented by three other data sets, namely (1) the Welsh Social Survey (Welsh Office, 1992); (2) the most recent schools' censuses; and (3) the Welsh Examinations Database. Taken together these data sets provided a multi-level analysis of language in social context.

Two prerequisites for community language vitality are the influence of the family and the role of bilingual education in language reproduction. The mother tongue of marriage partners and within-family language transmission are still the most critical determinants of acquiring Welsh fluency. However, a major issue for language policy is that Office of Population Census and Surveys (OPCS) Household Composition data for 1991 suggest that many Welsh speakers are isolated at home and cannot communicate in Welsh with any other member of their household. Whereas 26.4 per cent of all households contained Welsh speakers, 56.6 per cent of these households were 'fully Welsh-speaking', yet only 10.9 per cent of these households contained children (Aitchison, 1995). This is a worrying demographic characteristic, and does not augur well for the domestic vitality of the language: 43 per cent of all Welsh-speaking households do not contain any children.

Household composition data suggest that the general trend is one of fragmentation and relative isolation, despite an increased use of Welsh in many new public domains. Having based our hopes on bilingual education as the chief pillar of language reproduction, it is only recently that we have measured the effect of the school system on successive generations of first- and second-language Welsh speakers. The school effect needs to be interpreted carefully and supplemented by data on issues such as pupil self-identification, the quality and variety of Welsh used in different contexts, continuity within the educational system, the adoption of various teaching methods and learning strategies, especially among second-language learners in English-medium schools. Some of these issues were teased out of the data sources in Chapter 2.

COMMUNITY FRAGMENTATION AND ATROPHY: INEVITABLE SPECTRES?

We saw in Chapter 1 that attempts to introduce territorial language planning measures based upon a set of shrinking cultural regions are doomed. However, if scale, location and regional context continue to be critical to the identification of linguistic practices, it behoves us to develop newer perspectives rather than abandon spatial analysis altogether (Ambrose and Williams, 1981: 53–71). This in turn suggests that social agencies for language reproduction are more critical then ever. Consequently the Community Research Project sought to investigate how individuals and social agencies may be able to construct strategies to overcome the lack of daily contact between Welsh speakers in identifiable/ acknowledged circles and social contexts.

As a supplement to aggregate census data, a social survey analysis was undertaken to identify language behaviour by domain and group characteristics. The research was premissed on the following questions:

- If the old social circumstances no longer maintain Welsh to the same extent that they did, are there new circumstances which can be created to strengthen the use of the language in the community?
- If there are, what are they?
- Who should establish and manage them?
- How should they be financed – privately or publicly or in a partnership?
- Should they emerge naturally from within the community or should they be established by local or central government, for example, in the shape of cultural resource centres?
- Should Antur Teifi, Menter Cwm Gwendraeth and Menter Aman Tawe extend their remit to establish and manage these new networks as part of the process of 'language intervention'?
- In order to intervene effectively in the language situation, is there a greater need for specific detailed data on the actual use of Welsh?

The project sample comprised 563 adults aged 17 and over (for full details and data analysis see Williams and Evas, 1997). Census data were used to identify the aggregate characteristics of local neighbourhoods and the respondents were selected from a random sample of addresses drawn from designated neighbourhoods. It is not claimed that the sample is representative, merely indicative of current trends in language attitudes and trends. (For a detailed critique of language use surveys, see Williams and Morris, 2000.) The sample's use of language in the four study areas was measured via a comprehensive questionnaire, having a core set of questions relating to the following issues:

- the use of Welsh and English in the local area;
- an assessment of the language skills of the population of the areas;
- the respondents' hopes in respect of a more comprehensive use of Welsh;
- the respondents' educational and occupational background by language status;
- the linguistic structure of the respondents' families;

- a description of how easy it was to use Welsh within different do
- which language the repondents would prefer to use within domains;
- the practical use of Welsh;
- an assessment of the respondents' self-confidence when using Wels
- the number of people who take the opportunity to use the current bilingual provision.

A second focus was the identification of various social communication networks and their relationship to institutional support agencies, some of which were specific to their locale. In Mold they were asked about the potential to launch a language initiative, in the Teifi Valley attention focused on the activities of Antur Teifi whilst in the Gwendraeth and Aman Valleys the role and effectiveness of the *mentrau iaith* were featured.

As the focus was the degree to which language planning intervention would affect the behaviour of individuals, the project investigated the extent to which individuals would wish to change the status quo so as to bring about a greater choice in the formal use of Welsh in society. This was done by asking: (i) which social networks are desirable and practicable? (ii) which social networks are desirable but impractical? (iii) which social networks are necessary following the implications of the statutory Welsh Language Act (1993) and Local Government Reform (1995–6)?

A third issue was the role of *mentrau iaith* as an instrument of community language planning. These community regeneration movements with a linguistic cutting edge were funded initially by the Welsh Office, through the Welsh Language Board, together with ancillary funding by local authorities (for a detailed case-study see Chapter 9). They provide one model of interventionist language planning at the community level. How are they to be assessed in view of the fact that they developed in a largely *ad hoc* manner? They each have a specific brief and interpret their responsibilities in a different fashion. As all have been established within the past decade it is difficult to measure their long-term impact on language use. However, it is important to ascertain the relationship between *mentrau* and language normalization.

## THE PRINCIPAL FINDINGS OF THE FIELDWORK

The number of domains in which Welsh is used has increased significantly over the past thirty years, especially in education, the media, leisure and selected public services. However, there has been a corresponding intensification of the influence of the English language, particularly in relation to new technology. Unless there is significant investment in the provision of effective infrastructural support for Welsh, the ability of the individual to use Welsh will diminish within strategic domains such as the workplace and daily business life.

Today, it is the home and the education system, rather than the community,

.vhich share the task of nurturing new speakers. The data analysis revealed that there was a failure to transmit the language from one generation to another in all the locations surveyed. One reason is the increase in the numbers of Welsh-speakers who choose a non-Welsh-speaking partner. There is considerable evidence to suggest that English tends to be the language of the home in some families. Notwithstanding this, one cannot attribute the failure to transmit the language to the home environment alone, rather it is reflective of wider social changes, chief of which is the decline of traditional social networks which used to support Welsh outside the home and the school. One should also note the decline in the opportunities children and young people have to mix with their contemporaries and a range of adults, reflective of the social fragmentation evident since the 1960s. One means of achieving cohesion is to encourage members of an older generation to use the threatened language with young people in social and community centres, drawing the youngsters into language networks. In time, it is hoped that the parents of such children, the semi-speakers, would also repossess the language. This is the real meaning of a community language, as many urge 'we should not be speaking about the language but rather speaking it on every possible occasion'.

The respondents reacted favourably to opportunities to use Welsh in situations where the choice offered to them was both obvious and convenient. For example, the frequency of choosing Welsh when using the bank and building society's automatic cash dispensing machines was relatively high because one is specifically prompted to select a transaction language. Where no such obvious choice is offered, and in circumstances where the customer has to search for a Welsh-medium provision (as is the case with BT Welsh-medium helplines), the opportunities available are underused.The means by which one is offered a language choice is thus critical to an increased use of Welsh.

There was a routine lack of expectation of using the language in formal social situations, and to some extent this derives from a lack of opportunity or an unwillingness on behalf of the individual to choose to use Welsh. Several factors account for this tendency. Often an uncomfortable experience in using or in asking for a Welsh-medium service predisposed respondents to opt for the English rather than the Welsh version. Many respondents felt that their linguistic skills were deficient, especially within formal contexts. Generally there was a lack of confidence among all age groups who chose English rather than Welsh, even in social domains which offered a genuine, stress-free language choice.

The respondents all ranked their core language skills of understanding, speaking, reading and writing slightly higher in English than in Welsh. This may be due to a lack of use of the language, the reaction by some to their experience within the education system, a lack of bilingual provision within the community and the cumulative impact of English on Welsh society generally. Several respondents reported feelings of inferiority concerning their Welsh linguistic abilities, especially in comparison with the perceived 'standard' variety of Welsh as used by the media.

Great concern was expressed surrounding the deleterious effects of unilingual English speakers moving into predominantly Welsh-speaking communities. Specifically, the influence of professionals such as doctors, ministers of religion, health visitors and managers on the patterns of Welsh used in the community also caused concern. In addition, there was a call for a reconsideration of the statutory planning process to protect the role of Welsh within the community.

In domains where there has been considerable investment, such as education and the public sector, there is a willingness to use the language. Our principal finding is that the general public is favourably disposed to extending bilingualism in the community. But, in order to realize language rights through offering a choice of service, there has to be a much more effective provision. Hitherto the prime emphasis in policy terms has been on increasing the numbers able to speak Welsh. But it is time that we also adopted effective bilingual working practices which are attractive to the public. Unless this is achieved, the enthusiasm displayed for the improved status of Welsh is a piece of self-deception.

Second-language speakers did not always feel themselves to be part of the available Welsh-language networks. Some who were learning the language reported that they found difficulty being accepted as proto-speakers of Welsh by fluent speakers, and as such felt that they were being excluded from the Welsh-speaking community. On the whole, however, the public displayed particularly favourable attitudes to increasing bilingual provision:

- in the advertising world;
- in incorporating the interests of Welsh within the town and country planning system;
- in promoting Welsh within the business environment;
- in the workplace generally.

There is a significant potential for the increased use of Welsh which was welcomed by the overwhelming majority of the sample. Similarly, there is also a high potential to increase the new opportunities to use the language. However, it should be acknowledged that there is a discrepancy between the explicit aspirations of the respondents to use more Welsh and their daily instrumental choices. There would be an increased employment of the language – across the whole continuum of language abilities – if greater provision were made for its use, and were this to be done new speakers would be drawn into the language networks.

To date, the potential of Welsh in the business sector has not been realized. Evidence from the fieldwork confirms that the lack of provision for Welsh militates against its use, especially in office work and in dealings with the public sector.

The essence of regenerating any community language is to inculcate a shared responsibility for its condition among all who speak it. The fieldwork revealed that some believed that it is only official agencies who should be actively working in favour of Welsh, and in consequence they shift the responsibility from their own shoulders, thereby weakening the degree of community ownership in the process of language regeneration. A number of factors influence the degree to which Welsh is used by the respondents in the study areas, though clearly not all the communities face the same problems. Nevertheless, action to influence these factors so as to bring about a change in the patterns of language use is possible by intervening in the normal social processes of the community.

## MENTRAU IAITH

The prime examples of intervention are the *mentrau iaith*. Menter Cwm Gwendraeth was established in January 1991 as a pioneering programme to promote Welsh at the community level and to provide a model for language planning which could be adapted to other parts of Wales. Its sister organization, also located in the anthracite coalfield of south Wales, Menter Aman Tawe was established in January 1994. The Community Research Project revealed that there was a widespread appreciation of the activities of the *mentrau iaith* which enriched the quality of life and provided a reinforcing effect on attitudes to Welsh and its use.

### Menter Cwm Gwendraeth

As will be discussed in the next chapter Menter Cwm Gwendraeth's strategy is based on the following aims:

- to create social conditions that will nurture positive attitudes towards Welsh and an increase in its general use;
- to normalize the use of Welsh as a medium of social and institutional communication;
- to highlight the close relationship between language and attitudes which relate to quality-of-life issues, the environment and the local economy.

Menter Cwm Gwendraeth attracted very able key personnel who have shown great acumen in developing an objective strategic development plan. This includes the setting of realistic targets (as discussed in Chapter 1), using a variety of primary and secondary data to analyse specific issues, the detailed monitoring of *mentrau* projects and a critical self-assessment of its language promotion activities. In this respect, the *menter* is a pioneering model of sound purposive planning.

To reduce overcentralized planning, the *menter* established local village committees able to share ownership in the processes of language intervention. These committees help integrate the community into the decision-making process and in turn implement *menter* policy. This has been rewarded in terms of the community's support, goodwill and restoration of community's confidence in using the language in public affairs.

The *menter* has demonstrated its readiness to create working partnerships with other bodies and agencies. It has extended its influence such that it is perceived as a community development enterprise which emphasizes the Welsh language and which uses it to accomplish its tasks. In its development as a community agency, the *menter* has succeeded in attracting financial support from new sources, including a substantial grant from the European Union. Success has not been without its own sources of tension, as Cefin Campbell demonstrates in the next chapter, but there is no doubt that Menter Cwm Gwendraeth is one of the most practical and inspiring agencies of language revitalization in contemporary Wales, well worthy of imitation.

### Menter Aman Tawe

The second *menter* surveyed was Menter Aman Tawe whose goals are to act as:

- a programme to promote the Welsh language in the Tawe and Aman Valleys;
- a programme to secure an appropriate place for Welsh in both valleys;
- a programme to stimulate enthusiasm and pride in our heritage.

Menter Aman Tawe functions as a co-ordinating forum for Welsh in a relatively depressed region. It consciously focuses on youth work and on adopting Welsh as a natural extension of daily life, including social activities, games and cultural events. One of the positive features revealed by the fieldwork focused on the Aman Valley was that participants very much enjoyed such *menter* activities; there is little feeling that they are attending such activities out of a sense of duty, rather they feel that such activities are core community youth projects. However, the continued effectiveness of *menter* activities is highly dependent upon a relatively small group of volunteers.

Menter Aman Tawe places a great emphasis on direct social involvement with people and pays far less attention to structural planning than other *mentrau*. Some might argue that Menter Aman Tawe's impact is thus more immediate and direct, adopting an essentially pragmatic mode of action. However, this style also reflects the social structure of the area which is predominantly working class and relatively poor. Initially some twenty-five village committees were established to expedite the work of the *menter*. By 1997 many had ceased to function due to a lack of sustained enthusiasm on behalf of the volunteers.

The main challenge facing Menter Aman Tawe is the lack of social leaders who can advance its cause. There is no lack of commitment or initiative displayed by its staff; what is lacking is a sense of community ownership of the *menter*, as opposed to a community interest in its success. The Community Research Project recommended concentrating on how social leaders are nurtured and integrated into the language regeneration process. There is a dire need for a framework whereby local community leaders can be trained. This could be incorporated as part of the *menter iaith*'s remit, together with its partners in the community, so as to ensure effective linguistic networks. In its current format, Menter Aman Tawe's long-term potential for self-sustaining development is moderate to slight.

The principal consequence of linguistic intervention in the industrial valleys was an upsurge in community confidence and pride as residents saw exciting things happen in the locality. It has also contributed to the re-formation of cultural and socio-economic networks. The *mentrau iaith* have prompted many of the region's institutions to offer a practical language choice in their service provision, thereby opening up new domains. These new opportunities should support a wide range of Welsh-medium activities in the following spheres:

- the language of popular culture in the area, for example rugby, cricket, drama;
- the health services and community care provision;
- children's chosen language of play outside the confines of school;
- working men's clubs and public houses;
- skills training courses and career development programmes.

### Mentrau iaith: *a framework for regenerating Welsh in the community*

Regenerating Welsh in the community is a long-term process and it would be naïve to assume that any interventionist agency could directly influence the lives of the majority of any area's residents in the short term, especially if it were externally initiated. One would not expect any social agency to influence the majority of people the majority of the time. Similarly, one would not expect different communities to react in a uniform manner to the same regenerative stimuli. The flexibility to react effectively to a particular area's specific needs is an integral element to the concept of a *menter iaith*.

*Mentrau* have become significant agencies for tackling linguistic fragmentation, especially in areas where there is a high proportion of Welsh speakers. The reasons for encouraging the establishment of a nation-wide network of *mentrau iaith* are the following:

- In locations characterized by strong language potential but weak socio-linguistic networks, which would otherwise lead to fragmentation, they offer a significant socio-psychological fillip for the reproduction of the language.
- As local language co-ordinating bodies, they can create new partnerships between the National Assembly, the Welsh Language Board, local government, statutory public bodies, health trusts and voluntary agencies and private companies.

Another advantage is that *mentrau* can encourage the use of Welsh in hitherto limited domains, and without constituting part of the official administration of any district. To maximize this autonomy *mentrau* have to display political acumen and demonstrate interpersonal skills, for they must operate as respected co-ordinating bodies, without necessarily accruing any political status or power. *Mentrau iaith* will continue to depend on established agencies for their existence and their shared success. Doubtless in time some will become assimilated and others may jettison their original linguistic focus and evolve into community economic organizations.

Thus, the likely development of the *mentrau* raises some intriguing questions. First, should any additional *mentrau* be conceived primarily as a language or community or economic development enterprise, or a combination thereof? Need *mentrau* necessarily be temporary adjuncts to other community initiatives? If *mentrau* are meant to be interventionist agencies able to encourage new networks and revitalize the language activities of a community, should they be short-term or medium-term ventures, or agencies charged with the co-ordination and encouragement of Welsh-medium activities initiated by others?

The Welsh Language Board has served as the facilitating agency providing initial expertise and financial support, but it is unlikely to assist new ventures to the same extent that it has assisted established *mentrau*. Local authorities will shoulder more responsibility for supporting the needs of new *mentrau iaith*. In political terms this is a positive move and is far more likely to enable *mentrau iaith* to co-ordinate their myriad activities *within* a variety of well-established statutory and voluntary organizations, enabling them to operate as cost-effective interventionist agencies engaged in the process of community regeneration.

One of the paradoxes facing *mentrau* is that they are destined to loose their catalytic element by becoming incorporated into the institutional system they were designed to affect through intervention. As any *menter iaith* is, in essence, a temporary expedient, it is fair to ask how this tendency may be overcome. There are few orthodox answers to this issue. It is unlikely to exercise the newly developed national network of *mentrau iaith* as they take account of how best to influence the cross-cutting responsibilities of local authority departments of education, health and welfare, etc. One maxim needs repeating, however: the essential task of a *menter iaith* is to persuade others to act; it is not the function of a *menter* to take unto itself the responsibility for all related activities. Herein lies a major conundrum for planners and activists alike. Unless there is a shared conception of basic terms like community, empowerment and partnership, there is every possibility that language policy will flatter only to deceive. It will seek to 'return' or 'transfer' to the community, power and responsibility for the reproduction of Welsh without also releasing the necessary political and economic investment to realize this wish-fulfilment as social practice.

By 2000 a network of eighteen *mentrau iaith* had been established, with support from the Language Board during 2000/1 totalling £430,390. The core principles of Menter Cwm Gwendraeth's *Strategy* have been influential in the thinking of successive *mentrau iaith*. However, future *mentrau iaith* should also include the following aims:

• to urge and encourage community ownership of the language, together with a transference of responsibility for it back to volunteers and the *menter*'s community organization partners;

- by means of social and leisure activities to increase the opportunities available for people to use Welsh;
- to work for the promotion of Welsh in the community through co-operation with movements, institutional representatives and individuals at local and national level;
- to raise the profile of Welsh in business in the local area;
- to promote bilingualism in the workplace;
- to encourage Welsh speakers to use the language and to make use of existing bilingual opportunities;
- to improve the command of fluent speakers;
- to regain uncertain speakers, or those who have lost their Welsh for whatever reason;
- to offer practical assistance to adult learners and pupils who are learning Welsh as a second language;
- to provide advice for parents on raising their children bilingually;
- to assimilate new speakers to the Welsh-medium community and inform the mother-tongue speakers about their needs;
- to undertake translation work, or direct enquiries to qualified translators;
- to lobby training agencies to prepare professional bilingual and language-friendly materials;
- to disseminate information about local Welsh-medium education and training;
- if appropriate, to promote issues which will lead to local economic development.

Consideration should also be given to several administrative issues when planning and launching a new *menter iaith*:

- an appropriate management structure for each new situation;
- a robust financial plan for the likely lifespan of the *menter* (initially some two to five years would seem appropriate);
- practicable formulations as to how to 'normalize' the *mentrau iaith* so that they gradually lessen their dependence upon government direct grant as they seek to become self-sustaining agencies, genuinely working within the community they serve and from which they sprang;
- detailed consideration of the target area's networks, together with a consideration of the socio-linguistic nature and wishes of those who might be described as 'the invisible Welsh-speakers', that is, those citizens who currently do not constitute an element of the existent Welsh-medium networks;
- consideration of the role and possible efficacy and/or baneful effects of recent forms of telecommunications in maintaining newer networks;
- consideration of the attractions that would accrue following the establishment of cultural resource centres, which would not necessarily constitute an integral part of the *mentrau*: they could be an additional element, in which case the element of co-operation in any proposed relationship should be stressed;
- consideration should be given to convening a series of seminars in association with the agencies, the local authorities and disciplinary specialists in order to discuss and evaluate the experience gained hitherto;
- preparation of an information pack which would review the concept of community planning; provide an overview of the strategies and efficacy of the existing

*mentrau*; offer examples of successful and unsuccessful initiatives together with a detailed interpretative account; provide data on probable annual investment so that all decisions are made upon a realistic basis.

All these elements depend upon a lucid exposition of the role of the Welsh Language Board in the process of stimulating practical developments in the field of language planning. A formal agreement between the Welsh Language Board and the *mentrau iaith*, which specifies the nature of the relationship and an outline of the responsibilities shared with others who provide bilingual services, has been developed and is discussed in Chapters 3 and 9 of this volume. The board's initial focus on patterns of language behaviour and encouraging *mentrau iaith* was reasonable, but consideration should now be given to additional variables which influence language revitalization efforts, such as:

- occupational structures and local economic development;
- unorthodox social networks, especially in urban contexts;
- research on the social and economic implications of telematic networks;
- demographic trends and age/sex differences by language acquisition and maintenance;
- a lucid understanding of community changes which may be independent of, though contributing to, those conditions which maintain Welsh as a dynamic element in society;
- an analysis of the contemporary 'Welsh way of life';
- consideration of the available methods whereby the linguistic abilities of Welsh-speakers could be improved;
- research on how the *mentrau* may evolve as agencies in the field of soci-economic development;
- investigation of comparative methods of language revitalization world-wide.

Three other means of revitalizing Welsh are also worthy of consideration: *mentrau* to promote Welsh as the county level, resource centres and linguistics *animateurs*.

LANGUAGE PROMOTION ENTERPRISES AT THE COUNTY LEVEL:
THE CASE OF CARMARTHENSHIRE

In 1996 Carmarthenshire County Council sought to advance the idea of a county-wide language planning framework. The ways in which current provision could be developed and enhanced was summarized by the Consultative Panel – which included several of the authors of this volume acting as representatives of the *mentrau iaith*, the Welsh Language Board and Cardiff University – as a choice among three options or a combination thereof:

- to establish additional *mentrau* throughout the county;
- to establish a county-level *menter iaith* with a number of outlier satellites;

- to develop the current *mentrau* and *anturiaethau*, together with a forum to co-ordinate their activities.

The county chose to amalgamate options 2 and 3 to create Mentrau Myrddin, details of which are provided by its director, Cefin Campbell, in the next chapter. Connecting Mentrau Myrddin to county council systems of administration will be of benefit in the long term as they can share experience, specialist knowledge, purchasing power and forward planning. This should also assist local authorities to implement their language plans. The network enables personnel from one *menter* to participate in projects initiated by other *mentrau* and external agencies, for example, work with special needs children, development work with new bodies or new ways of utilizing telecommunication facilities to teach through the medium of Welsh, to diffuse information and to network effectively. Resource information packs could also be prepared in association with county or national level organizations, drawing on the experience of staff from the *mentrau* and the proposed resource centres described below.

## COUNTY LANGUAGE RESOURCE CENTRES

The language resource centre would be the principal instrument for (1) developing the county's language plans, (2) promoting its statutory linguistic obligations, (3) improving delivery of the bilingual services and (4) securing the provision of adequate resources and appropriate materials. In respect of the statutory language processes, the language resource centre would supply specialist services for all aspects of the county's responsibilities. Specifically it would:

- proffer professional advice to councillors, the officers of public, private and voluntary organizations and all residents of the county;
- arrange seminars and training for county officers and *mentrau* workers;
- co-ordinate the relevant parts of the county's schedule of work so as to improve its internal organization, encourage communications in Welsh, provide advice on bilingual interaction with the public, offer professional language-related advice on publications, forms, public signs, leaflets for contracted services and various other county activities.

The centre would improve the public's bilingual service through effective co-operation with other county council departments, for example, by issuing specific advice on socio-linguistic targets to school governors, to the Department of Community Affairs, the Probation Service, the Rent Office, the Careers Service, focusing on specific issues in turn.

Such centres would conduct language-skill audits of county service providers, whether or not they are directly employed by it. This would include a needs analysis of the linguistic requirements of specific posts; the levels of written competence required; identifying what type of support both learners and bilingual officers would need. Thus a genuine choice of language of work and social interaction would be exercised, thereby increasing the Welsh-medium character of the county's civic culture.

The centre could provide instantaneous translation equipment, videos, Welsh-medium and bilingual software and share resources with the education authority and county council libraries, the marketing sections and the town and country planning department. Also, it is possible to develop a range of peripatetic and mobile services such as a Welsh-medium occupational training service, translation service, Welsh-medium children's play buses in which parents may also receive intensive Welsh lessons.

## A NATIONAL LANGUAGE RESOURCE CENTRE

The original research project recommended that the National Assembly and Welsh Language Board establish a National Language Resource Centre responsible for the following issues:

- Marketing the economic value of bilingualism to Wales, and to those businesses who are considering locating or investing here, especially within the context of a multilingual European Union;
- Monitoring, supporting and transplanting practical language planning activities, together with new theories in this field, by drawing on international precedents;
- Surveying and reviewing materials which facilitate the use of Welsh, especially in relation to software developments in the workplace;
- Creating a central data-base of Welsh materials so that individuals can profit from examples of good working practice which may be adapted to various circumstances;
- Preparing guides and materials to assist individuals and voluntary organizations to work in practical terms to promote Welsh in their communities;
- Providing a support help-line which the public could access to gain authoritative advice on the use of Welsh, for example, on how to express complex ideas when the language has to be very precise, as in preparing a contract or a legal document;
- Acting as a national information centre for translation services and other language-related services;
- Holding a national data-base for language planning.

Research is critical in formulating language policies. The proposed central database would facilitate the diffusion of information on applied bilingualism and the effectiveness of local language policies. It would monitor developments in the health services, the business sector, the voluntary sector and throughout the community. The centre could provide an appropriate structure for pioneering such activities as well as diffusing examples of language planning in Wales and in a European context, drawing on good practice from Catalonia, Ireland and the Basque Country as evidenced in Chapter 11.

## LINGUISTIC *ANIMATEURS*

If public services are serious about their response to the recent guidelines on developing bilingual policies, then they should *provide* a comprehensive bilingual service. Many institutions require an external stimulus to kick-start their reaction, and thus should embrace the idea of linguistic *animateurs*, who would function at three levels and with varying degrees of financial support and authority:

- At the local level, being active in society, social workers, nurses/health visitors/midwives, could, in some cases, be required to make more use of Welsh whilst discharging their responsibilities;
- Within a county or a specific region, *animateurs* could be given a wide brief to promote Welsh, either as part of preparatory action to the setting up of a *menter iaith* or completely independent of such possibilities;
- Within specific occupations or industries, linguistic *animateurs* could work *pro tempore* in, for example, the police service, local authorities or health trust, the ambulance and fire services. Their role would be to establish a new bilingual framework in order to improve good practice or to prepare the ground for the implementation of workplace language plans by adopting best-case examples from other sectors.

Linguistic *animateurs* could be supported financially by a consortium of para-public agencies, for example, the Local Government Management Board, or they could be employed directly by, or in partnership with, the Welsh Language Board on fixed-term contracts, for example, for five years to establish new bilingual working practices in a suite of para-public agencies or to prepare for new *mentrau*. They would need professional training and the following resources prepared by the Board: an information pack dealing with the principles and practice of language planning including worked examples of 'good practice' and 'bad practice'; a comprehensive analysis of the formal responsibilities agencies have in connection with the promotion of Welsh, together with information on key contact personnel in the local target area, so that effective networking can be initiated from the beginning of the appointment of any *animateur*; in-service training at a national level for all linguistic *animateurs*. To achieve these aims a stronger national network of *mentrau* personnel and *animateurs* would be necessary. Language-sensitive community leadership skills could be developed by an external agency along the lines suggested by CCETSW Wales, as part of its social-work training programe. International examples would also figure in the instruction which should be a shared responsibility of academic institutions, with input from respective Language Boards, the European Bureau for Lesser Used Languages and the European Union.

## REALIZING THE POTENTIAL: OVERCOMING BARRIERS TO WELSH IN THE WORKPLACE?

Hitherto, the chapter has presented the case for appropriate national frameworks and local structures for the normalization of the language. However, it is evident from the Community Research Project results that consideration should also be given to normalization from the standpoint of the individual, that is, the user, as well as the standpoint of the service provider.

The greatest difficulty facing the normalization of Welsh lies in the workplace. Unless this sphere is revolutionized, any free choice will be totally false for it is not an unfettered choice. Language rights are not genuine if they can be exercised only as a customer and not also as a worker – this is the operation of the market and not the assertion of democratic rights *per se*. Thus continuous provision of good-quality occupational education and training is essential. Professional language improvement courses are needed, focusing on language skills and self-confidence to enable individuals to work effectively in both English and Welsh. A national campaign for the promotion of plain, clear and accurate Welsh would form an important element in this process. The research highlighted the following barriers to increasing the use of Welsh in the workplace:

- an unaccustomed use of Welsh professionally;
- a lack of consistent and relevant terminology;
- a lack of confidence;
- a feeling of awkwardness when using Welsh in linguistically mixed contexts, either with individuals and families or with fellow workers;
- a lack of support from managers and superiors within particular establishments;
- a lack of proprietary feelings towards the language;
- a deficiency in several aspects of the mastering of language, such as grammar and confidence in its use;
- a tension between the formal language of reports and guidelines, and the natural language of conversation (but this could also be true of English);
- a personal tension between a professional self-image and the individual's ability in Welsh.

### *What is to be done?*

It is not the sole responsibility of the individual to solve all of the above problems. Many Welsh speakers found it easier to use English rather than Welsh in formal settings, because of the long-standing status differential of Welsh in comparison with English. In order to equalize language choice there needs to be:

- a change in attitudes through sophisticated strategic and marketing campaigns together with other effective methods;
- an increase in the provision of in-service training so that one may feel totally confident in using English and Welsh equally well;

nge in behaviour, through persuasion, encouraging interest and increasing
pportunities to use the language;
rease in the total who use Welsh on a daily basis, whether they be new speakers or semi-linguals.

## Changing attitudes

Changing attitudes originates with the education system and, as we have seen
elsewhere in this volume, both the bilingual education sector and the English-
medium sector face different challenges to normalize bilingualism. The second-
language population will receive far more attention in the future, whether they
are adult learners, parents of Welsh-medium schoolchildren, pupils encounter-
ing Welsh as part of the National Curriculum or those who were raised unable
to speak Welsh by Welsh-speaking parents. Any language planning process
should be keen to analyse the relative success of late immersion methods and
measure the contribution of centres seeking to assimilate linguistically those
who are described as 'latecomers' to a community. But there is an additional
need to be able to measure the success and failure of adults learning the
language in formal classes, and the difficulties such learners encounter as they
seek to be incorporated within Welsh-medium networks and communities. A
significant improvement would be the adoption of progressive 'brain-friendly'
language teaching methods. Where do such changes need to take place?

*In the mind:* Changing attitudes towards the role of Welsh in society is a difficult
task. Although the reluctance of some to work bilingually is understandable, the
research suggests that the principal difficulty is lack of provision and habit.

*In our expectations:* Currently many companies and public bodies who offer an
element of language choice operate a *patina* of superficial bilingualism.
Expectations have to change if the vision of a bilingual Wales is to be realized.
The public has to be convinced that the Welsh language belongs to all and that
they share a joint responsibility for its welfare. CCETSW's mission statement
captures the change in expectation well when it suggests that 'bilingualism is not
a problem, but a fact, and we have to acknowledge this fact if the service which
is offered is to be of a high quality and relevant'.

*In our civil rights:* The individual is a citizen with acknowledged rights. This is
one of the main themes of the CLP research, as many inhabitants were discov-
ered to be concerned that their civil rights are not currently being upheld by the
system.

*In the community:* There is a need to extend the boundaries of bilingualism
within the community, in the institutions and agencies which maintain the quality of life and offer better ways of coping with the social problems which beset

our age. The challenge is to create partnerships which will enable us to share and benefit from each other's experiences. The ability to choose the language in which we would prefer to be served is but an extension of this personal and social empowering. But securing the possibility of choice is itself dependent upon national and international political underpinning.

*In the political sphere:* The realization of language rights is dependent upon how responsive public bodies are to the Welsh Language Board and National Assembly on the one hand and to social pressure on the other. The reaction of local authorities to the need to devise a language plan is in part dependent upon their decision to allocate finance for its provision and the reaction of the people who will ultimately be affected by it, namely the electorate. It is thus a matter of some urgency to encourage the public to use the new opportunities to their full potential.

   These goals and priorities cannot be achieved without a great deal of social, political and economic pressure. Within the context of the Welsh Language Board's *Strategy*, the following recommendations were proposed by the Community Language Project.

### *The principal recommendations*

The concept of *mentrau iaith* should be developed and adapted to the needs of other areas in accordance with the framework proposed above, and that support be given to new *mentrau iaith* wherever it is appropriate.

The concept of County Language Initiatives should be developed and implemented in accordance with the illustration discussed herein.

The concept of County Language Resource Centres should be developed and implemented.

The concept of a National Language Resource Centre should be developed and implemented.

A network of linguistic *animateurs* should be established and developed.

A closer relationship should be nurtured between the Welsh Language Board, the *mentrau iaith*, the local authorities, and the public, private and voluntary sectors, and effective partnerships should be established in order to expand bilingual provision and enable communities to use the language in all aspects of life through offering the public an efficient language choice.

A marketing strategy for Welsh should be devised and sustained in order to draw people to use Welsh-medium networks, to encourage people to utilize the existing opportunities, to use the language and to promote a dynamic, contemporary image of the language.

A campaign should be launched to encourage people – especially second-language speakers – to raise their children through the medium of Welsh and to extend the natural opportunities for children and young people to socialize together and with a variety of adults both from within and outside their immediate family through the medium of Welsh.

A thorough investigation should be undertaken into the successes and failures of teaching Welsh to adults, and into the problems they have when attempting to blend into Welsh-medium networks and communities, so that effective frameworks for this sphere may be constructed together with significant investment.

Increased provision should be made for in-service language tuition; a permanent occupational training infrastructure of the highest quality should be developed and endowed so as to facilitate the effective use of Welsh in the workplace.

Appropriate information packs should be produced to facilitate the process of establishing *mentrau iaith* and Language Resource Centres, and the training of community leaders and linguistic *animateurs*; in particular, provision should be made for the relevant training of community leaders.

Consultation be undertaken with the Welsh Office/National Assembly with a view to redrafting those aspects of the statutory planning process which directly impinge on attempts to regenerate Welsh as a community language.

Co-operative work should be undertaken, in association with the Development Board of Rural Wales (or possible future successor bodies), Menter a Busnes and Antur Teifi, in order to develop their ideas and processes so as to encourage self-sustaining economic development in other areas.

### *Other recommendations*

A campaign should be launched to increase the use of the language through the provision of software and technology.

A comprehensive advertising campaign should be launched to increase the awareness of existing Welsh-medium services.

Suppliers should provide bilingual services as a matter of course rather than requiring the citizen to specifically ask for a Welsh service.

A framework which is supportive of bilingualism should be created: based on the process of realizing those civil rights which are incorporated within the Welsh Language Act, 1993 and recognized human rights charters.

More proactive methods should be developed to persuade second-language speakers to use Welsh more frequently.

Closer co-operation should be developed between the Welsh Language Board and a number of professional bodies in Wales in order to realize the concept of a bilingual service, to normalize the idea of the bilingual workplace, to prepare official documents in clear, simple and correct Welsh, to standardize the terminology used by bodies which provide a bilingual service, to convince private companies and bodies that they are a critical component in the broader strategy for the Welsh language.

Professional research is required into the relationship between language reproduction and the town and country planning process so as to realize a more holistic perspective. Similarly, we recommend that research be undertaken into the relationship between economic development, governmental intervention (for example, through the tax system) and the future of the language.

Co-operation should be developed with the media so as to present effective *role models* for learning and using the language.

Consideration should be given to adapting for Welsh purposes the decalogue used for the promotion of Catalan, as follows:

i. Speak Welsh on all occasions, especially with your family and friends. Try to speak Welsh with those people who can understand the language, even if currently you are used to speaking to them in English.

ii. Be polite to those who speak another language, but insist that they show the same respect to your language.

iii. Speak Welsh with all others; on the street, on the telephone, in work and elsewhere. If the other person understands you, keep at it in Welsh, even if you get a reply in another language.

iv. Give encouragement to those members of your family who do not as yet fully comprehend Welsh by speaking slowly and explaining occasional phrases to them.

v. When someone attempts to speak Welsh give him or her support by showing that you appreciate their attempts.

vi. Do not over-correct other speakers; teach by example.

vii. Respect the various dialects and nurture the richness of spoken Welsh.

viii. Support Welsh-medium newspapers and journals. Take advantage of all opportunities to enjoy programmes, live shows, books and modern exciting materials in Welsh.

ix. Use Welsh in your written correspondence, especially in dealings with large companies and public bodies – for example, write your cheques in Welsh. Make the Welsh language both visible and audible in your business profile, for example, in your signs, your advertisements and your messages to customers.

x. Insist on your right to use Welsh in your dealings with companies and institutions. Do this in a polite and constructive manner, and by adhering to the principles of the decalogue we will build a bilingual Wales which belongs to all.

The opportunity should be taken for strategic planning in order to predispose the general public toward a more favourable attitude to Welsh, paying especial attention to planning for young people.

The general public must be appraised of the fact that Welsh belongs to all and that all have a shared responsibility for it.

There is a need to extend the boundaries of bilingualism within the community, the institutions and the agencies that maintain the quality of life and deal with social problems.

A discussion should be initiated on the formation and financing of a daily Welsh-medium 'newspaper', taking advantage of the latest technology such as teletext, email and the Internet.

Welsh-medium medical and dentistry services should be available wherever possible.

A computer-generated automatic language choice should be made available for public and private customer enquiry help-lines, so that the individual does not have to ask specifically for the Welsh version. Wherever possible, the Welsh-medium service should not be allocated a different number from that given for the English-medium service.

There is scope for the specific planning to improve the marketing of the language as an economic asset and as an integral part of Welsh-medium communities.

Local authorities should increase their provision for the teaching of Welsh as a second language.


## CONCLUSION

The chief challenge facing language policy-makers is providing an appropriate community and national infrastructure wherein a genuine language choice may be exercised. A related challenge is normalizing Welsh so that it is in fact used as vehicle for normal communication in the widest possible range of domains. But this involves much more than the provision of opportunity and an ancillary right to language choice. It involves investment, training, encouragement and political conviction. The development of a comprehensive bilingual society is a project in social engineering. It also involves the institutionalization of bilingual services as an integral, not additive or deviant feature of public policy. The National Assembly, unitary authorities and bodies such as the Welsh Language Board have a critical role as legitimizing agencies pressing for a more comprehensive Welsh Language Act, marketing the advantages of bilingualism in the economy and constructing new forms of partnership through statutory obligations and pump-priming initiatives. In time such actors will set the parameters by which language-related issues will be debated, monitored and incorporated into significant policy measures. But the long-term infrastructural support will be non-governmental and grounded within local economies and communities. Hence the critical need to tackle the questions of empowering indigenous economic and social processes if Welsh is ever to realize its role as a self-sustaining language in society.

## *Acknowledgements*

The Welsh Language Board sponsored the research undertaken on *mentrau iaith*. The fieldwork was undertaken between January 1996 and March 1997 by myself and my colleague Dr Jeremy Evas whose collaboration and insights I am happy to acknowledge. A complete copy of the larger report, *The Community Research Project*, by C. H. Williams and J. Evas (1997) is available on the respective World-Wide Web sites of the Welsh Language Board and of the University of Wales Cardiff: http://www.cf.ac.uk/uwcc/cymraeg/index.html. An earlier version of this chapter was delivered as a plenary address to the Comhdháil Náisiúnta na Gaeilge annual conference, Dublin, 13 December 1997. I am grateful to Helen Ó Murchú for her gracious invitation and kind hospitality.

## *References*

Aitchison, J. W. (1995). 'Language, family structure and social class, 1991 census data', presentation to *The Social History of the Welsh Language Conference Aberystwyth*, 16 Sept.

Ambrose, J. E. and Williams, C. H. (1981). 'On the spatial definition of minority: scale as an influence on the geolinguistic analysis of Welsh', in Haugen, E., McClure, J. D. and Thomson, D. (eds.), *Minority Languages Today*, Edinburgh: Edinburgh University Press, pp. 53–71.

Appiah, K. A. (1994). 'Identity, authenticity, survival', in Taylor, C. and Gutman, A. (eds.), *Multiculturalism: Examining the Politics of Recognition*, Princeton, NJ: Princeton University Press, pp. 149–64.

Fforwm Iaith Genedlaethol (1991). *Strategaeth Iaith, 1991–2001*, Aberystwyth: Fforwm yr Iaith Gymraeg.

James, C. and Williams, C. H. (1996). 'Language and planning in Scotland and Wales', in Macdonald, R. and Thomas, H. (eds.), *Nationality and Planning in Scotland and Wales*, Cardiff: University of Wales Press, pp. 264–302.

Keating, M. and Loughlin, J. (eds.) (1997). *The Political Economy of Regionalism*, London: Frank Cass.

Loughlin, J. and Peeters, B. G. (1997). 'State traditions, administrative reforms and regionalization', in Keating, M. and Loughlin, J. (eds.), *The Political Economy of Regionalism*, London: Frank Cass, pp. 41–62.

Marin, B. and Mayntz, R. eds. (1991). *Policy Networks: Empirical Evidence and Theoretical Considerations*, Boulder, CO: Westview Press.

Menter a Busnes (1994). *A Quiet Revolution: The Framework of the Academic Report*, Aberystwyth: Menter a Busnes.

Welsh Office (1992). *Arolwg Teuluoedd*, Cardiff: Y Swyddfa Gymreig.

Welsh Office (1995). *The Welsh Language: Children and Education*, Cardiff: Welsh Office, Statistical Brief SDB 14/95.

Williams, C. H. (1989). 'New domains of the Welsh language: education, planning and the law', *Contemporary Wales*, 3, 41–76.

Williams, C. H. (1994). *Called unto Liberty: On Language and Nationalism*, Clevedon, Avon: Multilingual Matters.

Williams, C. H. (1999). 'The communal defence of threatened environments and identities', *Geografski vestnik*, 71, 105–20.

Williams, C. H. and Evas, J. (1997). *The Community Research Project*, Cardiff: Welsh Language Board.

Williams, G. and Morris, D. (2000). *Language Planning and Language Use: Welsh in a Global Age*, Cardiff: University of Wales Press.

# 9

# Menter Cwm Gwendraeth: A Case-study in Community Language Planning

## CEFIN CAMPBELL

Menter Cwm Gwendraeth is a community-based language initiative. Its objective is the promotion and development of the Welsh language as a medium of social and institutional communication. The geographical focus of its activities is a densely populated, deindustrialized area in the county of Carmarthenshire in south-west Wales known as Cwm Gwendraeth, the Gwendraeth Valley. Menter Cwm Gwendraeth was officially established in January 1991 as a pioneering language initiative. Its success over many years has led to the establishment of eighteen other *mentrau iaith* or language enterprise agencies in different parts of Wales. By initiating an innovative interventionist strategy based on a holistic approach to language planning – taking into consideration socio-economic as well as language-based factors – it has succeeded in establishing *mentrau iaith* as credible instruments for stabilizing linguistic fragmentation.

### HISTORICAL AND SOCIO-ECONOMIC BACKGROUND

Cwm Gwendraeth has a population of over 25,000, of whom 75 per cent, according to the census figures of 1991, speak Welsh. The valley, like any other typical south Wales valley, comprises numerous villages which are the remnants of a once thriving coal industry. The abrupt termination of Cwm Gwendraeth's main source of employment (as happened in the whole of the south Wales coalfield) has had a catastrophic effect on the local economy and general well-being of its close-knit communities. Consequently, the Welsh language has been similarly destabilized.

### LINGUISTIC BACKGROUND

If we look at the demographic evidence for the period 1870–1920 in the history of west Wales, it will highlight contrasting fortunes. Neighbouring rural counties like Cardiganshire and Pembrokeshire experienced a dramatic decline in their population, Cardiganshire witnessing an 18.5 per cent decrease. On the other

hand, the industrial belt of south-east Carmarthenshire saw a growth in population from 33 per cent of the total population of the county in 1871 to 55 per cent
by 1921. In fifty years the forces of industrialization had transformed the distribution of population within Carmarthenshire.

## CURRENT DEMOGRAPHIC CHARACTERISTICS

The post-war years have seen a significant population flux in Cwm Gwendraeth.
The area has witnessed two major influxes of incomers and a steady out-flow of
young, economically active personnel over recent decades. The first wave was
experienced in the 1950s when hundreds of miners were relocated from Durham
and Lancashire to work in newly developed modern mines at the bottom end of
the valley. This had a severe destabilizing effect on the language, especially in
villages like Carway and Trimsaran, but thankfully most of the miners' children
and grandchildren by now have acquired the language through natural absorp-
tion and the education system. The second wave occurred during the economic
boom of the 1980s when de-urbanization became a trend which led thousands of
families in large towns and cities to uproot and opt for a better quality of life in
the countryside. Wales was seen as an idyllic destination by many.

Cwm Gwendraeth, being mainly an urban locality with a rural periphery,
managed to avoid the worst effects of this population shift in terms of linguistic
dislocation. However, many rural villages in the outlying areas of the valley
have experienced difficulties in maintaining Welsh-language networks as
monoglot incomers create situations whereby the English language becomes the
*lingua franca* of social discourse. In recent years, evidence has come to light of a
growing social polarization between Welsh speakers and English incomers in
certain areas, giving rise to tensions and hostilities.

## SOCIAL AND ECONOMIC CHARACTERISTICS

Cwm Gwendraeth can be described as an area suffering from post-industrial
decay. The collapse of its main industry and the scale of the resultant difficulties
has led to a substantial deterioration in the physical and social conditions of the
valley. As a result, the community has been caught in an economic vacuum
between the decline in heavy industry and the growth of 'lighter' high-tech
industries and retailing outlets. Consequently, the current unemployment rate
for the valley is higher than the national average for the whole of Wales and is
particularly high for those under twenty-five, at between 10 and 15 per cent. The
trend for the long-term unemployed is also on the increase.

For language planners, this approach requires a shift in thinking from the
traditional focus on language as an abstract entity to language speakers and their
social well-being. It also means recognizing that, whatever the welcome gains

made in education, language rights or the media in recent years, in the long run these will only be sustained through economic means. This does not mean the prioritizing of economic over cultural-linguistic planning goals, but rather the integration of language and economic planning at local and regional levels.

## THE CURRENT POSITION OF THE WELSH LANGUAGE IN CWM GWENDRAETH

According to the census figures of 1991, 75 per cent of the population in Cwm Gwendraeth speak Welsh. This area has one of the highest concentrations in absolute numbers of Welsh speakers in the whole of Wales, and has therefore been identified as being an important barometer for language shift or revival. Closer examination of these figures elicits a number of interesting trends:

- a decrease in the proportion of Welsh speakers of 1.7 per cent over a ten-year period (1981–91), compared with a decrease of 1.4 per cent on a national level;
- a decline in actual numbers of Welsh speakers of only 479 over the same period;
- a lower rate of decrease in proportionate terms between the oldest and the youngest age groups in 1991 compared with 1981;
- a slump in the proportion of Welsh speakers in the sixteen to twenty-four and twenty-five to forty-four age groups in 1981, which is reflected in the twenty-five to forty-four and forty-five to sixty-four age groups in 1991 (a decline mirrored nationally);
- a fall of 14.2 per cent in the proportion of Welsh speakers over three generations in 1991, compared with a fall of 29.1 per cent in 1981.

The general picture therefore is one of relative stability in the overall proportion of Welsh speakers between 1981 and 1991. However, there is some cause for concern that in the latest census only 66.7 per cent are denoted as Welsh-speaking in the twenty-five to forty-four age group which are generally considered to be the members of the population who are embarking on parenthood.

Patterns of language use were also the focus of a recent study by Heini Gruffudd of the Adult and Continuing Education Department, University of Wales Swansea.[1] His study chose to concentrate on the choice of language made by young, bilingual adults (sixteen to twenty year olds) living in east Carmarthenshire and West Glamorgan; Menter Cwm Gwendraeth serves part of this area. A total of 329 young people were sampled.

Gruffudd reported that the main social domains which positively influence the use of Welsh are the chapel/church and activities run by Urdd Gobaith Cymru (the Welsh League of Youth) and the Young Farmers' Clubs, but sadly, as the study also highlights, these are the least popular attractions for young people interviewed, with only 10.3, 2.4 and 1.2 per cent respectively attending at least on a monthly basis.

The most popular venues were discos (28 per cent weekly attendance), sports activities (35.7 per cent), pubs and clubs (46 per cent) and a visit to the cinema (42.6 per cent attending monthly). Not surprisingly these social domains create the least favourable conditions for language interaction, with 68.2 per cent stating that they never use Welsh or use it for less than half of the time in a disco, 63.9 per cent in a pub/club, 62.5 per cent in sports activities and 70.7 per cent at the cinema. The one heartening feature, however, is that 68.8 per cent use the language almost always or more than half of the time in informal situations with friends.

Attitudes towards the Welsh language and the use of the language in differing social contexts were also the focus of a recent study conducted by Professor Colin H. Williams and Jeremy Evas of the Department of Welsh, University of Wales, Cardiff, which was sponsored by the Welsh Language Board.[2] The research data for Cwm Gwendraeth were compiled from 163 individual interviews which set out to measure the degree of language use in many different contexts. The researchers' main conclusions are that the potential exists for a far greater use of Welsh in many contexts if the opportunity were provided for a genuinely free choice of language, but at present we should recognize the fact that Welsh speakers in Cwm Gwendraeth view their four core skills (speaking, comprehension, reading and writing) to be more developed in English than in Welsh.

Although the perception of their linguistic skills in Welsh is inferior, the vast majority had no problems performing a number of functions in Welsh and a significant majority (80 per cent) reported that they would choose Welsh, or expressed no preference as to which language they used, in a variety of social situations. A large number (over 80 per cent) believed that local authority employees who dealt with the public should speak Welsh or agree to learn the language, while 66 per cent believed that companies who offered services in Welsh should be eligible for tax relief.

## THE PURPOSE OF A COMMUNITY-BASED LANGUAGE INITIATIVE

Many people questioned the need to invest money, time and effort in underpinning a language in an area which was one of the most predominantly Welsh-speaking regions in the whole of Wales. The detractors pointed to other parts of Wales where the language's position was much weaker. History, however, shows that the decision was the right one. The rapid language shift that has occurred in neighbouring communities over the last thirty years has highlighted the need in language terms to batten down the hatches and to strengthen the language situation from within.

## AIMS AND OBJECTIVES

By adopting a holistic approach to community language planning – following a lengthy consultation process – the following general aims were agreed:

- to create social conditions that would foster positive attitudes towards the Welsh language and an increase in its use;
- to normalize the use of Welsh as a medium of social and institutional communication;
- to highlight the close relationship between language and attitudes which relate to quality-of-life and socio-economic issues.

## ORGANIZATIONAL AND MANAGEMENT STRUCTURE

Prior to its official commencement on 1 January 1991 a steering committee had been appointed at a public meeting to oversee the development of Menter Cwm Gwendraeth. The steering committee later became the Management Committee responsible for strategic and financial accountability. One of its first tasks was to appoint a full-time director and assistant who started in their posts in January and February 1991 respectively. Another immediate goal was to register Menter Cwm Gwendraeth as a limited company by guarantee and secure charitable status.

Working groups consisting of local people were set up to look at the language situation in various sectors, to map out current provision of activities through the medium of Welsh in each particular sector, to assess opportunities and threats and to draw up a development plan including specific projects and work programmes. Working groups were established to consider ways of developing the use of the Welsh language among children and youth, Welsh learners, local businesses, voluntary groups, social institutions, sports and leisure activities and to promote the use of simultaneous translation equipment. Each group was to highlight needs, prioritize resources, set realistic targets, monitor developments and evaluate outcomes. In this way, a purposive planning procedure could be achieved which would ensure the validity of the overall developmental planning process.

In order to avoid the danger of overly centralized planning, Menter Cwm Gwendraeth also established a series of local village fora to share ownership in the process of language intervention. These village fora undertook the responsibility for organizing events and activities to promote the Welsh language and for acting as a local gauge to assess potential threats to the language and seek opportunities for language gain, albeit on a limited basis.

These working groups and village fora and the host of other volunteers who helped in many different ways also served another function, albeit unconsciously, which is the development of community participation. By sharing in the responsibility for language and community regeneration, each individual becomes empowered, develops skills and leadership qualities. It also increases their self-confidence and awareness as they become more and more involved in the democratic process of improving the quality of life in their local communities. As a result it increases the vitality of local communities, as it devolves responsibility to grass-roots level. In a sense it means empowering indigenous economic, social, cultural and linguistic processes which, if successful, could lead to long-term benefits for the area as a whole. This challenge is of crucial importance if Welsh is ever to recover its role as a self-sustaining language able to serve all in the community (see Williams's discussion in Chapter 8).

## PRESENTING A STRATEGY FOR LANGUAGE REVIVAL

Menter Cwm Gwendraeth's initial three-year strategy was based on a thorough diagnosis of the language's relative strengths and weaknesses and was the result of a lengthy and wide-ranging consultation exercise. The strategy was presented as a blueprint for language regeneration under the following headings.

### (i) Language and the community

> Whenever languages are in contact, they are in competition for users. They may be seen as commodities on a 'language market,' and they will live only as long as they find customers who will buy them.[3]

The link between an endangered language and the community it serves must obviously be the focal point of any attempt at reversing language shift. Traditionally, linguists have generally chosen to disregard the analysis of the social aspects of language, but have recently undertaken a conscious reappraisal of language planning techniques. In order to ensure effective language intervention from the beginning any language agency must seek to understand the true nature of the community as it is, and with every linguistic phenomenon it investigates it will be increasingly compelled to take account of the non-linguistic context in which it is embedded.

The Welsh language survived for centuries within the confines of specific societal domains that enabled it to flourish in the face of increasing anglicization. These were the domains of the home, the family, neighbourhood and workplace networks, and religious institutions like chapels, churches and Sunday schools. If the Welsh language is exposed to destabilizing external influences without the security of a number of well-cushioned and prominent social domains it risks following the road to decline and extinction. Huffries contends that a clear separation of functions is necessary to allow the development of persistent bilingualism:

> The use of two or more languages within one community is dependent on each language serving a function which the other does not. If two languages could be used inter-

changeably on all occasions by all speakers, one would be superfluous and ultimately dropped from the repertoire of languages serving the community. It is then the fulfilment of separate functions by different languages which permits persistent bilingualism within the community.[4]

This form of established diglossia is reiterated by Fishman as a means of achieving stable bilingualism: 'If a strict domain separation becomes institutionalised such that each language is associated with a number of important but distinct domains, bilingualism may well become both universal and stabilised even though an entire population consists of bilinguals interacting with other bilinguals.'[5] One of the main aims of Menter Cwm Gwendraeth at the outset was to consolidate and support existing domains, establish new domains of language use and extend the use of Welsh to those domains which functioned mainly through the medium of English, concentrating mainly on community activities. Clearly, attempts to retain a language as a living entity have to be endorsed by its communal usage within the public domain.

For Welsh to be the preferred language of use in a range of social contexts in circumstances where there is a gradual and perceptible shift towards the dominant language requires a programme of positive reinforcement to strengthen awareness of the language's intrinsic value as a community language. As John Edwards points out, the ultimate success of a regeneration programme depends on the will of the speakers of receding languages: 'If the will to revive a language rests, then, upon a desire to alter or reorientate group and individual identity it follows that the strength and scope of that will are vitally important in revival efforts.'[6]

A central plank in the process of creating favourable conditions for the language has been the committed extension of the provision of social opportunities for people of all ages to socialize and use the Welsh language in informal and leisure situations. This has been achieved by arranging a programme of popular activities and events which have underlined the importance of the language as an integral component of community life in Cwm Gwendraeth, appealing to both Welsh and non-Welsh speakers alike.

More detailed information on specific projects and events will be presented later on in this chapter, but generally they have included rock and pop concerts by leading Welsh-language bands, folk concerts, discos, sports quizzes, drama festivals, touring theatre companies, musical and sports festivals, literary events, traditional concerts, folk dances and various workshops. The pinnacle of the social calendar is the annual Gŵyl y Gwendraeth (Gwendraeth Festival) held every May, which is a week-long celebration of the best of Welsh-language culture. All in all about 120–40 events are organized annually, either directly by Menter Cwm Gwendraeth, by village fora, community groups and organizations, or local clubs and leisure associations with the support of Menter Cwm Gwendraeth.

The ultimate aim then, in embarking on a 'pump-priming' exercise, is to hand responsibility for organizing such events back to the local community, ensuring that their desire to see the language playing an integral role in community life is mirrored by their willingness to become stakeholders in the ownership process.

### (ii) Language status

> One can hardly overestimate the importance of some official status in maintaining a language. It gives it social status among its native users, and serves in part as a barrier against self-depreciation and embarrassment.[7]

Menter Cwm Gwendraeth was established at a time when the Welsh language had no official status. In December 1993, however, a Welsh Language Act successfully completed its passage through Parliament, giving the language equal status with English for the first time since the Acts of Union of 1536 and 1542. Certainly the Welsh Language Act of 1993 went a long way to make amends for the gross injustices suffered by Welsh speakers for more than four centuries, and significantly for the first time in seven hundred years a British government talked of promoting and facilitating the use of the Welsh language.

This Act has already had a huge impact on the way public authorities conduct their business and a marked bearing on the public's perception of the Welsh language in the context of its overall status and accessibility. The clear knock-on effect, in terms of self-awareness and confidence, and skills development from the point of view of the service provider and customer, will be enhanced as the service is fine-tuned and augmented over the next few years. Unfortunately, however, the private and voluntary sectors remain outside the provision of the Act. For many this was a regrettable omission as it meant that equal validity for the language in its use in the wider public domain would be sporadic and inconsistent. Nevertheless, the heartening feature of this increasingly conducive linguistic environment is the large number of private-sector businesses which have voluntarily expanded their bilingual provision.

Menter Cwm Gwendraeth's role since the passing of the Welsh Language Act has been to assist public bodies in preparing language schemes, responding to individual schemes during the public consultation process and monitoring the effectiveness of the schemes as they are implemented and developed. Brochures have also been distributed to businesses in the area outlining the commercial and social advantages of bilingualism. Menter Cwm Gwendraeth has assisted in setting up a Business Club for Welsh-speaking business managers and company owners who meet on a regular basis to invite guest speakers to address them (in Welsh) on a number of relevant business-related issues. It has also helped many small businesses to receive grant aid from the Wales Tourist Board and the Welsh Language Board towards bilingual signage and marketing material as well as assisting with some written translation work and the design of bilingual advertisements.

While there are clear signs that the Welsh language is enjoying a more prominent role in the public, private and voluntary sectors, the next challenge is to ensure that bilingual speakers take advantage of this increased provision.

### (iii) Language and education

Planning and policy development must include the education sector, but as a sub-structure of a larger more broadly conceived plan and implementation policy – the education sector occupies one niche in a larger plan.[8]

*Statutory education:* The growth in Welsh-medium education over the last twenty-five years has been one of the great phenomena of recent Welsh history. In 1998/9 over 30 per cent of Wales's schoolchildren were involved in Welsh-medium/bilingual education. Many of these pupils, particularly in anglicized south-east Wales, come from non-Welsh-speaking homes.

In Cwm Gwendraeth, out of a total of twenty-four primary schools, all except one (which is a Category A/B school) have been designated by the local authority as being Category A schools, which means that they teach primarily through the medium of Welsh – although English is used jointly as a medium of instruction between the ages of seven and eleven. In effect this means that all children by the time they leave primary school at eleven years of age are fully bilingual. Despite the remarkable developments of recent years and the thousands of children who have acquired Welsh through formal education, surprisingly little has been done until very recently to offer opportunities outside the confines of the school to use the language in a social context.

In view of the sparse provision of youth activities available through the medium of Welsh in the area, Menter Cwm Gwendraeth felt compelled to fill an obvious void. It also felt that the great efforts made to expand the acquisition of Welsh in the statutory education sector were not reflected in the level of community activity available through the medium of Welsh, which if instigated could supplement and solidify the gains made by schools. It would also serve another important purpose, namely to form a bridge between the language of education and the language of the community, so that Welsh in psychological terms would not primarily be seen solely as the medium of school-based activities, but rather as a continuum of the education domain.

*Further education:* Since the passing of the Welsh Language Act (1993) more and more organizations, businesses and public bodies are now implementing a fully bilingual policy, which has resulted in a steady increase in the number of jobs now advertising for bilingual skills. These have been mostly in evidence in the field of education, public administration, finance and social care. Coupled with the fairly recent growth in the Welsh-language media, the need for bilingual technical and administrative staff, and the demand for bilingual skills in the fields of journalism, printing, public relations and translation services, there has never been a greater demand for Welsh-medium or bilingual training in an array of different vocations offering lucrative terms and job prospects.

Carmarthenshire College seems to be out of step with these recent developments and has subsequently been the focus of intense lobbying from Welsh-language activists and organizations like Menter Cwm Gwendraeth. They have

consistently pressed the college for a radical rethink of its current provision so
that training courses match the real needs of employers in the context of bilingual skills instead of the perceived and somewhat outdated needs covered by its
current position. Another crucial consideration as far as the link between the
Welsh language and post-sixteen education is concerned is the fact that the
majority of young people who go on to do vocational training are likely to
remain in their home area and use their skills for the benefit of the community.
Providing a bilingual service, whether it is in the field of social services, child
care, hairdressing or car mechanics, in an area with over 75 per cent Welsh-
speaking has got to become the norm if the language is to be successfully utilized
in all walks of life.

*Adult education:* In terms of language revitalization the most significant development in recent years has been the remarkable growth in the number of adults
learning Welsh. In 1998/9, over 21,000 adults across Wales were attending Welsh
classes, the number having more than doubled in ten years.

As discussed by Gruffudd and Morris in this volume, there are a great variety
of courses available locally at different levels, ranging from courses for absolute
beginners to those on a more advanced level. There are also courses for reticent
speakers of Welsh who wish to enhance their language skills. They vary in
nature from the intensive 'Wlpan' courses that meet over a relatively short
period of time to once-weekly or weekend courses. Some colleges also offer
distance-learning packages for those who are unable to attend conventional
courses. The providers of Welsh for adults in all areas work together within a
consortium in order to ensure that a more co-ordinated and integrated approach
prevails and to avoid unnecessary duplication of resources.

### (iv) *Language awareness*

Language is the major symbol-system of our species.[9]

Raising the profile of the Welsh language and stimulating a greater awareness of
the integral role it plays in the community's make-up have been key priorities
for Menter Cwm Gwendraeth from the beginning. Due to historical circumstances many native Welsh speakers harbour a negative perception of the relevance and social value of their mother tongue, to the extent that a low
self-assessment of personal competence in the language and a reluctance to speak
it when afforded the opportunity is commonplace. Regrettably, many still hold
the view that the Welsh language is inferior, old-fashioned, inadequate and irrelevant to the needs of today's rapidly developing world – a view that has provoked
tensions and hostilities and has led to a 'talking down' of the language.

However, perceptions and attitudes are changing. Years of campaigning and
lobbying has ensured that the Welsh language has consistently remained on the
public agenda as a topic for lively debate. Thankfully the language issue attracts

fewer dissenting or antagonistic voices nowadays than it did in previous years, as shown in a recent review of the public's attitude towards the Welsh language conducted by NOP Consumer Market Research which was sponsored by the Welsh Language Board: 71 per cent supported the continued use of Welsh; 88 per cent believed that the language was something to be proud of; 75 per cent were of the opinion that Welsh and English should have equal status in Wales.

Marketing the Welsh language as a vibrant, contemporary and versatile medium of communication has been the main strand of Menter Cwm Gwendraeth's language awareness campaign over recent years. The main aim has been to raise the public's awareness of the unique and key role that the language plays in the community's social and institutional life, and foster positive attitudes towards it by encouraging a sense of ownership and shared responsibility for its future well-being.

As experts in the field of marketing know only too well, changing long-established attitudes and behavioural patterns can be an arduous task calling on a range of marketing techniques which challenge traditional customs and conventions. In terms of linguistic marketing the objective is to ensure a transformation in attitudes based on the following principles:

| | | |
|---|---|---|
| Enmity | → | Sympathy |
| Prejudice | → | Acceptability |
| Apathy | → | Interest |
| Ignorance | → | Knowledge |

Achieving these aims has involved vigorous publicity campaigns, including regular press statements, features and photographs in local newspapers publicizing events and activities, use of exhibition stands in schools, public libraries, festivals, eisteddfodau, local shows and carnivals, advertisements and sponsorships, sale of merchandise and other branding products, regular contributions on national television and radio as well as on local commercial radio.

All in all this has ensured that the name of Menter Cwm Gwendraeth, with the positive image of the language that it attempts to convey through its various activities, is seen and heard over and over again until it becomes synonymous with a sense of vitality, confidence, satisfaction and pride that are essential prerequisites of a successful revitalization campaign. One can only hope that, by association, people's attitudes towards the language will be more favourable and supportive and that it instils in them a desire to shape its destiny. Without such dedication by its speakers and main advocates language revitalization is unlikely to succeed.

To a large degree the roots of many of the problems facing the Welsh language today lie in the historical development of language usage and its contextual role in the locality. Historically, the Welsh language has not enjoyed any form of status in public life outside the confines of particular domains associated with religious worship or education. The English language has more often than not been the *lingua franca*, with Welsh confined to informal networks and leisure

activities. The challenge for language planning is to change old habits that have
been built up over many centuries – not only habits relating to language use but
also the image, status and social values associated with the Welsh language that
have become ingrained in the mind-set of generations of Welsh speakers.

Following the passing of the Welsh Language Act and the implementation of
language schemes by public authorities, a campaign was recently launched in
conjunction with the Welsh Language Board called 'Defnyddia dy Gymraeg! –
Use your Welsh!' Its aim was to encourage Welsh speakers to use the language
when dealing with public bodies. It involved advertisements on bus shelters,
billboards, on the backs of buses, in newspapers and in the form of posters and
leaflets in shops, doctors' and dentists' surgeries, hairdressers, train stations,
post offices, libraries, cinemas, job centres, schools and almost anywhere where
the public could access information. Although it ran for six months, its success
is difficult to measure, as it is only one of a series of campaigns aimed at increasing the use of Welsh between service provider and client in the public sector. A
long-term strategy using constant drip-drip techniques is needed to overturn
age-old habits.

An extremely successful project in terms of changing patterns of language
usage has been the utilization of simultaneous translation equipment in which
Menter Cwm Gwendraeth invested right at the very beginning. As referred to
above, English has been the language of officialdom and the administration of
public office in Wales for many centuries, a situation which has led to the development of a form of diglossia whereby English has mainly been the language
used by Welsh speakers in formal situations like meetings, committees and
public gatherings. The curious irony is that informal discussions relating to the
proceedings of these very same meetings were more than likely to be conducted
through the medium of Welsh, very often immediately prior to these meetings
or straight afterwards!

The introduction of simultaneous translation equipment into the bastions of
officialdom was initially a slow and frustrating process, as great efforts were
made to convince people that offering a choice of language in no way impinged
on the rights of Welsh or non-Welsh speakers to use English if they so wished,
that no one was stuffing Welsh down their throats! Rather, it was a case of the
democratic rights of Welsh speakers being recognized. Slowly and cautiously,
over the years support for its use grew, mainly as a matter of principle and as a
response to growing demands by Welsh speakers for their rights to be acknowledged. Amusingly, it was also used out of a sense of curiosity by many diehards
who became attracted to using highly sophisticated technology for the first time!

Another marketing tool that has been adopted to increase the profile of the
Welsh language has been the support given by Welsh-speaking sports and television celebrities for campaigns aimed at raising an awareness – amongst young
people especially – of the advantages of speaking two languages. The stars of
stage and screen, and particularly from the field of rugby and soccer, have been
effectively used as role models for young people who see, through their public

endorsement of the language, that speaking Welsh is something to be extremely proud of and a distinct advantage in terms of job opportunities in the media industry. These celebrities have taken part in sports festivals, workshops and 'it's a knockout' competitions, and have hosted various concerts and events – often free of charge, which is a further gesture of their goodwill towards the language.

Other projects have involved distributing Welsh-language tapes and CDs to retail stores and pubs to play as background music, the publication of a 'fanzine'-style newsletter for young people and the production of a bilingual leaflet, in conjunction with the now defunct Pwyllgor Datblygu Addysg Gymraeg (Bilingual Education Development Committee), aimed at parents and outlining the numerous advantages of bilingualism.

### (v) Housing and planning

In the field of housing and planning, local authorities and housing associations in recommending and developing policies shape the future of the local community. In designating land for housing, new roads and industrial development they lay the material foundations for living communities.[10]

On the subject of housing and planning – a very delicate issue that can often lead to the most intense controversy – Menter Cwm Gwendraeth has broadly supported the arguments put forward by Cymdeithas yr Iaith Gymraeg (Welsh Language Society) in their *Property Act Handbook* which was first published in 1992 as part of their campaign to pressurize the government to adopt a Property Act. This document was revised in April 1999 but still contains important principles in relation to the current housing and property situation in Wales today.

It calls on the National Assembly of Wales 'to adopt and implement housing and planning policies that will lay a secure foundation for the future of every community throughout Wales, the Welsh language, and the natural environment'. It argues that the Assembly should adopt the following principles as a basis for its housing and planning policies:

- that houses and property are regarded as a necessity rather than a marketable commodity;
- that local people's access to the existing stock of housing and property is encouraged and ensured;
- that house and property prices reflect the local market;
- that the planning system protects and serves local communities.

Menter Cwm Gwendraeth has actively supported these main principles and has urged local authorities to consider the Welsh language as a key factor in granting planning permission, and to give it the same professional consideration as other factors such as the local economy, transport, leisure and the environment. It has called on local authorities to consider, before approving planning applications, the effects of the development on the community concerned, both socially and linguistically, and to what extent it would satisfy the needs of the local community. The danger is that, by ignoring linguistic factors, local authorities could seriously undermine the nature and character of local communities and their cultural heritage.

The campaign involved a series of meetings with planning officers, participating in public consultations and on one occasion arranging a public meeting to oppose the development of 150 houses in a local village where over 80 per cent of the population spoke Welsh. It was argued that these houses did not meet a local need and that a sudden influx of people from outside the community would place a huge burden on local services, the local school and structural services like sewerage operations and water supplies, as well as undermining the viability of the Welsh language in terms of its communal usage. Unfortunately, the outline planning permission for this development was not relinquished by the local authority and remains valid to this day.

It is hoped that the National Assembly, having recently taken over powers from the Welsh Office, will be able to give greater protection to Welsh-speaking communities from the potential ravages of commercial exploitation and speculative development.

### (vi)  Economic development

> Language vitality and economic viability are two sides of the same coin. No language can survive for long without a sound economic base. And cultural-linguistic diversity can be an important source of innovation and local dynamism.[11]

Wales, at various stages in the history of modern industry, has possessed some of the most sophisticated technologies and one of the most skilled labour forces in Europe. By the end of the nineteenth century it was one of the most heavily industrialized and urbanized regions of Britain – itself one of the most powerful economies in the world.

It was the south Wales coalfield more than any other which became the dominant feature of the Welsh economy, with the anthracite coalfields of west Wales playing a significant part in the prolific exploitation of one of its most lucrative natural resources. Anthracite production in 1854 was a million tons a year, by 1913 it had increased to almost five million tons. When the coal-mining industry entered into a downward spiralling crisis, from the 1920s until it bottomed out in the 1960s, the economic consequences for Wales and each coal-mining community were catastrophic.

At present the government and local authorities have failed to attract inward investors of any great significance to the area to take advantage of brownfield sites that have been developed along the M4 corridor from Swansea and further west as far as Cross Hands. If successful these would put a large dent in the unemployment figures for the area in one fell swoop. There has also been criticism of government agencies and local authorities for the lack of priority given and uncoordinated approach to developing indigenous small to medium-size businesses in west Wales.

Whilst the unemployed, school-leavers, trainees and graduates wait for an economic miracle to occur, the steady haemorrhaging of the young, better qualified, highly skilled and more able-bodied and socially active bilinguals further erodes the social and language base to a degree that seriously threatens the linguistic and demographic characteristics of the area. One ray of hope is the growing realization among economists that language and culture can play a significant role in economic recovery, as examples from across Europe have highlighted in recent years. This has led to much debate on the role of culture in regional development and the way that the cultural and linguistic diversity of Europe's regions and localities can contribute to a stronger European economy.

Adam Price in his booklet entitled *The Diversity Dividend* probes the complex inter-relationship between language, culture and the economy. He concludes by stressing that language planning and economic development must go hand in hand if linguistic communities are to remain viable. He argues that it is essential for specialists from both these disciplines to be brought together to re-evaluate these separate approaches and seek practical ways for implementing integrated policies.

While underlining the need for language enthusiasts to influence economic development policies he adds that

> there is an equally urgent need for those with a business or economic background to make their voices heard in language circles. In so doing, they can influence the application of language policies in the private sector, encourage the use of management methods in language planning and ensure that language bodies themselves play an assertive role in building local bridges between the economy and the language. (p. 36)

Traditionally, those responsible in Wales for economic planning on a national and regional level have been somewhat reluctant in the past to acknowledge the link between the economy, culture and language and have only recently (and rather grudgingly) recognized its potential. As Adam Price (1997) explains, 'in the real world few problems can be said to be wholly economic in nature – their economic aspects are inter-twined with their social and cultural dimensions. Culture is in the economy and the economy is in culture. And language lies at the root of both' (p. 6).

In a world of mass communications, universal trading and gradual homogenization, there is a real fear that distinctive identities may become submerged in a process of 'wholesale globalization'. However, it could be argued that this growing uniformity also poses a challenge to those who foster cultural diversity and pluralistic values. This awareness of a unique identity based on cultural-linguistic values is particularly relevant at a regional level and begs for wider acceptance by policy-makers of the link between language and economic revival, a point highlighted once more by Adam Price: 'The link between language revival and economic resurgence needs to be explicitly recognised. Self-confidence can arise from cultural-linguistic assertiveness and a sense of identity worth preserving can motivate people to safeguard their future via economic action' (p. 33). He emphasizes further:

> Local self-confidence is the starting point of any development process – whether cultural or economic. As confidence is based on identity and identity linked to language, the lower status that has been accorded to minority languages historically can be expected to have had some implications for collective self-esteem. (p. 21)

Evidently, there needs to be a two-pronged approach to securing a sound economic and social base for language maintenance and community vitality: creating suitable job opportunities in a range of sectors, including 'leading edge' technologies, in order to retain the better qualified young people who are currently leaving their home communities to find work, and to create a culture of innovation and entrepreneurship, which is sadly lacking at present. The first is the ultimate responsibility of the Welsh Assembly and government bodies like the Welsh Development Agency, Training and Enterprise Councils, higher and further education colleges and local authorities. Whatever challenges they face, none will be of more significance for the future of Wales than closing the gap between Wales and other regions within the UK by increasing the current GDP level of 82–90 per cent of the UK average, which in post-industrialized areas like Cwm Gwendraeth and other south Wales valleys is as low as 72 per cent of the UK average. The underlying reasons for this prosperity deficit are all too familiar: low employment activity rates, low economic output, low investment in innovation and entrepreneurship, low levels of education and training attainment, and low wage structures.

The fact that the West Wales and the Valleys Region has become eligible for European Union Structural Funding under the Objective 1 priority designation must be viewed as a golden opportunity to create the necessary structures for economic prosperity in these deprived areas. £1.2 billion of development funding will be available for seven years between 2000 and 2006, so that Wales, in particular the areas blighted by the current imbalance, can achieve a significant increase in their economic prosperity.

The matter of innovation and entrepreneurship is a far more tricky problem, as historically Wales has largely not fared well in terms of setting up indigenous businesses. The reasons for this lack of enterprise have only recently been explored and the findings have highlighted a number of significant trends. Traditionally, the Welsh in general, and Welsh speakers in particular, have tended to view the public sector as an attractive career destination. Many theories have been put forward as to why this should be. One explanation is the worthy desire to be 'of service to the community'. Marc Classon expands further on this notion:

> Throughout the twentieth century there has been a general tendency for aspiring Welsh-speakers to seek preferment in national institutions related to education, local or central government and public administration. This may be described as the result of

the predominance of an 'other-regarding' rather than 'self-regarding' value system. Such that even those who do succeed in business often justify their commitment as an expression of community solidarity and support.[12]

Others have argued that it is a problem of identity, as Classon notes:

Self-doubt and an ambiguous relationship towards England and English ideas, culture and practice pervade many of the criticisms of the alleged relative under-performance of predominantly Welsh-speaking regions. It may be asked if there is a persistent, historic negative self-image in relation to business and the encouragement of an entre- preneurial spirit, which reflects a deeper lack of confidence predicated upon an uncer- tain identity? Or is this a myth of conquest, a perpetuation of differential power relationships which has been internalised by the subordinated 'minority culture'?

Two research studies commissioned in 1989 and 1993 by Menter a Busnes – an enterprise agency which was established to increase awareness of business and the economy amongst Welsh-speakers – found that the difference in attitude towards business enterprise between Welsh speakers and non-Welsh speakers (which included English in-migrants) was quite profound.[13] The overall percep- tion by Welsh speakers was that business success happened outside Wales, that there were very few Welsh role models in the field of business for the young to emulate and that the Welsh were generally less enterprising than other people. Thankfully these views had 'softened' somewhat between 1989 and 1993.

The fact remains, however, that attention needs to be focused on creating favourable economic conditions conducive to language and cultural develop- ment. Welsh-speaking communities like the Gwendraeth Valley need a mix of successful small to medium-sized enterprises and substantial inward investment programmes to sustain them. The 1994 report by Menter a Busnes entitled *Quiet Revolution?* maintains that this can be achieved by channelling the energy and dynamism exerted by various Welsh-language movements over the past forty years into the economic sector. It concludes:

If Welsh language culture is to undergo its own 'Quiet Revolution,' it will have to learn to channel some of the extraordinary energy, commitment and enthusiasm which have underpinned the linguistic and cultural revival seen over the last forty years into economic and community development . . . With many of the cultural battles now won, Welsh language culture is entering a new phase in which to sustain the cultural advances of recent years it will have to shift its focus more to the economic sphere. This does not mean the prioritisation of economic over cultural goals; it does mean re- making the connection between cultural and economic activity and rediscovering within the diversity of Welsh culture those positive attributes potentially supportive of a more dynamic economic life. (p. 30)

The main role of Menter Cwm Gwendraeth in terms of creating a sound economic base for the language and encouraging local enterprise has been its support of economic policies and training programmes initiated by various government agencies and local authorities. It has consistently encouraged these organizations to link economic development and language development and to see them as mutually interdependent elements in the social structure of Welsh-speaking communities like the Gwendraeth Valley.

In order to support indigenous Welsh-speaking businesses and to provide them with the skills and confidence to succeed in an increasingly competitive market, Menter Cwm Gwendraeth has established a Welsh-language business club which meets regularly to discuss relevant issues. The programme involves talks by business experts on various topics and visits to successful companies which demonstrate examples of good practice and a willingness to share experiences. Welsh-language training programmes have been put on to develop the linguistic skills of employees, especially those who are in direct contact with the public. Translation services have been provided to support the use of the Welsh language in the private sector, along with seminars on language awareness and sensitivity and a special course for dealing with the Welsh-language media.

### *(vii) Community development*

> Language decline and a crumbling economic and social base are interweaving features which have led to a lack of confidence, poor esteem and an erosion of basic life skills amongst the population over the last few decades.[14]

A truly successful community development programme is one which starts and ends with the needs and wishes of local people. It means focusing on individual communities and working closely with them, not for them, on regenerative programmes. Different from economic development, this approach is about people development and involvement, and requires a 'bottom–up' approach to identifying their needs and aspirations. Such a process is far more likely to promote personal growth and self-determination than simply providing services.

The success of any regenerative programme requires ownership by the community. Too often, a void can develop between communities and the agencies involved in their development. Agencies tend to drive their own agenda and justify decisions and actions against their own definitions of both the problem and the solution – by so doing they can ignore the often different perceptions and priorities of local people.

A community development programme is particularly necessary in economically and socially deprived areas as a tool for tackling social exclusion. Too many disadvantaged groups such as single parents, retired miners or poorly educated young people – by lacking in confidence and having a negative self-image – can remain excluded, alienated and unable to participate in the mainstream of community life. Community development is about:

- tackling social exclusion
- developing people skills

- increasing community participation
- encouraging community empowerment
- increasing confidence and self-esteem
- accessing knowledge and information
- developing skills in decision-making and advocacy
- capacity building

A recent Welsh Office Circular presents an overarching strategy for tackling social exclusion based on the need to build sustainable communities, encourage healthy living and improve educational achievement.[15] The programme is based on a number of fundamental principles of community development:

- that all the people in the community should have access either to work, to training or education or to another meaningful activity (such as community or voluntary work);
- that everyone should have somewhere decent and safe to live;
- that everyone should be able to lead healthy lives and to have access to appropriate health care;
- that all children in the community should feel safe and should be provided with appropriate education and opportunities for play;
- that people should be empowered to voice and contribute to decisions made about their community, so that there is collective ownership and 'capacity building'.

In 1995 Menter Cwm Gwendraeth accessed European funding to initiate a community development programme in which Welsh would play a key role in the administration and delivery of social enhancement projects. This would enable it to influence social networks that hitherto had not been affected by the more traditional and mainstream approaches undertaken.

This change of focus meant that the perception of Menter Cwm Gwendraeth was to change somewhat from a purely language-based initiative to a community development and language enterprise agency whereby the language would be a means to achieving social ends rather than as an end in itself. In the kind of socio-linguistic environment that presented itself in Cwm Gwendraeth at that juncture, the change of emphasis was as crucial as it was timely in ensuring the continued support of the local community.

It did not, however, mean the total abandonment of the kind of language-focused projects that had been the cornerstone of the organization's strategy from the beginning, rather a synthesis of energies combining interventionist language projects and a cross-cutting community development programme.

Prior to applying for European funding, Menter Cwm Gwendraeth had been working on an environmental enhancement scheme funded by the Welsh Development Agency which offered finance to develop small-scale capital projects. It involved liaising with local community councils and voluntary groups to identify needs in terms of improving the environment and working closely with interested parties on their implementation. Projects included creating riverside walks and cycle paths, play areas and nature reserves, improvements to village halls and recreation areas, general landscaping and flower planting. Many of these schemes provided employment opportunities for local people and training opportunities for the unemployed. During the eighteen months or so of its existence the project succeeded in realizing some significant visual improvements to the structural environment and contributed in no small measure to increasing the quality of life in many communities in the area.

In many ways it was the success of this project that provided the impetus for bringing a multi-agency group together to consider the best means of revitalizing the disadvantaged communities that existed in Cwm Gwendraeth. The original group that instigated and supported Menter Cwm Gwendraeth's application to the European Regional Development Fund, under the terms of the Industrial South Wales Single Programming Document, included the Social Services Department of the then Dyfed County Council, Dyfed Powys Health Authority, the Local Health Commissioning Team, Llanelli/Dinefwr Health Trust, Aman Gwendraeth Partnership, West Wales Training and Enterprise Council and the Gwendraeth Valley Community Education project. A total eligible expenditure of £241,000 was awarded to Menter Cwm Gwendraeth in October 1996 for a three-year period (which included 50 per cent matched funding) to employ two full-time and one part-time project workers and to cover administrative and developmental costs.

The main objectives of the project were to establish mechanisms:

- to enable communities to identify their needs and aspirations and highlight the extent to which these are currently being met by various agencies;
- to undertake a social audit and profile outlining weaknesses or gaps in provision by mainstream agencies;
- to set up village fora to increase community participation in decision-making processes;
- to enable agencies to help communities prioritize their needs and aspirations;
- to help the community to draw up a strategic action plan;
- to identify and access funding from various sources;
- to facilitate community capacity building through developing people's skills, knowledge, experience and confidence;
- to encourage the establishment or enhancement of effective inter-agency partnerships;
- to assist in implementing direct-benefit projects to do with capital expenditure programmes, training, environmental improvements, job creation, health awareness programmes and crime prevention schemes.

The Gwendraeth Valley Community Development Project has come to the end of its initial three-year term, but its impact on the area in such a short period of time has been quite remarkable. It has succeeded in bringing communities together to identify their needs, it has established effective village fora, accessed substantial funding for ambitious capital projects like a community leisure centre in Trimsaran costing in total over £570,000, set up training and adult education courses, accessed grants for bilingual signage, undertaken environmental enhancement schemes, created play areas, established child-care programmes, improved car parking facilities and has extended leisure provision for children and youth.

These of course are product outcomes – visual, definable and concrete – but on another level there have been significant process outcomes which have developed in an indirect, even subconscious way. These involve issues relating to confidence building, increasing the community's knowledge base, individual skills development, capacity building, leadership and advocacy skills, all indicators that underpin and support meaningful community development work.

By using the language as a natural, almost unobtrusive, medium of communication Menter Cwm Gwendraeth has succeeded in normalizing its use in domains where English has hitherto been predominant. This has been a most significant and invaluable development which has tangibly underlined the importance of creating a synthesis between language and community development and has created opportunities for Menter Cwm Gwendraeth to become involved in and influence all facets of community life. Josuah Fishman underlines the importance of integrating action on issues that concern language protagonists with those affecting the wider community thus:

> RLS [Reversing Language Shift] neighbourhoods must be battling neighbourhoods, struggling for social, cultural, economic, political and personal dignity. Action needs an image of community that local residents can identify with and that fosters commitment as a type of functional equivalence to kinship amongst non-kin. As distinct from its role among ideologists and linguists, Xish [e.g. Welsh] cannot be pursued in and of itself, for its own sake among ordinary folk. It must be part of the warp and woof of social life and make a meaningful difference in the neighbourhood . . .[16]

### (viii) Research and development

> In order to ensure effective language intervention from the beginning, any intervention agency must seek to understand the true nature of the community as it is.[17]

Research and needs assessment programmes have been the cornerstone of Menter Cwm Gwendraeth's strategic development from the outset. So that each project could be justified in terms of the financial and human resources expended on its implementation, a wide-ranging research programme was necessary in order to provide a multi-level analysis of the language in its social context.

A research study on the use of Welsh amongst businesses in the Gwendraeth Valley was undertaken in collaboration with the Welsh Department at the University College of Wales, Swansea. An evaluation of the progress made by Menter Cwm Gwendraeth on its initial three-year development plan was the subject of an M.Phil. thesis by a student from the Welsh Department at the University College of Wales, Lampeter, and a student from the Welsh Department of the University of Wales College, Cardiff, is currently looking at the links between the decline of the Welsh language and the rundown of the mining industry. Other studies by university students have looked at the use of Welsh amongst fourteen to twenty-five year olds, the use of Welsh in leisure and community activities, the impact of the education system on linguistic self-confidence and an in-depth study of linguistic networks based on the experiences of families living in one street in the close-knit community of Tumble, the largest village in the area.

A study on the social needs of young people in the valley carried out jointly with Trinity College, Carmarthen, formed the basis of a successful bid for National Lottery money to employ two part-time youth workers, whose main task was to provide a network of youth clubs and holiday play schemes in the area. Menter Cwm Gwendraeth also carried out some 'in-house' studies which involved community profiling and needs assessments and became the basis of many of the most innovative projects developed over recent years.

## THE TOP TWENTY INTERVENTIONIST PROJECTS

### (i) Language transmission in the home

By far the most innovative and potentially rewarding project initiated in recent years has been the campaign to raise awareness amongst parents of the importance of intergenerational transfer (IGT) of language in the home. This pilot project, run jointly with the Welsh Language Board, seeks to influence parents of child-bearing age via information leaflets and talks at ante-natal and post-natal classes.

The idea developed from a seminar organized by Menter Cwm Gwendraeth in October 1996, where experts from the field of language planning, child care, midwifery and health visiting, general practice, education, academic research and marketing came together to discuss the findings of a specially commissioned paper by the Statistical Directorate of the Welsh Office on the extent of mother-tongue transmission in the Gwendraeth Valley. By comparing the 1991 census and figures in the Social Survey of Wales 1992, with school-returns data in the Statistics of Education and Training in Wales, 1995, which denotes children from the age of four as being either first- or second-language speakers, it was possible to highlight a trend in language use in the home. The statistics for the Gwendraeth Valley showed a startling 34 per cent approximate loss in terms of language transfer.

These figures resulted in some feverish brainstorming, with the aim of drawing up a list of ideas which, if urgently implemented, could halt the decline of mother-tongue transfer and make a positive contribution to language maintenance in Cwm Gwendraeth. Josuah Fishman highlighted the danger signals for language planning which did not focus on IGT activity thus: 'The road to societal death is paved by language activity that is not focused on intergenerational continuity, i.e. that is diverted into efforts that do not involve and influence the socialisation behaviours of families of child-bearing age.'[18] One of the main recommendations of the seminar was the importance of targeting expectant mothers and their partners so that they could be positively influenced before their baby was born. Another idea put forward was the provision of fun activities for the whole family through the medium of Welsh (or bilingually where appropriate) so that everyone involved could see at first hand the social value of being able to speak Welsh.

The process of involving key agencies like the local health trusts and GP practices began immediately. Meetings were arranged with teams of midwives and health visitors working across the whole of Carmarthenshire in order to seek their support and co-operation with this pioneering project. Following lengthy discussions it was agreed that an information pack be compiled which would include details of the advantages of bilingualism, a question-and-answer booklet on raising children bilingually, information on local *cylchoedd* Ti a Fi (Welsh-language mother and toddler groups) and *cylchoedd meithrin* (pre-school playgroups), Welsh-language classes for adults, the provision of Welsh-medium education in the area and a simple introduction to baby-talk in Welsh! Sets of these information packs would be given to midwives and health visitors for distribution or used as resource material in ante-natal and parent-craft classes.

During the process of developing the information pack and producing relevant leaflets and booklets aimed at parents, the project's significance was reinforced by the publication of a research study carried out by Professor Colin Baker of the University College of Wales, Bangor, for the Welsh Language Board which highlighted, on a Wales-wide basis, the extent of intergenerational transfer in the home.[19]

The result of his study published in 1998 showed that, in cases where both parents were Welsh speakers, there was a 92 per cent chance that the children would be mother-tongue speakers. In cases where the mother was the sole Welsh speaker this figure drops to 52 per cent and where the father is the Welsh speaker it further diminishes to 48 per cent. To make matters worse, this downward spiral is further exacerbated by the fact that the most critical decline occurs in geographical areas which include Cwm Gwendraeth and the neighbouring Aman, Tywi and Tawe Valleys, which are densely populated communities with particularly high percentages of Welsh speakers. The significance of these findings in terms of language maintenance further underlines the crucially important role that the project plays in changing attitudinal and behavioural patterns. Fishman describes this evidence of language shift as 'speech communities whose native languages are threatened because their intergenerational continuity is progressing negatively, with fewer and fewer users'.[20]

Booklets, leaflets and other resources (including a short video on the advantages of Welsh-medium education) were included in information packs that were subsequently distributed widely by health visitors and midwives. An arrangement was secured between the Welsh Language Board and Bounty Services whereby leaflets outlining the advantages of bilingualism would be included in 'Bounty Packs' which are automatically sent to all expectant mothers in Wales via their local GPs. Altogether about 31,000 Bounty Packs have been sent out every year since August 1997.

Together with the dissemination of information packs, trained *animateurs* which include staff of the local *mentrau iaith* have arranged brief talks to all ante-natal and post-natal classes across the whole of Carmarthenshire (fifteen in total) outlining the social, educational and economic advantages of bilingualism. A programme of social activities for families has also been arranged with the emphasis on creating an environment of linguistic inclusivity and interaction. The project is currently being evaluated by an independent assessor and has included questionnaires to parents, midwives and health visitors. The results of this evaluation exercise are to be produced in a report to be published shortly by the Welsh Language Board. Early indications suggest that this extremely important project has paid huge dividends.

### (ii)  Saturday Morning Clubs

Research on the language skills of Welsh speakers in Cwm Gwendraeth has consistently shown that written and reading skills are deemed to be inferior to comparable skills in English. Aitchinson and Carter,[21] Williams and Evas[22] and Morgan[23] to name but a few have all in recent years referred to this linguistic deficit as being particularly characteristic of the Welsh-speaking communities of the traditional coal-mining valleys of south Wales.

Space does not allow for a detailed explanation of why this is so, only to suggest that it has its roots in the demographic make-up of the valleys following the discovery of coal – a period when thousands of workers migrated in droves to Wales from England, Ireland, Scotland and from Europe to seek work. Many of these immigrants learned Welsh and became assimilated into local Welsh-speaking communities, but their mastery of the language was based mainly on oral skills.

The aim of the *Clybiau Bore Sadwrn* (Saturday Morning Clubs) is to encourage children to read in the Welsh language as various activities, which are presented in a fun and lively way, are developed from themes explored in books that are read as a group. These clubs, which are aimed at children from the ages of five to eight, are held in various locations but usually in village halls or chapel vestries for two hours on a Saturday morning. Specially trained club leaders and assistants are employed to develop an inspiring programme of activities which includes painting and drawing, singing, puppet making, face painting, role play, mime, dance, word games, written exercises and puzzles. In total over 275 children attended these Saturday Morning Clubs in 1999, which ran for fifteen weeks in six different locations.

In response to questionnaires sent out to parents at the end of the series the benefits accrued in terms of their children's linguistic development were perceived as follows: 34 per cent saw an overall improvement in their children's

Welsh, 26 per cent saw an increase in confidence when speaking Welsh, 23 per cent said their children developed better reading skills, and 14 per cent stated that it had encouraged reading at home. Other interesting findings were: 69 per cent of the children were able to repeat the story read in the Saturday Morning Club at home; 34 per cent had asked their parents for a weekly Welsh book to read at home; and 29 per cent had from time to time asked for a Welsh book to read.

### (iii) Fun Clubs

In the absence of Welsh-medium activities in the evenings for children between the ages of seven and eleven a series of *Clybiau Hwyl* (Fun Clubs) were launched early on in the development of Menter Cwm Gwendraeth, with the aim of providing a wide range of fun activities for an age group that is considered to be vitally important for the language's future. These clubs seek to enhance the linguistic skills developed in schools by providing leisure opportunities in the evening through the medium of Welsh. The main objective is to bridge the gap between school-based and community-based activities and normalize the use of Welsh in recreational hours. These clubs meet once weekly in village halls or other suitable locations – deliberately avoiding school premises – usually over a period of twenty weeks. The activities, which are both socially and educationally orientated, include games, arts and crafts, gymnastics, swimming, self-defence, first aid, talks by the police, fire officers, local GPs and the like, visits to various places of interest, personal health, charity work, etc.

On average during the past year over thirty children have attended each of these clubs located in six different villages, each run by qualified play leaders and assistants. Because of their success the *Clybiau Hwyl* have remained permanent fixtures in Menter Cwm Gwendraeth's programme of activities over the years.

### (iv) Youth Clubs

The need to provide young people with opportunities to socialize in a safe and stimulating environment is self-evident but with cut-backs in expenditure severely constraining local authorities, very often the need remains unmet. A survey conducted by Menter Cwm Gwendraeth in 1996 into the needs of young people in the area highlighted the gaps in provision that existed. The survey also focused attention on the kinds of activities that young people were keen to support in their local community.

This was the first survey of its kind conducted in Cwm Gwendraeth aimed exclusively at young people and it included a total of nearly 1,000 respondents. It produced some interesting results:

- over half of the young people questioned did not participate in any formal youth provision;

- 70 per cent stated that, for practical reasons due mainly to transportation problems, they could not travel more than five miles to any activity;
- over 87 per cent wanted the youth clubs to meet at least once a week.

As a result of this survey, an application for funding was made to the National Lottery Charities Board, which resulted in a three-year grant totalling £80,000. Coupled with funding received from the local health authority under its Healthy Communities Scheme, in all, seven youth clubs were established in various locations meeting once weekly over a forty-week period.

The clubs sought to provide an attractive programme of activities through the medium of Welsh which would be educative, participative, empowering and expressive. These activities included games, competitions, self-defence, first aid programmes, environmental schemes, charity work, community aid, talks on drug, solvent and alcohol abuse and safe sex, visits to theatres, ten-pin bowling, ice-skating, visits to television studios, debates, arts and crafts, drama, music and computer games. The youth clubs were very well supported and greatly appreciated by those communities who had hitherto been deprived of such an important social provision.

### (v) After-school clubs

After-school clubs, Learning and Homework Clubs, have become extremely popular over the past few years as they provide care provision for children during after-school hours. This allows parents to carry on working or attend training courses which might enhance their prospects of gaining employment. Government grants have been made available through organizations like the Training and Enterprise Councils, Kids' Clubs Network and more recently the New Opportunities Fund administered by the National Lottery Charities Board.

Three such after-school clubs were established in the area, in conjunction with local primary schools, meeting on three to five afternoons a week between 3.00 and 6.00 p.m. Again the provision was through the medium of Welsh as the primary schools concerned were Category A schools which meant that the main language of education was Welsh. The high take-up showed that these clubs served not only an invaluable social need but also a hugely important economic one in an area suffering acute socio-economic degeneration.

### (vi) Social events

In an area that was largely unaccustomed to having Welsh-language entertainment on a social events programme in the local rugby or workingmen's clubs on a Friday or Saturday night, it was felt that breaking into the entertainment circuit by introducing the very best Welsh-language artists to new audiences was vital if the language was to have any credibility in the non-traditional social networks of the valley. It was a matter of parachuting the language, often in a covert manner, into the popular meeting-places of the young and not so young and proving to often sceptical audiences and local organizers that Welsh-language entertainment was both hugely popular and financially viable.

Over a period of many years it can be noted with some satisfaction that both goals have been achieved. One of the great successes over recent years has been the significant increase in the number of clubs and organizations which have transformed their programme of events in order to accommodate the enthusiastic demand for Welsh-language acts. The organizers were assisted in the beginning with lists of popular artists and with marketing, but gradually over time they were able to assume responsibility themselves for the organizing – in itself an important empowering process.

The events and activities that Menter Cwm Gwendraeth helped to 'pump-prime' in the early years ranged from folk evenings and concerts to karaoke evenings and rock concerts. There were also children's discos, touring theatre companies, eisteddfodau, sports quizzes, inter-village quizzes, 'It's a knockout' competitions, literary recitals, children's pageants and sports competitions.

The objective clearly was to raise the profile of Welsh and introduce the language to social networks that had hitherto been fed a diet of bland, middle-of-the-road entertainment in English. It also sought to create an awareness of Welsh as a contemporary medium of enjoyment and normalize its use in the domain of leisure and recreation. During the year 1996–7 a total of ninety-five activities were arranged either directly or indirectly, which works out roughly as one activity every four days of the year – quite a remarkable feat in linguistic engineering. Over recent years, as more and more social clubs have assumed responsibility for their own arrangements, fewer events have been organized centrally by Menter Cwm Gwendraeth thus allowing regenerative efforts to be concentrated on other important social domains and sectors.

### (vii) Gwendraeth Valley Festival

Gŵyl y Gwendraeth, which is a week-long festival held at the beginning of May every year is the pinnacle of the social calendar. The first festival, which was the brainchild of Menter Cwm Gwendraeth's marketing subcommittee, was held in 1992 and it has grown in size and popularity ever since. Its aim is to cater for all ages and interest groups, Welsh speakers, Welsh learners and non-Welsh speakers alike. Although all the activities in the programme are conducted through the medium of Welsh, efforts are made to include non-Welsh speakers via simultaneous translation equipment or written summaries.

A typical programme would include an eisteddfod, a folk evening, a rock concert, a sports forum, children's sports day, a public lecture, a grand concert, the final of the inter-village quiz, a children's pageant and a *cymanfa ganu* (hymn-singing festival). A total of approximately 4,000 people attend the festival every year, which does not include the large number of teams that compete beforehand on a village basis for the honour of representing their community in the grand quiz final. It is estimated that between 900 and 1,000 people take part in these village quizzes, in what is a test of general knowledge in a fun atmosphere. Gŵyl y Gwendraeth is certainly going from strength to strength and has long established itself as an integral part of the social calendar of the Gwendraeth Valley.

## (viii) Workshops

The aim of the workshops is to provide new and exciting opportunities for young people between the ages of seven and twenty-five to experience a range of activities which are both enjoyable and educative. These workshops, which could be a short series during the evening or a day-long programme usually held on a Saturday or during school holidays, have tried to cater for as many leisure interests as possible and have included tuition by a team of specialist instructors in disciplines like drama, dance, script-writing, rock music, sport, photography, video production, self-defence, instrumental music. Not only are young people provided opportunities not normally afforded them but these workshops serve another very important purpose, namely to ensure that extremely attractive recreational options are available to them through the medium of Welsh, thus increasing the language's appeal to a critical age group.

## (ix) Youth Theatre Company

The Youth Theatre Company which started in 1994 was set up in response to a demand by a large number of young people in the area for an opportunity to develop their skills in the performing arts. This followed a huge interest in the drama workshops that had been held previously. There is no doubt that the increased popularity of S4C (the Welsh-language television channel) and the growth of indigenous independent production companies, many specializing in drama and docu-soaps, has fuelled the imagination of a generation of young Welsh speakers attracted by the glitz and glamour of the television industry.

The Theatre Company, catering mainly for the twelve to twenty-one age group, has been meeting weekly for the past five years and has staged numerous productions of the highest standard using different genres such as drama, pantomime, reviews. Most of these productions have been written in-house and based on themes pertinent to the lives of young people, often containing allegories reflecting everyday experiences. The company has received many offers to perform in public and has been invited on a number of occasions to participate at the National Eisteddfod. The latest production called *Talu'r Pris yn Llawn* (Paying the full price), based on the theme of drug misuse, received the backing of Dyfed Powys Police Authority, who asked the company to tour primary schools in the area to raise awareness of the dangers of drug and solvent abuse.

On average some fifty young people attend on a weekly basis to develop their skills under the guidance of expert tuition in a number of different aspects of theatre production, including script-writing, make-up, costume design, set production, acting, lighting and sound, and directing. Many young people who have been active members of the Youth Theatre over many years have gone on to become successful actors, singers, cameramen, sound recordists and producers with television companies.

### (x) Visits by celebrities

In an attempt to raise the profile of the Welsh language, efforts have been made to seek the co-operation of well-known celebrities who are Welsh speakers by urging them to come along and speak to schoolchildren and young people who attend the Fun Clubs and Youth Clubs during the evening or sports workshops on the weekends.

The stars of sport and screen idolized by children can be used purposefully to promote the advantages of bilingualism. They are often seen on television, being interviewed or presenting programmes in Welsh, or representing their country in rugby and other sports, which in itself gives a positive image of the language. Getting them along to meet their young supporters and getting them involved in coaching or question-and-answer sessions gives the language an important psychological platform. In the past Menter Cwm Gwendraeth has been very fortunate to attract the support of some of Wales's most famous rugby players who have been more than willing to take part in projects aimed at promoting the Welsh language. Well-known actors and television presenters on S4C have also eagerly supported similar campaigns. Using Welsh-speaking sports and television personalities who are attractive role models for countless thousands of young Welsh speakers across the whole of Wales as practical advocates for the language can only have an immense positive influence on the perception of Welsh as a modern, thriving language.

### (xi) Village quizzes

These village quizzes form part of Gŵyl y Gwendraeth. As a forerunner to the festival, quizzes are held in every village throughout the area to decide which team represents each village in the grand final held during the festival week. On average between ten and fifteen teams take part on a village level, each comprising of four members. Very often these represent local organizations, sports clubs, societies, chapels, etc., which form a broad cross-section of society. The general knowledge questions and general banter is in Welsh, with team members assisting those non-Welsh speakers or learners who are present with a translation. These are generally fun evenings enjoyed by all those participating and watching from the sidelines. The good-natured competitive spirit also adds a little spice to proceedings.

The winning team has the honour of representing their village and pitting their wits against the best from the other seventeen villages taking part in the annual quiz, with the overall winners receiving a memorial shield to display in their local pub or post office for a year. In all, about 1,000 people actively take part every year in these village quizzes which prove to be extremely popular and entertaining.

During the winter months sports quizzes are held between local rugby, football and cricket teams which are again very successful. They follow much the same format, with a grand final held on the same evening as a Sports Forum during Gŵyl y Gwendraeth. These quizzes serve a dual purpose – not only do they ensure an enjoyable evening of fun for all concerned but they also introduce the Welsh language, and in particular technical terms in Welsh in subjects like sport or general knowledge, into domains that have hitherto been associated mainly with the English language.

### (xii) Children in Need project

Following a successful bid for £30,000 to the Children in Need fund over a three-year period, Menter Cwm Gwendraeth was able to focus its attentions on providing opportunities for children experiencing economic, social and educational deprivation.

First this involved providing care and play opportunities for children with special education needs through:

- sensitive integrative programmes in conjunction with the local education authority and professional and voluntary organizations specializing in care delivery;
- the provision of training courses for play leaders and carers;
- initiating marketing campaigns to raise awareness of the importance of sensitive social integration of children and young adults with special needs.

The second strand was of Pastoral Care programmes, which included:

- an educative programme to raise awareness of the dangers of alcohol, solvent and drug abuse, HIV and AIDS, under-age pregnancies, road traffic accidents, etc.;
- the setting up of advice centres and help-lines;
- arranging a series of workshops focusing on the above issues.

A third aspect was the provision of social and leisure opportunities for children who have missed out on such opportunities because of economic and social deprivation.

During the lifetime of this particular project many important developments were achieved. These included the setting up of a data-base of information on organizations, agencies and counsellors who could assist individuals with problems related to alcohol, solvent or drug abuse and other issues of particular concern to young people. Leaflets, posters and videos were also distributed and shown in youth clubs and Fun Clubs run by Menter Cwm Gwendraeth and the local education authority, which included contact addresses and help-lines.

Talks were arranged by trained specialists outlining the dangers of drug and solvent abuse. Talks were also given on subjects like personal health, contraception, anti-social behaviour, joy-riding, vandalism and theft, with the aim of raising awareness and encouraging responsible citizenship. In order better to understand the extent of solvent, alcohol and drug abuse in the area a working party was set up by Menter Cwm Gwendraeth to carry out research amongst eleven to sixteen year olds. The group included Trinity College, Carmarthen, local GPs, Health Promotion Wales, Llanelli/Dinefwr Health Trust, Carmarthenshire Social Services, teacher representatives from the two local secondary schools and Prism (a voluntary organization giving advice and support on alcohol and drug misuse). As one of its main tasks it published a detailed report on its research findings which concluded in general terms that drug and alcohol abuse amongst young adults was far more prevalent than had been at first considered.

Menter Cwm Gwendraeth's two part-time youth workers (twenty-five and fifteen hours a week respectively) took particular interest in these issues and attended numerous training courses and conferences on related themes. They were extremely keen to arrange workshops and invite guest speakers to talk about various subjects and to enhance their own knowledge of these matters.

The programme of 'Integration and Social Activities' for deprived children also proved very successful. A number of children with acute educational needs, for example, Down's syndrome and cerebral palsy, were successfully integrated into mainstream activities assisted by specialist care workers. This proved to be hugely rewarding for all concerned and greatly appreciated by the parents in particular.

An attractive programme of activities was also put on in communities with a high incidence of social and economic deprivation, which needless to say was especially welcomed. As expected, the exercise did not proceed without its teething problems, and it was as much of a learning curve for the providers as for the recipients. Putting on a fairly structured programme of activities in communities that were socially disintegrating proved to be a major challenge and an invaluable learning experience for all involved in the restructuring process.

The fact that most if not all of the work carried out on this 'Children in Need' programme was done through the medium of Welsh on a one-to-one basis, or bilingually via written promotional literature, proves that Welsh can be a more than adequate medium for discussing all kinds of issues and concerns relating to young people in Wales today.

### (xiii) *Promoting Welsh in the business sector*

The business sector is an important part of the linguistic landscape and as such deserves special attention. The main thrust of the work undertaken to promote the use of Welsh amongst local businesses was based on research carried out by an M.Phil. student from the Welsh Department, University College, Swansea, on the use of the Welsh language by businesses in the Gwendraeth Valley.[24] This research showed that, in general terms, consumers welcomed an increase in the use of Welsh and that managers and owners of businesses were sympathetic to the cause of Welsh if costs would not be too prohibitive.

As a result of this research a glossy bilingual leaflet outlining the advantages of bilingualism was produced – which included reference to the commercial and social advantages of bilingualism. Using the extensive data-base of companies compiled from various sources, a leaflet was sent out to each business in the area with a voucher worth £50 which could be credited when using any of the support services that Menter Cwm Gwendraeth could offer to local businesses, for example, translation work, teaching Welsh to staff, developing language policies, undertaking language audits, bilingual design. In total, over 1,000 leaflets were distributed.

The fact that only five were returned meant that lessons had to be learned on how to deal with the business sector and grab their attention on first contact. One thing was clear, leaflet 'drops' did not work unless followed up with a personal call. Along with the mountain of 'junk mail' sent out to businesses daily, the leaflet offering a discount on Welsh-language services was probably binned in seconds along with other similar brochures offering special deals and reductions.

Undaunted, a decision was made to change tack and arrange personal visits instead with company owners or managers in order to encourage them to extend their use of Welsh. A list of businesses was drawn up reflecting a mix of sectors, which varied according to the size of companies, location, number of employees, and visits were carried out systematically over a given period of time. Armed with information on research studies carried out by NOP for the Welsh Language Board outlining the public's support for increased bilingualism and statistics showing the commercial benefits accrued by companies who reflect a positive attitude towards the use of Welsh, together with visual examples of bilingual design and lay-out on promotional literature and signs, and details of grants available for bilingual signage, members of staff sought face-to-face meetings with decision-makers within companies or individual owners.

This approach proved to be far more successful, and over a four-year period over twenty-five businesses have developed bilingual signage on shop fronts, business premises and vehicles, bilingual letterheads and promotional material. This development has had quite an impact on the linguistic topography of the area and has had a significant snowballing effect on the business sector in general.

In addition to the above developments, badges and desk displays were also distributed free of charge to as many businesses as were willing to participate, denoting those staff members who were bilingual speakers. This was part of the Welsh Language Board's marketing campaign, entitled 'Iaith Gwaith/Working Welsh', which was initiated across the whole of Wales. Menter Cwm

Gwendraeth also produced Welsh-language versions of 'Open/Closed' which could be displayed by local businesses. These again proved to be extremely successful, with over a hundred sold in a very short space of time. It is heartening to note that these displays can be seen today hanging on doors in local shops and businesses dotted around the valley.

Another campaign with which Menter became involved in conjunction with the Welsh Language Board was a competition run on an all-Wales basis which rewarded companies that best promoted the Welsh language – either in terms of staff training and delivery, bilingual design and packaging, or bilingual signage and promotional material. Each year winners in different business categories of businesses were presented with prizes at the National Eisteddfod.

In order to provide opportunities for Welsh-speaking business people to meet, share experiences and invite guest speakers to discuss topics of common interest a Business Club or 'Cwlwm Busnes' was set up in the area, meeting monthly over the winter period. This venture has also proved to be very successful in enabling the language to be a medium of delivery and discussion in a domain that has traditionally been associated with English. Tapping into the business sector is notoriously difficult but what Menter Cwm Gwendraeth has undoubtedly proved is that a great deal of goodwill exists towards the language and through encouragement and patience significant breakthroughs can be achieved.

### *(xiv) Promoting Welsh in the voluntary sector*

The voluntary sector is comprised of a myriad of various organizations representing a wide variety of interests. Some are very localized, others work on a Wales-wide basis, while most represent UK-based or even world-wide organizations and charities. In Carmarthenshire alone there are over 1,500 registered voluntary organizations and charities, each with their own agendas and objectives. Most voluntary groups work on a shoestring budget and fund-raising is probably their main activity from year to year. Most of the volunteers are elderly and in many cases English people who have settled in Wales on retirement.

For a large number of active volunteers, supporting the Welsh language is a costly and time-consuming business. Others, mainly Welsh speakers (although that is not always the case), recognize the advantages of a bilingual approach to promoting the work of their organization. Despite the efforts of the Wales Council for Voluntary Action and Carmarthenshire Association of Voluntary Services, which is the umbrella organization responsible for co-ordinating the work of the voluntary sector in the county, very little progress has been made thus far in extending the use of Welsh. A lack of money to pay for translating written material into Welsh, for employing simultaneous translators so that meetings can be held bilingually and for bilingual type-setting and design is often put forward as a reason for inaction.

Menter Cwm Gwendraeth's approach involved targeting those voluntary organizations which had active branches in the area with key personnel known to be supportive of the Welsh language. By working closely with these individuals, significant progress was made on many fronts, with some local organizations developing a fully bilingual policy. In order to encourage more use of Welsh a leaflet was produced outlining the advantages of bilingualism which included guidance on producing bilingual letterheads and literature. This leaflet was sent out to all voluntary groups in the Gwendraeth Valley. Unfortunately the response was disappointing, which meant reverting to establishing links with individual organizations and working with them to develop examples of good practice.

Because of the voluntary nature of the work, along with the perceived costs of implementing a bilingual policy and the limited number of individuals who can act as catalysts for change, progress has been rather restricted. Nevertheless, a sizeable investment in time and effort has been made to try and encourage a more positive response from the voluntary sector which may pay dividends in the long term. In the mean time efforts are continuing with individual organizations which have shown an eagerness to embrace the Welsh language as a tool to increase their effectiveness and efficiency in dealing with a bilingual community and in providing a quality service for their clients and supporters.

A survey undertaken by the Wales Council for Voluntary Action in 1995 of the use made of Welsh by voluntary organizations seems to reflect the difficulties they face in providing more of their services through Welsh: 82 per cent of those questioned had already adopted a bilingual name, but only 21 per cent had a Welsh-language policy in force. However, 72 per cent wished to extend their use of Welsh while 19 per cent had no intention of doing so. These figures on the face of it are quite heartening, but there remain significant barriers to the positive adoption and implementation of bilingual policies and the removal of discrimination and oppressive practices in the relationship between service providers and users.

### (xv) Simultaneous translation equipment

As mentioned previously in this chapter, the increased use of simultaneous translation equipment has been one of the great success stories of recent years. After an uncertain beginning when entrenched prejudices regarding the role of Welsh in the lofty world of officialdom hindered its development as a credible alternative to English, the idea that Welsh could coexist slowly caught on. It was a combination of enthusiastic support, a willingness to recognize the rights of Welsh speakers and the 'novelty factor' that finally persuaded various local bodies and organizations to adopt the use of translation facilities as an integral part of their service provision.

In order to defuse any tensions that may have arisen surrounding the cost of hiring the equipment and paying for a translator, the provision from the beginning was given free of charge – a situation that remains to this day, but which is currently under review. The balance on the expenditure was made up from income accrued from the hiring of the equipment to public- and private-sector bodies at a commercial rate. Fortunately, at the end of every financial year, the translation service managed to show a slight profit. So that an able team of simultaneous translators would be available on stand-by at all times and often at short notice, regular training courses were put on for those who were either complete beginners or who wanted to advance their skills further. These were often run in conjunction with the University Colleges of Wales, Aberystwyth and Swansea.

The issue of paying for services in Welsh often prompted the familiar response from some quarters of 'We all speak English anyway!' to which a measured reply underlining the basic rights of Welsh speakers to use their language without fear or prejudice was often necessary. This process of ensuring equal status for Welsh at the lowest level of formal community involvement has been slow and arduous as it challenges deep-rooted mind-sets, but using unobtrusive simultaneous translation equipment has been one extremely effective way of dismantling age-old habits, thereby allowing the Welsh language to develop in the domain of local governance. An interesting side-effect of this 'breaking down of barriers' is the increased confidence that Welsh speakers have gained in grappling with unfamiliar specialized terminology and jargon in their first language.

The fact that the use of the simultaneous translation equipment has increased by 30 per cent over a seven-year period underlines this new-found confidence, together with the growing realization that the basic rights of Welsh speakers are enshrined in the Welsh Language Act of 1993, something it is incumbent on service providers to recognize.

### (xvi) Youth entertainment

Survey after survey has highlighted the fact that for most young people the Welsh language projects an image that is associated with an old-fashioned, chapel-going and culturally worn way of life which has led in many cases to deep resentment of the language by some of today's youth and a negative perception of its role in contemporary society. In an attempt to counter these uninspiring views, a programme of events was put together which specifically targeted young people. In trying to cater for their interests via the Welsh language it was hoped that many of the psychological barriers surrounding their attitude towards Welsh could be broken down.

One of the saving graces in recent years has been the resurgence of a vibrant rock scene in Wales, with bands which started life singing in the Welsh language developing to become internationally renowned supergroups like Catatonia, Super Furry Animals and Gorky's Zygotic Mynci. Although these groups sing mainly in English they do include lyrics and songs on their CDs that are sung in Welsh – a fact that is appreciated by their fans from Japan to the United States.

This has certainly helped create an 'in your face', bullish image of Welsh which has been accentuated by the emergence of young Welsh-speaking actors who have recently made their mark in the highly attractive world of TV and film. The effortless, even nonchalant way that Ioan Gruffudd, Rhys Ifans and Mathew Rhys, for example, portray themselves as bilingual speakers exudes a self-confidence that is refreshing in the way that it is unfettered by inherited stigmas and hang-ups.

Menter Cwm Gwendraeth was fortunate to have arranged many gigs over recent years which had some of the above groups in the line-up (before they became too expensive to afford!) and others – hugely popular – that are on the verge of breaking through into the UK charts who sing in both Welsh and English. It is hoped that the positive images conveyed by these groups and the experience of enjoying live music of the highest quality has had some effect on the attitudes of young people towards the language.

In order to encourage and support new and up-and-coming bands, competitions were also held – 'The Battle of the Bands' – to promote new talent. In conjunction with Radio Cymru the winners were given a cash prize and an opportunity to play their songs on the radio. These sessions again proved to be immensely popular and an important springboard for those wishing to develop a career in the music world.

As part of the same campaign, Welsh-language discos were held in primary schools and bands were sometimes invited to play in secondary schools during the lunch hour. Welsh bilingual karaoke evenings also proved very popular and hugely entertaining. In so doing they once again ensured that the Welsh language could be successfully introduced into the world of popular entertainment – which is a significant breakthrough in psychological terms and in the context of language intervention.

### (xvii) Community education courses

Very few adult education and recreational courses have been offered through the medium of Welsh by the traditional providers of such courses in the area, namely the local authority's Community Education Department, the Adult and Continuing Education Department of the University of Wales, Swansea, the Workers Education Association (WEA) and Carmarthenshire College. The once-weekly Welsh-for-adults courses certainly feature prominently in most programmes, as does the odd Welsh literature or local history course through the medium of Welsh. It would also be true to say that many courses use Welsh informally as a means of instruction, but generally speaking the choice is very limited.

Following pressure from Menter Cwm Gwendraeth a slight increase has been achieved over recent years in the number of courses now offered through Welsh. These have ranged from computers, creative writing and photography to line-dancing, cookery, self-defence and aerobics. By attracting good enrolments they have underlined the fact that there is a demand for adult and recreational courses through the medium of Welsh. It is hoped that their success will lead to further such courses being provided in the future, as education establishments come to realize that the linguistic make-up of the area they serve is not reflected in the amount of Welsh included in their provision.

### (xviii) Welsh in the workplace

As all public-sector bodies have to draw up language schemes under the provision of the Welsh Language Act, Menter Cwm Gwendraeth saw that there would be a demand for employees to be taught Welsh in the workplace or for those employees who were Welsh-speaking to be given opportunities to develop their work-based skills in the language. In 1996 Menter Cwm Gwendraeth successfully applied to City and Guilds – one of the main awarding bodies in vocational training – to become an NVQ (National Vocational Qualification) Assessment Centre, specializing in particular in assessing candidates for the NVQ Language Units that are linked to six specific sectors: Business Administration, Care, Leisure and Recreation, Catering, Customer Care and Hospitality.

At the same time the organization was asked by the Welsh Office to co-ordinate a Wales-wide project to promote NVQs through the medium of Welsh. As a result its involvement in vocational training increased significantly, as the scope of the work developed over a much wider geographical area. It also meant that links with training providers and businesses further afield secured opportunities to cater for the needs of employers who needed Welsh-language training in the workplace.

As the only NVQ Assessment Centre in Carmarthenshire, Menter Cwm Gwendraeth was ideally placed to provide a variety of courses for employers, ranging from absolute beginners to the more advanced speakers. The training and assessment would normally concentrate on four key skills – speaking, listening, reading and writing – which would be considered from a range of levels from 1–5. Candidates could mix and match between any of the four key skills and the levels they considered to be most appropriate to their needs and abilities. In most cases the needs of the employer in relation to business output and their aim of achieving a fully bilingual service for their customers was also a prime consideration. This development not only provided important links with the training and business sector but also provided opportunities for Menter Cwm Gwendraeth to generate substantial income from training sessions which mirrored its fundamental aims and objectives of extending the use of Welsh in as many social and institutional domains as possible.

### (xix) Local history video

The idea for producing a video on the history of the Gwendraeth Valley developed from one of the regular consultations between Menter Cwm Gwendraeth and local headteachers. It was felt that a video which concentrated on the main periods of the area's history would be an invaluable educational resource, especially for a generation of children who are the first to be brought up in a community where the mining of coal and the traditions and customs so inextricably linked to that particular industry have all but disappeared.

In conjunction with a local independent television company – Agenda Productions based in Llanelli – steady progress has been made with the aim of ultimately producing three half-hour tapes, the first two concentrating on the Norman period up to the time of the Rebecca Riots and the third dealing exclusively with the development of the coal-mining industry and its effects on the local community. A project team has been appointed to oversee the development of the video which includes teachers, script-writers, producers and local history enthusiasts. In addition to the video, it is intended to produce information packs and resource material that could be used by schools, local organizations and community groups. The interviews and 'voice-overs' on the video are in Welsh but an English subtitle service will also be available. Not only will the video serve as an important educational resource but it will also be an invaluable archive for future generations, in particular the video portraying the local coal-mining community, as it contains interviews with former miners and their families about a way of life that has rapidly diminished over recent years.

### (xx)  Resource and information centre

Over the years Menter Cwm Gwenraeth has developed to become an important resource and information centre on matters relating to the Welsh language and community development for a wide geographical area. It is seen as a convenient 'one-stop-shop' for those wanting information or advice on anything to do with the Welsh language or the Gwendraeth Valley in general.

The fact that there are two main offices, conveniently situated at Cross Hands in the upper end of the valley, and Pont-henri towards the lower end, has ensured that accessing information has been relatively easy. People have always felt free to walk in or phone at any time. Individuals, local organizations, voluntary groups, sports clubs and many others have readily used the resources available to them at Cross Hands and Pont-henri to promote their work. Computers have been made available for community use as well as photocopying facilities, fax machines, printing and design services, simultaneous translation equipment and overhead projectors. Other resources available are Welsh-language spellcheckers and grammar checks (Cysill and Cysgair produced by the Welsh Language Board), badges and desk displays denoting Welsh-speaking staff (which form part of the Welsh Language Board's Iaith Gwaith/Working Welsh scheme), along with various leaflets and brochures for example: 'Carry on with Welsh – Guiding your child into the next stages of education', 'The Welsh advantage – bilingual food and drink packaging', 'Two languages twice the choice – why speak Welsh to your baby?', 'Bilingual from the beginning', 'Working Welsh – the choice is yours', 'Developing Welsh in the community', 'Get talking Welsh – a guide to Welsh for adults', 'Table talk – using Welsh for business advantages in hotels, restaurants, pubs and cafes'.

Also available are Welsh-language dictionaries and thesauruses, information on Welsh-language classes for adults, local *cylchoedd meithrin*, a list of recognized translators and language tutors, as well as an extensive database of local organizations and contacts. The office in Cross Hands is also used as a 'drop-off' point for articles and other contributions to the local Welsh-language community newspaper, *Papur y Cwm*.

In order to assess the extent of community use an audit was undertaken during January to March 1997, at the main office in Cross Hands, where staff were asked to make a record of all telephone calls and visits and the nature of the enquiries. Over the three-month period 1,562 telephone calls were received and 285 visits were made to the office in Cross Hands. A breakdown of these statistics highlights some interesting facts:

- 12 per cent of telephone calls sought information of a general nature;
- 8 per cent enquired about translation equipment while 9.5 per cent wanted information on social activities;
- 4 per cent wanted to order tickets for various events while 8 per cent wanted information on Welsh-language classes or the NVQ project;
- 7 per cent of calls were made by the press or media and 4 per cent by local schools;
- 33 per cent of visits were for prearranged meetings with members of staff;
- 17 per cent came in to design and print tickets and posters;
- 21 per cent made use of photocopying and fax facilities;
- 16 per cent borrowed and hired translation equipment or the overhead projector;
- 6 per cent delivered articles for the community newspaper, *Papur y Cwm*;
- 8 per cent used other resources, for example, leaflets, spellchecker, etc.

The volume of calls and visits over a twelve-week period reflects the amount of activity and interest generated by the work of Menter Cwm Gwendraeth since 1991. It also highlights the close link between the organization and the community it serves and underlines its success in generating grass-roots involvement in the wide range of projects that it has promoted over many years.

## QUALITY MANAGEMENT

One of the initial prime considerations of Menter Cwm Gwendraeth when it was established in January 1991 was that it should develop a model for community-based language planning and provide examples of best practice which could be adapted to other parts of Wales. The responsibility for developing such a pioneering model meant that the director and his staff along with the management committee had to be constantly aware of the importance of devising a blueprint that reflected a truly professional approach to language and community planning. The appointment of a new chairman in 1994 provided the organization with an opportunity to take stock of the situation and reflect in a constructive but honest manner on what had been achieved over the initial three-year period.

The new chairman, who is a general practitioner in the area, brought with him a wealth of experience in planning and management delivery which not only enhanced the administrative and management structure but also generated an awareness of the importance of sound working practices. These were based mainly on the principles of Total Quality Management and included aspects relating to Corporate Management, Risk Assessment, Team Working, Monitoring and Evaluation, Training and Marketing.

This led to a tightening up of the planning and delivery processes, which meant a far more disciplined and focused approach to project management whereby each project would be set targets and outcomes and individually costed. An individual project file was also devised which recorded details relating to income and expenditure, project members and partners, targets, outcomes and an evaluation report. The setting of targets and outcomes subsequently became an integral part of the bid for money from the Welsh Language Board and later Carmarthenshire County Council, and formed part of the service delivery agreement. All *mentrau iaith* across Wales now follow the same procedure which allows funding bodies accurately to assess the value of their investments.


## DEVELOPMENT AND RESTRUCTURING

Two years after the launch of Menter Cwm Gwendraeth, and following the huge amount of publicity that ensued, a second *menter iaith* was established – Menter Aman Tawe – to serve the adjoining communities of the Amman and Tawe Valleys. These also are largely urban, densely populated, former coal-mining communities with a high percentage of Welsh speakers. In addition, in 1995 Menter Iaith Llanelli was set up to work mainly in the former steel town of Llanelli, but its catchment area also included neighbouring villages which were traditionally, and still are to a lesser degree, predominantly Welsh-speaking. As a result, the south-eastern corner of Carmarthenshire, which geographically is about one-quarter of the county's total land area, had three *mentrau iaith* serving its communities while the mainly rural and less densely populated remainder of the county had no such provision.

It was about this time that local councillors and other dignitaries, along with language protagonists representing these areas to the north and west of Cwm Gwendraeth started voicing their concerns about this apparent anomaly. Consequently Carmarthenshire County Council and the Welsh Language Board started discussions with the three *mentrau iaith* and other key organizations with a view to setting up new *mentrau iaith* in other parts of Carmarthenshire and creating a body responsible for supporting and co-ordinating them. The Welsh Language Board was also keen to see the provision of *mentrau iaith* reflecting the geographical boundaries of local authorities.

Mentrau Iaith Myrddin (Carmarthenshire Language Initiatives) was established as an umbrella organization in April 1998, with the aim of setting up three new *mentrau iaith* in the county. It would also be responsible for supporting and co-ordinating the activities of the three existing *mentrau iaith*, developing county-wide projects and forging partnerships with key public-, private- and voluntary-sector bodies in Carmarthenshire in order to encourage wider use of the Welsh language in the services they provide for the public. The director of Menter Cwm Gwendraeth was appointed director of the new organization, which meant that the experience he gained over a period of seven years in Cwm Gwendraeth, and the numerous examples of good practice gleaned during that time, could now be utilized for the benefit of the whole of Carmarthenshire.

A successful bid for money from the National Lottery Charities Board in early 1999 meant that three new *mentrau iaith* in the north and west of the county could subsequently be established. Menter Bro Dinefwr and Menter Bro Myrddin (covering the Dinefwr area and west Carmarthenshire respectively) came into existence in October 1999 while Menter Bro Teifi (in the Teifi Valley) completed the network in April 2000. The three original *mentrau iaith* and the central co-ordinating body, Mentrau Iaith Myrddin, are funded by grants from the Welsh Language Board and Carmarthenshire County Council.

Although it is far too early to measure the success of this new county framework, early signs suggest that it could develop into an exciting model for successful language intervention. Already a synergy has evolved between the requirements of the local authority's Welsh Language Scheme and the community-based strategy of the *mentrau iaith*. If implemented to its full potential, the impact of the authority's language scheme upon its staff, elected members and the general public will be significant. To this end discussions have taken place between Mentrau Iaith Myrddin and officers and members of some of the key departments which have a direct effect on the health of the language, such as education and community development, economic development and leisure, as well as housing and social services. As these departments are directly responsible for appointing personnel to work in front-line sevices that deal mainly with the public, it is imperative that they are constantly reminded of the needs of the community in terms of language provision. In the context of economic development and housing they can also have an indirect but crucially important influence on the language's well-being.

In conjunction with the county council and Iaith Cyf, which is a Welsh-language consultancy based in Carmarthenshire, talks have been held with some of the main statutory bodies in the area, such as the health authorities, the police, fire brigade and ambulance services, training and enterprise agencies, further and higher education colleges, chambers of commerce and government agencies like Customs and Excise and the Inland Revenue, in an attempt to persuade them to sign language compacts which would commit them to undertake a thorough reappraisal of their language policies. This would include not only the use of Welsh on public displays, brochures and signage but also staff training and recruitment policies. If successful, this would go to the very heart of a purposeful language planning framework.

One advantage of having a centrally co-ordinated network of language initiatives in one county is the possibility of moving personnel who have an expertise or considerable experience in a particular field to work on projects initiated by other *mentrau* or similar organizations. This enables individuals to disseminate information, exchange ideas and to network effectively. This is particularly important in view of the fact that the recently established *mentrau* differ considerably from those operating in Cwm Gwendraeth, the Amman Valley and Llanelli. The fact that they serve a broader geographical area with widely dispersed rural populations, albeit with a relatively high percentage of Welsh speakers, suggests that their approach could be quite different.

Almost in parallel with developments in Carmarthenshire, a large number of new *mentrau iaith* have also been constituted in different parts of Wales, reflecting the keen interest in and enthusiasm for these exciting language enterprise agencies. The fact that eighteen such *mentrau iaith* exist across the whole of Wales, with at least another two in the offing, has led to the creation of a Wales-wide network called Mentrau Iaith Cymru (Language Initiatives of Wales) which meets on a fairly regular basis to share experience and exchange ideas. It is currently in the process of becoming a Limited Company by Guarantee and a registered charity, thus enabling it (and its constituent members) to take advantage of the substantial European Union Structural Funds that are now available under the Objective 1 programme. In conjunction with the Welsh Language Board, it is hoped that the framework provided by the creation of Mentrau Iaith Cymru can stimulate a concerted approach to community-based language planning in Wales.

## EUROPEAN PARALLELS

In order to expand the knowledge base, share experiences and exchange ideas, links have been developed with similar organizations involved with language promotion in Europe. Although no examples exist of the kind of innovative community language planning model developed by *mentrau iaith* in Wales, some interesting parallels have been identified, especially in Catalonia, the Basque Country, Ireland and Friesland. Links have been established through study and exchange visits supported by European Union funding and by attending European and International Conferences on Language Planning. The director of Menter Cwm Gwendraeth has presented papers to various conferences and seminars, stimulating a great deal of interest, on the part of language planners, in the concept of a community-based language initiative.

## WHERE NEXT?

As the nature of society and of local communities changes apace so, too, do the challenges facing language planners. Keeping the balance between consolidation on the one hand and development on the other can sometimes be a difficult exercise. Whilst some projects described in this chapter will continue to play a key role in the interventionist language programme, others will have to make way for new ideas which reflect the ever-changing social, technological, political and environmental trends that impact on the community. The successful organization is one which is able to respond accordingly and effortlessly to these new challenges and be realistic in its aspirations.

In view of these developments, Menter Cwm Gwendraeth and the county-wide network of *mentrau iaith* under the auspices of Mentrau Iaith Myrddin will certainly be focusing on the following domains in the short to medium term as a matter of priority:

- establishing a county-wide network of resource and training centres;
- intensifying the campaign to raise awareness of the importance of language transmission in the home;
- expanding the provision of Welsh-language courses in the workplace;
- further promoting the use of Welsh in the business sector;
- initiating projects to assimilate in-migrants to Welsh-speaking communities;
- marketing the availability of bilingual services and encouraging a change in pattern of use;
- reinforcing established links and developing new partnerships with key sectors, for example, further education, health, social services and economic development;
- realizing the potential of information and computer technology to the advancement of the Welsh language;
- conducting a reappraisal of current Welsh to Adults methodologies;
- sponsoring further research studies on patterns of language use.

## CONCLUSION

Menter Cwm Gwenraeth started off in 1991 as a three-year pilot project aimed at promoting the use of Welsh as a community language. Nobody associated with the initiative at the beginning knew exactly how things would develop or what could be achieved in such a short space of time. It was a journey into the unknown. As no one had previously done anything similar in Wales or for that matter anywhere else in Europe, there were no examples to follow or models to replicate. It meant starting with a blank piece of paper which after a long period of consultation eventually developed into a purposeful strategy for language intervention.

Nine years on, and existing from year to year on a grant allocated by the Welsh Language Board, its achievements have gone beyond the expectations of those who nervously gathered in the early days to consider what could be done to continue with the enthusiasm and support for the language which became evident during the visit of the Urdd (Welsh League of Youth) National Eisteddfod to the area in 1989. Little did they realize at the time that their aspirations would develop into one of the most effective models of language planning seen in Wales in recent years. The success of Menter Cwm Gwendraeth could not have been achieved without the tireless efforts of its extremely dedicated staff, the invaluable guidance and support of the management board and the enthusiastic way that a host of volunteers in the community have responded to the challenge of reviving a language that forms part of their collective inheritance.

In their evaluation of Menter Cwm Gwendraeth, Colin Williams and Jeremy Evas note a number of reasons why the concept of a *menter iaith* is important as a tool for language regeneration.[25]

- In situations which are characterized by strong language potential but have weak sociolinguistic networks, they offer a significant socio-psychological fillip for maintaining the Welsh language in contexts which would otherwise lead to fragmentation.
- They can function as a focus to create a new set of partnerships between the Welsh Assembly, the Welsh Language Board, local authorites, statutory public bodies, the business sector and a variety of voluntary agencies.
- They can initiate novel and pioneering forms of encouraging the use of Welsh and take advantage of social and institutional opportunities as they arise.
- The great strength of *mentrau iaith* is that they seek to serve the needs of the local community and encourage a shared responsibility for the language's future.
- They are viewed as pioneering interventionist agencies which seek to change expectations, create new networks and enable communities to regain ground which they have lost in linguistic terms.
- They are also perceived as worthwhile, cost-effective agencies engaged in the process of community regeneration.

In conclusion, it is too early to judge whether the holistic and innovative approach to community language planning developed by Menter Cwm Gwendraeth and other *mentrau iaith* has the capacity to realize meaningful and long-term gains for the Welsh language, but what is clear is that their existence in recent years has generated a great deal of goodwill and support from all quarters which must bode well for the future of the language.

Colin Williams and Jeremy Evas in their report on the *mentrau iaith* underline their immense potential thus:

> It is a little premature to assess the full impact of the 'Mentrau Iaith' in seeking to regenerate the Welsh language in their respective areas, but one should not underestimate their potential. To date, this is the most effective means of initiating and maintaining a regenerative strategy at the local level. 'Mentrau' are likely to become the key instruments [in Wales] for stabilising linguistic fragmentation in areas where there is a high proportion of Welsh-speakers.[26]

## Notes

[1] Heini Gruffudd, *Y Gymraeg a Phobl Ifainc* (Adran Addysg Barhaus i Oedolion, Prifysgol Cymru, Abertawe, 1996).

[2] Colin H. Williams and Jeremy Evas, *The Community Research Project* (Cardiff: Bwrdd yr Iaith Gymraeg/Welsh Language Board, 1997).

[3] Einar Haugen, 'Language fragmentation in Scandinavia: revolt of the minorities', in Haugen, E., McClure, J. D. and Thomson, D., *Minority Languages Today* (Edinburgh: Edinburgh University Press, 1981), p. 114.

[4] M. L. Huffries, 'Pennsylvanian German: maintenance and shift', in J. A. Fishman (ed.), *Readings in the Sociology of Language* (The Hague: Mouton de Gruyter, 1968).

[5] Josuah A. Fishman, *Reversing Language Shift* (Clevedon, Avon: Multilingual Matters, 1991), p. 14.

[6] John Edwards, *What is Language Revival?*, Proceedings of a conference on 'Language Planning' in Galicia (Santiago de Compostella: Galicia, 1991).

[7] N. Glazer, 'The process and problems of language maintenance', in J. Fishman (ed.), *Language Loyalty in the United States* (The Hague: Mouton, 1966), p. 63.

[8] R. Kaplan and G. Baldauf, *Language Planning* (Clevedon: Multilingual Matters, 1997), p. 9.

[9] Fishman, *Reversing Language Shift*, p. 6.

[10] Cefin Campbell, *Strategaeth Menter Cwm Gwendraeth Strategy* (Cross Hands: Menter Cwm Gwendraeth, 1991), p. 16.

[11] Adam Price, Caitríona Ó Torna and Allan Wynne Jones, *The Diversity Dividend* (Brussels: European Bureau for Lesser Used Languages, 1997), p. 20.

[12] Marc Classon, 'Language culture and enterprise', in A. Price (ed.), *Quiet Revolution?* (Aberystwyth: Menter a Busnes, 1994), p. 13.

[13] Carmel Gahan, *Agweddau at Menter a Busnes ymysg Siaradwyr Cymraeg* (Aberystwyth: Menter a Busnes, 1989) and Beaufort Research, *Agweddau Tuag at Fusnes ymysg Siaradwyr Cymraeg* (Aberystwyth: Menter a Busnes, 1993).

[14] Cefin Campbell, *Alliance*, 1(1), Gwendraeth Valley Healthy Community Project (1997), p. 3.

[15] 'People in communities: a programme to tackle social exclusion in Wales', Welsh Office Circular 24/98, Cardiff (1998).

[16] Fishman, *Reversing Language Shift*, p. 36.

[17] Colin H. Williams, *Community Language Planning* (Cardiff: University of Wales Press, 1997), p. 25.

[18] Fishman, *Reversing Language Shift*, p. 43.

[19] Colin Baker, *Intergenerational Transfer in the Home* (Cardiff: Bwrdd yr Iaith Gymraeg/Welsh Language Board, 1998).

[20] Fishman, *Reversing Language Shift*, p. 16.

[21] J. Aitchinson and H. Carter, *The Welsh Language Today* (Cardiff: University of Wales Press, 1985).

[22] Williams and Evas, *Community Research Project*.

[23] Ruth Morgan, 'Gwerthuso Menter Cwm Gwendraeth', M.Phil. dissertation, University College of Wales, Lampeter, 2000.

[24] Tracey A. Morgan, 'Y Gymraeg mewn busnes yng Nghwm Gwendraeth', M.Phil. dissertation, University College of Wales, Swansea, 1996.

[25] Williams and Evas, *Community Research Project*, pp. 26–7.

[26] Ibid., p. 26.

# 10

# Declining Density: A Danger For The Language?[1]
## JEREMY EVAS

The late twentieth century witnessed a substantial boost in the fortunes of the Welsh language (and, paradoxically, an enormous decrease in the number of those able to speak it). As we saw in Chapter 1, the Welsh language was subject to several enhancements of its legal and official status (with the Welsh Courts Act 1942 and the Language Acts of 1967 and 1993), its place in the mass media has also been secured (with the founding of S4C in 1982, and its digital offshoot in 1998). Coupled with these welcome developments, the number of school-children learning Welsh as a second language has increased apace (mainly as a result of the 1988 Education Act, which made Welsh a compulsory subject in all the schools of Wales). Moreover, the number of adults learning Welsh *ab initio*, or improving their grasp of the language, is also increasing at breakneck speed. Nevertheless, not all is well; a cursory glance at governmental survey results (for example, Welsh Office, 1995) affords a better understanding of the demographics of Welsh-speaking Wales. The story is well-known, the draining of the heartlands and the collapse of Welsh's community base: very familiar. The statistics have been thoroughly analysed by Aitchison and Carter (1994). It would only serve further to depress advocates of bilingualism by reproducing them here. Or would it? Is this change mere challenge rather than sheer threat?

According to the 1995 Welsh Office survey, the pyramid of linguistic decline is being inverted. For example, 32.4 per cent of the population between three and fifteen years of age are Welsh speakers, in comparison with 24.2 per cent of those over sixty-five and barely 17 per cent of those between thirty and forty-four. However, only 8.6 per cent of this youngest age group has Welsh as its mother tongue, in comparison with 18.9 per cent of the older age group.[2] It must be emphasized from the outset that scant comfort should be taken from these absolute figures.

In this chapter it is alleged that second-language speakers of Welsh, who form around 47 per cent of Welsh speakers (according to Welsh Office, 1995), are less likely to use their linguistic skills. If so, this is a true barrier against bilingualism. The hope of a fully bilingual Wales, and not merely one with passively bilingual citizens, is pie in the sky if the language is merely a badge of identity, not an actively used medium of communication.

There is no one panacea for all the barriers to the creation of a bilingual country. Linguistic plans and ventures must be bespoke for the particular linguistic situations which can differ enormously from place to place. The research presented in this chapter analyses the linguistic make-up of the Teifi Valley, a high-density Welsh-language speech area, in the traditional 'Bro Gymraeg' or heartland of the language. In so doing, it will touch upon a rather neglected target group within academic language planning activity in Wales, namely those who do not speak the language being planned. Very many of the steps taken to promote Welsh affect non-Welsh speakers, and bearing their importance in mind, we should consider the caveats raised by G. A. Williams (1985: 294).[3] Some non-Welsh-speaking commentators (for example, C. A. Davies, 1997a, 1997b; and even some who *do* speak the language, such as T. I. Williams, 1997) see the prosperity of the language as the fruit of the efforts of a linguistic cabal, a metro-politan élite or a 'Taffia'; their accusation being that citizens are quasi-oppressed into learning the language.[4] This is empirically disproved in Evas (1999). Their concerns do, however, reflect the fact that second-language speakers are becom-ing increasingly important as time goes on. For example, unpublished govern-mental statistical estimates show that the growth in the number of Welsh speakers will continue, and even accelerate well into the next century.

Many things have changed for Welsh; it is, by now, an urban as well as – if not more than – a rural language (see Jobbins, 1999b). It is on the increase in some areas and in decline in others. I shall now examine this contradictory situation in one area that contains some of the communities with the highest percentages of Welsh speakers in Wales.

## BACKGROUND TO THE RESEARCH

One of the main obstacles facing many lesser used languages is that the ability to use them at the micro level cannot be taken for granted. Consequently, in those areas where such assumptions *can* be made, conservation of the language is of the utmost significance. The Teifi Valley is one such area. This chapter's findings are based on a research project published in full in Williams and Evas (1997). The research brief was to analyse the linguistic situation of the region, elucidating 'weak spots' which interventionist language planning could then target. The area experienced a substantial change in its demographic base during the last two decades of the twentieth century and this change, which includes a large influx of people who do not speak the local language and the departure of many Welsh-speaking natives, has caused much worry for the future of the language in the area.

## WELSH IN THE TEIFI VALLEY AREA

According to the latest census figures (1991), 43.7 per cent of the population of Dyfed (which contained the Teifi Valley at the time this research was carried out) spoke Welsh. As a result of the comparatively high immigration rate to some areas in the county, this figure had dropped by 3.1 per cent during the previous decade, a higher percentage drop than the all-Wales figure. Despite this, Dyfed County Council (1994) stated that it was in these very areas that the highest success rates were to be had for those who were brought up as non-Welsh speakers but who now spoke the language. In Ceredigion, in the heart of the study area, 12.9 per cent of the Welsh speakers were born outside Wales. It is not evident where these people acquired their Welsh, but much of their success in language acquisition can be attributed to the compulsory education system. However, as shall be seen below, mere knowledge of a language is not synonymous with its use, even where the opportunity to use it exists. Once again, we should not take solace from absolute figures, as such oversimplification takes no account of the contributory mental, sociological and psychological factors. Notwithstanding this, it would appear that the foundations for further bilingualism in the county are quite firm, as the percentage of Welsh-speaking five to fifteen year olds (49.5 per cent, compared with 41.5 in 1981) is *higher* than the raw figure for all Welsh speakers in the county (43.7 per cent). As noted above, much of this can be attributed to the compulsory education system but, as we shall see below, it would be foolish to entrust the task of linguistic regeneration to the school system *alone*.

## RESEARCH RESULTS

The aim of this chapter is not to reproduce empirical statistics; rather, the aim is to portray the 'big picture' of the language in the area. Readers interested in the finer details may consult the entire research findings at http://www.cardiff. ac.uk/cymraeg/ymchwil/.

### Age of respondents

The study was undertaken in 1996 and the 219 respondents in the sample were drawn from the resident population of the Teifi Valley (for details see Williams and Evas, 1997). The majority of the sample (77 per cent) were born since 1940 and this age group contains three-quarters of the second-language speakers of Welsh. Very many of these second-language speakers are about to reach child-bearing age and, consequently, the current period is a most significant period for the linguistic balance of the region. Williams and Evas (1997) recommended that concrete steps should be taken to ensure that the children of this group become fluent in Welsh and have every opportunity to use Welsh socially outside the home. Appropriate linguistic provision must also be made available for future parents as a matter of urgency, whilst remembering Fishman's (*passim*) all-important language reproduction *nexus* between parent and child.[5]

## Language of the home and the workplace

The research aimed to create a picture of language use in the study area, starting with those locales where most time is spent, namely the home and the workplace. As Figure 10.1 shows, of all Welsh-speaking respondents, only those who were mother-tongue speakers spoke only Welsh in their workplace. Of Welsh-speakers, 28.6 per cent spoke Welsh and English equally, while 18.8 per cent spoke English most often at work.

The facile conclusion to be drawn from this is that those most likely to use Welsh are the mother-tongue speakers, and that those who have Welsh as a second language are less likely to use the language. Moreover, it is evident that the second-language group contains a wide range of linguistic competence, and it is axiomatic that language use depends upon the availability of fellow speakers in any given sphere. This is surely the reason why Glyn Williams (1992) is so critical of the 'domain' concept: it is inherently a static and restrictive notion. Notwithstanding this, the low levels of workplace language use in an area where the density of speakers is so high, especially for the second-language group, creates real concerns for any language planning initiatives. The socio-psychological implications for language planners are explicit in these figures. It must be emphasized that education, acceptance and socialization procedures for new speakers of minority languages are of paramount importance, and that the current lack of these is one of the major barriers to the further promotion of bilingualism. The research findings relating to the language of the home serve only to reinforce this general point.

According to the results shown in Figure 10.1, 51.4 per cent of Welsh speakers speak only Welsh at home but again, of this group, 98.8 per cent have Welsh as their first language. Patently, the results of the second-language group become more obvious on analysing the results of those who tend to speak more English at home: 11.8 per cent of the Welsh-speaking respondents are in this group, but

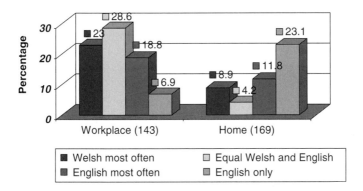

**Figure 10.1. Language use of Welsh-speaking respondents in the
home and the workplace**

the vast majority of them (75 per cent) are second-language speakers. An unpalatable truth for some is that a small, but significant, number of mother-tongue Welsh speakers also tend to speak English at home.

## Ease of use of Welsh and language preferences

Often, it is a lack of confidence or ownership of a lesser used language which is responsible for its non-reproduction. In this section, I will analyse the linguistic difficulties which the respondents experience when performing a number of language-related tasks. Such difficulties may contribute to a speaker's lack of self-esteem and to the far too common opinion that 'my Welsh/Basque/Breton/ Friesian isn't "good enough"', a self-deprecating comment typically heard in lesser used language speech communities. Respondents were asked to record the difficulty they faced on a three-point scale. The results, which are shown in Table 10.1, are presented first for mother-tongue Welsh speakers, and secondly, in brackets, for second-language speakers. There are substantial differences between the two groups' answers.

Once again, less favourable results are reported for the second-language group. Its respondents have more trouble in all nine situations. On average, 34.2 per cent of the second-language group were in the 'no difficulty' column, compared with 76.6 per cent of the mother-tongue respondents; 53.8 per cent of the second-language speakers had some trouble, compared with 16.9 per cent of the mother-tongue group and 12 per cent of second-language speakers had much difficulty, compared with 5.4 per cent of the mother-tongue speakers. It is obviously no surprise to find that the second-language speakers are that much less confident in their Welsh than their fellow first-language respondents, but more worrying than this is the lack of any supportive framework within the area

**Table 10.1. Self-evaluation of difficulty of performing tasks in Welsh (second-language group in brackets)**

| Task | N= | No difficulty % | Some difficulty % | Much difficulty % |
|---|---|---|---|---|
| Pronunciation | 110 (55) | 90.9 (43.9) | 5.4 (52.7) | 3.6 (4.3) |
| Making yourself understood | 112 (55) | 85.7 (32.7) | 8.9 (61.8) | 5.3 (5.5) |
| Speaking correctly | 113 (55) | 77.0 (20) | 17.7 (69) | 5.3 (10.9) |
| Using new words | 112 (55) | 64.2 (27.2) | 32.1 (60) | 3.5 (5.5) |
| Expressing what you mean | 112 (55) | 86.6 (38.2) | 9.8 (56.3) | 3.5 (5.5) |
| Thinking quickly enough to keep up with conversations | 112 (55) | 89.2 (41.8) | 6.3 (40) | 4.2 (18.1) |
| Finding correct words for special topics | 112 (55) | 53.6 (14.5) | 36.6 (58.2) | 9.8 (27.2) |
| Getting used to accents/ dialects in Welsh | 112 (55) | 72.3 (43.6) | 20.5 (43.6) | 7.1 (12.7) |
| Dealing with the Welsh in this questionnaire | 111 (52) | 79.2 (46.1) | 14.4 (42.3) | 6.3 (11.5) |

which could build on the existing second-language foundations. The foundations of the mother-tongue group are sound, although there is room to improve on them. These results call for skilled acquisition planning in the area. In this respect, the Welsh Language Board's call for a National Co-ordination Centre for this activity on the macro level, following the example of movements such as HABE in the Basque country (Welsh Language Board, 1999) is to be welcomed. Sadly, central government funding for this much-needed initiative has yet to be realized.

The research project also analysed actual micro-level use of Welsh in the community. One of the main findings – which provoked criticism of the authors in the media – was that there was scant opportunity for use of Welsh in key support sectors, for example, in encounters with doctors, dentists, health visitors, police and local shops. Strategic consideration of the fieldwork results led Williams and Evas to state the need for language planning in the following fields in the Teifi Valley:

- normalization of the concept of bilingual service provision;
- promotion of the idea of 'Welsh in the workplace';
- preparation of official documents in Welsh which are as understandable as their English equivalents (a 'Plain Welsh Campaign');[6]
- convincing companies and other bodies that they are part of a wide strategy for the revitalization of Welsh.

This last point would entail their making comprehensive provision for customers, ensuring that their staff have every opportunity to become fluent in Welsh, either via language 'polishing' courses (*cyrsiau gloywi iaith*) for those unsure of its written form, or by teaching the language *ab initio* to those who do not speak it, and, very importantly – within a neglected group – retrieving semi-speakers, that is, those with passive knowledge of a language, or those exposed to a language during childhood, but never directly addressed in it. One way of facilitating these programmes would be to vary tax rates for companies engaged in various language promotion schemes (see below). It is also evident that much work is needed into the myriad forms of marketing and bilingual economic activity, all connected with the process of language reproduction.

In such high-density speech communities as the Teifi Valley, it is possible to build upon strong linguistic foundations, but how long these foundations will last without interventionist language planning is a matter for further debate. For example, it is encouraging to note that 95.4 per cent of the mother-tongue group spoke Welsh at least half the time with colleagues, but it is less encouraging to note that only 79 per cent spoke Welsh to their superiors. Those speaking Welsh over half the time with the doctor fell to 68.7 per cent, with only half this group speaking Welsh on all occasions – one of the lowest figures for the mother-tongue group. Similar usage patterns obtained for interaction with dentists: 54.5 per cent of the mother-tongue speakers spoke Welsh to the dentist over half the time, but only 31.8 per cent all the time. It was not possible to ascertain concretely whether lack of linguistic confidence in formal/significant situations was responsible for mother-tongue Welsh speakers using English in this sphere, or whether it reflected a lack of Welsh-speaking staff. Anecdotal evidence suggested that a lack of Welsh-speaking staff was responsible for these different language usage patterns. In such a Welsh-speaking area, medical and dental treatment should be made available in Welsh wherever it is practically possible. If training programmes in non-violent communication skills (NVC) were started to encourage proaction on the part of those staff that are Welsh-speaking, then maybe the pitifully low percentages of the second-language group who speak Welsh could be increased.[7] At present, most second-language speakers use only or mainly English with doctors and dentists. Notwithstanding this, the percentages of Welsh speakers of all types who speak Welsh with the receptionists of doctors and dentists is markedly higher, which would suggest a paucity of Welsh-speaking staff in the senior levels of the health service.

## LACK OF OPPORTUNITY TO USE WELSH

Although a high proportion of the residents of the study area are able to speak Welsh, they do not, or they do not get the opportunity to, do so everywhere in society, as was seen in the last section. During the preparation stage of the research, anecdotal comments suggested that there was much less opportunity to use Welsh than might have been expected, given the high percentage of speakers in the area. The questionnaire examined these assertions in respect of language-related behaviour, the membership of social clubs in the region, and two rather more abstract elements: the repondents' enjoyment of life and their rights as citizens.

Of the mother-tongue respondents, 78.3 per cent felt that the lack of opportunity to use Welsh had a general effect on their language behaviour, and 84 per cent of the second-language group felt this. These figures fuel the argument that, in lesser used language circles, 'supply creates demand', rather than the axiomatic converse. Further justification for this presupposition will be examined later. For the interim it is significant that similar proportions of respondents felt the effects of a lack of opportunity for use on their self-confidence in using the language in public (64.8 per cent mother-tongue, 73.8 per cent second-language). However, the lack of opportunity impeded the reading habits of respondents less (62.7 per cent mother-tongue and 69.1 per cent second-language). The results for written use of Welsh revealed a similar pattern (63.2 per cent of first-language respondents and 69.1 per cent of second language felt this effect). However, the lack of opportunity to use Welsh impinged less on respondents' enjoyment of life (61.4 per cent first-language and 44.5 per cent second-language).

The most significant statistics of this section, and among the most important in the whole research project, were gleaned from a final question. The vast majority of mother-tongue respondents (72.5 per cent) and exactly half of the second-language cohort felt that the lack of opportunities to use the Welsh language had a direct bearing on their rights as citizens. This finding has far-reaching implications, and can be used to convince others of the need for further bilingual provision; it is indeed an extra motivation for the area's fledgling language planners to expand their work. The key implication emerging from these results is that the civil rights of the respondents have been neglected for too long – and this is likely to be a significant political issue in the near future.

The replies of second-language speakers to the civil rights question would suggest that Welsh does not *touch* them in the same way as it does mother-tongue speakers, in other words they feel a 'lack of ownership' for the language. This sentiment must be addressed, especially when one considers the all-important fact that the majority of the second-language group are about to reach child-bearing age. The fact that the region is facing a critical transformation in its linguistic balance cannot be overemphasized.

The *leitmotif* of this section is that the lack of opportunity to use the Welsh language produces a lack of confidence in its use in those situations where language choice is actually available. This vicious circle could easily be broken by increasing the presence of Welsh and the concomitant opportunities for its use in every possible situation. This is the basic premise of the Catherine Wheel eruditely presented by Strubell (1997) and should serve as a useful heuristic device for language policy-makers in the region.

### Future choices: what is to be done?

The respondents were asked to assess the relevance of several statements which related to issues which interventionist language planning could change within the Teifi Valley. Fieldwork interviews revealed that mother-tongue speakers felt an acute lack of opportunity to speak face to face with the staff of the local council in Welsh, and that no firm policy of language tuition was implemented in the council.

The high density of Welsh speakers in the valley is reflected in the number of respondents who believe that most people who work in the local council should speak Welsh or agree to learn it (see Figure 10.2: all respondents are included in the figures, regardless of linguistic ability, that is, these include the answers of non-Welsh-speaking respondents): 80.2 per cent of the total sample agrees with the statement the 'everyone working in the local council in this area should speak Welsh or agree to learn it' (96.5 per cent of the mother-tongue Welsh speakers and 69.1 per cent of the second-language group). This is an undeniable call for an increase in language provision in the local councils of the study area.

After examining this basic linguistic provision, the questionnaire then asked about bilingualism in the world of advertising, to ascertain to what degree the respondents felt that 'all types of advertising should be in Welsh or bilingual in my area'. Once again there was strong support for the concept of bilingual

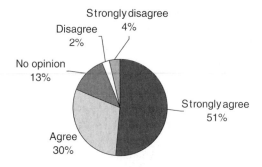

**Figure 10.2. Everyone working in the local council in this area should speak Welsh or agree to learn it**

advertising, a key element in the linguistic landscape which can create a positive effect on the public's perception of a language (see, for example, Bourhis, 1984). At the time this survey was held, the majority of Teifi Valley advertising, whether in newspapers, on posters or signs, was in English only. A monolingual linguistic landscape in a bilingual area can affect ethnolinguistic vitality negatively by depreciating one of the two languages. Of the entire sample, 73.1 per cent agreed with the statement that 'all types of advertising should be in Welsh or bilingual in my area' (91.3 per cent of the mother-tongue speakers, 58.2 per cent of the second-language group). A small group of 5.5 per cent disagreed with the statement, the majority of its members being non-Welsh-speaking.

The questionnaire then analysed a more unfamiliar and possibly more controversial issue in the British context. This concerned the contention that variations in company tax bands for those organizations which promoted active bilingualism could be extremely useful for the production of Welsh in the workplace. We

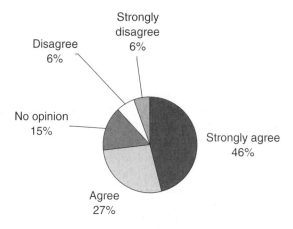

**Figure 10.3. All types of advertising should be in Welsh or bilingual in this area**

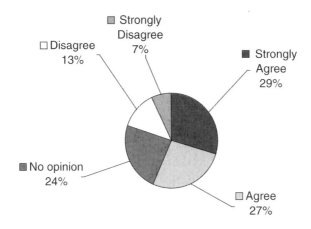

**Figure 10.4. Small companies should receive a reduction in their tax bills for offering bilingual services**

know that the economy in general, and the workplace in particular, is a critical location for the development of new Welsh speakers and the sustenance of those present speakers who have no connection with the language in other spheres (C. H. Williams, 1999b). In addition, this is an extremely effective device for developing a bilingual linguistic landscape where monolingualism has been the norm. It has been used in other bilingual societies after a long history of *de facto* monolingualism, such as Quebec and Catalonia. In fact, the frequent complaints in relation to the over-zealous Quebecois 'tongue trooper' language police are often unaware of the fact that the provincial government paid for large parts of the linguistic measures it imposed, through tax relief.

In the Teifi Valley, the unfamiliar nature of changing the tax system in favour of bilingualism affected the level of support such a measure received. Notwithstanding this, 56.5 per cent of the sample agreed that small companies should receive concessions on tax bills in order to offer services in Welsh (73.6 per cent of mother-tongue respondents and 38.9 per cent of the second-language group, but only 29.3 per cent of the non-Welsh-speaking groups). If a comparison is made between this and the previous statement in this section, it will be seen that larger proportions of each group noted that they had no opinion on this matter; 19.9 per cent of the sample disagreed with the statement (over half these were non-Welsh-speaking). Time after time the project elicited answers in a worryingly segmented fashion: the entire Teifi Valley community is not convinced that increasing the status of Welsh is a good thing. This suggests that more socio-psychological research is needed here to ascertain whether opponents of bilingualism feel under threat from advances in Welsh because they may have experienced enmity from native Welsh speakers. The project concluded that it was essential that skilled marketing techniques be employed

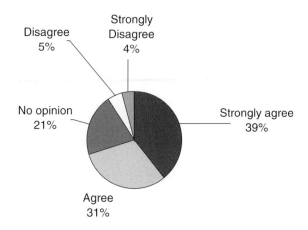

**Figure 10.5. It is important that Welsh is considered in the planning
process in my area**

when planning pragmatic strategies to ease/assuage these tensions at the micro
level.

It is likely that the lower levels of support for the varying of the taxation
system in favour of bilingualism were obtained because of possible controversial
connotations. If this is true then the answers to the subsequent question were
even more noteworthy. In 1995, shortly before this research project was
launched, another controversial issue flared up in Ceredigion, the district in
which the study area is located. This concerned the place of the Welsh language
in housing policy and local planning, issues which had been debated at length
by the Welsh Language Society.[8] The society had drafted a detailed agenda for a
Property Act to protect the fabric of communities experiencing population shift.
The society considered that urgent attention should be given to satisfying local
housing needs out of existing housing stock, rather than initiating new housing
developments. It has harshly criticized Tai Cymru (Welsh Housing, a quasi-
autonomous non-governmental organization, quango) that it sees as creating
unneeded new housing whilst paying no attention to the local housing stock. It
also argues that the number of holiday homes in Wales (up to 20 per cent of the
entire housing stock in Meirionnydd and Dwyfor and up to 40 per cent in some
zones of those areas) should be reduced (Welsh Language Society, 1992b: 3). It is
patently unjust that in many Welsh villages (as in the English Lake District, and
in other parts of Europe) local residents cannot afford to stay, or cannot find suitable housing, although high proportions of the houses are empty for the majority of the year. The society therefore believes that dwellings should be controlled
by statute. It is evident that the attendant depopulation and migrant influx,
which is so typical of such situations, can affect the inherent character of an area,
of which the local language and culture is an integral part.

Ceredigion District Council, which had authority over most of the study area at the time the research was carried out, was one of the few authorities in Wales to attempt to implement planning regulations in order to defend the community base of the language. Their plans were much exposed in the media in 1995; and withdrawn only to be reintroduced, with a new veneer, in 1997 by the new Ceredigion Unitary Authority. Despite its controversial nature, it would nevertheless appear that the majority of the sample agrees with the statement that it 'is important that Welsh is considered in the planning process in my area' (90.3 per cent of the mother-tongue respondents, 50.9 per cent of the second-language group, and 43.8 per cent of the non-Welsh speakers). A small minority (9.2 per cent) disagrees with the statement, and 65 per cent of this group are non-Welsh speaking. The influx of non-Welsh speakers, or 'mewnlifiad', the loaded Welsh term for this phenomenon, is an important issue in the Teifi Valley and the difference between language groups' responses to this statement could be proof of this and a sign of the micro-level tension in the area. Of course, if planning rules had been tightened, many of the non-Welsh-speaking group may not have been allowed to settle in the area in the first place.

Until recently, the high percentage of Welsh speakers in the Teifi Valley area enabled the inhabitants to live their lives on the local level almost entirely through the medium of Welsh. However, for several years, this has not been so easy. Paradoxically, while the number of high-percentage Welsh-speaking communities is decreasing, it is generally recognized that the status of Welsh is increasing in many other non-geographically based spheres, and that this could bring in its train more opportunities to use Welsh in situations hitherto unconnected with the language. This is what the next section of the questionnaire examined by reference to a number of contact situations.

On the one hand, the percentage of first-language Welsh speakers who state that they would use more Welsh if opportunities were increased (an average of 56.6 per cent) is larger than the percentage of those who would use the same amount (40.9 per cent). On the other hand, 2.5 per cent of mother-tongue respondents stated that they would use less Welsh if more bilingual opportunities were offered. The figures for the second-language group are far less encouraging: on average, only 23.1 per cent would use more Welsh if they had the chance, and the vast majority would use the same amount; 10.3 per cent of the second-language group would use less Welsh! Here again we see evidence of the second-language group's less favourable attitude towards the language, and the need to encompass every group in efforts to promote Welsh.

It also appears that new speakers could be gained for the language if the opportunities for the use of Welsh were increased. A small percentage of the non-Welsh-speaking group (3.6 per cent) not included in Table 10.2 stated that they would increase their use of the language if they were able to.

All the above statistics prove that there is indeed fertile ground for promoting the use of Welsh in the Teifi Valley area. Although substantial percentages of the first-language respondents state that they would not avail themselves of

Table 10.2.  The percentage of Welsh-speaking respondents who would use more or less Welsh if they were able (second-language group in brackets)

| | N= | More Welsh | About the same amount | Less Welsh |
|---|---|---|---|---|
| Local authority officials | 109 (54) | 63.3 (25.9) | 35.8 (64.8) | 0.9 (9.3) |
| Local councillors | 109 (54) | 62.4 (24.1) | 36.7 (66.7) | 0.9 (9.3) |
| Member of Parliament | 108 (54) | 62.0 (20.4) | 37.0 (70.4) | 0.9 (9.3) |
| Post Office | 113 (54) | 61.9 (27.8) | 36.3 (61.1) | 1.8 (11.1) |
| Small private businesses | 110 (54) | 54.5 (24.1) | 43.6 (64.8) | 1.8 (11.1) |
| Banks | 113 (55) | 54.0 (23.6) | 44.2 (67.3) | 1.8 (9.1) |
| Supermarkets | 112 (54) | 61.6 (29.6) | 36.6 (63) | 1.8 (7.4) |
| Insurance | 110 (55) | 52.7 (16.4) | 42.7 (70.9) | 4.5 (12.7) |
| Public transport | 109 (54) | 57.8 (29.6) | 40.4 (64.8) | 1.8 (5.6) |
| Large shops | 112 (55) | 62.5 (30.9) | 34.8 (60) | 2.7 (9.1) |
| Garages | 110 (46) | 59.1 (25.9) | 39.1 (64.8) | 1.8 (9.3) |
| Building societies | 111 (55) | 55.0 (20) | 42.3 (69.1) | 2.7 (10.9) |
| Hospitals | 113 (54) | 58.4 (20.4) | 39.8 (66.7) | 1.8 (13) |
| Directory Enquiries | 111 (46) | 56.8 (22.2) | 40.5 (64.8) | 2.7 (13) |
| Police | 111 (54) | 56.8 (24.1) | 40.5 (68.5) | 2.7 (7.4) |
| Inland Revenue | 108 (55) | 50.0 (18.2) | 43.5 (70.9) | 6.5 (10.9) |
| Travel agents | 108 (54) | 50.9 (22.2) | 45.4 (68.5) | 3.7 (9.3) |
| Fire service | 110 (54) | 52.7 (22.2) | 44.5 (68.5) | 2.7 (9.3) |
| DHSS | 107 (54) | 45.8 (16.7) | 49.5 (68.5) | 4.7 (14.8) |
| Ambulance service | 108 (54) | 53.7 (18.5) | 44.4 (68.5) | 1.9 (13) |

increased opportunities which language planning should bring in its wake, the majority of this group are still minded to use more of the language. It is true to note, that, as may be expected from previous results, the second-language group is not so enthusiastic to change its language usage patterns.

## CONCLUSION

The community foundations of the Welsh language in the Teifi Valley are amongst the strongest in Wales. Despite this comparative strength, they are facing many threats and many barriers to their further development. One of the main threats is the influx of non-Welsh-speaking families and individuals to the area, and an outflow of native Welsh speakers. The majority of the incomers in the sample discussed above are not, as the story often goes, of retirement age, and many of them have moved to the Teifi Valley area from other parts of Wales and not from England. The education system in its present form does its best to cymricize the children of incomers, but the second-language speakers produced as a result of these valiant efforts, as seen time and again above, have a tendency to feel less ownership of the language than do their fellow respondents who speak Welsh as a first language. This recent second-language phenomenon offers a great challenge to language planners in the Teifi Valley, a challenge which needs to be speedily met, in order to encourage those second-language speakers to bring up their children in Welsh – or at the very least to transmit positive attitudes about the language to them. It should be emphasized that the second-language grouping in the sample is relatively young; exactly half of them were born after 1975. As noted above, these people are of child-bearing age, and the need for tailor-made language planning provision for them cannot be overemphasized. Another fact which could cause headaches for those who wish to reverse the weakening of Welsh in the community is the number of adults who are in the process of learning the language. Of a non-Welsh-speaking population of 153,042 in Dyfed, only 2,606 registered for adult Welsh language classes at *any* level in 1992–3 (the latest figures available at the time of research). To put a finer point on this statistic, only 1.7 per cent of the non-Welsh-speaking population are learning Welsh – and it can be taken for granted that the vast majority (up to 94 per cent according to Asher, 1977) of language learners will abandon their lessons before attaining fluency, whether they are involved the crucial process of child-rearing or not.

While undertaking fieldwork in the Teifi Valley, the researchers witnessed hardly any direct marketing of the Welsh language. Such marketing has had great success in Catalonia and Quebec, and this could greatly contribute to the ethno-linguistic vitality of the Welsh language in both this and other areas. Williams and Evas (1997) argued for a much-needed, and long-overdue language marketing strategy for the area which should concentrate on the following elements:

- educating the non-Welsh-speaking population in the Teifi Valley about the importance of the language and its traditions;
- attracting new speakers to Welsh;
- changing behaviour patterns and the attitudes of native speakers and encouraging integrative behaviour towards learners;
- emphasizing the use of Welsh in official spheres as a completely natural, taken-for-granted act;
- encouraging a proactive, rather than reactive, attitude towards the language in the business sphere.

It is evident that the local schools should play an important part in the promotion of the necessary mind-set for all the above measures. However, it is in these very schools that the root of some of the area's linguistic problems are to be found – for example, the existence of secondary schools which are, to all intents and purposes, English-medium schools in such a highly Welsh-speaking community is deleterious at several levels. A minority of mother-tongue Welsh speakers are taught through the medium of English in these schools, and some of these pupils complain that they do not feel part of the wider Welsh-language social networks in the area. The second-language Welsh-speaking pupils in these schools do not have sufficient opportunity to be immersed in a completely Welsh-language atmosphere.

The research ascertained that the second-language group tended more towards English both in their homes and in their workplaces, and that a substantial proportion of the non-Welsh speakers had no Welsh speakers in their homes. If we are serious in our approach to planning the future for Welsh as a community language of any character, these problems must be tackled immediately, or the language will continue its slow ebb in the area, and linguistic ignorance will grow ineluctably.

During the fieldwork in the Teifi Valley, several anecdotes regarding tension between linguistic groups were noted, and several of those interviewed insinuated that two parallel communities were developing in the area, one Welsh-speaking, the other English. Such a situation is neither desirable nor productive for the future of the language in the area. Consequently there is an urgent need for post-intervention evaluation, while socio-psychologically sound research cannot be overemphasized in the field of language planning.

Non-reproduction of language continues to be a small, but significant problem here according to the statistics which the research collected – and if linguistic exogamy continues in the area, it can only be concluded that this problem will grow. For whatever reason, 22.2 per cent of mother-tongue respondents' eldest children in the Teifi Valley sample are less fluent in Welsh than their parents. Without a sound framework to re-energize the language in the area, it cannot be sure that these children will reach the same level of fluency as their parents, or that their offspring will ever become as fluent as their grandparents. If there is no intervention in the process of language reproduction in the area, there will be an ever-decreasing spiral of language loss. This *can* be prevented.

Although there are many elements in the linguistic situation of the Teifi Valley which are perturbing for language planners, there is considerable potential to improve the penetration of Welsh to more locations in the area. Indeed, the majority of mother-tongue speakers in the area had no difficulty in performing a given list of tasks in a number of situations in Welsh (although, understandably, the second-language group fared somewhat worse). Following this encouraging statistic, the survey results reveal that there would be much more use of the Welsh language if its status were increased. Over half the first-language respondents and 30.2 per cent of the second-language group said they would use more Welsh if opportunities were available. This is connected to the answers received regarding the effects of the lack of opportunity to use Welsh – 78.3 per cent of the first-language respondents and 84 per cent of the second-language groups found that the lack of opportunity affected their general use of Welsh, a suggestion, perhaps, that supply indeed does create demand. In these days where Citizens' Charters reign supreme, it was most significant to note that large groups of Welsh speakers in the area felt that the lack of opportunity to use Welsh affected their rights as citizens.

The respondents showed strong support for increasing the ability of the staff in local councils to speak Welsh. The majority of the sample believed that the language should be considered as an integral element of the planning process and there was considerable support for reducing the taxes of those companies which offered services bilingually. Cross-tablulation of these answers by language group proved that the supportive respondents in this respect were the first-language speakers, and the non-Welsh-speaking groups were less supportive of such measures. It is therefore fair to say that a special campaign for the hearts and minds of these people is needed if the revitalization movement is to encompass the entire community in the area.

Doubtless there is a way of building on the sound linguistic foundations and securing them for the future by intervening in sociolinguistic processes in the area. The changes being experienced by the Welsh language in the area are not all negative factors, merely a challenge for all members of the community to deal with. The language needs to be made attractive to those who can already speak it, and to the growing monoglot English-speaking minority in the area. One of the main reasons for the worries over the language's future is the lack of provision for it, and not lack of will on the part of its speakers. There was considerable agreement that the profile of Welsh should increase in the area and, in this respect, there was a great desire to see the establishment of a *menter iaith* (language initiative/agency) in the area along the lines discussed in Chapters 4 and 5 above. Such an agency, Menter Teifi, was launched in September 2000.

One all-important way of increasing bilingual provision is the creation of a meso- and micro-level framework for increasing bilingualism, that is to say, the implementation of the civil rights implications which came as a consequence of the statutory Welsh Language Act (1993). The core of this social change should be the deepening of the superficial bilingualism already in existence and its extension to the workplace and the private sector. In addition, if public services are at all serious in their response to bilingual policy guidelines, then they should *offer* a bilingual service to the customer without giving the impression that it is a compromise won by compulsion.

There would be a large welcome for an organization to re-energize the Welsh language in the Teifi Valley on the micro level, to meet the changes currently occurring on the meso and macro levels. Such an organization would be a great boost for Welsh, a fine way to harness the potential mentioned above, and – if it were effectively managed – a means of bridging between different groups of the community and promoting Welsh in the area. Although incomers are not the only target group for the spreading of Welsh, it is of paramount importance that we consider the full range of needs of the non-Welsh-speaking groups in the area. Members of these groups must be welcomed into the Welsh-speaking community in order to eliminate sociolinguistic ignorance and suspicion. They too will partly influence a wide range of policy issues, as they are: possible partners to Welsh speakers; present and future parents; customers and colleagues in the bilingual service sector; voters, taxpayers and citizens.

If the Welsh Language Board's *Strategy* (1995) and its Corporate Plan (1999) for the Welsh language are to be realized, this will only come about with the ready support of the majority of Wales's citizens, who do not, of course, speak Welsh. The Teifi Valley area is of general interest because it is linguistically similar to so many other areas with a high concentration of L1 first-language speakers. Questions for further research are the degree to which the Welsh language networks in the area cater sufficiently for the complete needs of all Welsh speakers in the area. It is feared that the current networks are not sufficient even for all the mother-tongue respondents, especially in the younger age groups, without making mention of the second-language group or the increasing non-Welsh-speaking groups in the area. The core message which the research provides is that the aspiration for further use of Welsh in this heartland area is very evident. The next step is to increase bilingual provision and thereby establish behaviour patterns which will institutionalize and stabilize Welsh in a number of social spheres in the area (C. H. Williams, 1999b). Decreasing density may cause some worries, but ostrich-like inaction will solve nothing. Quick work, and, above all, political will, can alleviate much of the danger faced by the language in this and all similar areas in contemporary Wales.

## Notes

[1] The research work reported was supported by a research contract from the Welsh Language Board undertaken by the Department of Welsh, Cardiff University. Other aspects of the work are reported on in Chapters 2 and 8 above. For a comprehensive discussion and analysis of the findings please consult Williams and Evas (1997).

[2] According to the Government's Schools Survey carried out in 1994 (Welsh Office 1996), only 6.5 per cent of the pupils in the primary schools of Wales speak Welsh at home and are fluent speakers of the language – this represents a decrease from the 8 per cent registered in 1977. The large difference between this figure and the 32.4 per cent mentioned above is to be appropriated, partially, to the success of the education system in creating new speakers. Unfortunately, the research presented below suggests that these second-language speakers are less likely to use their Welsh and, therefore, much research is needed into the group's process of language acquisition and their attitudes towards the language.

[3] He echoes the concern of many thousand of non-Welsh speaking Welsh people especially in 'Welsh Wales' (the post-industrial valleys of south-east Wales, as described in Balsom, 1985), frequently heard in the 1970s and 1980s. Thankfully, such accusations are much less frequently heard nowadays. Referring to increasing advertisements for bilingual staff in the *Western Mail*, the 'national newspaper of Wales', he states: 'Essentially, English-speaking Welsh people are increasingly being denied membership of Wales. Such people constitute four-fifths of the Welsh populations and over two thirds of those who could be considered biologically Welsh. What sort of Welsh nation or even Welsh people is going to survive this?'

[4] See Fletcher's excellent article (1997) which analyses this Welsh metropolitan élite or *crachach*.

[5] It should be noted that, since this survey took place, experimental provision for the aiding of language reproduction in areas where otherwise fragmentation would occur is being jointly undertaken by the Welsh Language Board and Mentrau Iaith Myrddin (Carmarthenshire Association of Language Initiative Agencies).

[6] I am pleased to note that this has been developed since the fieldwork by Dr Cen Williams of Canolfan Bedwyr at the University of Wales, Bangor.

[7] See http://www.seal.org.uk for more information on non-violent communication, and other issues of interest to successful language teaching.

[8] The Welsh Language Society (Cymdeithas yr Iaith Gymraeg) is a voluntary, non-violent direct-action pressure group whose campaigning has been very influential in bringing about an increased official status for Welsh. See http://www.cymdeithas.com for further information, together with the discussion in Chapter 1 above.

## References

Aitchison, J. and Carter, H. (1994). *A Geography of the Welsh Language 1961–1991*, Cardiff: University of Wales Press.

Asher, J. A. (1977). *Learning Another Language through Actions*, Los Gatos, CA: Sky Oaks Publications.

Balsom, D. (1985). 'The three-Wales model', in Osmond, J. (ed.), *The National Question Again: Welsh Political Identity in the 1980s*, Llandysul: Gomer Press.

Bourhis, R., ed. (1984). *Conflict and Language Planning in Québec*, Clevedon, Avon: Multilingual Matters.

Davies, C. (1997a). 'The last gasps of a dying tongue', *Times Higher Education Supplement*, (4 July).

Davies, C. (1997b). 'Minority language and social division: linguistic dead ends, linguistic time bombs, and the policies of subversion', in Frost, G. (ed.), *Loyalty Misplaced*, Reading: Reading University, pp. 39–40.

Dyfed County Council (1994). *Yr Iaith Gymraeg yn Nyfed/The Welsh Language in Dyfed*, Carmarthen: Dyfed County Council, mimeo.

Evas, J. (1999). 'Rhwystrau ar lwybr dwyieithrwydd [Barriers to bilingualism]', unpublished Ph.D. thesis, Cardiff University.

Fishman, J. A. (1991). *Reversing Language Shift: Theoretical and Empirical Foundations of Assistance to Threatened Languages*, Clevedon, Avon: Multilingual Matters.

Fletcher, P. (1997). 'Crachach's assault on England', *Western Mail*, see news archive on *http://www.totalwales.com*.

Jobbins, S. (1999a). 'Gwerin ac erin yw'r gelyn', *Tu Chwith*, 10, 41–52.

Jobbins, S. (1999b). 'Caerdydd – dinas newydd', *Barn*, 436, 20–25.

Nelde, P. H., Strubell, M. and Williams, G. (1996). *Euromosaic: The Production and Reproduction of the Minority Language Groups of the European Union*, Brussels: European Commission.

Welsh Language Board (1999). 'Strategaeth Cymraeg i Oedolion: Welsh for Adults Strategy', Document 39/4, *http://www.bwrdd-yr-iaith.org.uk*.

Welsh Language Society (1992a). *Ffordd Well i Gymru: Gwleidyddiaeth y Gymuned Rydd – Nid y Farchnad Rydd*, Aberystwyth: Welsh Language Society.

Welsh Language Society (1992b). *Property Act Handbook*, Aberystwyth: Welsh Language Society.

Welsh Office (1995). *Arolwg Cymdeithasol Cymru 1992*, Cardiff: Welsh Office.

Welsh Office (1996). *The Teaching of Welsh in Secondary Schools*, Statistical Brief, SBD 33/96, Cardiff: Welsh Office.

Williams, C. H. (1999a). 'The Celtic world', in Fishman, J. A. (ed.), *A Handbook of Language and Ethnic Identity*, New York: Oxford University Press, pp. 267–85.

Williams, C. H. (1999b) 'Governance and the language', *Contemporary Wales*, 12, 130–54.

Williams, C. H. and Evas, J. C. (1997). *Y Cynllun Ymchwil Cymunedol/The Community Research Project*, Cardiff: Welsh Language Board (also available on *http://www.cardiff.ac.uk/cymraeg/ymchwil/*).

Williams, G. A. (1985). *When was Wales?*, Harmondsworth: Penguin.
Williams, Glyn (1992). *Sociolinguistics: A Sociological Critique*, London: Routledge.
Williams, T. I. (1987). 'Futile linguistic engineering', *Times Education Supplement* (20 Feb.), 20.
Williams, T. I. (1997). *The Patriot Game: Reflections on Language, Devolution and the Breakup of Britain*, Beddau: Tynant Books, vol. 1.

# 11

# Language Revitalization in Comparative Context: Ireland, the Basque Country and Catalonia

## NICHOLAS GARDNER, MAITE PUIGDEVALL I SERRALVO AND COLIN H. WILLIAMS

The European dimension to social policy is a vital element of the language revitalization trends identified in Chapter 1. Until relatively recently, whenever Welsh-language concerns were set within a comparative context, it was to other Celtic lands that Welsh eyes turned, particularly to Ireland and Brittany. Today, language policy experts are more conscious of the value of drawing upon the wider experiences of our European partners, particularly Spain. Beyond Europe, it is to Canada/Québec, New Zealand and South Africa that language planners look for examples of good practice. In this chapter we reflect on the lessons to be gleaned from systematic comparisons with Ireland as a long-standing comparator, and Euskadi (the Basque Country) and Catalonia as European leaders in the field of language revitalization. Our message is that Welsh-language policy framers should be relying less on the tired cliché of Celtic solidarity and adapting several of the proactive measures developed within Euskadi and Catalonia. Consequently, after summarizing several of the key features of the Irish case, we concentrate our attention on the experience of Euskadi and Catalonia.

## IRELAND

One of the central features of the nineteenth-century Gaelic revival and the move towards independence achieved by the Treaty of 1921, was the need to distance and further differentiate Irish culture and values from British mores and interests. The three most prominent agencies for cultural liberation in the national struggle were Catholicism, the land and the language. Compared with Wales, Euskadi and Catalonia, the language issue *per se* was not as central in Irish nationalist thinking as one might have expected. Ireland's quest for national recognition was based upon the wider cultural platform of Catholic identification, even though, paradoxically, the nationalist drive was animated most forcibly by Protestant intellectuals. A specific language revival focus was offered by Conradh na Gaeilge (the Gaelic League) established in 1893 by Douglas Hyde and Eoin Mac Néil. It sought to teach Irish to adults, produce literature and magazines and put pressure on political authorities to devote more resources to the promotion of Irish (Hourigan, 1999). Professor Eoin Mac Néil in particular had a conception of a national struggle, which was non-sectarian, but nevertheless had profound politico-religious implications. 'For, by defining Ireland as a Gaelic rural culture brought to nationhood by a patriotic clergy and by denouncing the tradition of political nationalism established by the "neo-classical" patriots of the eighteenth century, he implicitly subverted the Protestant contribution to Ireland' (Hutchinson, 1987: 127).

### Goals

Following the 1916 Rising, the reorganization of Sinn Fein as a Republican Party under de Valera in 1917, and the subsequent struggle for national freedom in the War of Liberation, there was unanimity about the necessity of restoring the Irish language as a normal means of communication (Ó Gadhra, 1999). Following a national parliamentary mandate in the December 1918 general election, a conscious decision was taken to hold the proceedings of the new Dáil Éireann, the sovereign Irish Parliament for all thirty-two counties, in Irish. A Department of Irish was established with the president of the Gaelic League, Sean Ua Ceallaigh, as its minister. Government economic policy was geared to supporting native speakers of Irish through strengthening the agricultural sector and maintaining viable rural communities which were the lifeblood of the Irish-medium social networks. The teaching of Irish, geography, history and Irish economics was made compulsory in all schools where there were sufficient competent, if not always qualified, teachers. Irish, after a long struggle, was made an essential subject for entry into the new National University of Ireland, which had been established with three constituent colleges in Dublin, Cork and Galway in 1908. In 1922 the newly independent state launched a comprehensive strategy for the restoration of Irish as a national language. Thus Irish speakers were given preference in public-service positions such as gardai, army officers, teachers and civil servants, thereby creating a new middle-class Irish-speaking population. The 1937 Constitution gave recognition to two languages, Irish and English, but declared Irish to be the first official language. There followed a policy of incremental reform to establish state initiatives to promote the use of Irish, to stabilize Gaeltacht communities and to encourage a nation-wide system of voluntary language organizations, the most prominent of which is Comhdhail Náisiunta Na Gaeilge.

State support for agriculture did not stabilize the Irish-speaking communities and, as a result of education and planning policies, large numbers of Gaeltacht residents quit the predominantly Irish-speaking areas for employment opportunities in urban, anglicized locales. As Ó Riagáin (1997: 275) makes clear in his excellent study of language policy and social reproduction, government intervention 'changed the "rules" of the social mobility process', creating an important middle-class sector with at least a moderate competence in Irish (Dorian,

1999: 128). But, as with so many other instances of lesser used language behaviour, though required to use their Irish-language skills in a professional capacity, many of the new middle class chose not to reproduce their language within the family or the new neighbourhoods, although of course they continued to use Irish when they returned to their home communities.

### Policy and achievements

The government committed itself to a two-pronged attack to arrest the decline of Irish. The first policy was to define and defend the Irish-speaking areas, the Gaeltachtai. The government engaged in territorial language planning, hoping thereby to bolster the already fragmented Irish-speaking districts. In their detailed analysis of the vicissitudes of Gaeltacht delimitation Hindley (1990, 1991) and Williams (1988, 1991) review the statistical evidence and political motivations which underlay the exaggeration of any contribution the Gaeltacht might have made to language revitalization, Hindley (1991: 92) advances five lessons, which with hindsight might have made the Irish language policy less dependent upon ill-advised territorial language planning. The implementation of government policy was characterized by the following.

1. Lack of policy precedent. There were no precedents in 1925 for any attempt to revive a national language which had already become a minority tongue within its own national territory.
2. Lack of socio-spatial planning. There were no precedents, other than native reserves in the colonies, for demarcating minority language areas in order to preserve their cultural identity – except when, as at Versailles, the minority was a majority elsewhere.
3. Lack of census interpretation experience. There was little experience of the inadequacy of census enumeration of language ability as a guide to language use or genuine command.
4. Lack of conceptual awareness. There was no awareness of such concepts as 'critical mass' below which a language ability as a guide to language could fall in numbers or proportions only at its extreme peril, nor of village and urban 'systems' command of Irish, at least one of which was essential for language survival.
5. Lack of theoretical sophistication in terms of policy options. There had been no conceptual exploration of the territorial or individual alternatives in language planning strategies, nor indeed had much need been felt for language planning in the English-speaking world to which all *Irish*-speaking scholars belonged.

And in a monumental testimony to the role of the young state's yearning for success in reviving Irish in unpromising circumstances, Hindley simply concludes 'Ireland pioneered the field and we learn from her experience'.

The second policy initiative of the young state was to increase the numbers of Irish-speaking inhabitants through the education system. Terence Brown (1981: 85) demonstrates how Mac Néil, as Minister of Education, saw a commitment to education as a means to revive Irish civilization. In 1925 he asserted:

Nationality, in the best sense, is the form and kind of civilization developed by a particular people and distinctive of that people. I believe in the capacity of the Irish people,
if they clear their minds, for building up an Irish civilization. I hold that the chief function of the Irish State and of an Irish Government is to subserve that work. I hold that
the principal duty of an Irish Government in its educational policy is to subserve that
work. I am willing to discuss how this can best be done, but not to discuss how it can
be done without. (Mac Néil, 1925)

Brown adds that the National School teachers were enlisted in this crusade,
their role being to clear the minds of the nation's children through intense exposure to the Irish language.

Mac Néil was very conscious that one should not place an undue burden on
the school system to bring about a revival. Nevertheless, as Minister of
Education he was to preside over the legislative steps which made such a
dependence possible and inevitable. Ó Gadhra (1999: 7) phrases the dilemma
thus:

Central to this language restoration policy was the idea that it was possible to restore
Irish through the schools – with little thought being given to matters like incentive, or
the simple linguistic reality we now all accept i.e. teaching Irish even well in the class
is NOT sufficient. You need motivation, you need planning; you need political support
and moral support from leaders and role models. Above all you need to place an
emphasis on chances to use the language you have learned, written and oral. Above all
else, you have to convince the native Irish speakers of the value of their own heritage
which they must be encouraged to hand on to their own children and indeed to everybody else who is interested.

By the early 1960s, the declining viability of the family-farm sector, out-
migration of the young and low levels of participation in tertiary education
necessitated a change of economic policy. Instead of protectionist agricultural
policies and a concentration on the internal market, Ireland developed the export
market, together with small and medium-sized enterprises (Dorian, 1999). In this
modernizing context, severe doubts were raised as to the linkage between
educational success and competence in Irish. Consequently, in 1973 Irish ceased
to be a compulsory examination subject at the conclusion of secondary education. Ó Riagáin (1997) demonstrates the painful disjunction between economic
policy and language policy, first prior to the 1960s and then after the 1970s.
Initially, such socio-economic mobility as was available depended on inherited
economic capital in the form of family landholdings or small shops; thus, as
Dorian (1999: 128) explains, the incentives for Irish built into the educational and
government-employment systems affected relatively few young people. By the
1970s many young people sought upward social mobility through the higher
education system, but by then the incentives for achieving competence in Irish
had been weakened by changes in language policy.

Furthermore, Ó Riagáin's (1997) study demonstrates that government initiatives in economic, social and regional planning spheres have more important

effects on language patterns than do government language policies themselves. For example, a striking finding from the 1983 Irish language survey is that, as a result of economic policies and demographic change, more Irish was being used in An Daingean at that time than previously, but that less Irish was used in homes on the peninsula, particularly in the strategic western region. Dorian (1999: 129) comments that since Corca Dhuibhne homes in which both parents had high ability in Irish produced nearly twice as many high-ability children as homes in which only one parent had high ability, the changing marriage patterns of the region had significant implications for social reproduction of Irish.

Since the 1960s the quality and centrality of Irish-medium education has been subject to serious erosion. A Bord na Gaeilge (1986) report summarizes the cause and effect of this decline as follows:

> The number of pupils in all-Irish post-primary schools declined substantially. It became possible to obtain a State examination certificate without having to pass Irish. The instrumental value of the language declined in other respects e.g. it became unnecessary for entry to the Civil Service or to some third-level colleges. Though greater numbers and proportions of young people got the opportunity to study Irish increasing percentages of pupils either failed State examinations or decided not to take Irish in those examinations. While acknowledging the relationship already mentioned, between examination performance, communicative ability and high levels of usage, it is nevertheless arguable that many students who succeed in examinations obtain academic certification rather than competence to speak the language freely. For the minority who attain high communicative competence by the time of leaving school there is the difficulty of finding sufficiently cohesive networks of Irish speakers within which they may use the language.

The same may be said of many Welsh, Basque and other lesser used language contexts. Commentators discussing the implications of Ó Riagáin's (1997) research argue that he has demonstrated a retreat from a national policy ever since the ending of compulsory Irish in 1973. The government continues its support for all-Irish schools but has weakened the rule that all secondary students should learn Irish and the Irish-language requirement for second-level teachers. Restructuring of the National University has also meant the abolition of Irish as an essential requirement for university entry. The implication is clear, for 'there is no certainty, therefore, that Irish will not become an optional subject again, just as it was before the foundation of the state' (ITÉ, 1997). The principal features of twentieth-century language policy may be summarized as in Table 11.1.

### Top–down and bottom–up planning

The need for a national action plan was spelled out by Bord na Gaeilge (1988). The strategic policy initiatives identified then are still valid now, albeit within the context of a healthier Irish economy. It was reported that only around 5 per cent of Irish citizens use Irish extensively in their homes, neighbourhood or at

**Table 11.1. The main provisions for the maintenance of the Irish language**

| | |
|---|---|
| 1913 | Irish became compulsory for matriculation to the National University |
| 1922 | Irish was designated the 'national language' and competence in it became compulsory for entry to the civil service, police and army |
| 1926 | The Official Gaeltacht was defined and demarcated |
| 1937 | The status of Irish was reaffirmed in the Constitution |
| 1943 | Comhdháil Náisiúnta na Gaeilge was funded as a co-ordinating agency for voluntary language organizations |
| 1952 | Bord na Leabhar Gaeilge was established to supervise the allocation of funds for the publication of books in Irish |
| 1956 | State Department for the Gaeltacht was established (now the Department of Arts, Heritage, Gaeltacht and Islands) |
| 1956 | Gaeltacht Areas Order redefines the Gaeltacht to cover *c.*1860 sq miles, 7 per cent of land surface of the country |
| 1957 | Gaeltarra Éireann, a semi-state industrial development agency for the Gaeltacht, was established by the authority of the Gaeltacht Industries Act |
| 1972 | Radió na Gaeltachta, an Irish-language radio station, was established |
| 1973 | On joining the EU, the Irish government requested a 'treaty' status rather than an official language status for the language. As a consequence the primary treaties are translated into Irish as well as giving other rights to the language |
| 1978 | Bord na Gaeilge, a state body for the promotion of Irish, was established |
| 1979 | Údarás na Gaeltachta (the Gaeltacht Authority) replaced Gaeltarra Éireann |
| 1986 | Bord na Gaeilge published *The Irish Language in a Changing Society* |
| 1997 | TnaG, a national television station, was established |
| 1998 | A new Irish Language Act was prepared for submission to the Houses of the Oireachtas |

*Sources*: Ó Flatharta, 1999; Williams, 1990, 1999b.

work, although a further 10 per cent of the population use Irish regularly if less extensively. Weak rates of language reproduction lead the authors of the report to suggest urgent remedial action along the following lines. The state should take the initiative in changing the operating context of Irish usage and in changing the popular consciousness about Irish identity. In essence, the state should recreate an ideological basis for Irish-language loyalty and learning. To this end it advocated that Bord na Gaeilge be given wider powers to counter the generally marginalized position of Irish within other government agencies. It argued that central government itself, through its discourse, sense of complacency and lack of leadership, was one of the key agencies militating against promotional measures on behalf of Irish. Secondly, the report called for a popular cultural movement, both to resist provincialism and the downgrading of Irish, and also to act as a fulcrum for the re-creation of virile Irish-medium social networks. In contrast to the Welsh and Basque experience, where the social movement and the authorities were in open conflict the one with the other, the Irish case suggested a complementarity between popular demands and interventionist state action. Thirdly, the basic rights of Irish speakers in their dealings with state agencies needed much greater specification. While Article 8 of the Bunreacht na hEireann set out the constitutional standing of both official languages, there was little in the Irish system which set out the detailed practical legislative provisions. Calls for a revised Irish Language Act, then as now, have been welcomed but very little political commitment has been forthcoming. A further need was for infrastructural provisioning and planning, the key element for the realization of any relatively free language choice in a multilingual society. Four other needs were identified: to give legal effect to the concept of the bilingual state; to strengthen Irish in the public service; to increase the visibility and usage of Irish in the state-sponsored media and to arrest the decline of Irish in the Gaeltacht (Bord na Gaeilge, 1986).

Since then the main government agencies, the Department of the Gaeltacht, Údarás na Gaeltachta and the Bord na Gaeilge, have been accused of failing to achieve a high degree of policy integration. While it would be fair to say that co-ordination between and within organizations has not always been as smooth as might have been expected, there is a genuine consensus that the chief issues which still need to be tackled today are the following: Irish language speakers outside the Gaeltacht; migration and the Gaeltacht; language learning; traditional conceptions of the role of the Irish language in society and economy; television and the media occupying an important niche; TnaG TV station; Irish as an economic resource; and the work of Gaelscoileanna.

> It is now clear that the 'broad brush' Gaeltacht language policy has failed, that reliance on the schools has failed to halt Irish decline, and that accurately targeted major industrial investment in the real Irish-speaking core of the two principal Gaeltachtai has been accompanied by intensified decline. (Hindley, 1991: 93)

Despite the efforts of many countless hundreds of volunteers, community activists, agencies and government, the task of revitalizing the Irish language has proved greater than the resources and commitment hitherto shown. The basic fault seems to have been an over-optimistic assessment of the capacity of state intervention to restore Irish as a national language without a concomitant investment in socio-economic planning to bring about the necessary conditions to regulate the market forces which encouraged widespread anglicization. The Irish experience is a very good example of the clash of discourses which have been analysed in relation to Welsh by Williams and Morris (2000). They argue that language planning intervention from a market perspective is a highly irrational activity in

> the orthodox conception of language planning, where planning is viewed as the intervention of the state in order to overcome market forces on the ability of the group to reproduce itself . . . language planning also seeks to conform with a conception of rational organization, but given the opposition between planning and the market, the implication is that the market system is irrational as least insofar as it acts in opposition to the idea of a democratically elected government rationally to control the destiny of those who – presumably on rational principles – have elected it into office. (Williams and Morris, 2000: 249)

## How healthy is the Irish language?

In 1991, some 1,095,830 persons (32 per cent of the population) were returned as Irish speakers in the Census of Population. National percentages mask wide regional and class variations. The designated Irish-speaking areas, the Gaeltachtai, contain only 2.3 per cent of the state's population, but 45 per cent of all Irish-speaking families. In the north the language has shown an increased vitality and has been incorporated as a significant feature of the Good Friday settlement and subsequent arrangements for the operation of the Northern Irish Assembly (for details see Williams, 1999b; Mac Póilin, 1999). Ireland, at the end of the twentieth century, had 260 voluntary Irish-medium playgroups serving 2,500 children; 120 Irish-medium primary schools, twenty-six post-primary schools, serving some 22,000 children outside the Gaeltacht.

The range of use of Irish in post-primary schools is, however, limited, as revealed by Table 11.2. If the Irish language is to be used more intensely both within the public and the private sectors then clearly greater attention needs to be paid to the quality and range of Irish-medium education. To date, too little effort has been expended on the professional and vocational elements of Irish-medium education, and educationalists constantly raise the issue of the decline in standards of written Irish, with a particular concern being aired as to the authenticity of expression. This, it should be said, is not merely the special pleading of language purists, but the normal reaction of an older generation faced with the frustrations of dealing with a younger generation whose whole language repertoire is deeply influenced by the dominance of English.

A belated concern with holistic language planning now characterizes the Irish experience. But for far too long it was assumed that dedicated language initiatives, based in part on goodwill and in part on a symbolic adherence to Irish as a token of national identity, would suffice. Too often in the literature related to lesser used languages, the Irish example is quoted as a missed opportunity, or as an illustration of how difficult it is for government top–down planning to initiate processes of language revitalization. The reality, of course, is far more complex and we accept Ó Riagáin's view that language policies 'cannot be

**Table 11.2. Teaching medium/type of school: post-primary**

|  | Total no. of schools | All-Irish | Irish stream | Irish used for at least one curricular area |
|---|---|---|---|---|
| Secondary | 445 | 13 (3,695) | 1 (84) | 3 (260) |
| Vocational | 246 | 17 (2,268) | 5 (308) | 1 (74) |
| Community | 61 | 2 (530) | 0 | no data |
| Comprehensive | 16 | 1 (434) | 0 | no data |
| Total | 768 (369,865) | 33 (6,891) | 6 (192) | 4 (334) |

*Source*: Department of Education, 1996.
No. of students in brackets.

treated as an autonomous, independent factor' (1997: 283). They must be related to other trends and initiatives, grounded in the socio-economic context of everyday life, but always with the force of state legislative power and redress if public organizations and state institutions are to respect the language rights of citizens.

Many of the hopes of Irish language planning today rest on the reinvigoration of the public sector through the passage of a new Irish Language Act. It is a much-needed reform, for there is little 'parity of esteem' between the services offered through the medium of English and that of Irish. Comhdháil Náisiúnta na Gaeilge (1998) argues that there is a need for a new Language Act so as to give practical effect to the existing language rights of citizens. It recommends that the new Act should: 'Define and set out the State's duties and obligations in respect of the Irish language and give effect to the rights of citizens in relation to that language.' It also advocates that the new Act should provide for:

1) Institutional arrangements concerning the implementation of the said rights and duties.
2) Amendments to existing legislation and Government schemes to ensure that they are in accordance with the status of Irish as the 'national language' and the 'first official language'.
3) Institutional arrangements to ensure that all legislation enacted in the future is in accordance with the status of Irish as the 'national language' and as the 'first official language'.
4) The establishment of structures that will be responsible for the execution and implementation of the Act and for ensuring that State services through Irish are freely available to Irish speakers and Gaeltacht communities. (Comhdháil Náisiúnta na Gaeilge, 1998: 27–8)

The proposed Act should define the state's duties in relation to the Irish language, in relation to citizens' linguistic rights and in relation to the provision of Irish-medium public services. The appointment of an Irish Language Ombudsman together with an Oifig Choimisinéir na Gaeilge (Office of the Irish Language Commissioner) with functions similar to the Employment Equality Agency, should enable the new Act to be monitored and implemented more effectively. At the time of writing Éamon Ó Cuiv, TD, Aire Stáit, Roinn Ealaíon Oidhreachta Gaeltachta agus Oileán, the cabinet minister responsible for Irish-language matters, is seeking to present a Language Bill before the Houses of the Oireachtas. His principal justification for such a move is to convince state organizations that Irish-speaking citizens have constitutionally guaranteed rights to receive public services in Irish. He acknowledges that many fine policy proposals over the past decades have simply been ignored, for state organizations have been lukewarm in their implementation of guaranteed bilingual services.

It seems that non-legislative guidelines must be replaced by a formal constitutional system which will oblige the state system to grant the Irish language community their rights. I accept of course that a major change of mentality will be required in the public sector. (Ó Cuiv, 1999)

His judgement as to the reticence of public officials in implementing acknowledged language rights is a major feature, not only of the Irish and Welsh situations, but also of the Basque and Catalan cases to which we now turn for a more thoroughgoing attempt to guarantee a bilingual service at the point of individual local contact.


## LANGUAGE PLANNING IN THE BASQUE COUNTRY

### *Introduction*

The Basque Country, a traditional cultural unit, not a state nor even a single administrative unit, with an area very similar to that of Wales, is situated in the south-east corner of the Bay of Biscay, partly in France but mostly in Spain. It is home to about three million people most of whom consider themselves Basque,[1] though only close on a quarter claim to be able to speak Basque, in addition to either Spanish or French. Superficial parallels with Wales are numerous, both with regard to the position of the minority local language and to other aspects of local life. Indeed, it seems that the present weakened state of both Welsh and Basque owes much to very similar factors: primarily, the change to the present capitalist mode of production,[2] based on mining (coal in Wales, iron ore in the Basque Country) and steel production in the middle of the last century, which brought with it the need for a single language in common with the rest of the state. That language facilitated communication with non-speakers of the traditional local language, whether they were fellow workers and overseers who had migrated into the area or company owners. The state languages were also given a considerable role in schooling, in preparing the next generation of workers, in military service, whether compulsory or voluntary, and, to a greater or lesser extent, in the religious sphere.[3] Within the framework of those parallels there are differences too: in the Basque case two state languages (French and Spanish), not one, are involved; Welsh achieved a widely accepted written standard much earlier than Basque; and Welsh speakers have been relatively more literate in their mother tongue than Basques.[4] Little remembered now, there were substantial contacts between Wales and the Basque Country during the last century and a half: Basque ore was transported to Wales and Welsh coal travelled back to fuel Basque blast furnaces. The Spanish Civil War brought about a broader social contact, as Basque refugees were welcomed in Wales and Welsh socialists headed to Spain to fight against fascism (see Francis, 1984).

Conscious language planning for Basque, if one excepts earlier individual and small-group exertions whose effects were not widespread,[5] can be traced back to the last quarter of the nineteenth century. In 1876 the second Carlist war (so-called after a pretender to the Spanish throne by the name of Carlos) was brought to an end by a clear victory of the governmental forces. Basque speakers had fought on both sides: both for the pretender in defence of charter rights and the maintenance of a traditional organization of society where the influence of the church and local rulers bulked large; and, perhaps fewer in number, on the liberal side, in favour of state-wide administrative standardization. Be that as it may, the removal, subsequent to the war, of certain traditional rights (different taxation system, limited intervention by state in internal affairs, non-liability to military service; see García de Cortázar and Lorenzo Espinosa, 1997: 118–23) led to a widespread sensation of loss which many Basque speakers also associated with the increasingly evident loss of their own language, particularly where the introduction of the new capitalism was strongest. Thus, although the first attempts through local literary festivals to lend Basque a prestige that it had lost practically everywhere else had started about mid-century, it was the last quarter of the nineteenth century that became a time of formulation of a possible language policy. One of the clearest thinkers of the time was the initially liberal Campión. His and his companions' language programme has a clearly modern ring about it (Erize, 1997: ch. 8, especially pp. 477–82), including for example:

- ensuring language transmission within the family;
- promotion of a scientific approach to the language, including the production of a grammar and a dictionary and the creation of a Basque-language library;
- with regard to non-Basque speakers, the promotion of positive attitudes towards Basque and the criticism of negative ones; and petitioning the public authorities for support, particularly to achieve Basque-language education in the Basque-speaking heartland of Navarre by requiring teachers in those areas to know Basque and by creating chairs in the language in various teacher training colleges;
- proposal of a degree of co-officiality for Basque, though without ever using such a term: specifically, the right to use Basque as well as Spanish in official documents in Basque-speaking villages and requiring a knowledge of Basque of all public servants in those villages.

But their achievements were pitifully few in view of the widespread loss of the language. Indeed, the main success of language planning at that time was in the field of corpus rather than status, laying the ground for a spelling system specifically designed for Basque, rather than simply borrowing the conventions of French or Spanish orthography.

The ferment in Basque language activity led to the first language planning conference for Basque, held in 1901–2 on either side of the Franco-Spanish border. Though it led to no new practical measures, the arguments used at it reflect the flowering of a new awareness of the need for a 'social restoration' of the language, to use the terminology of the time. Sabino Arana, founder of the Basque Nationalist Party and present at the conference, was actively interested in both corpus[6] and status questions. Race and religion were perhaps the primary elements of his conception of Basqueness, but the Basque language was always a major accompaniment. Once he had abandoned his initial radical independentist political formulations, he set the agenda for a cultural nationalism, including a sort of Basque identity planning, in which the language was an essential element. It was this programme which inspired many of the language planning activities undertaken from then on until the Spanish Civil War: the first concerted attempts at establishing publicly financed Basque-medium schools; the promotion of a whole new generation of Basque writers and readers; the creation of an academy of the Basque language with a mission to establish a common standard form of Basque spelling and of the language as a whole, to ensure mutual comprehensibility in a language where dialectal traditions were increasingly divergent. All this activity came to an abrupt end in 1937 during the Spanish Civil War, when Franco's troops captured Bilbao, putting an end to Republican legality in the area, though the war continued for two more years in the rest of Spain. The public use of Basque, both orally and in writing, was virtually banned on the Spanish side of the border. It was proscribed in the schools, publishing almost ceased, pro-Basque language institutions barely survived if they did not disappear. The major figures of the pre-war movement were either dead, in exile or in prison. It was the end of an era. For many Basque speakers, Franco and the language policies he represented have been Basque's cruellest enemy, but a dispassionate look at pre-war language policies suggests that, with or without Franco, they were a long way from achieving the success of which their promoters dreamed. The shift to Spanish continued practically unabated, those who continued speaking Basque showed increasing signs of Spanish influence, access to public funds was very limited, Basque failed to gain a foothold in town life or modern mass entertainment, much of the pro-Basque propaganda was delivered in Spanish, and, in general, the whole effort was just too weak, too unsupported and opponents too strong, to be successful. It has been suggested that the purist lexical tendencies of some nationalists, with the intention of strengthening the linguistic border, were also responsible for the decline of the language; but such activities were but marginal to the daily life of the language (Zalbide, 1988: 402–5; 91–5 in English version).

Exiles made their contribution to the written language, but their influence on the fate of Basque was inevitably limited. The next major revival must be situated in the mid-1950s, when a number of factors coincided to make a modest planning of the language possible: the major Basque linguist of the day, Koldo Mitxelena, began his professional career; the activity of the Academy of the Basque Language began to recover; Basque-language publications began to increase; most importantly of all, some parents decided to take steps to ensure that their offspring were educated in Basque. This latter initiative, planning more or less consciously for the use of Basque in education, has been the prime motor of Basque-language planning and in terms of sheer volume it is, even today, still the prime area for such planning. This first phase of the second major planned effort at reversing language shift (RLS) back towards Basque is a clear case of grass-roots, bottom–up planning, carried out at best with the tolerance of the authorities, but more usually with their active opposition. By the time of Franco's death in 1975 the achievements were, by today's standards, modest but the whole movement had clearly succeeded in putting planning for Basque back on the agenda. An intense transitional period started up at that point which, for convenience, can be regarded as culminating with the passing of the Law for the Normalization of the Use of the Basque Language[7] by the Basque Parliament in 1982. The rest of this section will discuss policies in place since then.

### *The present framework: rights and goals*

*Rights:* Before proceeding further it is essential to underline that, unlike in Wales, there is no single overall legal framework of rights regarding use of the Basque language, nor a single national language planning policy. The present-day territory of the Basque Country falls in two states (France and Spain) and the territory within the latter is further subdivided into two different regions (Basque Autonomous Community (BAC) and the Charter Government of Navarre). The resultant policies are, as we shall see, very varied. The distribution of speakers between these three areas and their relative weight in each is also very varied: over 80 per cent of all Basque speakers live in the BAC, but it is only in the French Basque Country that Basque speakers constitute over a quarter of the population, although the proportion is rapidly approaching that in the BAC.[8]

Taking the French Basque Country first, legal rights *vis-à-vis* Basque are almost non-existent,[9] in accordance with the French state's unstated policy of letting its mainland minority languages die of inanition. There have been some recent signals of potential change in this policy, but so far no such support as the ratification of the European language charter would imply.

In Spain the 1978 Constitution marked a major turnaround in the legal situation. Article 3 states:

> 1. Castilian [Spanish] is the official language of the Spanish state. All Spaniards have the duty to know it and the right to use it.
> 2. The other languages of Spain will also be official in the corresponding Autonomous Communities [i.e. regions] in accordance with their [the regions'] statutes.
> 3. The wealth of different linguistic modalities of Spain is a cultural heritage which shall be the object of special respect and protection.

Paragraph 2 of the above article was, in fact, further developed in both the BAC and Navarre.

In Navarre the founding law of the region[10] contains the following precepts (article 9):

> 1. Castilian [Spanish] is the official language of Navarre.
> 2. Basque shall also have the character of official language in the Basque speaking areas of Navarre.
>   A charter law shall determine the aforementioned areas, shall regulate the official use of Basque and shall organise the teaching of this language within the framework of the general legislation of the state.

The subsequent Navarrese law on Basque[11] established three zones:

- a Basque zone in the north of Navarre, roughly corresponding to the present-day extension of the traditionally Basque-speaking area;
- a mixed central area including Pamplona, capital of the region, where numerous Basque speakers live;
- a non-Basque area in the south of the region, where percentages of Basque speakers are much lower and where part of the territory at least has never been Basque-speaking.

Rights of speakers in the Basque-speaking zone are very similar to those of people living in the BAC (see below). In the mixed area, citizens have the right to use Basque with the administration, but no guarantee of a response in that language; the public authorities may optionally require knowledge of Basque of certain civil servants; in education, teaching of and in the Basque language is optional. Finally, in the Spanish-speaking area, citizens dealing with the administration in Basque may be required to present a translation; in education, teaching of Basque as a subject, but not as medium, will be financed by the administration. In short, the law is directed at maintenance, not normalization in its habitual Spanish state sense of gaining speakers and domains.[12]

Finally, in the BAC the mention of Basque in the Statute of Autonomy was included in the following form (article 6):

1. Basque, the Basque people's own language, shall have, like Spanish, the character of official language in [the Autonomous Community of] the Basque Country and all its citizens have the right to know and use both languages . . .
3. Nobody shall be discriminated for reasons of language.[13]

Other paragraphs of the same article pave the way for the law for the normalization of Basque, name the Royal Academy of the Basque Language as an official consultative body and authorize the BAC to propose international agreements for the protection and promotion of the language. The law itself is clearly directed at RLS and includes specific measures for a number of domains commonly tackled by such legislation: education, the media, administration, justice and so on.

It should be evident from this rapid run through the language legislation relating to Basque currently in force that, given these differences, the language is subject to potentially very great variation in language policies, even without taking into consideration the further variation that may be wrought by governmental agencies of a lower order (departments of the regional government, provincial (county) councils, town and village councils) or in Spain by the behaviour of agencies under the control of the state-wide government. The approach adopted in the legislation is based primarily on the principle of personality, though there are also minor elements of territoriality visible, particularly in the Navarrese legislation.[14]

Some explanation of these contrasting legislative Acts seems necessary to set the scene. Since the rise of Basque nationalism at the turn of the century, language policies for and against Basque have been closely intertwined with politics, with very differing legal outcomes in the three areas discussed above. Thus, in the French Basque Country, Basque political nationalism has always been weak. One can, however, talk of a widespread cultural nationalism which, nevertheless, has been able to achieve relatively little in the face of the continuing French state policy of *one state, one language*, out-migration of native speakers, in-migration (particularly for retirement) of non-speakers and the partial collapse, from the 1960s on, of intergenerational language transmission.

On the Spanish side of the border, much of the impetus for reversing language shift in the present century has come from political nationalism. This nationalism, expressed in an ever-changing range of political parties, has had both an independentist strand and a devolutionary one. Whilst it is clearly inaccurate to propose the simplistic equation 'Basque speakers are nationalist voters', it is equally clear that many are.[15] Further, the vigorous pursuit of independence by some Basque nationalists has led many in non-nationalist parties to be highly suspicious of a language proclaimed as the nucleus of Basque identity by their political opponents. Basque is viewed by some non-nationalists as being used to constitute a Basque identity which excludes Spanish monolinguals and is designed, they claim, to reduce them to second-class status. The outcomes of these tensions have been different in Navarre and the BAC.

In Navarre where one of the major parties has fomented a Navarrese regionalism, to stand against Basque nationalism and reaffirm the links with the Spanish state, where Basque political nationalism is relatively weak and Basque speakers constitute less than 10 per cent of the total population, it is hardly surprising that the resultant law described above only provides limited opportunities for maintenance and hardly any for expansion. Not a single nationalist party voted in support of the law (Cobreros, 1989: 143–51). The Government of Navarre has hindered the installation of repeater stations for the Basque-language TV channel, on the grounds that it is a vehicle for nationalist propaganda.

In the BAC, on the other hand, nationalist parties have constituted a majority in the Basque Parliament since its inception in 1980, although the proportion of votes seems to have been falling slowly since the mid-1980s.[16] The Basque government has frequently been a coalition, but the dominant party has always been nationalist, as reflected in the fact that the government's *lehendakari* or president has always been a nationalist. In the matter of the 1982 language legislation, the nationalists were aware of the need to seek a broad consensus and the law obtained support from the Spanish Socialist Party, though not from the statewide centre-right Popular Party (Cobreros, 1989: 101). This relative consensus has, however, largely come to an end, as the resultant policies began to alter the status quo.

In short, Basque nationalism has been central in achieving an improved legal status for Basque. But Basque language loyalism's relationship with nationalism also has its down side, visible in the rejection of some or all pro-Basque-language legislation and policies by some of the opposition parties. Further, the need of some nationalists to strengthen the border between 'them' and 'us' has on occasion, particularly in the first third of the century but also less frequently within the present attempt at RLS, had consequences in corpus planning, as it has led to a certain purism in vocabulary, neologisms[17] being coined on the basis of real or supposedly authentic Basque roots, avoiding any romance input. This purism, though satisfying for the élite proposing it, has not facilitated the spread of new vocabulary and has possibly alienated some users. Finally, the interests of nationalist parties do not necessarily fully coincide with those of Basque language loyalists.[18]

*Goals:* Leaving aside for the moment the lack of supporting policies in the French Basque Country and the maintenance promoted in part of Navarre, what are the goals of a language policy for Basque clearly directed at RLS as it occurs in the BAC? The law seems to presuppose that its aim is a bilingual society, but offers little idea of what that might mean in detail. It is not a topic which has been much debated. There is a broad acceptance among Basque language loyalists of the idea of 'normalization', usually interpreted as extending Basque to new speakers and to new domains. This definition requires further elucidation:

- It is a definition which ignores the continuing attrition on the home front: where parents are Basque speakers, one might well expect the home to be one of the domains that Basque maintains, but Basque is now often simply a co-mother tongue, especially as a result of the large number of mixed marriages but also in many families where both parents are Basque. In many such cases it is not even the dominant mother tongue, but simply a weaker partner;
- New speakers are being gained through schooling and adult education, but it is not clear whether these new speakers are strengthening intergenerational language transmission;
- It is the new domains which are particularly difficult to define. Where should the limits be placed? Can Basque aspire to all functions, all domains? Fishman has repeatedly criticized some Basque language loyalists for setting impossible goals.[19] In so far as some Basque language loyalists do seem to pursue a monolingual Basque society, the criticisms are fully justified. But if Basque cannot have it all, how much can it aspire to?

The diglossic society[20] (Latin, Spanish, Occitan in its Gascon form, Navarrese romance and French all having played the role of H (High Status), with Basque and other languages in the role of L (Low Status)) had been relatively stable over the centuries. Some languages had lost their role in the Middle Ages. But the major losses for Basque came in the eighteenth century, when the diglossic arrangement began to break down in the southern part of traditional Basque-speaking territory; it subsequently crumbled in the Spanish coastal provinces during the second half of the nineteenth century and finally collapsed in the French Basque Country in the second half of the twentieth century. There is no possibility of a straightforward return to that relatively stable diglossic situation, which may be sustainable in traditional societies but seems untenable in the face of successive waves of state industrialization followed by economic globalization. The rural area which may be considered the Basque hinterland and which stretches across the three areas outlined above is itself under threat in the French Basque Country and has had its potential influence curtailed in Navarre. With the possibility of faster travel and the rapid spread of new forms of communication, Basque speakers are engaged in relationship networks which no longer necessarily have a local geographical basis. The question is how many of these networks can be reserved for Basque, alongside the more traditional domains.

### Policies and their makers

*Policy-makers:* Policy-making bodies need some presentation here as, although in many cases the policy-making and implementing functions fulfilled are roughly the same as in Wales, their organization and assignation to different bodies vary rather more. Thus, at the highest level, mostly that of the basic legislative framework, two states not one are involved. The French state has done little beyond circumscribing the role of Basque. The Spanish state's central authorities, on the other hand, in addition to having established the basic legal framework for Basque language planning, seem to perform two further roles: that of acting as a brake on what are considered excessive measures in favour of the minority language and that of adapting the state's own existing legislation to the new constitutional framework. They are, with few exceptions, rarely involved in promotional activities. The second level of planning-from-above, as we descend the hierarchy, corresponds to the *département* of Pyrénées Atlantiques in France and to the regions of Navarre and the BAC in Spain. At this level, the appointment of a single language planning official (responsible for both Basque and Occitan!) was under consideration in 1998 on the French side of the border. The primary point of reference, however, is the officially funded Euskal Kultur Erakundea. South of the border, much more developed structures are in place. In the BAC, overall responsibility for language planning lies with the subministry for language planning, an integral part of the Department of Culture of the Basque government. The head of the subministry and the management team are all, in accordance with southern European practice, political nominees. The subministry is assisted in its policy-making by a part-time advisory body, the Advisory Council for Basque. Some other government departments, notably the Department of Education, have posts for language planning officials dealing with matters arising from the departmental remit. The next level down is that of the three provincial or county governments of the BAC. These each have a number of language planning officials. Thereafter, we reach the final level of top–down planning, the local councils, many (but by no means all) of which have an official specifically to deal with matters Basque, whose functions may range from that of mere translator to that of proactive implementer of council language policy. There is no single agency corresponding to the Welsh *menter*

*iaith*, though similar functions are sometimes fulfilled by such local council officials in conjunction with private-sector bodies. The Department of Education, in
addition to the officials at its headquarters in Gasteiz, has a total of eight officials
in its three provincial offices, a further twenty-two full-time 'language normalization' workers in its teacher-support centres round the BAC and, finally, at
over 300 primary and secondary schools there is a teacher on part-time release
from classroom duties to deal with the implementation of language policy
within the particular school. In Navarre the structure is similar, though much
more modest.

Finally, we reach the bottom–up planners, non-governmental grass-roots
organizations. In the days before governmental support these bodies were the
main sources of organized support for the Basque language. Amongst these the
Euskaltzaindia or Royal Academy of the Basque Language, now largely funded
with public money, stands out for its role in many aspects of Basque language
promotion up until the early 1980s. Since then it has concentrated on its corpus
planning role, passing most of its teaching, examining and cultural organizing
roles on to specific public and private bodies, whilst retaining an overview of
status planning for Basque.

Pro-Basque language organizations can be split into three groups: technical-
entrepreneurial, professional-cum-trade union and citizen-activist (following
Agirrebaltzategi, 1999: 58). In the first group one can include modern Basque-
language cultural companies (such as the terminological centre UZEI, local
Basque-language publishers, private language schools, Basque-language press,
language planning consultancies working in the private sector) almost invari-
ably set up within a conscious language planning perspective, sometimes as
non-profit-making bodies, sometimes in pursuit of profit. There seem to be relatively few examples of the second group; the most notable is perhaps the union
of Basque-speaking lawyers, pursuing the creation of Basque-language courts.
The third group includes amongst others Euskal Herrian Euskaraz, a small association of activists, well-known throughout the Basque Country for its confronta-
tional tactics in favour of Basque. More powerful and, on the whole, more
attractive to the majority of the population are the numerous[21] grass-roots
Basque-language associations, based on specific towns, villages or small
geographical areas. Many of these have spawned initiatives belonging to the first
group, particularly in the sphere of local mass media. A noticeable development
of the last couple of years, following on the initial efforts to co-ordinate the
private sector by EKB, has been the banding together of many of these non-
governmental organizations in a single umbrella organization called Kontseilua.

*Achievements:* A brief list of language planning achievements over the past quar-
ter-century seems vital if the reader is to have some idea of the strengths and
weaknesses of the Basque situation. The total number of speakers is now rising
at each census (Eusko Jaurlaritza, 1995, 1997; Eusko Jaurlaritza et al., 1997).
Education is, not surprisingly, the sector where most has been achieved, with

most native Basque speakers now attending Basque-medium primary school (Gardner, 2000; Zalbide, 1990, 1999). Basque-medium secondary schooling (but rarely vocational training or FE) is also widely available in the BAC and parts of Navarre. The number of degree courses that can be studied entirely in Basque is limited, but a number of universities offer courses partly or substantially in Basque, as do teacher training colleges. Language training is also available to adults. With regard to the media,[22] there is one Basque government-owned Basque-language TV channel, several local TV stations run in Basque, a number of private and publicly owned radios broadcasting wholly or partly in Basque, a daily newspaper, a considerable number of local magazines published on a regular basis as well as a number of children's comics and general and specialized periodicals. Annual book production, including original, translated and bilingual works, runs to well over a thousand, with a notable presence of school texts and children's books in general. Basque music, both traditional and modern, is readily available on tape and CD. Three language planning consultancies offer their services to private-sector companies wishing to use more Basque.

The provision of Basque-language services in the public sector (general administration, health, police, courts) has improved to some degree, but the language profile scheme whereby civil servants have to certify they have achieved the level of Basque required for a particular post has been repeatedly weakened over the years and is not infrequently subverted. There has been a very modest improvement in the offer of Basque-language consumer services in the private sector; otherwise, opportunities to work in Basque are extremely limited.

The ability of bottom–up Basque language planners to secure mass mobilization is a notable feature of the Basque planning scene: some events are one-off, perhaps a dozen (sponsored walks, cultural products fair) annual and some less frequent. Many attract visitors, both speakers and non-speakers of the language, in tens of thousands and represent a considerable, year-round, organizational commitment as well as an additional source of finance for the promoting organizations.

*Degree of policy integration:* Language policies, as with policies in other fields of endeavour, are likely to be stronger if they are all pulling in the same direction. The degree of co-ordination of policies can be measured in various ways. In the Basque context it seems appropriate to ask at least the following three questions:

- How far are policies co-ordinated between and within organizations?
- How far are language policies integrated into other types of planning?
- How far are top–down and bottom–up language policies co-ordinated?

Corpus planning is one field where there has clearly been at least a degree of joint planning across territories: the Royal Academy of the Basque Language, principal body for corpus planning, was founded by the provincial councils of the four provinces of the Spanish Basque Country and has always included academics from all parts of the Basque Country, though has it yet to achieve full official recognition of its work on the French side of the border. The new written standard it has promoted, *batua*, has been implemented with a considerable degree of success, though some people have never fully accepted it, particularly north of the border and in Biscay. Similarly, UZEI, now under the auspices of the Academy, has also involved scholars from across the country. But corpus planning is relatively easy to co-ordinate. The problems arise more obviously in status planning. Considerable differences in the legal frameworks were outlined above and it can thus hardly come as a surprise to readers to learn that the degree of co-ordination is relatively modest. To some extent, the Basque government acts as major partner in joint initiatives: thus, its Advisory Board includes representatives from throughout the country; it has also led the two major sociolinguistic surveys carried out in the past few years (Eusko Jaurlaritza, 1995; Eusko Jaurlaritza et al., 1997); and there have been other minor instances of collaboration over the years.

Within the Basque government, planners do co-ordinate their work to a modest degree. What weakens their effect is the fact that other government services often tend to assume that making Basque official is the unique responsibility of those planners and need not therefore have any effect on their own practices. In short, the maintenance and promotion of Basque is just one of the many objectives pursued by governmental agencies and, for many of their members, a fairly minor one at that. At worst, language legislation is skirted round and ignored. At best, that same legislation can serve to attain considerable advances in the promotion of the language, when, say, in a small town,[23] politicians favourable to the promotion of the language, officials competent to carry out the planning and grass-roots organizations coincide in the pursuit of the same objectives.

Finally, a number of specific co-ordinating bodies exist. Thus, all of the following have or have had co-ordinating bodies: small, predominantly Basque-speaking local councils (UEMA); local council language planning officials (UETS), private-sector language loyalist organizations (see below), language planners of the Basque government, the BAC's provincial councils and their provincial capitals (HAKOBA); local language loyalist organizations with a geographical base and related media (Topagunea).

In relation to co-ordination with other sorts of planning, the way in which language planning for Basque was integrated in a broader cultural planning for a Basque identity at the beginning of the twentieth century has already been mentioned. Relatively little remains of that attitude today, perhaps because for the majority of Basques, urban as they are, the traditional Basque identity rooted in rural life is ever less familiar. Connections with other sorts of planning, economic planning or land use planning for example,[24] are very limited.

Practically all language planning for Basque from the 1950s until Franco's death in 1975 can be considered bottom–up planning.[25] Even in the transitional period, from 1975 to, say, 1982, much that was done also falls in the same category. It was a period of numerous new initiatives in support of Basque. What had until then been a very modest private sector of organized Basque language loyalists underwent a notable boom. From 1981 on the Basque government took on a major planning role in the BAC, first in education and more gradually in other spheres. With regard to this aspect of co-ordination the past twenty-five years are perhaps primarily a story of initial conflict between top–down and bottom–up planners, leading to reflection and, increasingly it seems from about 1992 on, to the adoption of a *modus vivendi*. Grass-roots associations old and new turned to local government for finance (rather than to central Spanish state or European sources). But along with public finance came various other requirements, not always to the liking of the language loyalist associations. In addition, government attempts to set up its own organizations fulfilling what often seemed to be identical objectives, thus threatening competition with the private sector, led to further conflict. The political split within the Basque nationalist camp between radical independentists outside the Basque government (whose views one can caricature as 'devolution is worthless') and the other nationalist parties usually in the government (similarly, 'devolution is a valuable start') meant that the basic conflict about who should be doing what was often overlaid with mutual political suspicion. Major conflicts have arisen over the following topics: the creation of a Basque-language newspaper, the organization and financing of Basque-language classes for adults and the financing of the *ikastola* school system and its integration in the state or private school system. All of these conflicts and other, more minor ones have achieved at least partial resolution over the past few years. At the same time, this conflict has not led to a complete breach, as government money has continued to flow into many of the private bodies involved and there have been occasional joint projects.

A second aspect of relationships between public and private sectors concerns the role of the co-ordinating bodies that the private sector has developed. EKB, set up in 1983, at times seemed to act as a shadow language planning body, often critical of the Basque government, particularly of the failure to produce a thoroughgoing strategic plan for the language. This demand was not satisfied until 1999 when the Basque government finally made its plan public (Eusko Jaurlaritza, 1999). By then EKB was winding down, giving place to the broader based, rather more co-operative Kontseilua. The new ambience is reflected in the recent increase of the number of members from NGOs on the Advisory Council for Basque.

### Conclusions

*How healthy is the Basque language?* The fact that, according to successive censuses, the number of Basque speakers is now on the increase hides the gradual death of Basque north of the international border. This information is of course based on self-report. Other sources, such as language examinations, while also suggesting an increase, give a far more modest assessment of numbers competent in Basque. Reported use of the language in any case falls short of claimed knowledge; actual use has only been measured on a local basis and, there too, similar results have been found.

The term 'Basque speaker' itself deserves analysis. At the beginning of the century it would have referred to a monolingual or to a native speaker who also had some command of Spanish or French. Nowadays, it refers to bilinguals whose mother tongue and/or dominant language may well not be Basque. The only obvious area of improvement is the sharp increase in the number of people literate in Basque. Many who report themselves to be Basque-speaking on the census have a poor command of the language and are not necessarily frequent users of it. At the present time many Basques consider that one can be 'an X-man via Y-ish': this does not bode well for the compartmentalization of domains necessary for language survival.

The *Euromosaic* study gives a comparative idea of the strengths and weaknesses of the three component communities of the Basque Country: in a study of forty-eight EU language minorities the BAC was placed eighth in rank order, Navarre twenty-first and the French Basque Country twenty-sixth. Welsh was assigned eleventh place. An unpublished Basque government report, *Reclus*, forecasts that, assuming maintenance of present policies, the percentages of Basque speakers will continue to rise in the BAC, will be very dependent on the details of implementation in Navarre and will continue to decline in France. But there are other factors to consider as well. In-migration to the Spanish Basque Country practically came to a halt in the 1980s. With low birth rates at home and increasing Europeanization, however, a new wave of immigration is likely both from other parts of Europe and from North Africa. Thus, Arabic and English may well become increasingly visible in the Basque Country. Indeed, many parents are already seeking an early start in English for their children.

In the *Euromosaic* study one of the concerns is to determine whether a given speech community has fared successfully in the face of the alterations in the social distribution of language wrought by successive waves of economic change. From this perspective we can say that Basque has been moderately successful in surviving the expansion of capitalism since the nineteenth century, even though it has weakened in the process. It is not yet clear whether it will be equally successful in the face of globalization.

*Is planning appropriate?* The original domains chosen for governmental intervention in the Basque Country are familiar enough in Western Europe: education, mass media (and, increasingly IT), administration. Bottom–up planners, with some financial support from the authorities, have paid some attention to community. If we compare this with Fishman's insistence on family, neighbourhood, education and lower work-sphere, we can see both coincidences and differences:

- In the Basque Country the family has been left to fend for itself, with the mixed results mentioned above. Even given the difficulty of intervention by planners, there is clearly room for a task force to offer support, both to endogamous marriages in the French Basque Country and to mixed marriages everywhere.
- The *neighbourhood* of American language planning terminology seems to correspond fairly closely to the use of the term *community* in Europe: this, as suggested, has received some attention from planners, particularly at the local council and grass-roots levels. Within the community sphere there have been some noteworthy initiatives in the subdomain of religion.
- Education has far and away received the most attention: the Basque RLS effort was excessively dependent on the school initially and to some degree still is (Fishman, 1990; 1991: ch. 13), but with a curious lack of attention to vocational training at the secondary level and FE, precisely those aspects of education especially relevant to planning for the lower work-sphere.
- the public-sector work-sphere has received considerable attention, but once again the advances in subdomains which have major impact in local communities, such as health, the police and the courts, are very modest indeed. Very little attention has been paid to the private sector, though a small number of initiatives are now in place. In particular, the gains in terms of modern, urban, cultural service companies tend to hide the continuing losses in what we might term 'traditionally Basque firms', usually related to the primary sector, which have retained some degree of Basqueness to the present day without conscious planning and which constitute an obvious area for intervention. On the whole, the presence of Basque is extremely limited in industry and commerce.

Ultimately, in addition to contrasting underlying models of intervention, this discussion on priorities requires hard data on effectiveness, at present unavailable; even if economists' work on measuring effectiveness is fascinating it is still in its infancy.[26] In any case, achieving a Basque-language TV service comparable to that available in major languages, maintaining an up-to-date supply of basic computer software or even ensuring a broad range of university degrees in the minority language are going to continue to be difficult and may, with time, prove to be impossible, especially if more essential language planning activities are to be given greater attention.

*What lessons can be drawn from the Basque case?* A few features possibly relevant to other bilingual situations may be mentioned:

- some legal backing and access to governmental resources is essential for the minority language, as the very different fate of Basque north and south of the international border shows;
- language policies and their success or failure are conditioned by many factors: administrative organization, political and sociological features of the society are all relevant;
- the Basque case illustrates clearly the pros and cons of having one's language taken up by a political cause;
- Basque language loyalists are not agreed on objectives: this has led to conflict on more than one occasion;

- excessive reliance has been placed on education: other domains have been largely ignored (family, health, police, justice, work, commerce);
- the willingness of many in the administration to leave Basque language planning implementation to those specifically charged with carrying it out suggests a lack of ownership of the whole process on the part of government outside the language planning élite;
- some Basque language loyalists seem blissfully unaware of the need to attract goodwill and support from the monolingual majority: some proposals, not usually endorsed by the government, seem particularly provocative to the majority;[27]
- the relative success of planning in the BAC has brought about an increasingly negative reaction from Spanish monolinguals: this is most evident in the educational sector;
- language planning has yet to be integrated with other forms of planning;
- the university has failed to provide intellectual backing: there are plenty of linguists and to some degree experts in the literature and in educational sciences, but hardly any sociolinguists, historians of the language or economists with an RLS interest;
- insufficient evaluation work is being carried out.

## LANGUAGE PLANNING IN CATALONIA

### Introduction

Catalonia is one of Spain's seventeen autonomous communities and is situated in the north-east corner of the Iberian Peninsula. However, the Catalan language is not only spoken in the Autonomous Region of Catalonia alone, yet another example – like the Basque Country and many other cases in Europe – of a lack of correspondence between administrative and linguistic borders. Catalan is spoken in four different European countries: Andorra, Spain, France and Italy. Within Spain, it is spoken in four autonomous regions: the Principality of Catalonia, most of Valencia, the Balearic Islands, and a part of eastern Aragon known as the Franja de Ponent (Western Strip). In France, Catalan is spoken in almost all of the *département* of Pyrénées-Orientales (also known as Northern Catalonia or Roussillon), which was surrendered to France under the Treaty of the Pyrenees in 1659. Finally, as a result of the Kingdom of Aragon's territorial expansion in the Middle Ages, Catalan is spoken in Italy, in Alghero, a town on the island of Sardinia.

The social, political and legal condition, as well as the sociolinguistic situation, of the Catalan language varies considerably in each of the above-mentioned territories. From a legal point of view, it ranges from complete absence of recognition in Roussillon to the exclusive official status it enjoys in Andorra.[28] In Aragon, the 1982 Statute of Autonomy recognized different linguistic varieties which deserve protection and support without giving them co-official status, and in Catalonia, Valencia and the Balearic Isles, Catalan is co-official with Spanish. In Italy, the Catalan language spoken in Alghero has recently been

**Figure 11.1.   The administrative divisions of Catalonia**
*Source*: reproduced with the kind permission of M. Folch-Serra, Department of
Geography, University of Western Ontario.

given official status. Some eleven million inhabitants live in these territories, out of which seven million speak Catalan, and almost nine million understand it. Comparatively speaking, the autonomous community of Catalonia, the territory on which we shall concentrate in this section of the chapter, is where the Catalan language enjoys a 'healthier' situation.[29] This is due to its more active promotion by the Generalitat, the autonomous Catalan government, which considers the language to be a cornerstone of its policies and, since the recovery of Catalonia's democratic institutions, has undertaken a large array of measures to promote and expand its knowledge and use.

Nevertheless, purposeful language planning in Catalonia goes back to the beginning of the twentieth century, mainly in the field of corpus planning. In this period the Catalan language was standardized, which turned out to be a crucial moment in the recovery of the language after centuries of decay. Following the Catalan literary revival in the early nineteenth century, known as the *Renaixença* (Renaissance), there began a process of functional and social expansion of the Catalan language, which reached its peak during the Second Spanish Republic (1931–9), which declared Catalan to be an official language. The diffusion of Catalan created concerns about correct usage and gave rise to controversies between the defenders of a form of written Catalan closer to the spoken language and those who preferred a more archaic form (Siguan, 1993: 32). The First International Congress of Catalan Language took place in 1906 with a dual objective: to proclaim to the world that Catalan was indeed a language, and not a Spanish or Occitan dialect; and to discuss how to make Catalan a unified language which would be a useful means of communication among all its speakers, adapting the language to be a modern functional instrument for all purposes, from scientific and technical to commercial and popular use. As a result of these discussions, the Congress concluded that fundamental work in codification of the language was needed. Pompeu Fabra (1868–1948), grammarian, lexicographer and former industrial engineer, was the artificer, the *seny ordenador* (the organizing mind) of modern Catalan. He is the author of the *Normes Ortogràfiques* (orthographic norms) (1913), the *Gramàtica Normativa* (grammar) (1918), and the *Diccionari General de la Llengua Catalana* (dictionary) (1932). These works were accepted and adopted by public authorities, institutions, literary figures, publishers and the press, and eventually became accepted in all Catalan language territories. They continue to constitute a major reference point for contemporary written Catalan.

This large and rigorous task would not have been possible without the institutionalization of Catalan political nationalism, with the establishment in 1907 of the Institut d'Estudis Catalans (IEC, Institute of Catalan Studies) and, more specifically, its Philological Section (1911), under whose patronage Pompeu Fabra undertook the above-mentioned works. The IEC, which adopted and continues to perform the role of academy of the language, was created by Enric Prat de la Riba, one of the fathers of Catalan nationalism and one of the most important exponents of the modern idea of Catalonia as a political entity. The establishment of the Mancomunitat (1914–25) – a precursor of the Generalitat, but with more limited political prerogatives – underpinned the process of Catalan standardization, for the Mancomunitat carried out remarkable cultural and educational policies in favour of the Catalan language. The driving force behind these cultural and linguistic developments lay in the profound political and economic changes that Catalan society underwent during this period. In the context of a predominantly agricultural Spanish state, Catalonia experienced a relatively early process of industrialization that brought about the emergence of a wealthy and educated autochthonous bourgeoisie. From the mid-nineteenth century onward this Catalan-speaking bourgeoisie, unable to secure a dominant political position in a Spanish state ruled by a centralist land-owning class, and disappointed about the loss of the last Spanish colonies in Cuba, Puerto Rico and the Philippines (1899) – a bitter blow to Catalan industry and trade – turned its back on Madrid and invested its energy in the transformation of a 'region' into a 'nation' (Vilar, 1964: 63). A robust process of nation-building and cultural revitalization began alongside the progressive growth of modern Catalan nationalism, and the Catalan language became even more central to the definition and articulation of a Catalan national identity.

The relatively normalized situation that Catalan enjoyed in the first decades of the twentieth century – chiefly in the short period of the Second Republic – was violently disrupted by the outbreak of the Spanish Civil War. When, in 1939, General Franco's rebel forces won the war, the ensuing dictatorial government abolished the Catalan government, which had sided with the Republic, and imposed a highly centralized regime, not only politically, but also linguistically and culturally. For just under forty years, only Spanish could be used in public life throughout Spain: in government, in the classroom, the press and the media, etc., with the sole exception of religious services, where, after the Second Vatican Council (1965), Catalan was adopted as the language of the activities of the Catholic Church in Catalonia. These conditions relegated Catalan to the status of a 'family language', kept far away from the echelons of prestige and power.

One of the goals of the dictatorial regime was to make the whole of the Spanish state politically and culturally homogeneous. Special efforts were made to eliminate the use of other languages spoken in the Spanish State: Catalan, Galician, Basque, Asturian, Aragonese and Aranese. The methods used to eliminate these languages included severe direct repression and other, more sophisticated, means of changing identity. In Catalonia obvious repressive activities involved the removal and burning of Catalan books from libraries and bookshops; the abolition of non-Spanish-language newspapers and periodicals; the banning of Catalan in the radio, theatres and cinemas; the translation of signs, place names, personal names and surnames into Spanish. Examples of more subtle attempts include Franco's permission, from 1946, of the publication of books in Catalan (under political censorship, of course) which had to be written in pre-standardized Catalan.[30]

Alongside political action against the Catalan language and culture during this period, other social and economic developments occurred which resulted in the Catalan language being further removed from its use in formal domains. In 1959 Spanish Television (RTVE) began to broadcast. This meant a big step forward towards the substitution of the Catalan language. Due to RTVE's broadcasts, the Spanish language penetrated deep into most Catalan domains which it had never reached before. It was the beginning of the most effective process of bilingualization yet, even more so than state schooling. The process has persisted up to the present when, as a consequence, not a single monolingual Catalan speaker exists any more. As in the Welsh, Irish and Basque cases, the complete bilingualization of minority-language monolinguals has profound implications for language policy. This represents a significant step towards linguistic and cultural homogenization in which minority-language claims can no longer be formulated on a basis of ignorance of the language of the state.

Catalonia's economic development during the 1950s and especially the 1960s, on the one hand, and the underdevelopment of other regions of Spain – particularly Spanish-speaking Andalucía, Extremadura and Murcia – on the other, meant that a large number of unskilled agricultural labourers in search of jobs, mainly in industry and tourism, migrated to Catalonia. One of the reasons why these immigrants decided to move to Catalonia instead of Germany or France, as many others certainly did, was that they remained within Spanish territory, and therefore expected an easier adaptation to their new home, in terms of culture and language. A large number of these immigrants settled down in the new industrial belt around the Catalan capital, Barcelona, and other urban complexes. For decades they and their offspring had little or no contact with Catalan within the new 'linguistic enclaves' into which they moved, where linguistic endogamy within the Spanish-speaking group was the common pattern. Even today, most of these areas are still mainly Spanish-speaking. For the first time in Catalan history, the language of social integration had become Spanish, not Catalan. These immigrants and their descendants now constitute nearly half of Catalonia's population.

Throughout the years of the dictatorship, Catalan individuals and organizations, both from the clandestine underground and those in exile, strove, often in highly adverse circumstances, to protect Catalan culture and identity (Samsó, 1995).

- The Generalitat kept functioning in exile.
- The Institute of Catalan Studies continued covert activities in Catalonia.
- Literary festivals and the publication of books and magazines such as *Quaderns de l'Exili* (Notebooks of the Exile) took place in different places in Europe and America, in order to keep the use of Catalan in literary and intellectual activities.
- In the later stages of the Francoist regime, a more tolerant cultural policy allowed the teaching of Catalan language. Omnium Cultural, a Catalan-culture NGO, was founded in 1961 by a group from the leading industrial bourgeoisie and a circle of intellectuals, in order to provide patronage for schools teaching the Catalan language, subsidize Catalan publications and to promote literary awards.

Following the death of General Franco in November 1975 there began a complex and fragile process of democratic transition. This process meant the restoration of Catalonia's self-government, together with the return of the Catalan language into public life and the beginning of its recovery.

## *The legal framework*

*Spanish Constitution, 1978:* Article 3 of the 1978 Constitution was the first step towards the official recognition of non-Spanish languages of the Spanish territory. Nevertheless, the recognition of linguistic plurality was not on the level of federal countries such as Switzerland, Belgium or Canada, as the central government remained monolingual[31] and a principle of territoriality was applied in the autonomous communities with their own language.[32] The Constitution established Spanish as the official language of the Spanish state, and required all citizens to know it. It also guaranteed the officiality of other Spanish languages within their own territory[33] and according to their respective regional constitutions.

*Catalan Statute of Autonomy, 1979:* The second big step for the recognition of the Catalan language in Catalonia was the 1979 Statute of Autonomy, very similar to other statutes in autonomous communities with languages other than Spanish. Article 3 of this statute declares that Catalan is Catalonia's 'own language' (*llengua pròpia*); that Catalan is the official language of Catalonia as is Spanish (which is official throughout the Spanish state) and that the regional government, the Generalitat, will guarantee the normal and official use of both languages, will take the necessary measures to ensure adequate knowledge and will create the conditions to allow both languages to attain full equality with respect to the rights and duties of the citizens of Catalonia. It mentions also that Aranese, an Occitan dialect spoken in the Pyrenean valley of Aran, will be the object of special respect and protection. In addition the Generalitat was given exclusive control over public education, enabling it to decide the language of instruction.

*The Catalan Language Promotion Acts of 1983 and 1998:* In order to fulfil its statutory aims of defending and promoting the Catalan language, the autonomous government, after a long period of consultation with political parties and other NGOs, adopted, in 1983, the first Catalan Language Act (*Llei 7/1983 de 18 d'abril de Normalització Lingüística*), endorsed by the Catalan Parliament with no votes cast against and only one abstention. The principal aim of this Act was to legalize the use of Catalan and Aranese and promote them in order to overcome the damage of a long period of systematic repression and ostracism from all public uses, which had left those languages in a precarious situation. This Act mainly addressed the use of Catalan in three key domains: public administration, education, and the mass media and cultural production:[34]

1. Section 1, article 5, declares Catalan to be the habitual language of internal procedures of the public administration, both in the Generalitat and other local authorities. It also guarantees that citizens are able to deal with and demand information
   from these authorities in the official language of their choice with no need to
   submit a translation. In order to be able to supply these services, public officials
   are required to show proficiency in both languages when entering the civil service.[35] Article 9 allows citizens to address the judiciary in whatever official
   language they prefer without the need to provide a translation. In practical terms
   this is very difficult, because the judicial body remains largely monolingual
   Spanish,[36] as is the case in all other central state and semi-state organisms in
   Catalonia.
2. Section 2, article 14, declares Catalan to be the language of education but the
   teaching of Spanish is also compulsory in all levels of state education from nursery schools to advanced level, with the exception of university education where
   teachers can choose the medium of instruction. Students have to show competence in both languages at the end of their primary education. Furthermore, the
   Act pre-empts any demand that pupils should be separated in different schools
   for reasons of language. Native Spanish speakers can be taught through the
   medium of that language in early education (three to six years old) and, after a
   period of 'language immersion', when students advance in their knowledge of
   Catalan, the latter progressively becomes the vehicular language of teaching.
3. Section 3 states that the Generalitat is obliged to promote Catalan language and
   culture in public radio and television; it is entitled to subsidize newspapers and
   other periodical publications written totally or partially in Catalan and boost
   publication of Catalan books; it is obliged as well to promote public cultural entertainment in Catalan.

Fifteen years after passing the 1983 Catalan Language Act, in order further to
protect and strengthen the territorial language, the Catalan government – in the
hands of CiU (Convergence and Union), the moderate nationalist coalition –
proposed updating this Act in the light of new circumstances. The CiU government argued in the introduction of the Act that the process of recovery of the
language had ground to a standstill not only due to economic forces, particularly
the globalization of communication, information and cultural industries, but to
a change in attitudes towards Catalonia and the Catalan language across
Spanish-speaking Spain. In the run-up to the 1996 state elections, some Madrid-
based private media started a campaign describing Catalonia's language policies
as a 'cultural genocide' directed against Spanish speakers living in Catalonia
(Strubell, 1996: 266–8). The Partit Socialista de Catalunya (Catalan Labour Party)
criticized CiU's decision to bring forward a new Act in order to 'hide' the
support given to the conservative Partido Popular (People's Party) in forming a
government in Madrid (Bañeres, 1999: 143), which also left the Catalan nationalist party 'exposed to criticism from its own more nationalist support' (MacInnes,
1999: 9). The passing of the new Act would affirm the CiU's commitment to the
Catalan language and therefore to their more nationalistic agenda. Hence the
political climate for the approval of the Act in the mid-1990s was very different

from the early 1980s *entente cordiale* among the political parties.[37] Initial popular support for the new Act was low, in comparison with the previous one. However, as a result of stinging criticism by PP politicians directed against both Catalonia and the Catalan language, popular opinion shifted to more favourable attitudes towards the Act (MacInnes and Gore, 1998: 29–31).

Some of the reform proposals were highly ambitious, involving a new 'duty' to know Catalan, further promotion of Catalan as the main medium of education at university level, requiring teachers to have a knowledge of Catalan, imposing sanctions on private companies which did not provide their services or products in Catalan and establishing quotas on the use of Catalan in radio, television and cinema. In the end, after a very heated political debate, CiU had to forego and water down many of these measures in order to gain the support it needed for the Act's approval by the PSC (Catalan Socialist Party). The 1998 Catalan Language Act (*Llei 1/1998 del 16 de gener*) was passed by the Catalan Parliament by a majority of votes from the CiU and PSC, but the conservative PP and nationalist ERC (Catalan Republican Left) voted against the Act, albeit for completely opposite reasons.

Nevertheless, and despite the controversy that surrounded the reform of the Act, very few substantial changes were made. If the previous Act paid paramount attention to the use of Catalan in public administration, education and the public media, the 1998 Act[38] draw attention to areas of social and cultural life where the use of Catalan was not yet guaranteed but where it was safe to legislate, as censuses showed that the level of understanding of Catalan was very high. Those areas where the reform was most evident included the private mass media, some cultural industries and economic activities, as detailed below.

Private radio and TV stations located in Catalonia are required in chapter 4, article 26, of the new Act, to broadcast at least half their output in Catalan. A reasonable number of songs produced by Catalan artists, and at least 25 per cent of songs played in music programmes from these TV and radio stations have to be broadcast in Catalan or Aranese.

The Act provides for the promotion of Catalan-language computer software and linguistic technologies (article 29). Article 26 of the same chapter 4 states that the Generalitat can demand quotas requiring the use of the Catalan language in films. The Decree 237/1998 *de 8 de setembre* establishes distribution and screen quotas in order to guarantee the translation of 'blockbuster' films into Catalan. Under this decree, at least half of the copies of those films with more than sixteen copies distributed (eighteen until December 2001) have to be in Catalan; 50 per cent of children's animation films have to be dubbed into Catalan; at least 25 per cent of films distributed by each distribution company in Catalonia have to be in Catalan; and the same percentages are applied to subtitled films. The decree provoked a severe disagreement between the Generalitat and the Spanish film distributors who in retaliation threatened to distribute fewer than the required sixteen copies, thus avoiding any obligation to dub films into Catalan. In the last analysis the crisis extended to the North American film producers, the 'majors', who opposed the decree and threatened to withdraw from distributing their films in Catalonia (Bañeres, 1999: 145–51). In May 2000 this decree was abolished as the Catalan government and the distributors failed to reach an agreement.

Public and privatized utilities, such as water, electricity, gas suppliers, communication and transport companies, have to use Catalan in signs and tannoy announcements as well as in their written communications, such as advertisements, contracts or bills, with their customers, without prejudice to the rights of citizens to receive a Spanish version if they request it. Furthermore, companies linked to any level of the Catalan government through contracts, aid grants, subsidies or other support are required by chapter 5, article 33, to use Catalan in signs and in their communications with clients when these communications are linked with the object of the support received.

## The goals and stages of language policy

*The normalization of the Catalan language:* The central objective of the language policy of Catalonia is fully to *normalize* the Catalan language, that is, to return to normality the use of the language in all areas of public life. As stated in the *Llibre Blanc de la Direcció General de Política Lingüística* (a White Paper) the government had the intention: 'to abolish the relationship of oppressive vs. oppressed language without reversing the situation, placing the two languages in a basis of legal equality and respecting the individual rights of all citizens' (Departament de Cultura de la Generalitat, 1983: 7). Nevertheless, the term 'language normalization' is an ambiguous one and has been used by politicians across the party spectra to mean quite different things. This may explain the popularity of the concept, which has expanded to other minority-language communities, both in Spain, such as the Basque Country and Galicia, and also in Wales. Although everyone more or less agrees that normalization is the process of reversing language shift after years of systematic decline, together with securing a better future for any self-sustaining language, the disagreements start when attempts are made to establish the rationale and methods by which this is to be achieved (Boix and Vila, 1998: 317).

According to the Catalan sociolinguist Albert Branchadell, the Catalan government's definition of normalization corresponds to what he calls a 'weak objective' or a 'weak normalization', involving a process which leads from a situation of formal double official status to a real (functional) double official status. This implies that all citizens who wish to use Catalan in every situation *could* do so, and Catalan would then become the main language of all institutions (Branchadell, 1996: 18). This definition contrasts with what Branchadell and many other sociolinguists believe to be the only way to achieve full normalization: when Catalan becomes the first language of the majority of the population and therefore the spontaneous preferred language of any social activity, implying that effectively everyone *will* live in Catalan (p. 19). This would also mean the disappearance of a Spanish linguistic community in Catalonia (p. 10).

Nevertheless, this is not the criterion of the Catalan government, which considers the normalization of the Catalan language to be compatible with the continuing existence of a Spanish-language community in Catalonia.

*Stages of language policy:* The creation in 1980 of the General Directorate for Language Policy (DGPL), as the main body in charge of the recovery of the Catalan language, represented the resumption of language planning by the Catalan government after more than forty years of language repression. This time the bulk of its policies were to be directed towards planning the status of the language, without neglecting the planning of its corpus. Since 1980 the language policies implemented by the Catalan institutions have evolved through two stages, broadly from 1980 until 1990 and a second phase from the beginning of the 1990s until today, the end of the twentieth century.

At the beginning of the 1980s there were no overall reliable data about the knowledge and use of the language in the whole territory of Catalonia. As we saw in Chapter 2, intelligent data gathering is a *sine qua non* for sound language policy. In the absence of such data, language planning officials used the only language data available to them, a 1975 census for the province of Barcelona. Extrapolating this data to the rest of Catalonia[39] it was assumed that 59 per cent of the population were able to speak Catalan, 80 per cent could understand it and 48 per cent used Catalan as a family language. The majority of Catalan families continued to use Catalan at home and for informal social purposes. However, the previous dictatorial regime's deleterious policy had undermined their self-image and confidence, and had an undeniable negative impact on Catalan use and competence, both oral and written. Only very young pupils, the elderly who had learned Catalan before the war and a few adults were proficient in written Catalan. The use of the language was very limited in newspapers, magazines, cinema, radio or TV, as well as in the administration, where civil servants had a very poor command of Catalan (Departament de Cultura, 1983: 11–12). Empirical research on language attitudes and behaviour at the beginning of the 1980s revealed two key attitudes.

1. The non-autochthonous population did not want the Catalan language to be imposed on them and rejected its compulsory use; they did not want to face discrimination on linguistic grounds; in general, they believed that the knowledge of Catalan could be advantageous in the workplace; they did not know the recent history of the Catalan language and considered the imbalance between the two languages to be normal; they agreed that Catalan should be taught in schools and they wanted their children to learn it; they were afraid of looking foolish by speaking Catalan in public and, in general, they accepted that Catalan speakers should be able to use Catalan freely.
2. The autochthonous population wanted to be very respectful towards the immigrant population; they did not want to be accused of racism, and switched easily from Catalan to Spanish, even if they were asked not to do so, as they did not want to be impolite; they wanted to forget forever the history of repression of Catalan

language and therefore they did not transmit it to the younger generations; in business and commerce they used only Spanish because everybody could understand it; they did not exercise their statutory rights, especially when dealing with public institutions, due mainly to inertia and shyness; they were afraid that they could not write properly and were conscious of the many mistakes they made when speaking Catalan, even if they did nothing to change this situation; they agreed that there should be an increase in the use of Catalan in the mass media, in schools and in the streets, but they did practically nothing to help change the situation; they did not want to cause any trouble, even if they were convinced that they were right. (Departament de Cultura, 1983: 13–14)

In view of this sociolinguistic situation DGPL decided to concentrate its action on, first, the extension of the knowledge of Catalan to all citizens of Catalonia, among students and adults alike. In order to do so, it had to create the necessary conditions at all levels of schooling, offering Catalan training or refresher courses for teachers, establishing language 'immersion' courses for children from Spanish-speaking homes and providing Catalan courses for adults, all of which were financed almost completely by the General Directorate and local authorities. Second, the DGPL sought to change the population's attitudes and norms of behaviour towards the use of Catalan through a series of campaigns aimed at informing, sensitizing and creating a consensus among the population. If the authorities wanted popular support to bolster language normalization, they had to inform the citizens that, without positive discrimination in favour of Catalan in some domains, the process would not be initiated. In 1982 the DGPL launched a campaign, popularly known as 'Norma', with the slogan: *el català és cosa de tots* (Catalan is everybody's business), where a cartoon figure of a ten-year-old girl encouraged the population to practice a 'bilingual conversation'. This sought to encourage Catalan speakers to speak in Catalan even if their interlocutors addressed them in Spanish, as many Spanish speakers in Catalonia understood Catalan. This campaign also argued that it was better to speak Catalan with some errors than not to speak it at all (Direcció General de Política Lingüística, 1983; Strubell, 1993: 185–7).

During this period, the Catalan language was extended to many new domains, especially those legislated for under the 1983 Act. The expansion of the use of Catalan in the administration was making progress as civil servants were taught and trained in Catalan. Moreover, the establishment of the Corporació Catalana de Ràdio i Televisió (Catalan Broadcasting Corporation) and of TV3 (1983), the Catalan-medium TV channel, a second Catalan channel, Canal 33 (1988) and a network of five public Catalan radio stations – Catalunya Ràdio, Ràdio Associació de Catalunya (today privatized), Catalunya Música, Catalunya Informació and Catalunya Cultura – expanded the use of Catalan within the modern mass media.

In the field of corpus planning, the works of codification by Pompeu Fabra needed to be adapted to the minor changes of the oral language, but nevertheless represented a significant starting-point for the diffusion of a common standard. However, as the functional expansion of Catalan spread over many new domains, the creation of terminology and the elaboration of different specific registers were urgently needed. In this field the DGPL commissioned universities and professional organizations, with the joint collaboration of the IEC, to carry out works of terminology and elaboration of new registers for all domains, from administrative and juridical to technological, scientific or commercial purposes. A major diffusion task of the standard language was carried out by the DGPL, with the publication of booklets, small vocabularies and many thematic posters, giving the correct Catalan names of such things as fruits and vegetables, tools for different jobs or car and bicycle components.

The extension of the Catalan language to new functions, especially in the mass media (Tubau, 1990a), again brought about a heated debate concerning two different language models, popularly known as 'Català *heavy* vs. Català *light*', that is, between the defenders of a more 'purist' model, or a model with fewer concessions to Spanish lexicon and syntax (Pazos, 1990); and those who favoured a model closer to the urban spoken language, more influenced by Spanish (Pericay and Toutain, 1986; Tubau, 1990b). In the end, no major changes in the Catalan standard took place; however, it could be said that the 'light' rather than the 'heavy' model prevailed in the media. In 1985 the Termcat, a terminology centre, was set up by the Department of Culture and the IEC as the responsible body for terminology research in all fields, especially the more dynamic scientific and technological fields, and the publication of specific vocabularies and glossaries.

At the end of the 1980s some Catalan sociolinguists and planners realized that the measures undertaken until then by the Generalitat were not sufficient to change the language behaviour of the population. Despite the fact that surveys showed an increase in the understanding and knowledge of the language, this knowledge, as has been noted earlier of Welsh in this volume, did not translate automatically into use (Colomines, 1990: 52–3). Despite the success of the 'Norma' campaign in creating goodwill among the population about the need to promote the language and pave the way for the acceptance of the first normalization Act, it did not achieve its goal of changing the deeply rooted social norm among Catalan speakers, a legacy from the years under the Franco regime, of accommodating to Spanish whenever addressed in that language (Direcció General de Política Lingüística, 1991: vol. 1, p. 12; Strubell, 1996: 267–8). This confirmation gave rise to yet another controversy, this time the 'debate about the future of the language' (Branchadell, 1996: 7). The contenders were popularly known as 'pessimists' who believed that the language was in danger of disappearing if normalization[40] was not achieved (mainly Prats et al., 1990) and 'optimists', those who believed that the Catalan language enjoyed good health, at least in Catalonia, and was no longer in danger (Vallverdú, 1990). This debate was the catalyst of a change in direction by the policies of the DGPL and meant the end of a first stage of promotion of the knowledge of Catalan and the start of a second phase where all the stress was to be placed on the extension of the use of Catalan (Direcció General de Política Lingüística, 1991: vol. 1, pp. 1–12; Boix and Vila, 1998: 40).

If there was to be a change of direction or the creation of a new paradigm for language planning and policy, major research was needed in order to acquire in-depth knowledge of current sociolinguistic reality and to understand better the social mechanisms which both hindered and favoured the extension of the use of the Catalan language. Thus the DGPL, comprising not only language planners and sociolinguists but also scholars from other social science disciplines, produced a document with up-to-date research about the real sociolinguistic situation of Catalan. This became the scientific basis on which the government sought to design a strategic plan in order to implement future policies. The results were published in 1991 in a four-volume study under the title *Estudis i propostes per a la difusió de l'ús social de la llengua catalana* (Studies and proposals for the extension of the social use of the Catalan language). Attention was also paid to analysing and learning lessons from other minority-language communities in Europe and elsewhere (Direcció General de Política Lingüística, 1991: vol. 4).

Therefore, the two most important developments during this second period are, first, the elaboration of the so-called General Plan of Language Promotion, published in 1995 and after a long period of elaboration and consultation, as the main strategic framework for the design and implementation of language policies. Secondly, there was in-depth analysis of the legal framework both of the Spanish Constitution and the Statute of Autonomy, in order to maximize Catalan-language promotion policies and either reform and update the 1983 Language Act or, as happened, to elaborate a new Act.

Nevertheless, the first suggestion for the need of a global strategic plan for the promotion of Catalan came as early as 1986 from the conclusions of the Second International Congress of the Catalan Language. This Congress mobilized large sections of the society to reflect about the process of language promotion not only in Catalonia but in all the Catalan-language territories, known as 'Països Catalans' (Catalan Countries). The need for a general plan was later stressed and supported by other sociolinguists (Bastardas, 1991: 75–9), who regarded the plan as a means of jettisoning improvisation and targeting efficiently the most crucial domains in which to intervene (Bastardas, 1990: 21).

If the plan was to be inclusive and accepted by Catalan society at large there was a need for wide consultation with the civil society, which is why in 1991 the Consell Social de la Llengua Catalana (Social Council of the Catalan Language) was created. The Council is constituted by representatives of all kind of organizations, public, voluntary and private, and acts as a consultative and advisory body on social implications in language policy.

The General Language Normalization Plan (Generalitat de Catalunya, 1995), which was finally approved in 1995, set out seven main areas within which to target language promotion: public institutions, education research and youth; the media; the socio-economic world, including trade unions, business organizations and private businesses; health and social institutions; cultural and territorial relations with the other Catalan-speaking territories; and finally diffusion of the standard language and sociolinguistic research (see Marí, 1997; Solé, 1997). The aim of the General Plan

> is to achieve the maximum respect for the personal language of each citizen and the maximum linguistic availability from the public and private organizations – as citizens, an effective linguistic option – as professionals, a sufficient knowledge of the two languages to allow them to respect the linguistic option of everyone. (Solé, 1997: 50)

The philosophy behind the policies undertaken in this second stage is well captured in the following statement:

> Not every domain is equally controllable or easy to inspect from the Administration. Catalans know this better than anybody: the whole of the repressive machinery of the Franco régime could not succeed in the abandonment by Catalan speakers of their language for family and intimate relations. Therefore, in a democracy, the capacity to legitimately impinge on cultural, social and family domains is very limited. This means that the objectives that can be established by the Administration, in accordance with popular will and always respecting the rights of the citizens, cannot be pursued by direct actions, but only through information, encouragement and support to *institutions which can legitimately influence in a more immediate and direct way the behaviour of the citizens.* (Direcció General de Política Lingüística, 1991: vol. 1, p. 12)[41]

From the beginning of the 1990s, the centre of attention of language policies and campaigns formulated by the DGPL switched from the individual to what Bastardas calls 'comunicacions institucionalitzades' (1991: 59); that is, to influence the communications produced not only by the public or semi-public institutions, where Catalan was comparatively more widely used, but to non-official organizations, from private companies, or leisure and sports organizations, to voluntary ones. As Bastardas points out, the communications of all kind of organizations or institutions have a remarkable impact on the communications by individuals because of their status and continued presence in the everyday life of citizens. They are more easily modifiable, if the political will exists to do so, than the more rooted interpersonal communication habits, which will adapt to the context only if it is necessary and advantageous (Bastardas, 1990: 13–19).

This change of direction, from trying to modify the communication habits of individuals to emphasizing efforts to influence those of all kinds of organizations, was reflected in the campaigns undertaken by the DGPL in this second stage. It was expected that, in return, these communications would have an impact on those of the citizens and help, with time, to shape their opinions about the value of the language and, most of all, their linguistic behaviour. If the slogans and messages of the previous campaigns, such as *el català depèn de vostè* (Catalan depends on you), *el català és cosa de tots* (Catalan is everybody's business) or *el català per respecte a tu mateix i a els altres* (Catalan for self-respect and respect to others), were very general and directed at changing the attitudes of the whole population, in this stage the campaigns were to be focused on important aspects of the every day life of citizens, such as restaurants, bars and hotels, commercial signs, supermarkets, tourism, sports, leisure, automotive sector (driving schools, garages, car sales shops, insurance companies), cinema and video, and with slogans like *es nota prou que sóm a Catalunya?* (It is clear enough that we are in Catalonia?), *català eina de feina* (Catalan is a working tool) or *el català sobre rodes* (Catalan on wheels), a campaign for the promotion of Catalan in the automotive sector (Strubell, 1993: 188–90). These campaigns were complemented by the publication of bilingual vocabularies, glossaries and other promotion materials such as posters and stickers, articulating the relationship between status and corpus planning.

The DGPL was also engaged in the creation of mechanisms to evaluate better the impact of their policies in the targeted sectors and other aspects of the every-day life of citizens, with the programme INUSCAT (*Indicador d'ús del Català*, Language use indicators), an index which enables the quantification and comparisons of the degree of use of Catalan in specific places and times (Romaní et al., 1997).

After all the steps taken prior to the elaboration and approval of the General Plan – research, revision of the legal framework and the creation of a consulta-tive body representing civil society – there was still a need to adapt the govern-mental implementation bodies to the new strategy. Thus the development and extension of a network of language centres, bureaux and services was given priority. In 1988 the Consorci per a la Normalització Lingüística[42] (Consortium for language promotion) was established by the Generalitat. The Consortium, a decentralized public organization, co-ordinated and financed by the DGPL and local authorities, was created to adapt targets and measures to the needs of different areas of the territory and sectors of society in view of the diversity of sociolinguistic features of each region and sector. Taking the form of a territorial network of language centres, the consortium was to be involved not only with the teaching of Catalan to adults but more actively with language invigoration through specific programmes directed to different sectors (sectorial programmes) and with language consultancy in their respective territorial areas of action. The Consortium developed the INDEXPLA, a software programme aimed at measuring and obtaining a graphic representation of the use of Catalan in all kind of organizations, from small or medium companies to more complex organisms, as a starting-point in developing and applying a made-to-measure plan and to evaluate afterwards the impact of this.

During this period there began as well the progressive creation of units of language services inside complex organizations such as chambers of commerce, trade unions and other entrepreneurial organizations, universities, professional bodies, public and private companies, etc., which were expected to influence and create a multiplier effect in the use of Catalan in the areas in which all these bodies worked.

## The language planning institutions: areas of activity

As in the Basque case, practically all Catalan-language promotion from the end of the 1950s, when the so-called *aperturismo* of the Franco regime relaxed its policies against the other languages of Spain, up until the first years of the Spanish democratic transition, can be considered 'bottom–up' planning. However, with the advent of Catalan democratic reforms, the government of the Generalitat began a process of institution-building and the creation of a number of policy-making and implementation bodies within all levels of government. Legitimization and institutionalization of the Catalan language led to a process of demobilization for linguistic reasons. Even if there are some civic organizations which still mobilize and campaign for more active promotion of Catalan,[43] and others which protest against the neglect of the rights of Spanish L1-speaking citizens, claiming that language policies by the autonomous government go too far,[44] 'top–down' planning is the predominant form of language planning in Catalonia.

*Top–down language planning:* Since the foundation of the General Directorate of Language Policy in 1980, the institutional structure charged with the promotion of Catalan language has grown into an impressive and complex organization (see Figure 11.2) which links all levels and departments of government and extends its actions to other organizations in civil society. With the growth of the structural support for the Catalan language we have seen also the development of a real field of expertise in language planning, with some 600 'tècnics de normalització lingüística' or professional language planners working within this complex organization.

Soon after 1980, when the DGPL[45] was founded as the main regulatory body of Catalan-language promotion, the Servei d'Assessorament Lingüístic (Language Advisory Service), Servei de Normalització Lingüística (Language Promotion Service) and the Institut de Sociolingüística Catalana (Institute of Catalan Sociolinguistics) were created, and today they are answerable to the Subdirectorate General. The Advisory Service is mainly in charge of the promotion of the quality of the Catalan language, used by public and private organizations alike, and the promotion of the teaching of Catalan in areas with special needs and abroad. The Promotion Service is responsible for the promotion of Catalan in all areas of social activity through campaigns and other means. The Institute is a centre for research and expertise in sociolinguistics, it has the function of monitoring, documenting and evaluating the results of language policies undertaken by the DGPL. In addition, it undertakes research about the use of Catalan in different sectors as well as analysing the sociolinguistic situation of the Catalan language.

Moreover, all government departments have a language unit[46] which has the dual function of advising civil servants on linguistic matters and diffusing specific terminology among all kinds of organizations and professionals linked

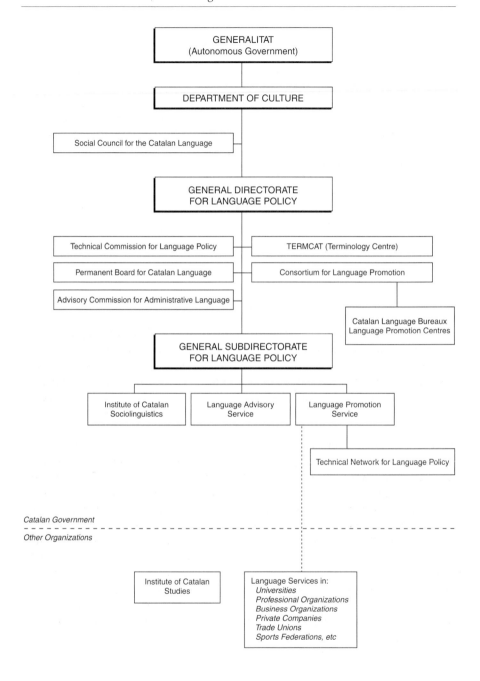

**Figure 11.2. Organization chart of language policy in the Autonomous Government of Catalonia**

to each sector of activity. The Generalitat has created a network of organizations in order to co-ordinate and draw together all these internal services:

- to guarantee the even application of the linguistic rules and regulations within every department (Technical Commission for Language Policy);
- to inform the DGPL about actions concerning language policy undertaken by the different departments; to fulfil the language use legislation in the administration and the norms about the knowledge of Catalan among civil servants and to supervise the correct and uniform use of terminology in close collaboration with the Termcat (The Technical Network);
- to advise the DGPL on matters relating to the administrative and judicial language (The Advisory Commission for Administrative Language);
- to devise and organize examinations for the award of general and specific certificates of proficiency in Catalan (Permanent Board).

There are also language units in the territorial representation of the Generalitat in all four of the provincial capitals of Catalonia.

## Conclusions

*Achievements and failures:* During the democratic period Catalan language and culture has been recovering well from a period of repression and subordination. The ability to understand and speak the Catalan language by the Catalan population has increased considerably since the beginning of the 1980s, especially among the younger generations, thanks mainly to developments in the education system. Adults have improved their language skills, thanks to the many available language courses for adults offered by the Consortium and other organizations. As a result of the steady support for the language by the autonomous government via active language planning and policies, the Catalan language is widely used in public institutions and has increased its presence, although at different strengths, in many domains of everyday life: media, workplace, businesses, leisure, culture, shops, new technologies, etc. Catalan is used more in the domain of the public institutions than in informal and everyday activities. A main cause of this is the tendency of Catalan speakers to a loss of linguistic loyalty towards Catalan due to the decrease of conflict in the linguistic contact between Spanish and Catalan. This tendency is most evident among youngsters, who have a general feeling of indifference regarding the language, due, as Emili Boix points out, to a poor understanding of the linguistic situation of the Catalan language (1993: 203–12). Thus, despite many campaigns to encourage 'bilingual conversation', Catalan is still not the habitual language of exchange between Catalan and Spanish speakers.

The mass arrival of Spanish-speaking immigrants ceased in the early 1970s, and by the early 1980s the migratory balance was negative. Immigrants who moved to Catalonia in the 1950s and 1960s are growing older, while their second- and third-generation descendants are growing up in a society where Catalan language has acquired a new prestige and currency. Due to the class structure of the Catalan society, whereby Catalan was spoken more extensively by middle and upper middle classes, by those with above average education and occupational skills, the Catalan language acquired a concomitant status and prestige. For many Spanish-speaking immigrants, upward mobility would involve acquiring a command of Catalan. However, despite their proficiency in Catalan, Spanish continues to be their preferred language in every day activities. The Spanish L1-speaking community in Catalonia is a permanent feature of the sociolinguistic landscape and, although they feel Catalan, their first-choice language is not Catalan.

Catalan is the habitual language of over half of the total population of Catalonia, and almost all of the population of Catalan origin. The intergenerational transmission of Catalan seems narrowly secured as different studies show that 50.4 per cent of parents say they speak Catalan with their children; 51 per cent speak Catalan with their partners (Strubell, 1999: 18) and 65 per cent claim to have a better competence in Catalan than their mothers (Bañeres, 1999: 134). Nevertheless, and quite worryingly, 40 per cent of the couples surveyed did not have children (Strubell, 1999: 22–5). If this trend continues, it will have an obvious impact on the vitality of Catalan in the near future, independently of any language policy that the government might implement to compensate for the effects of such a low demographic index.

Another problem which works against the normalization of the Catalan language is the loss of militancy in favour of Catalan, derived from a general feeling that Catalan is already 'normalized', or at least that it is no longer in danger. Indeed, the important presence of Catalan in public life, chiefly in public organizations, corroborates this feeling. At the same time, this vision of the preponderance of Catalan in public life favours the pro-Spanish reactions that claim that there is an unfair imposition of Catalan on the Spanish speakers in Catalonia, reactions which work for the delegitimization of the promotion of the Catalan language.

*Future challenges:*  There are many challenges ahead for the Catalan language if it is to be the hegemonic or preferred language of all citizens of Catalonia.

- The Spanish state is still a monolingual state and still has much latent animosity against the 'other' languages. Although legally these other languages are equal or co-official with Spanish, Spanish continues to be the only language that Spanish citizens have a duty to know. At present, Spanish is the language that guarantees the mechanisms of integration-discrimination almost without any restriction in Catalonia.
- There are still many sectors of life where Catalan speakers do not have the opportunity to choose between the two languages. Despite the limited subsidy policies practised by the Catalan government, globalization, Spanish and foreign markets and the omnipresence of mass media and cultural industries all favour Spanish and work against Catalan.

- The phenomenon of immigration from outside the European Union into Catalonia is not as large as in other countries like France, Germany or the UK. However, it certainly has an impact on Catalan, as the language of social integration of these new immigrants is likely to be Spanish, especially in urban areas. This issue is the litmus test for modern social and cultural policies. Official Catalan policies framed by the Generalitat, together with state policies from Spain, France or Italy, are unable to deal with this matter adequately.
- Finally, global language policy or joint action for the promotion of Catalan in all the Catalan linguistic territories does not seem to happen. Certain threats to the unity of the Catalan language are posed by some political sectors in the Valencian community which favour a different codification for the public use of Valencian. This lack of co-ordination leads to a missed opportunity for the creation of a wider Catalan market as there are more than eight million potential consumers for its products and services.

## FRUITFUL AREAS OF EUROPEAN CO-OPERATION

Given the wealth of evidence contained within these comparative cases, it is vital that other lesser used language communities benefit from the sharing of information. To that end Williams (1999a) has suggested the following programme for increased European co-operation, not only for lesser used language communities within the EU but also for those in Central and Eastern Europe.

1. Joint venture projects by respective language boards in Europe, for example, sharing resources on social motivation campaigns, language marketing and advertising campaigns.
2. Preparation of a Community Language Planning Handbook for the European Union.
3. Technological developments for community language development, for example, co-operation on spellchecker software and on-line dictionaries/thesauri between language groups and in co-operation with major international software houses (for example, Microsoft/AppleMac), thereby taking advantage of economies of scale in the production of such facilities.
4. Exchange and development of progressive and successful, stress-free, holistic teaching methods for community language eduction, especially for new speakers and those whose skills need to be boosted.
5. Marketing strategies to convince the general public of the material relevance of the lesser used language in the wider society, for example, a commercial and economic edge to more common culturally based justifications for language promotion. In the original research project, this was a particularly acute consideration which should be harnessed in promoting the target language within the business environment, in the advertising world and in adult education both as a medium of teaching and as a subject in itself.
6. Within the statutory system of democratic representation, language promotion should be a consideration in the following areas: in the workplace generally, in incorporating the interests of the target language within public administration,

the legal profession and senior civil service and developing professional competence of its usage within these key sectors (this is particularly acute if we wish to realize a truly bilingual civil society, wherein the communities in question may be served in the language of their choice by a professionally trained service provider), in incorporating the interests of the target language within the town and country planning system.

7. Facilitating community development activities which are not necessarily dependent upon government support, but reach out to other agencies and to the commercial sector. There is a real danger in tying the future of individual communities to the largesse of the local state. How one maintains the relative autonomy of community-level action is one of the most profound challenges influencing the vitality of contemporary democracy.

8. To initiate practical strategies which will relate aspects of community language planning in a more focused manner than hitherto to economic and regional development programmes.

9. To focus on the training of multipliers (language *animateurs*) in the community who would: develop practical aspects of policy, drive implementation and innovation, offer specialist assistance to target groups with acute/special needs.

10. To devise multilateral action-research projects wherein the interests of community language planning is one consideration among many. An overconcentration on language issues rather than social issues may fragment rather than integrate community interests – the medium must not become the message.

11. To foster collaborative policy initiatives with agencies such as the Committee of the Regions, selected Regional Assemblies and Parliaments, and NGOs; so that language considerations become embedded in all aspects of policy, where relevant, rather than being considered as add-on measures.

12. To establish a Europe-wide related set of websites for the dissemination of good practice, research findings, financial sources and socio-political initiatives.

## Notes

[1] According to Eusko Jaurlaritza et al., 1997: 28–9, 83 per cent of the population of the Basque Autonomous Community considers itself Basque, about 70 per cent of the French Basque Country and 56 per cent of Navarre.

[2] It is nevertheless somewhat of a puzzlement to historians of the shifts in language use in the Basque Country as to why Basque was so readily substituted by Spanish in parts of the inland rural provinces of Araba and Navarre in the eighteenth and nineteenth centuries, a process which had been promoted by church and state well before the capitalist developments in the coastal provinces of Biscay and Gipuzkoa starting in the second half of the nineteenth century and thus which cannot be explained in the same way.

[3] For a full development of these parallels in the changing fortunes of the two languages in the face of this change in the mode of production, see Basterra (1999).

[4] For a description of the modest attempts at schooling in Basque in the past, see Zalbide (1990), Chapter 1.

[5] In this respect one can mention Larramendi, Anton Abadia, Louis-Lucien Bonaparte and their collaborators.

[6] He unsuccessfully proposed a base ten counting system to replace B tional base twenty system; he proposed further modifications to the B system; he invented neologisms and was the inspiration for many others to do so.

[7] Published in the Official Gazette of the Basque Country of 16 December 1982. English translation available: see Basque Government, The Secretariat of Linguistic Policy.

[8] Data taken from Eusko Jaurlaritza, Nafarroako Gobernua and Euskal Kultur Erakundea.

[9] The 1951 Deixonne law allows some use of Basque in teaching; but the French state's primary concern in its most recent language planning law seems to be to defend French from English.

[10] Literally, the Organic Law for the Restoration and Improvement of the Charter Regime of Navarre.

[11] Published in the Official Gazette of Navarre on 17 December 1986.

[12] 'In spite of the fact that this law occasionally goes as far as using the expression "normal use" (art. 1.1.) and speaking of "protecting the recovery and development of Basque in Navarre" (art. 1.1.b), it is clear from the framework that the object is more one of maintenance or conservation of Basque in the Charter Community [of Navarre] than of setting in motion a process of language normalisation within a régime of effective bilingualism; more a case of halting the process of regression at the moment of initiating this piece of legislation than of promoting its reversal' (Cobreros, 1989: 145).

[13] Gardner's translation. An alternative translation, along with translations to other state languages of the EU including Irish, can be found in Berriatua.

[14] The one modest element of the use of the territoriality principle in BAC legislation, to wit the right of local councils in predominantly Basque-speaking areas to use Basque only, was declared unconstitutional by sentence 82/1986 of the Constitutional Court of Spain.

[15] According to a 1996 government survey reported in the newspaper *El País* on 28 September 1998, 75 per cent of Basque speakers in the BAC were in favour of independence. By contrast, this equation clearly does not hold in Catalonia where the use of Catalan and its defence is a cross-party matter.

[16] For data on elections in the BAC, visit www.eustat.es (Eustat is the Basque government's statistics organization).

[17] For example, earlier this century some tried to replace the traditional 'fruitu' (fruit) by 'igali'. When the word 'telefono' (telephone) came into use, an attempt was made to replace it by 'urrutizkin'. Only a small number of these purist inventions have achieved a broader acceptance and use.

[18] For this belief see Erize, 1997: 514 for an opinion expressed in the 1930s.

[19] See, for example, Erize's interview with Fishman in *Planet* (April 2000) or Fishman, 1989: ch. 12, particularly p. 394.

[20] Readers should be warned that Basque language loyalists frequently use the term *diglossia* in a way not supported by English-language academic literature, as an often insulting description of the present situation of the Basque language to be overcome by appropriate language policies. See Sánchez Carrión, 1987: 343–4 for a description of how this change in meaning came about.

[21] Over seventy such organizations, large and small, were active in the BAC in 1999. (Information provided by subministry for language planning of the BAC.)

[22] A recent doctoral thesis by Asier Aranguren on local media mentioned in *Euskararen Berripapera*, 91 (Dec. 1999), 3, lists forty-six local magazines (usually weekly, fortnightly or monthly), six local TV stations and five publicly owned local radio stations.

[23] A town often mentioned in this respect is Arrasate or Mondragón, which has

pioneered language planning initiatives subsequently taken up by other towns. Nevertheless, it should be pointed out that this town has dedicated nearly 4 per cent of its annual budget to language maintenance and promotion, at a time when the Basque government is proposing that local councils should aim at upping their funds to 2 per cent.

[24] We are unaware of any examples of the conservation of the Basque language being taken into account in the planning of land use. While it is true that massive in-migration to the Spanish Basque Country came to a halt in the mid-1970s, specific projects do occur which are likely to harm the use of Basque in a given area and, hence, some protection would be desirable, but none exists. In the economic sphere, there is no organization comparable to Menter a Busnes.

[25] The main source for this section is Agirrebaltzategi (1999).

[26] See Grin et al. (1999) for one such attempt, discussing examples from Wales and the Basque Country among others.

[27] For example, the oft-repeated proposal to do away with the model A (Spanish medium, Basque as a subject) option in primary and secondary education.

[28] Although Catalan is the only official language of Andorra, this does not imply that it is the only language spoken in this micro-state. Spanish mainly, but also French, are widely used, especially in commerce and tourism (Govern d'Andorra: 1996). The Andorran government is currently undertaking activities to promote the use of Catalan in this small country.

[29] According to the last census of 1996, 95 per cent of a total population of 5,984,000 claimed to understand Catalan (93.8 in 1991), 75.30 per cent claimed to be able to speak it (68.3 in 1991), 72.40 per cent to read it (67.6 in 1991), and 45 per cent to write it (39.9 in 1991) (Institut d'Estadística de Catalunya: http://www.idescat.es/)

[30] That is, Catalan before Pompeu Fabra's codification works.

[31] Article 3.1 of the Spanish Constitution is very similar to Article 2 of the French Constitution.

[32] Nevertheless, it cannot be considered a full principle of territoriality as the territorial languages are not exclusively official but they share joint officiality with Spanish. Even where they are co-official, there is a marked difference between them, as the use of Catalan is a right but the knowledge of Spanish is a duty.

[33] For the full statement of Article 3 see the earlier discussion in this chapter relative to the Spanish state and the Basque Country.

[34] See the full text of the Act in and further legislation implementing its provisions in Weber and Strubell, 1991: 55–76.

[35] Act 17/1985 on Public Offices of the Administration of the Generalitat was considered by the Socialist Spanish government to be anti-constitutional and was brought before the Constitutional Court. This Court considered that requiring knowledge of Catalan by candidates for public office did not breach the Constitution.

[36] The fact that the use of Catalan is still in a minority position in this domain is because there is a deficit of Catalan-speaking judges. This is made worse by the mobility inherent in this job, as judges tend to stay only temporarily in Catalonia and, mostly, see no reason to learn Catalan.

[37] It is worth noting that in 1983 the conservative party Alianza Popular, the PP's predecessor, had no representation at all in the Catalan Parliament.

[38] For a more in-depth analysis of the 1998 Language Act see MacInnes and Gore, 1998: 31–8.

[39] Because the linguistic situation of the province of Barcelona is very specific, this extrapolation was far from an adequate picture of the linguistic reality of Catalonia and

was made only for operational purposes (Departament de Cultura, 1983: 11). A complete picture is, of course, only possible with the type of Household Survey and Census Analysis instruments discussed in Chapter 2 above.

[40] Normalization here means to make Catalan the hegemonic language of Catalonia.

[41] Puigdevall i Serralvo's translation and italics. The Catalan original says: 'No tots els àmbits són igualment controlables o inspeccionables des de l'Administració. Això, els catalans ho sabeu millor que ningú: tot l'aparell repressiu del règim franquista no aconseguí que els catalans abandonessin la seva llengua en els àmbits més familiars i íntims. Per tant, en una democràcia la capacitat d'incidir legítimament en àmbits culturals, socials i familiars és molt reduïda. Això vol dir que els objectius que l'Administració pot establir, d'acord amb la voluntat popular i respectant sempre els drets dels ciutadans, no es poden perseguir mitjançant accions directes, sinó per la via de la informació, de l'encoratjament i del suport a entitats que poden legítimament influir de manera més immediata i directa en la conducta dels ciutadans.'

[42] Visit the Consortium's web page at http://www.cpnl.org/

[43] For example, Omnium Cultural, Organització pel Multilingüisme, ADEC-Associació en Defensa de l'Etiquetatge en Català or Plataforma per la Llengua.

[44] For example, Foro Babel, Convivència Cívica Catalana, Acción Cultural Miguel de Cervantes, CADECA-Coordinadora de Afectados en Defensa de la Lengua Castellana.

[45] For more information about the General Directorate visit its official web page at: http://cultura.gencat.es/llengcat/

[46] Some of them make extensive use of the internet in order to make their services more accessible and easy to use. For instance the Department of Territorial Policies and Public Works (http: //www.gencat.es/ptop/llengua/index.htm); the Department of Industry, Commerce and Tourism (http: //www.gencat.es/dict/serveis/servling/serveilingdef.htm) and the Department of Justice (http://www.gencat.es/justicia/llengua/).

## References

Agirrebaltzategi, P. (1999). 'Euskararen aldeko gizarte-mugimenduaren 25 urteok: EKBren ekarpena', *Bat soziolinguistika aldizkaria*, 31 (July), 55–73.

Arna Phoillsiú ag Oifig an tSoláthair (1965). *Athbheochan na Gaeilge: The Restoration of the Irish Language*, Dublin: Arna Phoillsiú ag Oifig an tSoláthair.

Bañeres, Jordi (1999). 'Quinze mesos intensos: L'ús social del Català al Principat (gener de 1998–març de 1999) (2a part)', *Revista de Catalunya*, 140, 131–54.

Basque Government, The Secretariat of Linguistic Policy (1986). *Basic Law of the Standardization of the Use of Basque*, Vitoria-Gasteiz: Central Publications Office, Basque Government.

Bastardas i Boada, Albert (1990). 'L'extensió de l'ús del català: Fonaments teòrics per a una nova etapa', *Revista de Catalunya*, 38, 13–23.

Bastardas i Boada, Albert (1991). *Fer el futur: Sociolingüística, planificació i normalització del Català*, Barcelona: Empúries.

Basterra, H. (1999). 'The sociolinguistics of iron and coal', unpublished Ph.D. thesis, Philips University, Marburg.

Berriatua, X., ed. (1983). *Euskal Herriko Autonomia Estatutoa*, Vitoria-Gasteiz: Eusko Jaurlaritzaren Argitalpen Zerbitzu Nagusia.

Blaney, R. (1996). *Presbyterians and the Irish Language*, Belfast: Ulster Historical Foundation and Ultach Trust.

Boix i Fuster, Emili (1993). *Identitat i llengua en els joves de Barcelona*, Barcelona: Edicions 62.

Boix i Fuster, Emili and Vila i Moreno (1998). *Socioligüística de la llengua catalana*, Barcelona: Ariel Lingüística.

Bord na Gaeilge (1986). *Irish and the Education System: An Analysis of Examination Results*, Dublin: Bord na Gaeilge.

Bord na Gaeilge (1988). *The Irish Language in a Changing Society*, Dublin: Bord na Gaeilge.

Branchadell, Albert (1996). *La normalitat improbable*, Barcelona: Empúries.

Brown, T. (1981). *Ireland: A Social and Cultural History, 1922–1985*, London: Fontana Press.

Clarke, D. M. and Jones, C., eds (1999). *The Rights of Nations: Nations and Nationalism in a Changing World*, Cork: Cork University Press.

Cobreros, E. (1989). *El régimen jurídico de la oficialidad del euskera*, Oñati: Herri-arduralaritzaren euskal erakundea.

Colomines i Puig, Joan (1990). 'Informe sobre la llengua', *Revista de Catalunya*, 44, 48–56.

Comhdháil Náisúnta na Gaeilge (1998). *Towards a Language Act: A Discussion Document*, Dublin: Comhdháil Náisiúnta na Gaeilge.

Departament de Cultura de la Generalitat (1983). *Llibre Blanc de la Direcció General de Política Lingüística*, Barcelona: Departament de Cultura.

Direcció General de Política Lingüística (1983). *La campanya per la normalització lingüística*, Barcelona: Generalitat de Catalunya.

Direcció General de Política Lingüística (1991). *Estudis i propostes per a la difusió de l'ús social de la llengua Catalana*, Barcelona: Departament de Cultura, Generalitat de Catalunya, vols 1–4.

Dorian, N. (1999). 'Review of P. Ó. Riagáin, *Language Policy and Social Reproduction 1893–1993*', *Language in Society*, 28 (1), 129–30.

Erize, X. (1997). *Nafarroako Euskararen Historia Soziolinguistikoa (1863–1936): Soziolinguistika Historikoa eta Hizkuntza Gutxituen Bizitza*, Iruñea: Nafarroako Gobernua.

Eusko Jaurlaritza, Kultura Saila (1995). *Euskararen Jarraipena*, Vitoria-Gasteiz: Eusko Jaurlaritzaren Argitalpen Zerbitzu Nagusia [in Basque, Spanish and French].

Eusko Jaurlaritza, Kultura Saila (1997). *II. Soziolinguistikazko Mapa*, Vitoria-Gasteiz: Eusko Jaurlaritzaren Argitalpen Zerbitzu Nagusia, vols 1–3.

Eusko Jaurlaritza, Kultura Saila (1999). *Euskara Biziberritzeko Plan Nagusia/Plan General de Promoción del Uso del Euskera*, Vitoria-Gasteiz: Eusko Jaurlaritzaren Argitalpen Zerbitzu Nagusia [an unpublished English translation is available].

Eusko Jaurlaritza, Nafarroako Gobernua and Euskal Kultur Erakundea (1997). *Euskal Herriko Soziolinguistikazko Inkesta 1996/Euskararen Jarraipena II*, Nafarroako Gobernua: Eusko Jaurlaritza; Vitoria-Gasteiz: Euskal Kultur Erakundea [also available in French and Spanish].

Fishman, J. (1989). *Language and Ethnicity in Minority Sociolinguistic Perspective*, Clevedon, Avon: Multilingual Matters.

Fishman, J. (1990). 'Eskolaren mugak hizkuntzak biziberritzeko saioan', *Euskal Eskola Publikoaren Lehen Kongresua*, 1, 181–8 [also in Spanish, pp. 189–96, under the title 'Limitaciones de la eficacia escolar para invertir el desplazamiento lingüístico'], Vitoria-Gasteiz: Eusko Jaurlaritzaren Argitalpen Zerbitzu Nagusia.

Fishman, J. (1991). *Reversing Language Shift: Theoretical and Empirical Foundations of Assistance to Threatened Languages*, Clevedon, Avon: Multilingual Matters.

Flynn, D. (1993). 'Irish in the school curriculum: a matter of politics', *The Irish Review*, 14, 74–82.

Francis, H. (1984). *Miners against Fascism: Wales and the Spanish Civil War*, London: Lawrence and Wishart.

García de Cortázar, F. and Lorenzo Espinosa, J. M. (1997). *Historia del País Vasco*, Donostia-San Sebastián: Editorial Txertoa.

Gardner, N. (2000). *Basque in Education in the Basque Autonomous Community*, Vitoria-Gasteiz: Eusko Jaurlaritzaren Argitalpen Zerbitzu Nagusia.

Generalitat de Catalunya (1995). *The General Language Normalisation Plan*, Barcelona: Generalitat de Catalunya.

Goldring, M. (1993). *Pleasant the Scholar's Life: Irish Intellectuals and the Construction of the Nation State*, London: Serif.

Govern d'Andorra (1996). *Coneixements i usos lingüístics de la població d'Andorra*, Andorra: Govern d'Andorra.

Grin, F. and Vaillancourt, F. (1999). *The Cost Effectiveness Evaluation of Minority Language Policies: Case Studies on Wales, Ireland and the Basque Country*, ECMI monograph 2; Flensburg: European Centre for Minority Issues.

Harris, J. (1984). *Spoken Irish in Primary Schools*, Dublin: Linguistics Institute of Ireland.

Hindley, R. (1990). *The Death of the Irish Language: A Qualified Obituary*, London: Routledge.

Hindley, R. (1991). 'Defining the Gaeltacht: dilemmas in Irish language planning', in C. H. Williams (ed.), *Linguistic Minorities, Society and Territory*, Clevedon, Avon: Multilingual Matters, pp. 66–95.

Hourigan, N. (1999). 'A comparison of the campaigns by European regional and lesser used language communities for radio and television services', unpublished Ph.D. thesis, Galway, National University of Ireland.

Hutchinson, J. (1987). *The Dynamics of Cultural Nationalism*, London: Allen & Unwin.

Institiúid Teangeolaiochta Éireann (1997). *Polasaithe Teanga an Stáit: Athbreithniú*, Dublin: Linguistic Institute of Ireland.

Kearney, R., ed. (1988). *Across the Frontiers: Ireland in the 1990s*, Dublin: Wolfhound Press.

Kiberd, D. (1996). *Inventing Ireland: The Literature of the Modern Nation*, London: Vintage.

Leersen, J. (1996). *Mere Irish and Fior-Ghael*, Cork: Cork University Press.

Mac Cárthaigh, D., ed. (1998). *I dTreo Deilbhcháipéise d'Acht Teanga Éireannach*, Dublin: Coiscéim.

MacInnes, John (1999). 'Consensus and controversy in language normalisation in Catalonia: the 1998 Act', *Journal of Catalan Studies/Revista Internacional de Catalanística*, 3; electronic version: http: //www.fitz.cam.ac.uk/catalan_journal/2/articles/maciness/index.html.

MacInnes, John and Gore, Sarah (1998). 'The politics of language in Catalunya', *Edinburgh Working Papers in Sociology*, 13.

McCrone, D. (1998). *The Sociology of Nationalism*, London: Routledge.

Mac Laughlin, J., ed. (1997). *Location and Dislocation in Contemporary Irish Society*, Cork: Cork University Press.

Mac Néill, E. (1925). 'Irish Education Policy 1', *Irish Statesman*, (17 Oct.): 168–9.

Mac Póilin, A., ed. (1997). *The Irish Language in Northern Ireland*, Belfast: Ultach Trust.

Mac Póilin, A. (1994). 'Spiritual beyond the ways of men: images of the Gael', *The Irish Review*, 16, 1–22.

Mac Póilin, A. (1999). *The Belfast Agreement and the Irish Language in Northern Ireland*, Belfast: Ultach Trust.

Marí, Isidor (1997). 'El pla general de normalització lingüística de Catalunya: Un marc estratègic per a la definició i l'execució de les polítiques lingüístiques', *Actes del congrés europeu sobre planificació lingüística/Proceedings of the Conference on Language Planning, Barcelona, 9 i 10 de novembre 1995*, Barcelona: Generalitat de Catalunya, Departament de Cultura.

Nelde, P., Strubell, M. and Williams, G. (1995). *Euromosaic: The Production and Reproduction of the Minority Language Groups of the EU*, Luxembourg: Official Publications Office of the European Communities.

Ó Cuív, E. (1999). 'Key note address to the International Conference on Language Legislation', Killiney, Dublin, Comhdháil Náisiúnta na Gaeilge.

OECD (1991). *Ireland: Review of National Policies for Education*, Paris: OECD.

Ó Flatharta, P. (1999). 'On the delivery mechanism of social and economic development in the Gaeltacht', paper presented at the ECMI International Seminar, Flensburg, ECMI, 18–20 June.

Ó Gadhra, N. (1990). *An Ghaeltacht (Oifigiuil) agus 1992?*, Dublin: Coiscéim.

Ó Gadhra, N. (1999). 'The Irish Gaeltacht communities on the eve of the third millennium', paper presented to the Nineteenth Annual Celtic Colloquium, Harvard University, 30 April 1999.

Ó Gadhra, N. (2000). 'Re-thinking Irish Language Strategy for the new millennium', *Saoirse* (Feb., 154), 8–9.

Ó Huallacháin, C. Fr. (1994). *The Irish and Irish: A Sociolinguistic Analysis of the Relationship between a People and their Language*, Dublin: Assisi Press.

Ó Riagáin, P. (1992). *Language Maintenance and Language Shift as Strategies of Social Reproduction: Irish in the Corca Dhuibhne Gaeltacht, 1926–86*, Dublin: Linguistics Institute of Ireland.

Ó Riagáin, P. (1997). *Language Policy and Social Reproduction: Ireland 1893–1993*. Oxford: Oxford University Press.

Paseta, S. (1999). *Before the Revolution: Nationalism, Social Change and Ireland's Catholic Elite, 1879–1922*, Cork: Cork University Press.

Pazos, Maria-Lluïsa (1990). *L'amenaça del català 'light'*, Barcelona: Tibidabo Edicions.

Pericay, Xavier and Toutain, Ferran (1986). *Verinosa llengua*, Barcelona: Empúries.

Prats, Modest, Rafanell, August and Rossich, Albert (1990). *El futur de la llengua catalana*, Barcelona: Empúries.

Romaní, J. M., Aragay, J. M. and Sabaté, J. (1997). 'INUSCAT: Un indicador de l'ús del Català', *Treballs de Sociolingüística Catalana*, 13, 15–23.

Samsó, Joan (1995). *La cultura catalana entre la clandestinitat i la represa pública 1939–1951*, Barcelona: Publicacions de l'Abadia de Montserrat.

Sánchez Carrión, J. M. (1987). *Un futuro para nuestro pasado*, Sánchez Carrión: Donostia.

Siguan, Miquel (1993). *Multilingual Spain*, Amsterdam and Lisse: Swets and Zeitlinger.

Solé i Camardons, Joan (1997). 'Planning multilingualism: the Catalan case,' in Ammon, U., Mattheier, K. L. and Nelde, P. H. (eds.), *Sociolinguistica*, Tübingen: Max Niemeyer Verlag, pp. 43–52.

Strubell i Trueta, Miquel (1993). 'Les campanyes de normalització lingüística de la Generalitat de Catalunya (1980–1990)', *Revista de Llengua i Dret*, 18, 181–92.

Strubell i Trueta, Miquel (1996). 'Language planning and bilingual education in Catalonia', *Journal of Multilingual and Multicultural Development*, 17(2–4), 262–75.

Strubell i Trueta, Miquel (1999). 'Una llengua sense poble?', in Pradilla, Miquel A. (ed.), *La llengua Catalana al tombat de mil·leni*, Barcelona: Empúries, pp. 9–33.

Tubau, Ivan (1990a). *El català que ara es parla: Llengua i periodisme a la ràdio i la televisió*, Barcelona: Empúries.

Tubau, Ivan (1990b). *Paraula viva contra la llengua normativa*, Barcelona: Editorial Laertes.

Vallverdú, Francesc (1990). *L'ús del català: Un futur controvertit: Qüestions de normalització lingüística al llindar del segle XXI*, Barcelona: Edicions 62.

Vilar, Pierre (1964). *Catalunya dins l'Espanya moderna: Recerques sobre els fonaments econòmics de les estructures nacionals*, Barcelona: Edicions 62, vol. 1.

Weber, Jude and Strubell i Trueta, Miquel (1991). *The Catalan Language: Progress towards Normalization*, Sheffield: The Anglo-Catalan Society.

Williams, C. H. (1988). 'Language planning and regional development: lessons from the Irish Gaeltacht', in Williams, C. H. (ed.), *Language in Geographic Context*, Clevedon, Avon: Multilingual Matters, pp. 267–301.

Williams, C. H. (1990). 'Political expressions of underdevelopment in the West European periphery', in Buller, H. and Wright, S. (eds.), *Rural Development: Problems and Practices*, Aldershot: Avebury, pp. 227–47.

Williams, C. H. (1991). 'Linguistic minorities: West European and Canadian perspectives', in Williams, C. H. (ed.), *Linguistic Minorities, Society and Territory*, Clevedon, Avon: Multilingual Matters, pp. 1–43.

Williams, C. H. (1999a). 'Legislation and empowerment: a Welsh drama in three acts', in Comhdháil Náisiúnta na Gaeilge, *International Conference on Language Legislation*, Dublin: Comhdháil Náisiúnta na Gaeilge, pp. 126–59.

Williams, C. H. (1999b). *Equality Issues Facing the Irish Language in Northern Ireland*, Belfast: The Northern Ireland Assembly Transition Programme, Central Community Relations Unit.

Williams, G. and Morris, D. (2000). *Language Planning and Language Use: Welsh in a Global Age*, Cardiff: University of Wales Press.

Zalbide, M. (1988). 'Mende hasierako euskalgintza: Urratsak eta hutsuneak', in *II. Euskal Mundu-biltzarra, Euskara Biltzarra/Congreso de la Lengua Vasca*, Vitoria-Gasteiz: Eusko Jaurlaritzaren Argitalpen Zerbitzu Nagusia, vol. 2, pp. 389–412.

Zalbide, M. (1990). 'Euskal Eskola, asmo zahar bide berri', in *Euskal Eskola Publikoaren Lehen Kongresua*, Vitoria-Gasteiz: Eusko Jaurlaritzaren Argitalpen Zerbitzu Nagusia, vol. 1, pp. 211–71.

Zalbide, M. (1992). 'Basque language loyalism at the beginning of the century: strengths and failings', in Hughes, Medwin (ed.), *The Challenge of Diversity*, Dublin: European Bureau for Lesser Used Languages, pp. 75–112.

Zalbide, M. (1999). 'Normalización lingüística y escolaridad: Un informe desde la sala de máquinas', *Revista Internacional de los Estudios Vascos*, 43(2), 355–424.

# 12

## Conclusion: Economic Development and Political Responsibility

### COLIN H. WILLIAMS

### INTRODUCTION

For far too long language revitalization has been assumed to be primarily concerned with issues of cultural maintenance, bilingual education and the attraction of new speakers to the myriad Welsh-medium social networks. However, as we have demonstrated in this volume, there is a need to address in tandem issues of regional development and economic opportunities for bilingual services and bilingual working practices.

Wales is characterized by an uncompetitive business environment. It ranks last but one of the British regions in terms of regional competitiveness, and in a broader European perspective innovative small and medium-sized enterprises (SMEs) are less export-oriented than matched comparators in Denmark and Ireland. If they engage with the innovation support infrastructure for technology grants and inter-firm collaboration, they prefer that to be within Wales rather than outside, again unlike the two small peripheral European comparator economies (Cooke and Wills, 1999). There is much talk of a knowledge-based economy where information and flexible, cumulative skills are prized above all. In such an economic climate the crunch question is to ask whether regional economic development policy has any room whatsoever for Welsh-language considerations. This is especially pertinent when orthodox economic thinking considers additional so-called 'minority languages' a burden, an extra cost and a potentially complicating factor that might dissuade hesitant investors and reluctant relocators from siting any new activities within Wales. (This is a general argument just as capable of being used, for example, to reduce bilingualism within the university sector for fear of dissuading foreign students from coming to Wales.)

Consequently, the role, range and reach of diverse interventionist economic and language enterprise agencies, within an inhospitable trading environment, are pressing concerns. Across a wide range of social and economic issues, regional planning experts such as my colleague Professor Phil Cooke have argued that 'Wales has been suffering from too little strategic thinking, not too much' (Cooke, 2000). I want to illustrate the paucity of current strategic thinking by providing four brief cameos of the differing approaches to the question of economic development and language regeneration. They are: (1) international and national level initiatives, as represented by Welsh Development Agency and European Union sponsored activities, (2) regional level involvement represented by Menter a Busnes and Antur Teifi initiatives and activities, (3) community level involvement as represented by *mentrau iaith* (language enterprise agencies), and (4) Objective 1 funding for regional regeneration.

## EUROPEAN AND WELSH PARTNERSHIP

As with Brittany, Catalonia, Flanders and Scotland, Wales represents a particular configuration where regional innovation has also led to a renewed sense of confidence in European-level institutions and networks. By relating Welsh events to European currents of thought and praxis, new opportunities are created for the development of so-called 'problem regions'. However, there is great ambiguity as to how one should play the European dimension, precisely because Wales simultaneously wishes to be seen as a dynamic leader of post-industrial development, as witnessed by its active participation in the Four Motors Programme, and as an eligible member for European Regional Development Funding (ERDF). Up until the late 1980s massive dislocation in the traditional industrial sectors of mining, steel-making and textiles had dealt a body-blow to Welsh economic performance. However, following the 1988 reforms, Wales has obtained an average share of 12.5 per cent of all UK ERDF funds, and 8.6 per cent of all UK European Social Fund (ESF) funds. Commenting on this trend, Mathias (1995) argues that this is a considerable success when one takes the restrictions in eligibility into account. Evidence of the reconstruction of the Welsh economy is provided by the increase in levels of inward investment from around £30m in 1985 to around £230m in 1992, most of which is private overseas capital (Cooke, 1993a).

There have been five European Union initiatives of relevance to Wales. RECHAR (I/II) was significant as the mining industry sought to adjust to the massive haemorrhage of men following the ruthless downsizing of the middle Thatcher years. RETEX was aimed at textile-manufacturing regions and did not perform well in Wales, even though the industry continues to struggle, especially in the north and west. LEADER was concerned with strengthening agencies of rural development and has been a considerable success, particularly in terms of local infrastructural development and introducing new farming practices. KONVER was established to assist areas in coping with problems stemming from the decline of the defence industry. Both Pembroke and Anglesey have benefited as compensation for the decommissioning of RAF production and maintenance facilities. INTERREG, aimed at facilitating cross-border co-operation, has become the most significant initiative, used extensively by local authorities in west Wales dealing with Irish partners and with Pembroke's new partnership with the greater Amsterdam region (Mathias, 1995).

Recent expansion in the use of European funds has seen a shift from invest-ment in capital infrastructure, such as transport and physical communication, to the creation of community projects which provide a network of support for sustained development and enhanced quality of life, including housing, educa-tion, access to information and telecommunication facilities (Mathias, 1995). Thus the Welsh RELAY Centre was established in 1993 with the express purpose of helping industry take advantage of the EU programmes such as ESPRIT, BRIDGE, BRITE/EURAM and STRIDE. In addition, the EU and the Welsh Development Agency have jointly funded the UK's first Electronic Data Interchange (EDI) Awareness Centre in Wales. Late in 1995 Wales was nominated as one of the newly created Regional Technology Plan (RTP) regions. Participants recognize that this is not a panacea for the long-term complications of structural adjustment, because of the difficulty in meeting all the requirements of additionality, consolidating networks and harnessing the potential of the region. In that sense, like many other EU programmes in Wales, it is essentially an exercise in network-construction and access to technology rather than an income-generating programme. But over time synergy becomes crucial as a trig-ger to innovation and mini-technopoles may develop as a result of the strategies identified in Castells and Hall (1994).

The discussion to date has tended to focus attention on aggregate structural factors which relate either to a predominantly rural economy or to the downturn effects of a post-industrial landscape as in Cwm Gwendraeth and Aman–Tawe. Issues of external investment, control and policy implementation have gradually given way to a concern as to how Welsh national agencies such as the Welsh Development Agency and other interventionist arms of the state can regenerate such communities, either through pump-priming schemes or infrastructural improvements.

## MENTER A BUSNES

A key question is to what extent there is a significant economic difference if the language promotion is undertaken on behalf of a target group by a state agency. To what extent are the considerations altered if the promotional work is under-taken by the minority speakers themselves within the community and local economy?

Menter a Busnes reflects innovative approaches to the challenge of promoting self-directed and targeted economic development and cultural change. The aims and objectives of this agency established in 1989 are:

- to maximize the economic potential of Welsh speakers;
- to create and operate a long-term action-based programme to make sure that Welsh-language culture adapts itself creatively in terms of economic attitudes and activities;

- to increase considerably the number of Welsh speakers who develop companies that already exist; work in and manage businesses of all kinds; invest in businesses; establish new ventures; initiate economically based activities in the community; operate in a wider range of sectors; and manage effectively in a variety of situations.

The practical means by which Menter a Busnes translates these aims into reality include comprehensive business and management training programmes; schools and adult education seminars on business enterprise opportunities, vocational training; agricultural enterprise and marketing information packs; promoting empirical research and policy initiatives; EU inter-regional projects co-ordinated by Agora, with an emphasis on cultural tourism and farm diversification; promoting new forms of bilingual intervention in both the rural and urban contexts (Menter a Busnes, 1997). Williams and Morris (2000: 236) claim that Menter a Busnes adopt a deprecating conception, in that Welsh speakers lack an entrepreneurial capacity. It is the sort of argument which lies at the heart of the modernist link between normality and reason. Nevertheless, Menter a Busnes perform a very strategic role in heightening the awareness of economic opportunities and the need to analyse the restructuring process at the local/ regional level.

## ANTUR TEIFI

Antur Teifi was founded in 1980 as a private company to stimulate economic enterprise in the Teifi Valley. An underlying concern was to revitalize aspects of the local economy so as to maintain a viable community in what was then one of the strongest Welsh-speaking areas in Wales. Its great strength is that it was grounded in the aspirations of local community activists to improve their region's economic condition. Initially it concentrated on diversifying the agro-economic base and providing telematic training and facilities to a hitherto poorly served rural area. The interventionist strategy has operated through the improvement of the local infrastructure, through the provision of professional marketing advice and economic development information, through a commitment to joint-venture partnerships and through experimental methods of restructuring local–global economic networks. Welsh is a natural means of communication, for over 90 per cent of the staff are Welsh-speaking, but the language is an extension of local involvement, not an end in and of itself. The value-added in operating in a bilingual context may be itemized as follows.

- It assists effective local and regional networking.
- It attracts backing from other agencies such as the Welsh Development Agency; the Development Board for Rural Wales; and European support through the LEADER Project.

- It facilitates the Antur's ability to respond quickly and effectively to local community needs, especially the demand for skills training.
- It assists the company to adopt a holistic and flexible approach to a rapidly changing economic context.
- By encouraging local people to seek employment within the region it is perceived as a community asset.
- Local support for the aims and methods of Antur Teifi have allowed it to penetrate into other neighbouring regions and to become a significant actor in the local economy of south-west Wales.

The company has realized much of its potential as a dynamic, self-sustaining enterprise agency. It has countered much of the traditional prejudice against a Welsh-medium enterprise culture and in consequence the experience of Antur Teifi is obviously of great significance to others seeking to harmonize economic development and language regeneration either in other parts of Wales or further afield. Taken together both Antur Teifi and Menter a Busnes serve to emphasize the acute need for far more indigenous agencies able to promote diversity-led development.

## COMMUNITY DEVELOPMENT AND *MENTRAU IAITH*

*Mentrau iaith* are set to be the primary means by which community language regeneration is attempted. Currently some twenty *mentrau iaith* are in operation and the revised strategy of the Welsh Language Board recommends that this form of language planning intervention should be extended into other communities, on a joint-partnership basis. The key issue is to what extent language planning agencies can influence long-term patterns of language-related behaviour. We saw in Chapters 8 and 9 that *mentrau* extended the use of Welsh into under-developed domains, such as sports and leisure, for example, cricket or after-school clubs, special interest groups, for example, walking holidays, local drama and pop festivals, community economic skills training, translation and production facilities. They also act as a local lobby to convince para-public agencies and commercial interests to expand their bilingual customer services. However, in their attempts to develop a holistic approach, community language planners are often hamstrung by the twin operational difficulties of (a) insufficient resources, both human and fiscal, and (b) the inability to co-ordinate activities across departments which impinge upon language, but which are always secondary to their prime departmental duties of fulfilling their statutory obligations in the health service, the education system, child support agencies, housing, social deprivation and the like.

*Mentrau iaith* occupy a delicate position for, though autonomous agencies, they are funded by the National Assembly through the Welsh Language Board and occasionally receive ancillary funding from local authorities and/or European Union finance. They provide one model of interventionist language planning at the community level. Because they are novel and have developed in a largely *ad hoc* manner, it is difficult to measure their long-term impact on language use. Price (1996) has warned that the need for competitiveness in the global economy has led many firms to shed labour, which has deleterious effects for the unskilled and semi-skilled workers in deindustrializing areas. Thus some *mentrau iaith* are likely to focus on skills-based training, adapting much of the rationale of the 'social economy' whereby a new sector of labour-intensive community-based enterprises based around people and environment-related services will be generated, as has happened between Menter Aman and Aman Valley Enterprise. In time, of course, it is possible that a hybrid agency will emerge in several parts of Wales drawn from the language promotion and economic restructuring backgrounds. If so, much greater work needs to be done in articulating the complex relationship between language, economy and civil society.

## THE OBJECTIVE 1 PROGRAMME

A second major initiative has been the granting of EU Objective 1 status to large parts of Wales which over the seven years 2000–6 will provide an additional £1.3 billion of development funding. This is a mixed blessing, for although it is a financial boost it is also a socio-economic indictment that regional deprivation has been allowed to slip to a level beyond the UK and European thresholds.

The West and Valleys designated area which qualified for Objective 1 support is characterized by:

- extremely low and declining GDP which was 72 per cent of the EU average, reflecting the Welsh national average which is 17 per cent below the UK average. Many parts of Wales fare much worse, for example, the Central Valleys figure is 64 per cent of the EU average while Anglesey is 68 per cent of the EU average;
- unemployment, especially the long-term;
- declining economic activity rates;
- high levels of social deprivation, with eighty-two of the hundred most deprived wards in Wales being within the designated area;
- an overdependence on declining industries, for example, energy, defence, slate and oil refining;
- a region dominated by the agricultural industry which has been hit by a number of crises in the past decade;
- relatively few dynamic indigenous medium-sized businesses with growth potential;
- a region which is economically isolated with poor communication network and infrastructure.

In the Single Programming Document for the Period: 2000–2006 which provides a detailed analysis of these features, great play is made of the role of culture and language. Welsh is described as a 'critical element which underpins the region's identity ... with nearly 75 per cent of the Welsh speaking population living in the region' ( Wales European Taskforce, 1999a: 5). Table 12.1 shows the proportion of Welsh speakers aged three or older within the Objective 1 region.

Measures to enhance the economic performance of the region which include a specific linguistics/cultural dimension include: (1) business development and enterprise priorities, which will be influenced by Menter a Busnes planning and policy; (2) a competitive environment, which will seek to enhance the enterprise initiatives; (3) community regeneration initiatives, which are likely to be modelled on the *mentrau iaith* experience; (4) promoting employability and a learning society based in part on bilingual skills training programmes; (5) rural development and sustainable use of natural resources, which will adopt more ecological and holistic approaches to the social and economic needs of the rural communities within the region. Wales, via the Objective 1 funding scheme, is beginning to mobilize the key structural determinants of economic performance, environmental sustainability and cultural reproduction within one integrated programme.

Other agencies which have entered the regional development–language enterprise nexus include (a) Newidiem, a spin-off from Menter a Busnes, which seeks to concentrate in the short-term on promoting bilingualism within the workplace especially the major retail and service sector; (b) refashioned *mentrau iaith*, of which the most recent have a far more hard-headed economic rationale to their work and engagement in community development; (c) major UK economic development agencies recognizing the significance of bilingualism in Wales as an economic value, rather than a social cost in the labour market; (d) the growth

Table 12.1. **Proportion of Welsh speakers, by age, in west Wales and the Valleys**

| County | 3–15 | 16–44 | 45–64 | 65+ | Total |
|---|---|---|---|---|---|
| Gwynedd | 90.9 | 75.6 | 65.6 | 68.4 | 74.3 |
| Anglesey | 78.1 | 62.5 | 57.4 | 55.9 | 62.6 |
| Ceredigion | 76.8 | 57.8 | 53.9 | 62.7 | 60.9 |
| Carmarthen | 56.6 | 46.0 | 53.0 | 65.3 | 53.5 |
| Conwy | 45.6 | 35.7 | 30.2 | 34.2 | 35.8 |
| Denbigh | 35.3 | 27.4 | 28.7 | 29.4 | 29.6 |
| Pembroke | 28.3 | 15.7 | 20.0 | 22.2 | 20.4 |
| Neath PT | 21.7 | 14.1 | 19.5 | 26.0 | 19.1 |
| Swansea | 16.0 | 8.5 | 15.1 | 21.8 | 14.0 |
| Bridgend | 19.3 | 8.8 | 5.4 | 10.5 | 10.1 |
| Rhondda CT | 17.0 | 8.1 | 4.6 | 10.9 | 9.5 |
| Torfaen | 29.2 | 3.8 | 3.3 | 3.1 | 8.3 |
| Merthyr | 3.7 | 6.6 | 4.8 | 9.5 | 8.1 |
| Caerffili | 17.4 | 6.1 | 3.3 | 4.5 | 7.4 |
| Blaenau G. | 22.6 | 3.4 | 2.7 | 2.6 | 6.4 |

*Source*: 1997 Welsh Household Interview Survey, in Wales European Taskforce, 1999b: 6.

of a significant number of consultancies spawned by devolution and constitutional change which seek to advise on Wales in the UK, Irish–British context and European sphere of economic interest.

Additional promising trends include the initial success of language marketing and promotion in three sectors: (i) elements of the agricultural sector, dairy products, food marketing and eco-business activities; (ii) small and medium-sized enterprises; (iii) information technology and communication/media companies. However, major barriers remain to the widespread introduction of Welsh/bilingual skills in the manufacturing and retail sector, outside the predominantly Welsh-speaking areas.

Cooke (2000) has argued that Wales is confronted by three crucial economic problems: the likely continuing decline of its heavy industry sector, difficulties in maintaining past high levels of foreign direct investment, and an indigenous SME sector that is ill-equipped to compete in the knowledge-based economy. Objective 1 business support funding, he argues, must be spent strategically on building clusters of specialist SMEs supplying traded and marketable business services from consultancy to design systems, more akin to economic processes which characterize the richer European regions. The crucial additional factor is the strengthening of knowledge-based businesses with capabilities in export markets. Language and communication processing skills are essential in such industries, so that while one may make a case for the wider use of Welsh in such contexts, it is also logical to develop the skills base of the Welsh workforce and future workforce by focusing greater resources on acquiring languages of wider communication. Economic and human investment must therefore be directed towards building clusters and integrated market-based networks in multimedia, software, systems design, biotechnology, advanced manufacturing, knowledge-intensive buisness services, optoelectronics and related industries. In order to develop the existing potential, Cooke (2000) argues that the public sector and government need to bump-start these initiatives and then withdraw so that they become self-sustaining entities. The link between strategic allocation of public resources and direct economic growth could not be more stark. Much depends on the partnership being forged between political leaders and the indigenous business base, so that regional economic development will be characterized more by innovation and sustained growth in the new economy, and less by the branch plant mentality of the *ancien régime*.

## A CHANGED POLITICAL CONTEXT

The establishment of the National Assembly for Wales, in May 1999, provides a radical reorientation of many of the themes of this volume, for it offers an institutional frame and political voice to develop a range of national strategies. Among the more important structural initiatives are: (a) a powerful economic committee; (b) structural change and internal merging of key agencies to produce a more powerful and integrated Welsh Development Agency (some initial questions have been raised as to the accountability of this agency and of its direction in economic planning); (c) the bilingual structure and operation of the Assembly; (d) vigorous education, training and language policies; (e) pressure by the National Assembly on a range of agencies and quangos, including the Welsh Language Board, to engage in more medium-term holistic, language planning and community development programmes.

The Assembly's political role is to identify the broad principles of Welsh-language policy, to decide how far to move along the spectrum from voluntarism to compulsory bilingualism, to identify priorities such as promotion, access or consolidation, and to integrate the interests of Welsh into all spheres of life in line with current holistic views on language planning. It is useful to distinguish between three different elements to the relationship between the Assembly and the Welsh language: (1) the place of the Welsh language in the operation of the Assembly itself; (2) the relationship between the National Assembly and the Welsh Language Board; (3) the key policy issues through which the Assembly's action (or inaction) will impact on the 'fate of the language'.

Hitherto unresolved issues include the fact that the standing orders will have to incorporate a general ruling whereby the issue of a disparity between two language versions can be resolved without necessarily giving automatic preference to one version over the other. Academic interpretations and analysis of the legal implications will be assisted by the production of a Legal Digest of Assembly Deliberations in co-operation with the Welsh Governance Centre at Cardiff University, which will also be a resource and documentation facility of National Assembly legislation. In addition, it is probable that a language standardization centre will need to be established at the earliest possible date, in line with the 1995 recommendations of the Official Welsh Panel of the Welsh Language Board.

Third, there is the question as to how extensive the bilingual translation facilities will be. Prior to the 6 May 1999 Assembly elections, critical voices cautioned that a significant problem related to the committees and subcommittees where the provision of translation facilities where no member spoke Welsh would have been farcical and generate ridicule. Now that the linguistic skills and preferences of the first Assembly Members are known, many of these unresolved considerations will be tempered by the reality that a greater number of bilingual speakers have been elected than was anticipated. A *Western Mail* (1999) survey categorized the sixty Assembly Members thus: twenty may be described as a fluent speaker, reader, writer; six as a semi-fluent speaker, reader, writer; eleven have a basic understanding as a learner, while twenty-three have no real understanding of Welsh. Since that date many of the non-Welsh-speaking AMs have undertaken to attend classes and seek a better understanding of Welsh. Significantly Plaid Cymru constitute the majority of competent bilinguals, while many in the Labour Party who have a basic competence have pressed for greater tuition in Welsh as part of the fulfilment of their Assembly duties. The fact that three of the party leaders and many of the significant players of the Assembly conduct media interviews regularly in both Welsh and English contributes to the normalization of bilingualism. However, even at this early stage, it is possible to forecast that while the Translation Unit will guarantee the open and effective use of either Welsh or English within the chamber, there will be structural barriers to the diffusion of bilingual working practices throughout the civil service which may strengthen demands for a dedicated Welsh civil service. This is particularly apposite as many of the senior civil servants, socialized under the old Welsh Office culture, consider their prime role is as representatives of a British public administration system within Wales, as opposed to a distinctly organic Welsh civil service which would work towards the functional implementation of both Welsh and English as working languages of the Assembly.

A final aspect deserves attention. In a small country like Wales, personalities are as significant as the structure of governance that they animate. Thus, in relation to language policy, the rapport between Ron Davies, Dafydd Elis-Thomas, Dafydd Wigley and Rhodri Morgan during the devolution process, and the subsequent appointment of Dafydd Elis-Thomas as Presiding Officer and Alun Michael as First Minister, eased the operation of a bilingual Assembly. This accord was not harmed when Rhodri Morgan became First Minister: in fact it naturalized the process, for Rhodri Morgan adopted a more thoroughgoing revision of the Welsh character of the Labour Party. One of the iconographic changes was to adopt the Welsh national colours of red, green and white, as used both by the Welsh Rugby Union and the Urdd Youth Movement. Another was to reposition the Labour Party as the 'national' as opposed to 'nationalist' party of Wales. An integral element of this repositioning is to recapture the Welsh-medium heritage of the Labour Party, which in the 1970s and 1980s had been jettisoned for fear of boosting the legitimacy of the nationalist message that, for politics within Wales, it was the Welsh context which was paramount. In addition, the commitment of experienced individuals such as Cynog Dafis, Christine Humphreys, Carwyn Jones, Ieuan Wyn Jones, Rhodri Glyn Thomas and Phil Williams, among others, will surely see the formulation of policies which recognize the social and economic reality of bilingualism in a wide range of domains. But how should the Assembly operate in respect of language planning and policy?

A central question for the National Assembly is the nature of the relationship it establishes with the Welsh Language Board. To what extent, and in what ways, will/should the Assembly seek to take over the role of the Welsh Language Board? Can the functions of the Board be better realized in a different, more democratic, organizational format, or is there an inherent tension in this field between legitimacy and accountability on the one hand and effectiveness on the other? Will we need a dedicated, specialist body to continue the work of the board, or could it be done by a committee of the Assembly working directly with the civil service?

There are grounds for arguing that the responsibilities of the Welsh Language

Board could be transferred to the Assembly, which would have a mandatory duty to promote Welsh through drawing upon its own Welsh Language Scheme. The Assembly has been bilingual from day one and its own scheme could build on its very different way of working from the previous regime of the Welsh Office. A democratic, publicly accountable, outward-looking Assembly would be a very different organization from the bureaucratic, inward-looking civil service and its scheme for using Welsh would need to reflect this (NAAG, 1998).

However, should this transfer of responsibilities happen, it is possible that any future Assembly *en masse* would be less committed to the language than is the Welsh Language Board. If this is likely, then there is little merit in initiating a transfer of responsibilities. Far better to strengthen the co-ordinating function of the Language Board, which would militate against the severe fragmentation that has bedevilled previous efforts at language promotion. In time consideration should also be given to additional reforms, such as a more powerful Welsh Language Act and the Welsh Language Authority outlined by Gruffudd in Chapter 6, together with the experience of our Basque and Catalan neighbours described in Chapter 11.

In addition to these organizational considerations, two other technical problems remain. First, which organization within the Assembly will be responsible for the development of language policy? Currently it is the Culture and Sports Committee chaired by Rhodri Glyn Thomas which has responsibility for overseeing linguistic matters, but it has delegated day-to-day functioning to the Language Board. It is too early to gauge the full impact of the success of the Welsh Language Board, especially in relation to its language schemes, but it has achieved a great deal in a short space of time. It is debatable whether the Language Board should accrue more powers to itself and be responsible for the disbursement of most, if not all, grants targeted toward the language or Welsh-medium organizations. Such a move may have a logical premiss but could be politically damaging as it would make the language over-dependent upon the nuanced values and policy directions of the Board. However, should the Language Board yield to the Assembly its influence in directing change through grant disbursement, it is difficult to envisage the Language Board having any real power and control over the fortunes of Welsh.

A counter to this position would be critical of the practice of direct reporting to the First Secretary and a subject committee, and assert that a commitment to democratic accountability would not brook Welsh-language policies and grants being handled outside the democratic framework. There would be a case for a special body other than the staff of the Assembly having a language standardization role, but the rather conservative civil service/quango-like arrangement for the Language Board would need to be brought into line with the rest of Assembly matters. This would not occasion a reform targeted specifically at the operation of the Language Board but a far more general rearrangement of the relationship between former quangos and the Assembly. Thus, in future, it is likely that the Assembly will devise alternative arrangements for dealing with bilingualism as a national feature. This is because operating a bilingual policy is one thing, having a watching brief for the fortunes of Welsh culture is quite another, and the two should not be conflated. There is a prima-facie justification for a committee concerned with the Welsh language and culture separate from, but directing, the activities of the Language Board, as well as determining national language/cultural policy.

Secondly, which internal body will consider appeals in relation to the content of language schemes and make a decision to request judicial advice to take action against a public body? The latter question is far from straightforward in legal and procedural terms. It is doubtful whether the Assembly has the authority under clauses 28, 29 and 33 of the Act to establish the office of a language ombudsman who could intervene in disputes over the language schemes of public authorities. This was clearly a significant omission from the 1993 Bill as the very fact of agreed language schemes begs the question of assuring compliance.

Regardless of the specific arrangements, the Assembly's priority will be in education through targeting eight needs: (1) the teaching of Welsh within community centres; (2) additional training for teachers on secondment; (3) language skills upgrading and professional training for government employees; (4) public-sector bilingual training; (5) private-sector bilingual training; (6) high-level bilingual computer training and information system analysis; (7) sustained empirical research on the efficacy of various teaching methods; and (8) the development of a strategy which harnessed the potential of current providers and resource-developers drawn from the Welsh-for-adults consortia, the Welsh Joint Education Committee, private-sector initiatives such as Acen and Y Coleg Digidol and the myriad smaller commercial suppliers in the system. Current attempts by the Welsh Language Board to provide such a strategy augur well for a reduction in the fragmentation and waste of energy which characterize the sector, but it also signifies more and more power being channelled to a central agency of government, rather than being diffused through the system. In time, of course, the Assembly will take direct action in regard to issues of bilingualism, equal opportunity, language policy and economic development. Hitherto it has shown only a modest interest in such issues, and in a recent comprehensive overview of its strategic thinking made only passing genuflections to the range of Welsh-language issues we discuss in detail in this volume (National Assembly of Wales, 2000).

Having surveyed the current state of language revitalization efforts we are left with a set of key questions, inherent dangers and policy implications as we search for appropriate methods to promote the development of a bilingual society.

## KEY QUESTIONS

1. Is fragmentation and collapse the inevitable future for the Welsh heartland regions?
2. If so, should we be far less concerned with notions of domination, of hegemony, of territorial control and of resistance to externally induced change?
3. What are the perceptions held by consumers, agencies and educationalists as to what constitutes an appropriate place for proficiency in Welsh?
4. Can linguistic minorities achieve sufficient relative socio-cultural autonomy through the adoption of mass technology and internal communicative competence ?
5. Will ethnicity, as a base for social mobilization and group development, increase or decrease with greater European political-economic integration?
6. What effect will the enlargement of the EU have on the internal management of its constituent ethno-linguistic and regional groups?
7. Will the National Assembly necessarily strengthen a new definition of national identity and with what consequence for the promotion of the national language?
8. Will the strategy advanced by the Welsh Language Board garner sufficient support among its social partners and key actors within the economy to enable the specific initiatives it proposes to be realized?

## INHERENT DANGERS

1. That we continue to talk of 'subsidizing' the language rather than of investing in people, high-quality services and the realization of community empowerment and democratic choices.
2. That we fail to offer a range of services in Welsh which is commensurate with those available in English, so that any resultant choice is made on the basis of personal preference not lack of equality.
3. That we fail to prioritize the maximum utility-benefit of public investment and let tradition and insider-dealing determine how money (and hence limited power) shapes the contours of our economic and cultural landscape.
4. That we pay too little attention to the liberating force of communication technology and maintain a semblance that the 'old order' of top–down planning from central bureaucracies is the only worthwhile development in Welsh-language revitalization.
5. That we continue to confuse language reproduction with cultural maintenance and hence confine the relevance of Welsh to issues of 'ethnic membership' rather than to the construction of a plural, multicultural civil society.
6. That we believe too much of our own hype and accept that the language struggle is over, whereas in fact it has merely entered a new, more sophisticated and hence more demanding phase of political negotiation.
7. That we fail to incorporate mainstream issues of economic theory and consequent issues of consumer behaviour, service-sector changes and regional development planning into our language revitalization schemas.

8. That in any redefinition of bilingual public-service provision which is wedded to the rise of the digital economy and the potential of information networking, we create a digital divide between those who embrace the new opportunities and those who are consciously or unwittingly excluded from these new forms of interaction with government and the local state.

## POLICY IMPLICATIONS

A pressing need is comparative work on bilingual policy and language equality issues within the UK and Ireland. Future policy could be directed toward research-based answers which sought (1) to contribute both a theoretical and a practical element to language planning and language policy in the UK and Ireland; (2) to assess the character, quality and success of the institutional language policies of the newly established political assemblies in Scotland, Wales and Northern Ireland; (3) to investigate the complex nature of bilingual educational and administrative systems in Wales together with regional specific systems in Scotland and Northern Ireland; (4) to assess the role of cross-border arrangements for the increased recognition of Irish on the island of Ireland, together with Northern Irish, Gaelic and Ulster Scots links with Scotland. An obvious, if hitherto unknown quantity here is the role of the Irish–British Council in terms of co-operation, and political bargaining at the UK and European level, together with bilingual education, civil rights and group equality issues in Northern Ireland. As a new political forum its role and impact should influence the deliberations of European Committee of the Regions and several other international bodies.

Issue (5) would be to investigate to what degree the institutionalization of Celtic languages *vis-á-vis* the established dominance of English can be a model for the relationship of other lesser used languages world-wide in their relationship with English. Potentially this issue is of global significance if one can transfer several of the lessons to be learned from the survival of the Celtic languages to multilingual contexts as varied as contemporary India, and much of Sub-Saharan Africa, let alone the evolving European political system. Policy (6) is to gauge the degree to which the information technology and media opportunities developed in connection with the National Assembly of Wales and the Northern Irish Assembly are capable of sustaining a wider range of bilingual practices in public life. It is noteworthy that the development of Sianel 4 Cymru, and to a lesser extent the Gaelic-medium television service, has created a self-confident and pluralist bilingual workforce which sustains a wide range of media activities. It is possible that both Assemblies will have a similar impact in relation to the information society in matters of public administration, education, legal affairs and the voluntary sector.

The remaining answers would seek (7) to analyse the economic demand for a skilled bilingual workforce in several sectors of the economy; determine to what extent bilingual working practices in Wales offer a model for subsequent parallel developments within a range of multilingual contexts within the English regions, for example, either in respect of several European languages or selected non-European languages such as Arabic, Urdu, Hindi or variants of Chinese languages of wider communication; (8) to investigate what effect the arrangements for the bilingual servicing of the National Assembly will have on the legitimization of bilingualism as a societal norm; (9) to assess how the experiences generated within the National Assembly will impact on the bilingual character of educational and public administrative services, together with the local government and legal system; (10) to analyse the extent to which European Union and Council of Europe language initiatives related to both Regional Minority and Immigrant Minority Languages are adopted in the various political contexts which comprise the UK and Ireland.

## CONCLUSION

Taken together, these questions, potential dangers and policy options comprise a formidable range of issues. The difficulty of course is that for some within society they are vital, whereas for others they are marginal or divisive. Central agencies such as the National Assembly, the Welsh Development Agency and the Welsh Language Board have a critical role as legitimizing institutions constructing new forms of partnership through their statutory obligations and pump-priming initiatives. Quite radical initiatives to strengthen the role of Welsh as both a community language and as a language of the workforce are under way following the recommendations of Williams and Evas (1997) and the Wales European Task Force (1999). But the long-term infrastructural support and dynamism will be non-governmental, largely located within the voluntary and private sectors and grounded within local communities which have already exhibited remarkable initiative in supporting regional economic enterprises. There is at last an acute awareness among Welsh decision-makers and economic policy practitioners that the conventionally held presumption of incongruity between the search for appropriate economic development and the need for sensitive, indeed vigorous, language promotion, can no longer be sustained. Instead of envisaging a narrow sectoral role for bilingualism within the Welsh economy and society, there is a growing recognition that only holistic perspectives and comprehensive analyses of the place of Welsh will satisfy the acute need for innovative regenerative thought and action. Hence the need to tackle the indigenous economic and cultural developmental issues raised in this case-study, so that bilingualism in Wales may become a situational norm. In truth, there are many difficult questions and issues yet to be faced, but there is also a new sense of realism based upon the intelligent application of research and a constructive melding of the various actors dedicated to improving the quality of Welsh life. Political leadership and direction is crucial now if the potential outlined in this chapter is to be fully realized. In tandem with our European partners we are learning to take responsibility for our own destiny, as far as that it practicable in a globalized world. Fresh visions of the possible, allied with the maximum amount of synergy and the application of intelligent optimism, are now required. Given the dedication of previous generations to the cause of advancing the interests of lesser used languages in education, public adminis-tration and the media, I have no doubt that a similar level of dedication will be expended on the cause of economic dynamism and community development once that central message has been absorbed by the general public, and it is to that end that I commend the collaborative work represented in this volume. We need, above all, realistic and critical assessments both of our own individual circumstances and the collective condition of our European partners, so that we can make it possible for there to be a truly multilingual and multicultural Europe which does not conflict with the aspiration to secure a dynamic and satisfying economic order.

This volume has focused on the implications – both the dangers and the opportunities – for the Welsh language of the new frameworks of governance and regulation that have been established in Wales. In the conclusion it has explored the implications for Welsh language revitalization of the establishment of the National Assembly. If the National Assembly is to succeed as a political institution people from all over, and from both main linguistic groups, must be able to engage with it and feel a sense of shared ownership. In order for this to occur, the potential sensitivities of the linguistic politics of Wales will need to be recognized and addressed. If, however, the Welsh language is seen in terms of a resource rather than as a problem or, indeed, simply a matter of rights and enti-tlements, then this will be an important contribution to the development of a common Welsh civic identity – the emergence of which is surely a precondition for the success of the National Assembly and ultimately for the complete reha-bilitation of Welsh as a co-equal language of everyday life in Wales.

## Acknowledgements

This research derives in part from work commissioned by the Welsh Language Board (1995–7) on Community Development Planning and by Menter a Busnes (1998–2000) on policy formulation aimed at increasing bilingual opportunities in the economy. Acknowledgement is also made of the research support provided by an ESRC grant, no. R000 22 2936, 'The Bilingual Context, Policy and Practice of the National Assembly of Wales'.

## References

Aitchison, J. W. (1995). 'Language, family structure and social class, 1991 census data', presentation to The Social History of the Welsh Language Conference, Aberystwyth, 16 Sept.

Arfé, G. (1981). 'On a community charter of regional languages and cultures and on a charter of rights of ethnic minorities', resolution adopted by the European Parliament, Strasbourg.

Bellin, W. (1989). 'Ethnicity and Welsh bilingual education', *Contemporary Wales*, 3, 77–97.

Casson, M. (1993). 'Cultural determinants of economic performance', *Journal of Comparative Economics*, 17, 418–42.

Castells, M. and Hall, P. (1994). *Technopoles of the World: The Making of 21st Century Industrial Complexes*, London: Routledge.

Cooke, P. (1989). 'Ethnicity, economy and civil society: three theories of political regionalism', in Williams, C. H. and Kofman, E. (eds.), *Community Conflict, Partition and Nationalism*, London: Routledge, pp. 194–224.

Cooke, P. (1993a). 'Regulating regional economies: Wales and Baden-Württtemberg in Transition', in Rhodes, R. (ed.), *The Regions and the New Europe*, Manchester: Manchester University Press.

Cooke. P. (1993b). 'Globalization, economic organisation and the emergence of regional interstate partnerships', in Williams, C. H. (ed.), *The Political Geography of the New World Order*, London: Wiley, pp. 46–58.

Cooke, P. (2000). 'Nowhere to run, nowhere to hide – regional economic development in Wales', paper presented to the Canada–Wales Forum, Welsh Governance Centre, Cardiff University, April.

Cooke, P. and Wills, D. (1999). 'Small firms, social capital and the enhancement of business performance through innovation programmes', *Small Business Economics*, 13, 219–34.

Council of Europe (1992). *European Charter for Regional or Minority Languages*, Strasbourg: Council of Europe.

Declaració de Barcelona (1996). *Declaració Universal de Drets Lingüístics*, Barcelona: International PEN and CIEMEN.

Hill, S. (1999). 'Understanding the prosperity gap', *Agenda* (Summer): 12–13.

Huggins, R. and Morgan, K. (1999). 'Matching a national strategy with European intervention', *Agenda* (Summer), 15–18.

Killilea, M. (1994). 'On linguistic and cultural minorities in the European Community', resolution adopted by the European Parliament, Strasbourg.

Kuijpers, W. (1987). 'On the languages and cultures of regional and ethnic minorities in European Community', resolution adopted by the European Parliament, Strasbourg.

Langevelde, A. P. van (1993). 'Migration and language in Friesland', *Journal of Mulitlingual and Multicultural Development*, 14(5), 393–411.

Mathias, J. (1995). 'Wales – the shift from Nationalism to Regionalism', mimeo, European Studies, Cardiff University.

Menter a Busnes (1993). *Nodweddion Siaradwyr Cymraeg mewn Busnes*, Aberystwyth: Menter a Busnes.

Menter a Busnes (1994). *A Quiet Revolution? The Framework of the Academic Report*. Aberystwyth: Menter a Busnes.

Menter a Busnes (1997). *Success Story: A Report on the Work of Menter a Busnes 1995–6*, Aberystwyth: Menter a Busnes.

Menter Cwm Gwendraeth (1991). *Strategaeth, Menter Cwm Gwendraeth*, Cross Hands: Menter Cwm Gwendraeth.

Morgan. K. and Price, A. (1998). *The Other Wales: The Case for Objective 1 Funding Post 1999*, Cardiff: Institute for Welsh Affairs.

NAAG (1998). *National Assembly for Wales: Final Report*, Cardiff: National Assembly Advisory Group Consultation Paper.

National Assembly of Wales (2000). www.betterwales.com, Cardiff: National Assembly of Wales.

Thomas, A. (1998). 'De-politicising the language', *Agenda* (Summer), 46–7.

Thomas, H. (1993). 'Welsh planners voice some lingering doubts', *The Planner*, (22 Oct.), 41–2.

Wales European Taskforce (1999a). *A Prosperous Future for Wales*, Cardiff: European Affairs Division, National Assembly.

Wales European Taskforce (1999b). *West Wales and the Valleys Objective 1*, Cardiff: European Affairs Division, National Assembly.

Welsh Language Board (1999). *The Welsh Language Fact File*, Cardiff: Welsh Language Board.

Welsh Office (1995). *The Welsh Language: Children and Education*, Cardiff: Welsh Office Statistical Brief SDB 14/95.

*Western Mail* (1999). 'A guide to Welsh speakers in the National Assembly' (16 June), 9.

Williams, C. H. (1989). 'New domains of the Welsh language: education, planning and the law', *Contemporary Wales*, 3, 41–76.

Williams, C. H. (1998). 'Operating through two languages', in Osmond, J. (ed.), *The National Assembly Agenda*, Cardiff: Institute of Welsh Affairs, pp. 96–10.

Williams, C. H. (1999). 'Governance and the language', *Contemporary Wales*, 12, 130–54.

Williams, C. H. and Evas, J. (1997). *Y Cynllun Ymchwil Cymunedol*, Cardiff: Bwrdd yr Iaith, Prifysgol Caerdydd.

Williams, G. (1980). 'Review of E. Allardt, *Implications of the Ethnic Revival in Modern Industrial Society*', *Journal of Multilingual and Multicultural Development*, 1, 363–70.

Y Swyddfa Gymreig (1992). *Arolwg Teuluoedd*, Cardiff: Y Swyddfa Gymreig.

# Index